Manufacturing
Celebrity

Latino Paparazzi and Women Reporters in Hollywood

VANESSA
DÍAZ

Manufacturing
CELEBRITY

DUKE UNIVERSITY PRESS

Durham and London

2020

Designed by Matthew Tauch
Typeset in Minion Pro and Futura Std by
Tseng Information Systems, Inc.

Library of Congress Cataloging-in-Publication Data
Names: Díaz, Vanessa, [date] author.
Title: Manufacturing celebrity : Latino paparazzi and
women reporters in Hollywood / Vanessa Díaz.
Description: Durham : Duke University Press, 2020. |
Includes bibliographical references and index.
Identifiers: LCCN 2019054806 (print)
LCCN 2019054807 (ebook)
ISBN 9781478008545 (hardcover)
ISBN 9781478009436 (paperback)
ISBN 9781478008880 (ebook)
Subjects: LCSH: Hispanic American mass media. | Hispanic
Americans in mass media. | Celebrities in mass media. |
Mass media and culture—United States. | Mass media—
Political aspects—United States. | Paparazzi—United States. |
Women journalists—United States. | Fame—Social aspects—
United States. | Popular culture—United States.
Classification: LCC P94.5.H58 d53 2020d (print) |
LCC P94.5.H58 (ebook) | DDC 305.5/2—dc23
LC record available at https://lccn.loc.gov/2019054806
LC ebook record available at https://lccn.loc.gov/2019054807

Cover art: *Vengeance* premiere, Cannes Film Festival,
2009. Photo by Georges De Keerle / Getty.

Duke University Press gratefully acknowledges the
Bellarmine College of Liberal Arts, Office of the Dean,
at Loyola Marymount University, which provided funds
toward the publication of this book.

THIS BOOK IS DEDICATED TO Chris Guerra and Natasha Stoynoff. And to my parents, Jean and the late Woodrow ("Nino") Díaz, who taught me the importance of and the power in speaking out against injustice and inequality at every turn, every day, even (perhaps especially) in the areas where it might be easy to overlook or ignore.

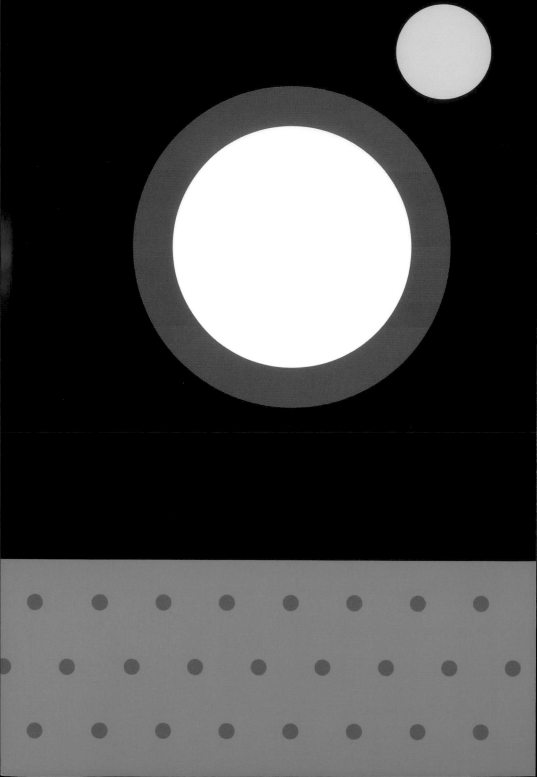

CONTENTS

III • Crafting the Media and the Sociocultural Consequences

ILLUSTRATIONS

ACKNOWLEDGMENTS

I never imagined that my first book would focus on celebrity culture in the U.S. Coming to this book project was an organic process that evolved as a result of several personal and professional factors. From the time I started working for *People* magazine in college to the reporting I did for them during my time as a graduate student, I constantly reflected on the racial and cultural politics of celebrity culture, and entertainment more broadly. As a child growing up in Southern California, the allure of Hollywood was omnipresent. Thus this book is a result of both highly concentrated times of research and lifelong reflections.

That research would be nonexistent without the openness and generosity of my research collaborators in the entertainment and journalism industries; from the paparazzi, to the red carpet reporters and photographers, to the staff reporters at the celebrity weekly magazines, and beyond, my life has been thoroughly invigorated by my experiences working with them. There are too many to name, and several requested anonymity, but you will get to know many of them through this book. A very special thanks to Galo Ramirez, Natasha Stoynoff, and Chris Guerra's mother, Vicky.

During my time at the University of Michigan, Ruth Behar, Kelly Askew, Daniel Herwitz, Conrad Kottak, and Barbra Meek kept me going. Ruth's constant encouragement of my writing is a central reason I completed this book. Several other U of M faculty also offered support and helped me develop intellectually, especially Janet Hart, Judith Irvine, Webb Keane, Lawrence La Fountain-Stokes, Bruce Mannheim, Damani Partridge, Yeidy Rivero, and Jennifer Robertson. Arlene Dávila has been an inspiration and a source of support since I walked into her classroom on my first day of college at NYU; thank you.

Dwight Blocker Bowers, Amy Henderson, and the late Marvette Pérez (1961–2013) helped make my time at the Smithsonian Institute productive and intellectually stimulating. Thank you also to the other former and current SI staff who welcomed me during my time there, especially Eduardo Díaz, Omar Eaton-Martinez, Margaret Salazar-Porzio, Taína Caragol, and Steve Velasquez.

I am so grateful to my UCLA friends, colleagues, and mentors, especially John Caldwell, Jessica Cattelino, Peter Hudson, Purnima Mankekar, Norma Mendoza-Denton, Safiya Noble, Chon Noriega, Jemima Pierre, Shannon Speed, and Abel Valenzuela. An extra special thank you to my UCLA mentors during my time on the Ford Postdoctoral Fellowship and UCLA Institute for American Cultures Visiting Researcher Fellowship in Ethnic Studies, Darnell Hunt and Sherry Ortner. I would have never made it through this process without the support of my friend and mentor Mark Sawyer (1972–2017), whom I miss dearly.

Thank you to: The staff at the National Academy of Sciences who administer the Ford Foundation Fellowships, and to the entire Ford family; Dartmouth's Program in Latin American, Latino and Caribbean Studies for hosting me during my time as a Postdoctoral Fellow; my Cal State Fullerton colleagues Christina Ceisel and Hunter Hargraves; and my colleagues in the Department of Chicana/o and Latina/o Studies at Loyola Marymount University.

Countless other friends, colleagues, and mentors helped shepherd me through this process. A special thanks to the current and former USC faculty who offered me intellectual support, especially Sarah Banet-Weiser, Macarena Gomez-Barris, Jack Halberstam, Josh Kun, Rhacel Parreñas, and George Sanchez. Thank you to Leo Chavez, Frances Negrón-Muntaner, and Frances Aparicio for your encouragement.

Thank you to John L. Jackson for continual support of my work; your positivity is infectious and inspiring. My monthly calls with Mari Castañeda during much of the book writing process helped keep me on track. Jason de Leon saw the heart and the value in this project from early on in its development—thank you. My soul-nurturing and life-affirming conversations with Aimee Cox seemed to happen at all the points I needed them most. Thank you to Aisha Beliso-de Jesús for your healing and wisdom. I am grateful for the inspiring theoretical debates with Jonathan Rosa throughout the development of this book. Thank you to Elana Buch for our L.A. work sessions over sushi and arepas. Thank you to Jane Lynch for your generous feedback on book chapter drafts, and to my other U of M cohort members: Elana Res-nick, Jane Lynch, Luciana Nemțanu, Bruno Renero-Hannan, and Nick Emlen. Thank you to Naomi Gordon-Loebl for teaching me so much, despite the fact that you were my student when we met. Kate Epstein, Margo Meyer, and Liz Crooks, thank you for your help during my editing process.

From the time I met editor extraordinaire Ken Wissoker at my first Ford Foundation Fellows conference, his encouragement of and interest in this project helped keep me motivated throughout the writing process. Thank you for believing in this book and in me. I am also so grateful to Liz Ault, Josh Tranen, Liz Smith, and the many other incredible staff members at Duke University Press who helped make this book possible.

Thank you to my friend and sister, Elizabeth Kai Hinton, who has provided me with careful guidance throughout my academic career and has remained a primary source of support. Thank you to my dear friend Loren Nunley, who somehow managed to get an MD *and* an MBA before I finished my PhD. Thank you to Bridget Callihan and Joey Forster, who always welcomed me with open arms when I returned home to Los Angeles. Thank you to Rafael "Papo" Zapata and my NYU crew; and Alana, Belén, and Cynthia, and my J. W. North fam. Gracias a mis hermanxs del alma: Alex Ortiz, Alexey Rodriguez y Magia López.

Thank you to my siblings, Angie, Larissa, and Woodrow "el tercero." Thank you for the love and support from my aunts, uncles, cousins. Titi Nanny, your joyful warrior spirit is what I aspire to. Dad, your life and work have made me who I am today; I carry you with me, and I take comfort knowing that you and your sister are with us in spirit and watching over us every day. Thank you to Jill Sargent, who was there for me like no other when I went through one of the hardest times of my life. Thank you to my mother, who has withstood some of the toughest of times and yet fearlessly continues to wear her heart on her sleeve in a way that most people would never imagine possible. Finally, words cannot express the level of gratitude I have for my brilliant partner, Ben, who served as my go-to at-home editor at every stage of my writing. Your indefatigable support has shown me your love, dedication, and belief in my abilities as a scholar. Thank you for helping me get to the finish line.

This research was supported with generous funding from the Ford Foundation, Smithsonian Institute, UCLA Institute for American Cultures, César Chávez Postdoctoral Fellowship at Dartmouth College, Loyola Marymount University (LMU) Bellarmine College of Liberal Arts (BCLA), LMU BCLA Dean's Office, LMU's Center for the Study of L.A., UCLA Chicano Studies Research

Center, Bunche Center for African American Studies at UCLA, the Mellon Summer Institute on Tenure and Professional Advancement, and the following funding from the University of Michigan: Rackham Graduate School, Institute for Research on Women and Gender, Center for the Education of Women, and Alliance for Graduate Education and the Professoriate.

INTRODUCTION

The Precarious Work of Celebrity Media Production

I met Chris Guerra in October 2012. The paparazzi photographer Galo Ramirez introduced me to Chris, a young, aspiring paparazzo who had only recently begun working on a freelance basis for the same agency as Galo. I photographed one of their training sessions as they waited outside Heidi Klum's Pacific Palisades mansion. My photos of Chris's training were shown during his memorial service three months later (see fig. I.1).

Chris was struck by multiple cars and killed on New Year's Day in 2013. Reports indicate he was attempting to comply with a California Highway Patrol officer's orders to return to his car after trying to photograph Justin Bieber's Ferrari in Los Angeles. He was twenty-nine years old. According to witness testimony and dashcam transcriptions, a police officer had stopped Bieber's Ferrari for speeding and was beginning to question the car's occupants about the scent of marijuana in the car. When one of the occupants told the officer that Chris was videotaping the stop, the officer released them to focus his attention on Chris instead.[1]

"What the hell are you doing?" the officer was recorded saying. He then uttered several undecipherable words, ending with "paparazzi." When Chris explained that he was a photographer and a member of the press, the officer asked, "Do you have any credentials other than you just standing there?"

I.1 **Photo of Chris Guerra training as a paparazzo near Heidi Klum's home. October 2012.** Photo by the author.

As the officer's tone became more aggressive, Chris responded, "Okay, all right! Relax!" The officer told Chris that paparazzi should not hassle people and demanded that Chris return to his car, which was parked across four lanes of traffic with no crosswalk nearby. Chris's last words were, "All right, brother." He was then hit by two cars and killed.

The driver of the first car, an SUV, was stopped, questioned, and sent on her way with no charges. Per the police report, the officer told the driver that "the accident was not her fault." The second driver never stopped, which constitutes a felony hit-and-run, but no investigation followed.[2] Although there is no evidence that Chris was killed instantly, the officer, who was trained in CPR, made no attempt to investigate whether he was still alive. The dashcam later recorded the officer saying to his partner, "Dude, I was just like, I just told him he couldn't stand there. Fucking idiot, man."

The singer Miley Cyrus echoed this sentiment in a Twitter thread reacting to the incident: "Hope this paparazzi/JB accident brings on some changes in '13. Paparazzi are dangerous! . . . It is unfair for anyone to put this on to Justin's conscious [sic] as well! This was bound to happen! Your mom teaches u when your [sic] a child not to play in the street! The chaos that comes with the paparazzi acting like fools makes it impossible for anyone to make safe choices."[3] These tweets were retweeted almost 100,000 times, and fans responded with such comments as "Your hate for the paparazzi is one of my favorite things about you."[4] Some comments from viewers of online video reports of Chris's death were even more vitriolic: "It's sad when people die. Paparazzi, not so much"; "Paparazzi don't count as human beings, so it's ok to laugh when one gets flattened"; "Poor Justin. I feel so bad for him. Fuck you, paparazzi"; and "More paparazzi need to die. If I see one on the road, I will swerve to hit the motherfucker."[5]

As part of her Twitter tirade against Chris, Cyrus tweeted at the E! News correspondent Ken Baker, "@kenbakernow you can have a big part in making that change if the photos stop being made entertainment. There's plenty of news without paps [paparazzi]!"[6] Baker, who had previously worked for People magazine and Us Weekly, agreed with Cyrus and condemned paparazzi work, despite the fact that his own work depends on it: "@MileyCyrus honestly, I can't believe this hasn't happened before. So many super sketchy street ambushes, all for stupid pics."[7]

Instead of being acknowledged as an integral part of the celebrity news machine, the work of paparazzi is popularly derided and framed as disposable.

That today's Hollywood paparazzi are predominantly Latino men, including U.S.-born Latinos and Latin American (im)migrants, is central to the nature of the public discourses around paparazzi. News articles refer to them as "untrained," "corner-cutting," "foreigners working on . . . questionable visas," while online reader comments call them "bottom feeders" and "illegals" who should "be deported."[8] The field has become dominated by Latinos because formal barriers of entry do not exist for paparazzi work. This is their way into the Hollywood system, outside the hierarchies and elite spaces inhabited by others in the industry, such as celebrity reporters. The paparazzi's informal labor and racially minoritized status position them as public scapegoats for what is wrong with celebrity media.

Celebrity reporters, on the other hand, contribute similarly to celebrity media production but are not scapegoated in the same way. This is due at least in part to such factors as race, gender, class, education, and perceived professionalism. Celebrity reporters are predominantly college-educated women, many from middle- to upper-middle-class backgrounds, and the vast majority are white, while the paparazzi were predominantly working-class men of color without a college education. However, celebrity reporters face different perils, as the story of the former *People* magazine reporter Natasha Stoynoff reflects.[9]

Before working as a stringer—a regular freelancer—for the magazine, I was hired as an intern at *People* in the fall of 2004. My cubicle was directly outside of Natasha's office. At the time, many of her reporting assignments were focused on Donald Trump, whose television show was soaring in the ratings (see fig. I.2). Indeed, the entire magazine was wrapped up in the success of *The Apprentice* and heavily promoted Trump. Talk of *The Apprentice* was so prominent during that time that it inspired a group of us at the office to dress up as Trump and his apprentices for Halloween. Only weeks later Natasha was conducting interviews at Trump's Mar-a-Lago estate for a story about the happy married life of the reality star and his third wife, Melania, who was pregnant at the time. When they were alone during the interview Trump attacked Natasha, forced his tongue into her mouth, and told her they would have an affair.[10] Despite the assault, the story Natasha was working on was published; it was titled "Happy Anniversary" and celebrated the couple's wedding anniversary and Melania's pregnancy.[11]

In 2011, during a taped interview for my research, Natasha confided in me about the attack since it was relevant to my focus on gender in the work of celebrity media producers. She said that she was writing a story about a "very famous person" that "was all about how he was so happy with his new wife.

I.2 Natasha Stoynoff (*second from left*) with Donald and Melania Trump in 2005. Despite Donald Trump's denying Stoynoff's accusations or even knowing her, photographer Troy Word took a photo of a smiling Stoynoff and Trump at Trump's Mar-a-Lago estate on the day Stoynoff was assaulted. Photo by Troy Word.

Meanwhile she was pregnant and he's making a pass at me. Literally pushing me against the wall sticking his tongue down my throat." She paused and whispered, "Donald Trump." I was still freelancing for *People* and thus a colleague as well as a researcher, and a friend. But even in a private setting with someone she trusted, she hesitated to say his name out loud, years before he was a presidential candidate. Natasha continued, "He called me up after the article ran and said, 'I just want to tell you what a great article you did. It was fabulous. I love it.'" At the time of the attack she told a superior, who asked if she wanted to press charges, but she decided against it. "I just thought, this guy felt so big." She explained that she felt dishonest about the story. "But I didn't know my power then. . . . I was in shock for those few moments that I couldn't react normally as I should have. . . . Donald Trump doesn't give a shit about what anyone thinks or feels. And then I talked to one of my best friends and she said, 'Oh, he made a pass at me once too. It's just common for him.'"

For fear of losing her job, she did not publicly tell the truth about Trump for years. She even allowed her story about Trump's very happy home life as a doting husband to be published. Stories like Natasha's are not unique. Women in the entertainment industry, in all kinds of positions, are frequently used strategically and mistreated for the benefit of the companies they work for or the pleasure of the men they are interacting with professionally. Celebrity reporters spend most of their careers at the mercy of celebrities, who are able to exercise a great deal of power over them and the media outlets they represent. To maintain her dignity, the reporter of course likes to think of herself as powerful, possessing the agency to shape a story and change the world. But as Natasha's story reveals, the power of the celebrity reporter can be quite limited. Faced with the possibility of disrupting the narrative about Trump in a very real way, she opted for the status quo, the path of least resistance—a testament to her vulnerability rather than her weakness.

Because Natasha had revealed to me years earlier that Trump had assaulted her, I was not surprised when the infamous *Access Hollywood* video was released during the 2016 presidential campaign, in which Trump said that as a "star" "you can do anything" to women.[12] The fact that the tape had only a limited impact on public opinion made me fearful about what the outcome might be if Natasha publicly shared her story, but I still hoped that she would. On October 12, 2016, *People* published the first report in which Natasha publicly told the story of her assault by Trump.[13] I reached out to her to remind her that she had described the assault to me in a recorded interview and named Trump as her assailant; my recordings became a potential legal asset to her as she faced criticism and threats of a lawsuit from Trump. My research on celebrity media had become wholly intertwined in the U.S. presidential race.

Maybe this should not have been entirely surprising. The practices of celebrity reporting, and celebrity media production more broadly, are now important to U.S. politics and world events. While there were always blurred lines between entertainment, celebrity, and politics, the distinction between entertainment and news media is not an empirical reality, but rather a function of a public imaginary—that there *should* be a difference between so-called hard news and entertainment news. The dynamics I talk about in this book are increasingly relevant to media in general, international politics, and to the state of American culture more broadly.

Chris's and Natasha's stories demonstrate why the topic of this book matters. Their stories are interconnected and divergent in significant ways, which is why this book focuses on both the reporters and the photographers whose work populates the pages of celebrity magazines. A central component of this book is understanding how the politics of visibility and invisibility affect these media producers and are critical to the maintenance of the celebrity system.

A narrative of invisibility and precarity connects Chris's and Natasha's stories. Natasha felt invisible and unimportant next to Trump, who was rich, powerful, and influential at her place of work and in the country. She had established her career in part by interviewing him. She might have the opportunity to meet and interview high-profile individuals, but she herself is not one of them. Her work is in the service of the celebrities and of the corporation that paid her to do this work. As a freelance celebrity photographer working outside of the confines of corporatized spaces and contexts, Chris's labor was even more precarious. Paparazzi work has historically depended on remaining as invisible as possible so as to obtain truly candid shots of celebrities. However, instances like the policing that led to Chris's death are a result of hypervisibility. Both Chris and Natasha were marked subjects, deployable and disposable in the service of prevailing formations of power. In the context of her assault, even while on the job Natasha's body existed for Trump to use, demonstrating the authority and power his celebrity status afforded him. In the context of Chris's death, even while on the job his body existed to be policed, demonstrating the forms of authority and power that he was unable to challenge. Neither Trump nor the police officer had to confront the consequences of his actions. In these two cases, Natasha and Chris shared a complicated relationship with (in)visibility. They were both positioned as highly visible, and yet, in terms of their own agency and ability to act, they were invisible. Thus even if someone is made visible, it is often in ways that don't honor, respond to, or disrupt prevailing formations of power. The experiences of Chris and Natasha very clearly, and very deeply, underscore the precarious nature of their labor in a glamorized field, in which visibility is always strategically produced.

Events following Chris's death and the assault of Natasha demonstrate the care and agency with which these two different precarious laborers are understood and treated in their socioprofessional contexts. Recently the entertainment industry has made institutional space for victims of sexual assault, but the physical assault of paparazzi largely continues without punishment. The industry and society in general still do not see the attacking of paparazzi as a social problem. This discrepancy raises questions around visibility, legality, gender, sexuality, race, privilege, and education that I explore in this book.

Race, Gender, and Power
in the Manufacturing of Celebrity

On the corner of Sunset Boulevard and Vine Street, in the heart of Hollywood, crowds of fans pressed as close as possible to the red carpet for the 2011 VH1 Do Something Awards. As I waited for the celebrities to appear for interviews, a process that had become routine after several years of reporting for *People* magazine, I overheard the conversations of the young fans. "Hillary Duff, I used to want to be her," one teenage girl told her friend. "She's so nice and so real. I feel bad for her sister, though. It's like Ashlee [Simpson] trying to compete with Jess[ica Simpson]. Oh, here comes [David] Beckham! I have fantasies about him all the time." Such everyday conversations demonstrate the deeply personal connections and imaginary social relationships that people form with celebrities in the United States.[14] For this girl and many Americans, celebrities are the people we emulate, fantasize about, and feel we know intimately enough to be on a first-name basis.

How is it that we often know more about celebrities than we do about many friends and neighbors we see in person every day? Images and talk of celebrity have come to dominate U.S. culture. In beauty salons and classrooms, at stores and dinner parties, people discuss celebrity gossip, such as the latest celebrity breakup or current Kardashian family drama, rather than discussing their own lives. While celebrity, stardom, and fame have been a part of global cultures for centuries, celebrity news has increasingly come to dominate media coverage and personal conversations during our lifetime.[15] Reality television, the internet, and social media make celebrities ever more accessible, while at the same time convincing people more than ever before that they too have a chance to become a celebrity. "We give people lip service that you have to be talented, but there's a generation of people that see Snooki [of MTV's reality show *Jersey Shore*] and think, 'It happened for her, it can happen for me,'" Ron, a freelance reporter who has worked for *Us Weekly* and *People*, told me. Research corroborates this observation. A 2005 Harvard survey revealed that 31 percent of U.S. teenagers think they will become famous.[16] A 2012 UCLA study on preteen values found that fame was the most important value to participants.[17] To understand why this obsession with and desire for fame has permeated U.S. culture requires understanding how celebrity and fame are portrayed in the media.

My research shows how the social relations of celebrity media producers affect how they compose images and shape stories and, ultimately, how

Americans relate to celebrities and understand fame. In doing so, it builds on the pioneering work of the anthropologist Hortense Powdermaker in postwar Hollywood, which examined how the lives of moviemakers affected film production. Since Powdermaker's *Hollywood: The Dream Factory* was published in 1950, Hollywood industries have multiplied, and their media have become more engrained in everyday life in the U.S., entering homes in an array of new forms.

To understand celebrity media production, it is vital to understand the racial, ethnic, and class politics involved in its labor. At the first celebrity event I attended, I introduced myself to an African American celebrity by explaining that I worked for *People* magazine. "I call that *White People* magazine," he joked. The relationship between the race and ethnicity of the reporters, interviewees, and consumers is layered. Reporters of color, like myself, are aware that they are mostly producing a magazine of white popular culture and are most likely to do the few interviews with celebrities of color whom the magazines deem white-consumer friendly. My own conversations with paparazzi photographers suggest that as many as 50 percent of the Los Angeles–based paparazzi are undocumented and that they are the backbone of an extensive informal economy of celebrity photographs. The racialization of paparazzi in Los Angeles and their exclusion from the formal production process of the magazines became a critical place of reflection as I examine the work of and relationships between the predominantly white female celebrity reporters and the predominantly Latino (both U.S.- and Latin American–born) male paparazzi. Through a focus on gender dynamics in celebrity media production, I demonstrate how the predominantly female reporters and male photographers together promote and amplify the pressure for women to conform to certain physical expectations, while validating the male gaze on women in American culture.

This study of the manufacturing of celebrity culture is, at its core, a study of labor, race, gender, and the neoliberal global political economy. Understanding the contemporary neoliberal moment requires taking seriously the "accounts of Western media production that finely delineate the complicated power relations of organizational hierarchies" therein.[18] These are not simply studies of popular culture or celebrity but rather studies of labor, economies, race, gender, and the hierarchies that define the global social order. The industries that make up Hollywood—which I conceptualize as the Hollywood-industrial complex—exist and thrive because of these hierarchies, like most other financially profitable economic institutions. In order to understand the power structures within these industries, we must understand who is behind the production of media and why it matters. Furthermore, it doesn't *just* matter who is behind the camera or who is involved in production; the circumstances of the labor performed by those producers matter as well. In the case of the paparazzi, the precarity and disenfranchisement of their labor affects the extent to which they are able to receive equal citizenship in the celebrity media industry.

While the politics of inclusion in both media production processes and media products themselves is important, it has been regularly addressed in scholarship.[19] This book points to a deeper and more nuanced story. Throughout *Manufacturing Celebrity*, I emphasize that the statistics of diversity in media production, and in corporate and institutional realms more broadly, are not the only concern. Even where so-called diversity is present, we must contend with the politics of labor in that production, including the ways the labor has been structured based on race, class, and gender, and the dynamic interplay between various media laborers and the content of the work they produce. As the comedian Chris Rock argued in a blistering essay about race in Hollywood, Latinxs are institutionally excluded from Hollywood industries despite being the dominant demographic of the region.[20] The preponderance of Latinx paparazzi allows celebrity media to capitalize on the vulnerability of Los Angeles's Latinx laborers. The inclusion of Latinxs as paparazzi was a side effect of an initial hiring practice at one particular photo agency (x17), resulting in a pattern that quickly snowballed because of savvy immigrant labor networks and Latinx understanding that this was their way into the industry. Paparazzi should not be thought of as bringing diversity to the industry. Framing the paparazzi as diverse reflects the neoliberal approach to diversity, in which diversity is defined as nonwhite. But the paparazzi community is actually not diverse; it is overwhelmingly Latinx. Allowing Latinx labor into one informal, delegitimized, and denigrated sphere within the industry is an example of tokenism and reflects the marginalization of these laborers.

As other ethnographers of culture industries have pointed out, the invisible laborers working behind the scenes wield tremendous influence over the cultural products we are all presented with as objects for consumption.[21] Much like the film and TV production communities that the media scholar John T. Caldwell describes in his book *Production Culture*, the communities of celebrity-focused media producers that I elaborate on in this book are as important to understanding celebrity culture, and Hollywood industries more broadly, as the content of the media they produce.[22] While it is fully possible to analyze media content without any understanding of the media producers themselves, as many scholars and journalists have done, these studies lack engagement with the stories, histories, feelings, opinions, and labor politics that directly affect the content.

My analysis of the politics and division of labor involved in the production of celebrity-focused media in the United States is based on ethnographic fieldwork—primarily in Los Angeles, and secondarily in New York—during which I conducted ethnographic interviews, archival research, and participant-observation through institutional, informal, and virtual ethnography. I explore the work and lives of the celebrity journalists, paparazzi, and red carpet photographers who create the content for the celebrity weekly magazines *People*, *Us Weekly*, *OK!*, *In Touch*, *Star*, and *Life and Style*. I conducted preliminary research during the summers of 2008 and 2009, full-time research from 2010 through 2012, and part-time research from 2013 to 2017. My previous experience as an intern and reporter for *People* beginning in 2004 also informs this work.

While issues of media consumption have been more thoroughly addressed in anthropology and related fields, media production remains underresearched, in large part because of issues of access to the media producers. During the course of my research, I continued my work on the red carpet for *People* as part of my participatory ethnographic methodology; this facilitated my extended access to the media producers I worked with on my project. Because I already had a wide network in what those who work in entertainment call simply "the industry," using the snowball effect to get references from reporters for other reporters and photographers was highly effective. In the industry, trust does not come easily, and my "in" was the reason I could do the work I set out to do. Having an online presence during fieldwork was also critical for the project's success; the reporters I worked with used social media (especially Facebook, Twitter, and Instagram) to keep in touch. Reporters and photographers alike often post images to demonstrate their "in" on red carpets. Failing to do so would raise questions among others in the industry: Did you get fired? Did you stop getting freelance work? I often started online conversations with potential interviewees, then met with them informally before doing a formal interview. "Liking" fellow reporters' posts was a necessary exercise for my research, as it facilitated such connections.

Sherry Ortner's insights about the meaning of "community" in the entertainment industry reflect my experiences. Referring to actors, directors, and movie and TV crews, she notes that while "Hollywood" is spatially discontinuous, there is a good deal of community.[23] As someone who has worked within the industry, I can attest that the feeling of community within it is undeniable; on red carpets most people, from publicists to reporters and photographers, know each other. Whenever I attended events as part of my participant-observation, I was surrounded by people I knew; former editors, former colleagues from *People*, and public relations agents I worked with regularly were all there. This distinct community of the people who write and place celebrity-focused stories in the press is tight-knit to the point of being incestuous. Connections tighten as people move from job to job; one person I worked with throughout my research had written for *Star*, been an editor for *People*, and was then working in public relations. To separate *People* from *Star* from *Us Weekly* is to forget that the people who shape those publications all intermingle and switch positions within them during the course of their careers.

The media professionals I interviewed during my Los Angeles–based fieldwork are journalists who work or have worked for one or more of the celebrity weekly magazines and photographers who regularly place photos in those magazines; they represent both the dominant demographics and the minorities within their industry. Taking full advantage of my position as a member of the same group of media producers that I research, I approach my research auto-ethnographically by making my own experiences a critical element of my ethnographic data.[24] Reflexivity is called for in the interest of disclosure, openness, and increased objectivity and has historically given voice to underrepresented peoples.[25] Given the space that has emerged for self-reflexive ethnography across disciplines, my personal experience reporting for *People* provides an important angle to my perspective on media production.

Although magazine editors are also relevant to the manufacturing of celebrities, the information gatherers—the photographers and reporters—are at the forefront of my research, as they craft content for the magazines.[26] While underscoring the precarity of their labor, my research simultaneously suggests that they maintain a significant amount of agency that allows them to shape U.S. popular culture and discourse on celebrity through their work. While older news ethnographies proposed that journalists play a "relatively unconscious role" in a standardized process of news production, my research shows that, rather than simply doing as others request, celebrity reporters actively shape trends in popular culture.[27] Bourdieu notes that journalists' job is to impose a "legitimate vision of the social world" on their audiences, yet "very few case studies have sought to empirically attend in detail to how journalists' preconceived story ideas (or 'frames') result in the deliberate pursuit of certain voices and commentary."[28] As celebrity news increasingly seeps into all forms of news media in the United States, it is critical to understand the "visions" celebrity reporters and photographers impose on U.S. culture, as well as the motives behind these visions.

Hollywood and the Hollywood-Industrial Complex

Hollywood is an anomaly. Perhaps no other place in the world evokes the same number of meanings, connotations, and global symbolic capital. While it was originally the name given to a small tract of land in Southern California, Hollywood has come to reference U.S.-based film, television, and an array of entertainment-focused industries.[29] Hollywood became a brand early in its history, as it was (and remains) a central part of the development and economy of the Los Angeles area. Hollywood's reach was quickly national and then transnational, as Powdermaker's research demonstrated.[30] Powdermaker studied how Hollywood films affected leisure activities in the U.S. rural South, how the films themselves were produced in Hollywood, and how the residents of a mining town in present-day Zambia watched and interpreted Hollywood film and local Hollywood-influenced film movements.[31] Over the course of more than two decades, she demonstrated the broad cultural, technological, economic, local, and global implications of Hollywood and its most prized product: the moving picture. Her work "blazed a pioneering path in media anthropology that subsequently lay untrodden, forgotten."[32] The everyday ordinariness of American interaction with Hollywood media makes this area critical for anthropology: What does contemporary Hollywood look like, and how does its media shape everyday life? Only recently have anthropologists "rediscovered" the need to study Hollywood from the inside as a critical center of cultural production.[33]

To much of the world, Los Angeles *is* Hollywood, and Hollywood *is* mass entertainment media and celebrities. Of course, Hollywood and Los Angeles are much more complex than the films that represent them. Despite its diverse, multiethnic, and multilingual history, by the mid-twentieth century, in part because of the Hollywood media industry, Los Angeles became the most "WASPish" major city in the United States.[34] Now more polyethnic than New York, Los Angeles shifts landscapes and demographics as quickly and frequently as the Hollywood film sets that have come to epitomize it.[35]

In 1887 a midwestern realtor named Harvey Wilcox registered the 120-acre subdivision of Hollywood in Los Angeles's Cahuenga Valley, which began as a rural community of farmers.[36] At that time, "pioneers on the far side of the continent and in Europe were inventing the movies, drawing on a century of experiments, and the latest advances in optics and photography."[37] Hollywood farmers began renting spaces to aspiring filmmakers; Cecil B. DeMille's first picture was filmed in a rented horse barn.[38] In 1903 Hollywood's population was 1,000, and it already had its first sightseeing bus.[39] By 1915 Hollywood movies were hugely profitable. The industry payroll was $20 million, and Charlie Chaplin's salary went from $150 a week in 1914 to $670,000 a year in 1916. Fan magazines, precursors to the ones I focus on in this book, helped fuel the industry.[40] The studio industry peaked in the 1940s, riding a wave that began in 1939 with epic films like *The Wizard of Oz*. But after World War II Hollywood looked different. "Strikes, trade disputes, anti-trust action, a flight of the audience to suburbia, [communist] witchhunts and television" hurt the motion picture industry.[41] In the late 1950s Hollywood was in a major decline and filmmakers began moving and working abroad. "In an ironic reversal of Hollywood's role as a haven for the oppressed, American writers and directors emigrate[d] to Europe and Mexico as refugees from McCarthyism."[42] Low-budget films like *The Graduate* (1967) and *Bonnie and Clyde* (1967) that featured young "budding stars" triggered a revitalization, shifting the focus to a more youthful-looking Hollywood and audience, a focus that persists today.[43]

As this brief overview demonstrates, Hollywood has a conservative history. Even before World War II, Hollywood films were subjected to government-sanctioned "moral" guidelines known as the Motion Picture Production Code, which included racist and sexist regulations. Hollywood productions have always "sold" the American way of life.[44] This means that films tend to establish white, suburban, capitalistic, heteronormative family life as the norm. Hollywood also tends to advance stereotypes and social norms about race, culture, gender, sexuality, beauty, and body image.[45] Most people do not believe that Hollywood representations deeply affect them, but in fact research shows they do affect opinions, values, and self-image.[46] The Hollywood-industrial complex creates media with the very *intent* of affecting imagined audiences.

Several scholars and journalists have invoked the term *Hollywood-industrial complex*. But what precisely is referenced by the term has varied and has never been theoretically framed. The term has been used to reference Hollywood's ties to U.S. political and military interests, and it has been used more generally to refer to Hollywood's conglomeration of businesses.[47] In her work on fame and celebrity culture, the journalist Maureen Orth used the term "celebrity-industrial complex," but this is not inclusive of the broader system that builds and sustains Hollywood.[48] Because this book focuses on the work that builds and maintains the entity I call the Hollywood-industrial complex, I provide my own clarifying framework for this term.

I use *Hollywood-industrial complex* as a way to reference the political economy made up of the totality of Hollywood's many subindustries and its laborers. This encompasses film, television, music, radio, agents, managers, celebrities, and media producers at all levels in the labor hierarchy. It also encompasses celebrity-focused media of all kinds, including reporters and photographers and those who employ them. In President Dwight D. Eisenhower's 1961 farewell speech, he warned of the "military-industrial complex"—the conglomeration of military and defense industries that promotes war to sustain itself, which Eisenhower was concerned would wield tremendous influence on U.S. government and society.[49] The Hollywood-industrial complex exists to sustain itself in a parallel fashion, with the celebrity system as its driving force. Celebrity personas are constantly created and promoted in order to stimulate consumption of Hollywood media, and vice versa. In his work on stardom, the philosopher Daniel Herwitz explains, "The celebrity system runs on itself; the celebrity is valued in virtue of mere participation in the system."[50] The military-industrial complex has such a grip on American society that members of the military are given automatic admiration and respect merely for participating in the military system. Similarly, as illuminated by Herwitz's quote, celebrities are admired and celebrated simply for being celebrities—for being pronounced worthy of celebration by the very system that manufactures them. The media producers I focus on are at the heart of this manufacturing of the celebrity system.

That Hollywood's political economic structure mimics that of such neoliberal forces as the military-industrial complex is no surprise, given the neoliberal agenda of Hollywood industries that I have outlined. Although there have always been films that critiqued the social order, Hollywood has been the purveyor of racist and xenophobic stereotypes that have served U.S. political interests domestically and abroad. Hollywood's relationship to the state may have evolved over the past several decades, but it still serves to profit from promotion of U.S. military and political interests, such as in representations of the War on Terror in film and television in the wake of 9/11.[51] Hollywood is and has always been an extension of the system, despite accusations of its liberalism (and its self-promotion as such). As an example, following the initial *People* story on Natasha's assault by Trump, the magazine continued to run follow-up stories going into further detail, including Natasha's response to

Trump's denial of the accusations and testimony from others corroborating her story.[52] But the day after Trump's election victory, *People*'s tone dramatically shifted. The magazine's website featured a story entitled "My Front-Row Seat to History: PEOPLE Senior Editor Charlotte Triggs Watches Trump Win the Presidency," featuring a photo of the president-elect with his arm around the editor.[53] More puff pieces quickly followed, including "27 Photos of Ivanka Trump and Her Family That Are Way Too Cute," "Melania Trump's First Lady Style: See Her Best Moments on the Campaign Trail," and a celebratory election story with the title "He's Hired!"[54]

People's quick switch from supporting Natasha as she spoke out against Trump to publishing laudatory postelection coverage of Trump exemplifies the nature of the Hollywood-industrial complex and its relationship to the state. The fact that Trump was a celebrity who did not hold any political office or military position prior to achieving the presidency at once highlights and concretizes Hollywood's link to the state, while also demonstrating that the power of celebrity and Hollywood stardom has never held more social, cultural, political, and economic power than it does now. The original purveyors of "fake news"—celebrity reporters and the media they produced that were colloquially called "rags"—built a system in which Trump could flourish. He now employs against "hard news" the rhetoric that celebrities have always wielded against "entertainment news" to derive empathy by accusing celebrity reporting of being false and performing aggrievement by the celebrity media. Trump treats CNN no differently than TMZ.

The Celebrity Weekly Magazine

> Let's not just let the tabloid be the scapegoat for all of us who have to take ultimate responsibility about what experiences we want to consume. | **ADRIAN GRENIER** | ACTOR, AT THE GETTY CENTER EVENT "ARE WE ALL PAPARAZZI NOW?," 2012

This book focuses on the content creators for U.S. celebrity weekly magazines, a genre that began with the launch of *People* in 1974. Before *People*, celebrity reporting was reserved for newspaper columns, trade publications, and less frequently published magazines. *People* did not always have the same glossy, picture-book look that it has today. In the 1970s the only color was on the cover and in the ads, which were for Virginia Slims, Beefeater Gin, and other alcohol and cigarette brands. Full-color printing of *People* began in the mid-1990s. The magazine used to include some news and human interest stories, but now there is a heavier focus on celebrity. As a *People* reporter told me, the magazine has a "huge backlog" of human interest stories because it devotes so little space to them. The look of *People* has also changed a great deal. The number of pages in "Star Tracks," the celebrity photo section, has increased over the years (from as few as two pages in 1978 to as many as seven pages in recent years), and its placement has shifted from the middle to the first section of the magazine. The cover now often has several photos instead of just one. Yet in spite of the greater number of celebrities mentioned or pictured, as a former *People* reporter named Phil told me, "*People* used to be a venue for growing stars, but now you have to be established to even get into the magazine. It's not a place or a way for people to 'break through' the way it used to be."

People had no direct competition in the United States until 2000, when *Us Magazine*, which had existed since 1977 as a more trade-focused bimonthly and then monthly publication, relaunched as a weekly.[55] Then, beginning in 2002, a wave of new magazines entered the market. Between 2002 and 2005 *In Touch* and *Life and Style* began publication, the tabloid newspaper *Star* was relaunched as a weekly magazine, and the British magazine OK! created a U.S. version. While the branding and reputation of these magazines vary somewhat, they all share a common focus on celebrity content and a glossy, image-heavy aesthetic.

The timeline of the weekly celebrity magazines reflects historical moments in which media producers saw a void and a cultural moment in time on which they might capitalize. A former Time Inc. employee provided me a never-before-published 1973 prospectus, which outlines the vision for the company's *People* magazine. It boasts:

> The times seem to be right for [*People*]. The war is over. Protest is at a minimum. The counter-culture has lost much of its steam. Except for what dismay and anger Watergate stirs up, people seem to be fairly relaxed. National and international problems don't impinge on the average persons' minds or consciences the way they used to. Their concerns after job and family (or job and mate) run to fun and games (or sex and sports). Enter *People*, reaffirming the indisputable fact that what really interests people is other people. . . . The 60's are finally ended; and now, too, the Nixon era. The uncharted, the real 70's, with their potential for new personalities, beckon.[56]

This prospectus demonstrates the (perceived) space that emerged in the 1970s for escapist journalism and a new fixation on personalities. Time Inc. saw the public as being tired of grappling with serious issues like the Vietnam War and Watergate. Of course, while the content of celebrity magazines may appear to offer diversion from the stressful realities and injustices of contemporary neoliberal life, it also reproduces those realities in both its content and its labor production processes. The media we consume and the celebrities we worship are part of the larger global political economic system, and not somehow the escape from it. These celebrity media products might feel like an escape because they offer a look at the lives of others—of the rich and famous. But much of this media is about creating the illusion that celebrity lives are like our non-celebrity lives, while reinforcing notions of what contemporary (white) American life is supposed to look like.

Like *People*'s founding, the rapid multiplication of celebrity weekly magazines from 2002 to 2005 was a similar attempt to capitalize on a moment of yearning for distraction and escapism in the U.S., this time following September 11. My own story suggests why they succeeded. As a first-year student at New York University, two weeks after classes began I witnessed a plane fly overhead as I walked down Bleecker Street in the West Village, then watched it make a distinct turn straight into the first tower of the World Trade Center. Traumatized, I sought solace in the following months by doing community activism and performing spoken-word poetry at the Nuyorican Poets Café. But after years of activism, my steam ran out. I just wanted to get away from it all. Perhaps, then, it is no coincidence that I became part of this cultural machine of celebrity media production while in New York as a student. I began working for *People* as a paid intern during my senior year at NYU; my primary job was to keep an eye on Mary-Kate and Ashley Olson, who were in their first year at the same university. As an intern, I did not get paid just to follow my famous classmates; I also got paid to interview celebrities on red carpets and to go to the clubs and bars where they hung out. If this is celebrity reporting, I thought, then I'm in. But I came to see that it was about more than just following celebrities and churning out an online story or an item in a magazine. It was about the production of a culture through media products that shape gender, racial, and class ideals, as well as the understanding of (and desire for) fame and celebrity in the United States. I was given this opportunity, a door into a world that is "exclusive" (as the magazine covers remind us in every issue). I hope to use it to share my stories, my understandings, and my analysis with the same world, the same consumers, and the same communities that voraciously produce and consume this product.

If, as *People*'s success proved, "what really interests people is other people," and the "potential for new personalities" needs to be exploited at particular historical moments, I believe that the creators of the newer magazines I examine found the post-9/11 U.S. a place where new personalities had the potential to emerge and attract attention.[57] Because lack of access to celebrities was a real problem for start-up publications, those magazines invested in the potential of the new television personalities—reality stars—who were easier to access, hungry for fame, and willing to share any and all personal information. As the sociologist Karen Sternheimer points out, "Celebrity culture is one of the hallmarks of twenty-first century America. Never before has it been so easy to know so much about so many people, even people we might not want to know about. We seem to be on a first name basis with them, give them nicknames, and sometimes even feel as if we know all about them."[58] We care so deeply about the minutiae of celebrities' lives today because we have been provided with the feeling of access to all information about certain personalities through the celebrity weekly magazines, reality television, and constant social media updates by celebrities themselves. This is the new baseline: we expect to have access to all personal details of celebrities, broadly defined. Access to this intimate information has shifted our own notions of community and our general discourse, with information about these personalities becoming the default conversation starters for many people, the shared imaginary community among Americans.[59]

Gatekeepers of Celebrity Culture: The People behind the Celebrity Weekly Magazines

> We're like the gatekeepers. . . . Half of what we do has to be what's important to people now. The other half has to be kind of like fortune telling: what *should be* important to people? | **MEGAN** | EDITOR AND WRITER FOR A CELEBRITY WEEKLY MAGAZINE, 2009 INTERVIEW WITH AUTHOR

Through analysis of the methods of celebrity media production, this book explains how the content creators for the celebrity magazines manufacture personalities that people feel they know and can relate to. Photo sections of these magazines tend to depict celebrities taking part in the practices of everyday American life—pushing their babies in strollers, shopping at the grocery store, buying a coffee at Starbucks—in an effort to humanize them and reinforce the possibility that not only can celebrities be like the reader, but the reader can be like celebrities. In fact, one section of *Us Weekly* is called "Stars: They're Just Like Us." However, the activities and characteristics that reporters choose to feature as examples of celebrities being "just like us" presume certain things about the reader and thus about the general American public. This book will shed light on expectations of modern American behavior and personhood by analyzing how celebrity reporters reinforce what it means to be one of "us."

To understand how celebrity reporters and photographers determine what makes a celebrity one of "us," we must consider who these media producers are. "In order to understand the complexities of media production, it is necessary to examine producers' sentiments and subjectivities in conjunction with questions of political economy."[60] That the majority of celebrity reporters are women is something widely acknowledged within the industry, but not critically examined. Based on my experience as a reporter and observations during my fieldwork, I investigate the sexualization of female celebrity journalists. Journalists are often encouraged to use their sexuality (usually presumed to be heterosexuality) to relate to female celebrities on the basis of so-called women's issues and to exploit their sexuality for the sake of obtaining information from male celebrities. Beyond pressure from editors, some reporters have personal motives for exploiting their sexuality to get close to celebrities. "I see people who think they're going to become a celebrity's girlfriend and get the famous lifestyle out of it," one weekly magazine reporter told me. At the same time, these women reporters set new and impossible-to-maintain beauty standards for women in American culture. In this book I explore the implications of women playing this critical role in the molding of popular culture.

I also explore the implications of the demographics of celebrity photographers, who are typically male and, in Los Angeles, primarily Latino. Entrance to the industry through paparazzi work has put these men of color in a place in which they can be surveilled, criticized, and placed in physical danger.

Despite the expansion of celebrity-focused publications (both print and online), work in the celebrity culture industry still carries a stigma. In the field of journalism, celebrity reporters are sometimes considered a joke. When I first began work at *People* in New York, my friends were flabbergasted. My working there seemed to undermine my social consciousness, to be out of character and even disappointing. However, I found my job fascinating, from the tasks to the colleagues and the end product. Within weeks of working for the magazine, a story I wrote about Mary-Kate and Ashley Olsen was featured as the top story on the America Online home page. (This was 2004, during the period of AOL's relevance.) A second story I wrote was picked up by CNN. Long before Donald Trump's presidency, it showed me that celebrity reporting and hard news were blurring and forcing a change in the understanding of news media in the United States.

Celebrity reporters are often conflicted about their role as producers of media that many of them believe is diluting news, journalism, and American culture. Instead I see the work as *deeply* affecting American culture, perhaps in problematic ways. But the people producing these changes need to be understood, as do their publications, their tactics, their reliability, and their intentions. Rather than focusing just on performative events like red carpets, celebrity reporters are almost always engaged in long-term assignments and are required to develop long-term and *meaningful* relationships with specific people or groups of people. Just as with anthropologists, deep relationships with sources are critical to the livelihood of a celebrity reporter's career. When observing celebrities, these reporters consider questions like the following: What do they eat? What do they say? What are they wearing? Who are they with? How do they live? I worked with journalists before, during, and after they wrote stories in order to understand the process they go through to develop celebrity personas. Using my own archive of interview transcripts, story outlines, and final published stories, I also reexamine my own approach to celebrity reporting and my own process of manufacturing celebrity personae.

There are some excellent examinations of the history of celebrity journalism, history of the Hollywood studio system, analysis of celebrity and fame, and contemporary textual analysis of celebrity magazines; there are also ethnographically informed analyses of Hollywood media products themselves.[61] However, there are no ethnographies on the production of these magazines or on the photographers and reporters who provide the content for these publications. Not since Powdermaker's 1950 ethnography of Hollywood has anyone truly captured the culture of mainstream Hollywood production. While focusing my attention differently, I follow the path Powdermaker carved within anthropology to argue for the importance of exploring this area of inquiry ethnographically.

Since Powdermaker, Hollywood and its many industries have consistently been described as factories, as sites of production and manufacturing. I continue that trend in this book, though I long debated it. I vacillated between the phrases *crafting celebrity, selling celebrity,* and *manufacturing celebrity* for my title. In using the last, I do not mean to imply that the media producers I studied do not have agency in shaping American celebrity today. I use the word *manufacturing* in part to pay homage to my predecessors, who illuminated the industrial nature of mass media and the Hollywood system.[62] Likewise I did not feel *crafting* or *selling* accurately represented the scope and complexity of the celebrity-industrial complex that produced the material I analyze.[63] The word *manufacturing* emphasizes that media content creators are part of a larger and more complex system of production.

From red carpet reporters and photographers to paparazzi and staff reporters for the celebrity weekly magazines, this ethnography will bring insight to the professional lives of the purveyors of celebrity culture. Without the human component, without the people who make *People*, we cannot truly understand the process, the history, and the material we are provided for consumption.

Methodology

The data for this project were gathered intermittently over the course of more than ten years. While I was engaged in full-time ethnographic research from 2010 through 2012, I also undertook both formal and informal part-time research before and after this time period. From 2004 to 2007 I worked as an intern and then as a stringer for *People* magazine. This experience and material informs my long-term fieldwork, though it is not the focus of the research. During the summers of 2008 and 2009 I spent months engaged in full-time ethnographic research in Los Angeles, laying the groundwork for the long-term fieldwork that began the following year. From 2012 to 2017 I also engaged in part-time ethnographic and archival research.

My ethnographic research was multisited and multimodal. In order to gather data on the manufacture of celebrity media, I engaged in participant-observation with celebrity reporters and photographers, took several hundred photographs, and compiled several hundred pages of field notes. Time I spent in the offices of weekly magazines and photo agencies as well as on the red carpet offered insights into the institutional configurations of celebrity media production.[64] I also conducted informal ethnography by spending time with the media producers at home and at casual work meetings, and by engaging with fans on the sidelines of red carpet events. While my work was predominantly with reporters and paparazzi, I also collaborated with celebrity managers, publicists, attorneys, and magazine ad agents and editors. In order to understand these broader networks, I also conducted virtual ethnography on social networking sites by tracking and engaging in online exchanges between reporters about media production.[65] Finally, as a participant-observer, I worked freelance as a celebrity reporter during the research, which provided me insider access to the community and inner workings of the industry—as did my accompaniment of paparazzi on shoots.[66]

The unique nature of freelance and contingent labor means that, while paparazzi have little agency in their financial dealings with the corporations that depend upon their labor, they do have agency in the ways they perform their labor. When working with paparazzi, I was able to spend time on the job with them, before, during, and after their workdays, with no corporate restrictions. Unlike almost any other work in the entertainment industry, in theory anyone can be a paparazzo or go to their job sites, which are public spaces. At the same time, working with paparazzi is restrictive for two reasons. First, social stigma has led them to be wary of others' interest in their work, as they anticipate ridicule, humiliation, or worse.[67] Second, the value of their photographs increases with exclusivity, so paparazzi are wary of those who may want to scoop their story. Due to my work as a celebrity reporter, the second point was of particular concern, but I made it clear to the paparazzi I worked with that my time with them was strictly about observing their work, not about celebrity reporting. However, with the permission of the photographer, I occasionally filed a report with *People* on what was happening at the time an image was shot in my presence, in case *People* decided to publish the photographs and wanted corresponding reporting.

My research on the red carpet relied almost entirely on my continued freelance work as a reporter for *People*, although occasionally reporter friends brought me as a guest when this was permitted. While I informed individuals I worked with and for at the magazine about my research, I also made it clear that my research would not detract from my reporting. If anything, my particular ethnographic attention to detail surrounding red carpet work enhanced my reporting. Just as reporter friends invited me to accompany them, when possible I invited guests to red carpets where I was reporting. I discussed with my guests their impressions of and questions about the red carpet ritual and the celebrity culture that surrounds it. My times in corporate spaces, such as the offices of celebrity magazines, were in the capacity of a researcher using their library to perform archival research, and thus I was not asked to sign any nondisclosure agreements. Other than this time in the offices of weekly magazines, almost all of my research was conducted in public spaces or homes of reporters and photographers.

I had an extensive network of reporters, photographers, editors, public relations representatives, and other industry figures willing to contribute to and participate in my project. In total, I completed in-depth ethnographic interviews with eighty-five informants and collaborators, including photographers, journalists, public relations representatives, magazine editors, and celebrities. The staff reporters, freelance reporters, and editors I interviewed include individuals who worked with each of the major celebrity weeklies: *People, Us Weekly, OK!, In Touch, Star,* and *Life and Style.* The photographers I interviewed, who largely work freelance, include individuals affiliated with each of the major photo agencies. Additionally I conducted roughly a hundred informal interviews with other industry figures and fans at red carpet events.

The research for this book was conducted predominantly in English, as that is the primary language of most of my research collaborators. However, my research with paparazzi was conducted in Spanish, Spanglish, and English; this is reflected in part I of the book.

For the most part, I use pseudonyms in order to protect the identity of my collaborators. However, some individuals, mostly paparazzi, asked me to use their real names. I analyze why this may be below. The title associated with each of my interlocutors is that individual's title at the time of the interview.

Since the internet has changed the process of news production and journalistic communication so greatly over the past several years, I also conducted virtual ethnography on social networking sites, celebrity weekly magazine websites, and other major celebrity news websites such as *Perez Hilton, Jezebel, Pink Is the New Blog,* and *Just Jared,* as well as individual celebrity-run websites.[68] On these sites I both observed and participated in conversations about celebrity news stories between celebrity reporters themselves, reporters and celebrities, reporters and consumers, and consumers and celebrities. Media-centered methods of my research also included mobile video ethnography, as I had celebrity photographers shooting first-person GoPro footage while on the job, allowing me to view their experiences from their own perspectives and discuss those experiences with them.[69]

Throughout the course of my research, I also reviewed photographic and textual archival materials from the *People* library (which includes archives of both *People* and other celebrity weekly magazines) and online media archives, as well as personal collections of notable stories, photographs, and videos from the reporters and photographers themselves.

My approach to the ethnography and theorizing in this book relies on working collaboratively with the media producers I studied. As John T. Caldwell points out, media producers "critically analyze and theorize their tasks in provocative and complex ways."[70] The recent work of the anthropologists Aimee Cox and Yarimar Bonilla provides helpful and contemporary examples of cotheorizing—that is, theorizing *with* community members in the course of ethnographic research.[71] Throughout my research I grappled with how to best engage with the individual laborers I relied on in ways that recognized them as equal intellectual citizens in this project, while also engaging with my own experience as an industry worker.[72] I sometimes heard that individuals I interviewed later said it was therapeutic and illuminating to discuss their professional practices with me, and this encouraged others to participate. I believe this sense of emotional release came from my tendency to analyze the work of the interviewees and process those ideas aloud *with* them. Their stories and answers informed my analyses; my ideas informed their own reflections. This approach of cotheorizing is at the core of my project.

In more recent work, Cox urges us to go beyond cotheorizing and fortify our ethnographies, and our ethnographic methodologies, with what she calls *unconditional relationality*. Unconditional relationality is a way to articulate the emotional, spiritual, and intellectual transformations that emerge *because* "the relationships formed during research have a life outside of the research and are not solely beholden to the condition that these interactions service the anthropological project." Unconditional relationality is not focused on theorizing ethnographic experience; it is about harnessing the complex transformations that occur through ethnography.[73] My relationship with Chris's mother, Vicky, is a case in point. As I describe in chapter 3, our dynamic and collective processing of Chris's death exemplified the unconditional relationality Cox calls for. Our processing was not carried out in the interest of theorizing but, rather, was a means of mourning and seeking justice. To reduce to cotheorizing the intellectual and collective manner of mourning in which Vicky and I engaged—which occurred in back-and-forth conversations and emails, reading the words I wrote about Chris's death, and observing presentations where I discussed his death—is to remove the humanity that our relationship embodies. In ethnography, especially when we are examining such serious matters as the violent death of Vicky's son or the sexual assault Natasha experienced at the hands of Donald Trump, we must embody empathy, we must be open to transformation(s), and we must acknowledge when we are doing much more than cotheorizing.

At Home in the Entertainment Industry

A central distinction between my work and that of others who have written ethnographically on media production is that my work emerged out of an existing relationship with the celebrity media industry. I worked in media (radio, documentary, newspaper, online, print magazine) for several years, including working for *People* magazine, before beginning my research. Other researchers who have chosen to embark on research in Hollywood or media production more broadly often decided to enter the industry *because of* and *for* their research interests.[74] My years of experience within the media industry naturally affected not only my access to it but also my relationships to interviewees. My relationship to the geographical locations in which I worked, and my identity as a woman and a Latina from Southern California, also had major impacts on my positioning of the self within my research and the ways in which I related to the individuals who collaborated with me.

I was born in Los Angeles to a father who was an aspiring musician. He tried his hand at acting and stand-up comedy as well. I had childhood aspirations of stardom and celebrity that shifted during college, as I became increasingly involved in political activism and hip-hop culture. But by the end of college, I was somehow in the thick of celebrity culture, working for *People*. Like Hedda Hopper, an actress who became a celebrity gossip columnist, many reporters interested in working with me on this project have a (failed) history of or aspirations of acting, screenwriting, and film producing, and either hoped or hope to become celebrities.[75]

I was a product of the greater Los Angeles area and had a strong desire and affinity for celebrity, entertainment, and fame. As a child I asked my mother to take me to open-call auditions, though I had no headshot or experience. I began writing fan mail to celebrities at a young age, including personalized birthday cards to my favorite stars. I knew their birthdays because I did the research and marked their birthdays on my calendar. I always made an effort to talk to celebrities I saw at events and was fearless about approaching them. I went to events like "Get Moving with Oprah" at Griffith Park in 1995 at age eleven, and attempted to make friends with every celebrity there, including Oprah Winfrey herself (until her security guard pushed me away). After years of consuming celebrity media I felt as if I was friends with all of them already.

Members of my family have attempted to enter the entertainment industry through a wide array of approaches, many of them involving reality television shows. Collectively my mother and three siblings have applied to be on twenty-five reality television series. One of my sisters keeps a list that includes the stage she has gotten to in the casting process (callbacks, interviews, etc.) of each show. She came close to being selected for *The Biggest Loser*, and this interaction with the industry led many other casting directors to contact her. Some of these she turned down because, she says, they were either "humiliating or demeaning" or just uninteresting. In fact the only member of my family who has appeared on television is my brother, who appeared on an episode of *The Dog Whisperer* with his ill-behaved English mastiff.

Once, when my family was going through one of our many rough patches involving drugs and financial problems, my oldest sister suggested we write to Dr. Phil and ask for help. This was presented in all seriousness as a potential solution to our issues. There is a real illusion of having access to celebrities, to fame, to the resources that we come to expect we are special enough to receive, like Dr. Phil's psychological services. Similarly, when we were going through another difficult time when I was a child, I wrote a letter to Oprah asking her to help my mother—a single mom whose husband, mother, and father had all died in the span of a year. I thought my mother was as deserving as all of the people Oprah helped on her show. I remember the feeling of sadness that came over me when I received a generic letter with Oprah's signature thanking me for my correspondence. Yet I kept the letter in my nightstand drawer for years.

After working at a radio station where I frequently interacted with celebrities, the nature of my enthrallment shifted. I no longer wanted or expected that I might be friends with celebrities, or that I might even become one myself. I became more captivated with the actual processes of interacting with celebrities at events, especially the rituals of interviewing and photographing them. Just like the readers, fans, and consumers who want to know every last detail about their favorite celebrities, I wanted that information, but I also wanted to know *why* and *how* that information was being amassed. My research interests are the natural product of growing up surrounded by communities obsessed with fame and celebrity.

My experience in media industries was instrumental to my ability to do this project. My work for *People* also enabled me to be a part of my own research; I am my own source throughout this book, and my own experiences are a critical part of it.[76] I understand this could raise concerns as to objectivity, a traditional goal of both anthropology and journalism. While I do not believe that objectivity is attainable for anyone, I do recognize the difficulties ethnographers encounter when attempting research within communities of which they are a part. I found myself wondering frequently whom I could trust and who my real friends were. Some of the individuals I worked with are close personal friends with whom I am still in very regular contact, and some of them are only professional contacts who kept up with me while I was on the red carpet. Being a red carpet reporter (especially for *People*) did carry a great deal of social and cultural capital. Savvy about the nature of this capital, public relations representatives, celebrity publicists, and celebrities recognized that their relationship to me could benefit them. As a reporter, I played a tangible part in determining the coverage of celebrities and brands in the magazine, so these industry figures put additional energy into our relationship while I was a regular on the red carpet. Now that I have largely transitioned out of this world, I am no longer considered a part of the community. Without the cultural and social capital that my position on the red carpet provided me, I'm not as important to them anymore. As Scott Huver, a longtime red carpet reporter in Los Angeles, told me, "No favors in Hollywood go into a bank." Completing my fieldwork or, rather, forcing myself to stop in order to focus on writing this book, was thus bittersweet. The red carpet was a home to me; it was familiar, filled with people I knew and routines and rituals I could do with my eyes shut.

I do not believe that we ever lose our homes completely; even if we, or our home, is physically gone, the home remains in the core of our being. Every place we have ever considered a home, for better or worse, is a part of who we are. Each home takes us through a different phase of our life, a period of growth. Even if we were taken from a home at a young age, as my father was taken from Puerto Rico as an infant, in an experience he described in violent terms, every single home we have ever known, whether we remember them vividly or not, make us who we are. In a world in which where we are born determines our nationality, in a country in which our national or ethnic background determines how we are socially read and understood, we may cling to or desperately try to negate our various homes. Though I lost my home on the red carpet, it still holds a piece of the ways I understand myself.

Manufacturing Celebrity

This book is divided into three sections. Part I contains three chapters focused on the paparazzi. Chapter 1 takes you on the job with the paparazzi, providing a window into the complex lives and work of this misunderstood group of laborers. It describes how the racial transformations in the workforce have impacted such issues as perceived skill and visibility, and how the photographers themselves conceptualize their work as a form of day labor. Chapter 2 explores the ethics and economics of paparazzi work, including both formal and informal economies shaped by the varying levels of precarity among the photographers. This chapter reveals the ways in which these racialized laborers understand their role producing images of mainstream white culture. Chapter 3 centers on Chris Guerra and the institutional circumstances that led to his tragic death on the job, including the broader structural violence that paparazzi face, the simultaneous disparagement and strategic use of paparazzi by celebrities, and the proliferation of anti-paparazzi legislation in California. I analyze these realities utilizing my conceptualization of media rituals of hate, as well as the framework of raciontologies, which Jonathan Rosa and I previously developed.[77]

Part II explores the work of celebrity reporters. Chapter 4 examines the red carpet as a space of media ritual that is more nuanced than popular imagery would suggest. It investigates how the red carpet shapes reporters' coverage of celebrities and, as a result, consumers' relationships to the stars. The chapter concludes by considering the perspective of photographers who document the red carpet process, producing a type of celebrity photography distinct from paparazzi images. Chapter 5 explores the other spaces in which celebrity reporting takes place, including nightclubs, public spaces, and one-on-one interviews. I illuminate the acute levels of precarity faced by reporters in these spaces, as they face pressure to push legal boundaries and are leveraged for their sexuality in ways that can be exploitative and sometimes traumatic, such as Natasha's experience with Trump. This chapter also underscores the ways in which the intersectional identities of the reporters further complicate this precarity.

Finally, part III provides a deeper analysis of specific tactics used by the celebrity weekly magazines to foster emotional investment in celebrity. Chapter 6 focuses on the magazines' "body teams," who report specifically on celebrities' bodies. The obsessive media evaluation of celebrity diets and pregnancies affects not only consumers but also the women reporters who produce this content. Chapter 7 examines the specific tactic of celebrity couple name combining, which is used by the magazines to promote feelings of intimacy with celebrities among fans. The name *Brangelina* is used as a case study in the very deliberate marketing of white heterosexual love. The book concludes by examining shifting boundaries of news and gossip and where the work of celebrity reporters and photographers fits in the contemporary media landscape.

Pappin' Ain't Easy

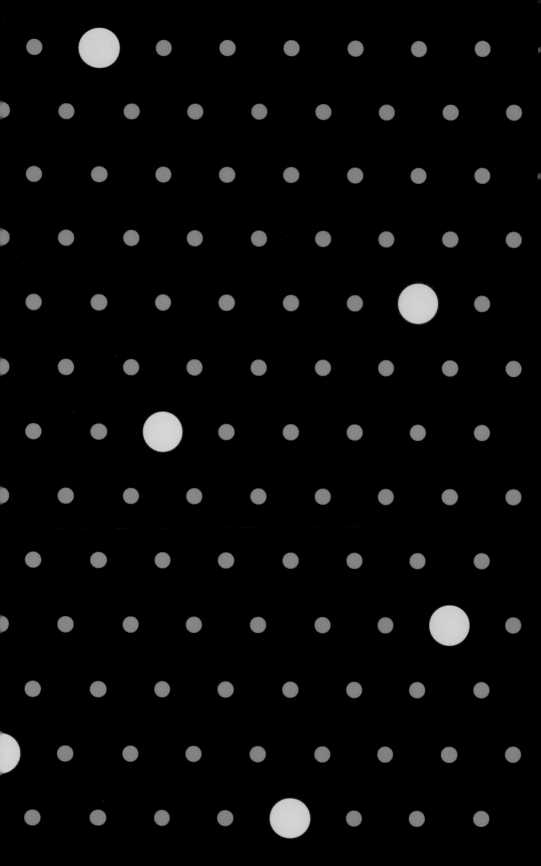

CHAPTER ONE

Shooteando: The Real Paparazzi of Los Angeles

T he paparazzi are a notorious fixture in Los Angeles. In contrast to other types of celebrity photographers—such as red carpet photographers and celebrity portrait photographers—paparazzi work on the street in an effort to capture candid, photojournalistic shots of celebrities (see fig. 1.1). Not only are they emblematic of Hollywood, celebrity, and Los Angeles culture, but they have also become a tourist attraction themselves. The official website of the Los Angeles Tourism and Convention Board has a page dedicated exclusively to paparazzi, encouraging people to go on "safaris" with paparazzi or to go where they can see paparazzi in action. Under the links on this page for "Activities and Recreation" and "Points of Interest," one finds the heading "Following the Paparazzi: 12 Places to Spot a Celeb." This content makes it clear that the paparazzi are seen as a vital resource for the tourism industry. The page reads as follows:

> Like swarms of bees searching for nectar, packs of celebrity-seeking paparazzi travel across Los Angeles every hour of the day in search of that next buzz-worthy shot. The encounter might be as ordinary as *Grey's Anatomy* star Katherine Heigl buying groceries, or as extraordinary as Reese Witherspoon having a romantic date at the beach. Witnessing the

1.1 Paparazzi in Los Angeles in 2014. Photo courtesy of Ulises Rios.

paparazzi portion of the star-making cycle is an authentic LA experience. The famous (and infamous) may go to great lengths to protect their privacy, but the paparazzi have uncovered their favorite public haunts. If you're eager for a celebrity sighting, check out some of the best paparazzi star-stalking spots in the city.[1]

Yet despite the paparazzi's central role in the celebrity culture of Los Angeles, reporters and editors of celebrity weekly magazines do not always consider paparazzi members of their profession and generally talk about them with disdain. "Paps are yucky, creepy people. They are stalking people for a living," said a former weekly magazine photo editor named Phoebe, who dealt almost exclusively with the selection and purchase of paparazzi shots for the magazine.[2] Similarly photographers who take celebrity photos on the red carpet become upset if referred to as paparazzi. "We are college educated, trained photographers. Paparazzi are animals who stalk celebrities," one red carpet photographer, Sam, told me. Based on public reaction to paparazzi both in person and online, it is clear that the general public largely has a negative perception of paparazzi as well. Perhaps no other figure in the entertainment industry is looked down upon as much as the paparazzo, particularly since Princess Diana's death in a car crash, for which paparazzi were initially blamed.[3]

Although paparazzi are looked down upon, their work appears everywhere. The majority of photos in the weekly magazines, and even a large number of celebrity photos used in news programs, are taken by paparazzi. A representative issue of *People* had twice as many paparazzi photos as non-paparazzi photos in the first twenty-five pages.[4] Because of the social stigma and physical risks involved in taking paparazzi shots, media outlets purchase photos only after they are taken; they do not officially employ paparazzi or assign paparazzi to take specific photos. Consumers might not even realize that the majority of the photos they see of stars walking down the street, lounging on the beach, or shopping are taken by paparazzi.

So who exactly are these people who perform such essential work in the celebrity media industry? As I have previously explained, the paparazzi are predominantly Latino men, including U.S.-born Latinos and both documented and undocumented Latin American immigrants. Though some are Brazilian and speak Portuguese, many are from predominantly Spanish-speaking countries. In my fieldwork, I worked most closely with Spanish-speaking paparazzi; hence I have titled this chapter "Shooteando," a term I heard used frequently. It is a Spanglish term that combines the English *shooting* or the Spanglish *shootear*, referring to shooting photos, and the Spanish suffix *-ando*, the gerund of regular verbs ending in *-ar*. The term is evocative of the way the Latino paparazzi have inserted themselves into an industry that historically had not made space for them. In Hollywood, industry insiders talk about various kinds of shoots and shooting all the time, but only paparazzi can be found *shooteando*.

As is the case with any realm of the Hollywood-industrial complex, gaining access to paparazzi is the first challenge in pursuing work with them.[5] Despite the ubiquity of their photographs, paparazzi continue to operate largely outside the formal economic channels of celebrity media. They are not on staff at any media outlet; they generally work on a freelance basis and provide their photos to one or more photo agencies in exchange for a percentage of any profits made on the photos. Some paparazzi sell photos under the table to a paparazzo who acts on their behalf as an image broker to the agencies.[6] Through my experience as a reporter and my network of friends and family in Los Angeles, I was able to get in with a few paparazzi, who then introduced me to others as someone who was cleared as trustworthy. Paparazzi are, ironically, quite private about their work, so having connections was critical to the success of my research.[7]

The generally informal, unregulated nature of paparazzi work reduces barriers of entry into the profession and helps fuel the celebrity media system, but at the same time it also positions paparazzi as a public scapegoat for what is wrong with celebrity media today. By looking critically at the paparazzi as both key media producers at the periphery of the formal media production process and vilified symbols of celebrity media, this chapter explores the exclusive and discriminatory nature of formal media production and the racial politics at play therein. Readers will get to know the rarely revealed paparazzi's point of view and learn why they feel that they are entirely misunderstood: as one pap put it simply, "We are good people. We are just doing our job."

Galo's Path to Becoming a Paparazzo

> People tell me to get a better job or a real job. What do you do? What gives you the right to say this? I make way more [than I could otherwise]. That's why I have this job. I'm not obsessed with celebrities. This is my job. If I hear that Brad Pitt is at a restaurant, you're damn right I'll go. It's my job. It could be a good job, or a bad job, but it's my job. I don't have to steal, lie, or hurt anyone to do this job. And I make a good living. I'm an entrepreneur. Don't criticize me based on what you see on TMZ. That's not me. | GALO RAMIREZ | PAPARAZZO, 2012, INTERVIEW WITH AUTHOR

In Los Angeles in particular, paps are regularly criticized and criminalized and thus are in the habit of defending themselves. As an Associated Press article summarized, "Paparazzi are disparaged by mainstream media, discouraged by the cops and despised by the same public that consumes their product."[8] Paps often assert that they are thick-skinned and don't let what other people think of them or say about them affect their work. Though this is generally true, they are still visibly affected by the way they are treated on the job. This is obvious in the quote from Galo Ramirez that opens this section. Galo was my main informant and collaborator among the paparazzi, and his defensiveness is not unique. In fact many paparazzi are hesitant to allow others into their professional lives for fear of being scooped or simply of being criticized.[9] But because Galo and I had a friend in common, he welcomed me into his world of photography.

1.2 Galo Ramirez on the job as a paparazzo in Los Angeles. Photo courtesy of Galo Ramirez.

Galo is thirty-one years old (see fig. 1.2). He usually wears jeans and a fitted T-shirt that shows off his lean, muscular five-foot, ten-inch frame. He is proud of the fact that no matter how hard or late he works, he makes an effort to go to the gym nearly every day. He is very concerned with eating healthy, but given his profession, he sometimes has to eat whatever he can get, which usually means going to whichever fast-food restaurant is closest to where he is working. He has large, piercing blue-green-gray eyes, full lips that are part of an infectious smile, tan skin, and dark brown hair. He drives a gray 2009 Toyota Prius (see fig. 1.3). He said the Prius was the best investment he could have made because his car is like his office, his photo studio, and, sometimes, his apartment and bathroom.[10] The car has a GPS screen built into the dashboard, and all his important contacts are saved into this system. When he pulled up a map with his contacts' addresses highlighted on the GPS, I could pick out nearly every A- and B-list celebrity with a home in Los Angeles: George Clooney, Jennifer Aniston, Ben Affleck, Sandra Bullock, and the list goes on. During the days I spent with him on the job, following celebrities or "door-stepping" outside of celebrities' homes, we had several hours to talk.[11] He liked having me around because being a pap can be quite lonely. Sometimes he has several friends around working on the same job, and sometimes he works completely alone. When he was alone, I brought him food and offered him

1.3 Galo editing photos in his car near the home of the actress Dakota Fanning. Photo by the author.

company; I had a lot to learn about his work and life, and I did it all from the passenger seat of his Prius.

At the time of my interviews, Galo was in the process of applying for citizenship, which he eventually obtained. As a young child, he was brought to the U.S. from El Salvador under political asylum; his home country was in the middle of a brutal civil war.[12] "We were trying to get away from all the shit that was going on," he told me. His mother left for the U.S. without him to try to set up a better life for them, leaving him with his maternal grandmother. He was then kidnapped and held hostage by his father, who was in the military; he was kept on a military base and left alone for days at a time.

> This one time he left and I don't know where he went, but I was starving. I was like three or four years old. This woman came by and was supposed to clean the room, but she saw that I was really small and so she asked me if I was hungry and I said yeah. So she took me and she had a bag of chips and some candy. So when I got back he was there and he was freaked the fuck out. I walked in the door. He yelled at her and fired her. Then when she left he beat the crap out of me with a military belt. It's like a batman-style belt, it's big and thick. That's when I was like, whoa, I don't want to be with him. Then he took me to his house and tried to force me to call his girlfriend "mom." And I said "No, she's not my mom." — Oh, was that Ben Affleck?

Galo broke off in the middle of this harrowing story to ask if Ben Affleck was driving the car that just passed us. It did not matter how engrossed in conversation he was, or how serious a conversation may be: his responsibility was to be on the lookout for celebrities at all times. Having decided that it wasn't Ben Affleck, Galo resumed his story of childhood trauma: "Then he made me get on my knees and he threatened me with this really thick chain and said he would hit me with it if I didn't call her mom. And then he was about to beat on me, but she got in the middle." Galo was finally rescued by his mother upon her return. "I was at [my dad's] house and I heard someone at the door. I didn't know it was her. He kept lying and saying I wasn't there. And she left. And I asked who it was and he said it was no one. She went straight to his boss in the military, and his boss gave him an ultimatum. And that was it. My mom came and found me, and then I came here [to Los Angeles]."

His mother had already found them a place to stay and had job prospects. It was 1987, and Galo was six years old. From elementary through twelfth grade he went to school in Hollywood, the heart of L.A.'s celebrity culture. He remembers picking up English quickly.

> They taught me how to count and say some stuff in English before I came here. So I picked it up really quick because I knew what they were saying. Otherwise I would have had a really hard time. Then the accent thing went away really quick too because I picked up English so young. I can sound really collegiate, or I can sound all slang. But I know I can speak proper English, I know how to spell, all of that. I learned that real quick. And it was hard because my mom didn't understand [English], so I had to really listen in class.

The rest of his family stayed behind in El Salvador; only he and his mother made the journey, and his brother was born in the U.S. shortly thereafter. When he got older and began thinking about careers, being a paparazzo was not his first choice. He stumbled upon the work accidentally. He was attending college at California State University, Los Angeles, when he began to feel guilty because his mother was working so hard to pay for his schooling and yet he wasn't excelling in or enjoying his classes. Against his mother's wishes, he quit school and started looking for work.

> I didn't focus, and I was like, I'm out of high school, I'm on my own, so I could do whatever I want. So I looked at it like I don't want this anymore; I don't want to go to school every day and scribble raps. That's what I

used to do, was scribble raps every day. As much as I wanted to concentrate, I wanted to focus on what I wanted to do. That's what made me happy, and I figured I wanted to do something that made me happy, so I was like, I'm gonna become a rapper or whatever. So every day I would go to school, write raps, get all right grades, and then I started falling off. And my mom was like, "What the fuck, I'm paying all this money." So I was like, "Okay, I can't do this to you anymore." She got depressed, but she got over it, because I said to her, "I can't keep doing this to you. I'm not going to school. I'm not learning anything I don't already know. I'm not taking any fun classes. It's all bullshit. Even if I get a diploma, it doesn't mean I'm going to get a job." So I dropped out, and I was like, I'm going to work really hard to make myself a successful person at whatever makes me happy, and photography just fell into my lap.

When Galo first dropped out of school, he didn't become a pap right away; he first worked for five years at a nonprofit company as a home caregiver for people with disabilities. From roughly 2000 to 2005 he helped care for people with conditions such as schizophrenia, paralysis, and autism. "I changed Pampers on adults. I can actually say that I attended UCLA for a semester because I was in class taking notes like crazy-style. I learned something sitting in the classroom. One of the people I worked for was in a wheelchair, so I was his proctor/caretaker. He couldn't write, so he used to sit there and listen and then he was like, 'Go. Write.' I had to take his tests, like be his proctor. So I went to class with him every day, English, computer science. I was like, oh shit, this is complicated shit." Although Galo grew as a person and enjoyed his work—he was especially proud of his time at UCLA—he said, "It wasn't exactly where I found true happiness. It was something that made me feel good because I helped people, but I was like, I can't do this all my life. I could only get so far doing that, and it wasn't the road that I wanted to take, so I kind of was like, I gotta figure something else out."

He quit his job as a caregiver. "I was just chillin' one day with my homie, and he was like, 'What's up, fool? You wanna come with me to work, dogg?' I knew he was a pap. So I was like, 'Aight, let's go. Fuck it.' So he said, 'You gotta be at my house early.'" He got to his friend's house at about 7:00 a.m. and they set out to find Brad Pitt. It was 2005, a time in the paparazzi industry in Los Angeles, according to Galo and many other paps, when there was an abundance of material to shoot (especially hot young celebrities like Britney Spears, Lindsay Lohan, Paris Hilton, and Nicole Richie) and not a tremendously large

1.4 Galo with Britney Spears in his car in 2006, when Spears asked him for a ride. Photo courtesy of Galo Ramirez.

number of paparazzi. Unlike today, when paps have to struggle to find photo opportunities that others have not already found, 2005 "was easy," Galo says (see fig. 1.4). He and his friend got into a "follow" with Brad Pitt, and the friend asked Galo to get into the driver's seat and take over.[13]

> So I'm following Brad Pitt going crazy. We get all the way to Malibu and I've been driving a Navigator and I'm after a motorcycle and [Brad Pitt] is smashing, so I caught up to him. He gets a fucking speeding ticket, and we get the shots. Then I get pulled over, so the homie has to take me to the office and explain to his boss, "This guy was driving your car. He was with me. He's my buddy and we got a ticket." And the boss is like, "What the fuck is he doing driving my fucking car? Who the fuck is he? What is he doing with you at work? What the fuck are you doing?" It's like this prestigious position working for Fame [Pictures], and, back then, it was

like, you don't get this opportunity often, so the boss was pissed. But my friend said to the boss, Jack, "Yeah, but it's because of him that we got Brad Pitt. He was able to keep up with him." And Jack looked at me and said, "Is that true?" And I said, "Yeah, I got a ticket." And he said, "Ah, don't worry about it. I got lawyers. We'll take care of it. You need a job? You want to work for me?" And I was like, "Yeah." He said, "All right, you're a lucky guy today." So I started training with all these guys.

Prior to landing this job at Fame Pictures, Inc., Galo had no formal training in photography beyond a high school photography class, where he learned how to develop his own film.[14] Now he was training with some of the top paparazzi in Los Angeles for a major photo agency. A few days into the job, Galo was training with another pap and they spotted an A-list actress who was then in a high-profile relationship with an A-list pop star:

> We stayed in the car for four hours and shot her "cheating" on her boyfriend. They sold the story like she was cheating, but we were outside of a studio where she was filming a movie and there were bushes and we had to shoot from the waist up. But we got her hugging and kissing this guy on the cheek. I think she ended up saying it was her producer, but it looked intimate and it looked papped. But when I shot the pictures, I didn't know he was a producer. I didn't know who it was. I just took the pictures and turned them into the agency, then they handled the sales. The photos sold for over three hundred thousand dollars, so there, again, the boss was happy.

Galo was hired as a staff photographer, which means he received a fixed salary in addition to small bonuses for high-grossing sales like this one. (This contrasts with freelance paps, who do not earn a salary but make a percentage of the total sales on every photo they take.) Two weeks after helping with this major sale for the agency, Galo got into a highly publicized car accident with Lindsay Lohan.[15] He was initially arrested under suspicion of assault with a deadly weapon.[16] Although the charges were eventually dropped, his career prospects changed.

> The boss was like, "Everything is fine. Don't worry. We'll have a new car tomorrow." And then he was like, "Hey, my lawyer advised me. I need to let you go." I wanted to cry out of anger, I was so pissed. It was liability towards the fuckin' owner. It was like, "Oh, he doesn't work for me no

more, they can't come after me. He doesn't belong to me no more." Some people go out with a bang. I came in with a bang. I went back to try to get a job from him, but he wouldn't hire me. I worked for the other guys briefly, but I wasn't making nothing.

Frustrated and demoralized, Galo decided to go back to a more traditional profession and got a job working for Cedars Sinai Hospital in the Radiology Department. He was excited about the position, but the week after he started the job, the *Los Angeles Times* published an article about the Lohan incident that mentioned him by name. He believes that this is why the hospital then immediately terminated his employment; hospitals in L.A. have experienced leaks of confidential celebrity medical information and thus are very careful about not employing individuals who have ties to entertainment or media industries.[17] Galo went back to trying to pap and was eventually hired by another agency, JFX. After working for them for a few years on staff, he decided to go freelance in hopes of making more money. At the time of our interview he worked freelance but sold his photos exclusively through one agency, AKM-GSI Media, where he felt he was able to determine his own financial fate.[18] Though paparazzi never actually know how much the agencies are making — their compensation is entirely based on an honor system dependent on the agencies actually giving them the percentage of sales they are promised — Galo felt confident that he was being treated right at this agency. "They won't steal from me, but I guess you never know," he said.

Galo and I had been in such deep conversation that I almost forgot we were following Heidi Klum's new bodyguard/boyfriend and her children. "Does he know all of your cars?" I asked Galo.

"He knows my car. He's trained to do that."

"But there are so many, how can they keep track?"

"License plates."

"It's funny, though, because even though I know there's overcrowding in terms of the number of paparazzi, it still seems like, whenever I'm with you, even that time over by Vanessa Hudgens's [house], there were a lot of paps over there, but it wasn't crazy out of control the way it gets on the streets. It's never like dozens of people."

"Because it's not a hot celebrity."

"So when do you feel like, 'Oh fuck, this is way too overcrowded?'"

"Big stories, like Brad Pitt maybe. There are a lot of guys, a lot of action, a lot of movement."

We were both yawning. Suddenly, "There we go," Galo said. He was look-ing at his smartphone while we were at a stoplight, something I was constantly asking him not to do, particularly since he had recently gotten into a minor fender bender while looking at his phone. He read a headline out loud: "'Don't look now, Seal. Heidi Klum's bodyguard turned boyfriend joins her brood at Starbucks.' And there's my shot." He was proud of the photos he took and loved to see them used.

"Look at this fucking idiot!" Galo said, pointing at another paparazzo in a car near us, who cut him off to get ahead and closer to Klum's bodyguard's car. "Now he's going to let his brother in. Great. Can you see how many of my pictures they used?" I started to scroll through the article he pulled up on his phone.

"A ton. It's a lot." He started to take the phone back and count the images. I snatched it back. "I'll count for you. You drive." I scrolled down the long article, counting each photo with a Stars Only Photography symbol by it; the outlet had used a combination of agencies' photos. "There are eleven that say 'Stars Only.'"

"Eleven. Nice!"

I noticed Galo looking off in the distance. "What are you looking at?"

"Mateo. He's going to Reese Witherspoon's."

"Oh, for real?" We sat in silence for a few minutes while Galo focused on driving. I was thinking about Heidi Klum and Seal's breakup.

I had talked to Galo earlier about one of my very first assignments for *People* magazine, which involved Klum. "That time that I first interviewed Heidi Klum that I was telling you about. When I talked to all of the Victo-ria's Secret Angels it was like right after she and Seal had gotten together and I interviewed her about it. It was our quote of the week in the magazine. And now they're split." Galo was looking at his phone again.

"You got a green light, stop it!"

"I know! I needed these shots on a Wednesday. Because on Saturday every-body's going to be here again trying to get it."

"So what now?" I asked.

"Go back and sit again until seven-p. We're just going to sit here and wait, see if they come out." He pointed out Gwyneth Paltrow's house as we pulled back up to Heidi Klum's street. He didn't want to show it to me earlier because he wanted to keep it a secret from the other paparazzi.

"Can I have some of your water?" Galo asked me.

"I think it's gone, but you can get the last trickles out of it." He took my metal water bottle, opened it up, and turned it upside down over his mouth, trying to get out any last drops. It had been a long, hot day. He did not have any more water; neither did his buddies, and he had to keep doorstepping for at least another four hours. He couldn't leave or he risked losing the shot, and with it his paycheck.

While we were waiting outside in the Brentwood–Pacific Palisades area near Klum's house, a pap named Hector Campos played me videos he took of all the paps saying their nicknames. Afterward Galo told me, "If you don't have a nickname, you're not 'in.' And if you're not 'in,' you're probably not going to make it. There is a certain brotherhood. I have respect for a lot of guys, but there are guys I can't stand because they don't get the business and they are ruining it." Paps routinely give each other nicknames, many of which reflect a connection to migrant labor, and they embrace the playful, if often insulting, names assigned to them by their fellow paps. That day I was with El Diablo ("The Devil"), Gallo ("Rooster"),[19] Cupcake Eyes, Señor ("Mister"), and a few new guys who did not yet have nicknames. They were all in their thirties and early forties, and they were all Latino—mostly immigrants from El Salvador—and most had been working as paps for between five and ten years. Their time in the business coincided with a demographic shift in the Los Angeles pap workforce that has been alluded to in the media but not thoroughly investigated or critically analyzed. This shift coincided with the expansion of the celebrity weekly magazine industry and an increased demand for paparazzi photos. More Latinos joined the workforce between 2002 and 2005, and by 2008 the shift from "all white guys" to mostly Latinos was noticeable.[20]

As I stood outside with the paps, I could see that in this wealthy neighborhood—the kind where paps do their work—the only other nonwhite faces were those of construction workers and landscapers. There was a Mexican food truck parked on the street for the service workers at the multimillion-dollar homes. Here the paparazzi were like the other service workers. They provide a type of service labor, but one that the people they shoot do not want, or at least pretend not to want, and do not pay for. But the paps occupy a similar social space; they are eyesores in the neighborhood. People want to pretend they do not exist, like all service workers, but they are an integral part of the Los Angeles and entertainment industry economies.[21]

Interestingly, paparazzi say their goal is to be invisible, which is often possible when they are working on a story alone. But when there are multiple paps on one story it is hard for them to remain discreet: a group of young, mostly brown-skinned Spanish-speaking Latino men in a rich, white, celebrity-heavy area becomes highly visible. The two new guys Galo was training, one of whom was Chris Guerra, seemed out of place because they were not speaking Spanish and were left out of a good portion of the conversation. Rooster and Señor spoke English, but it was clear that they preferred Spanish, or at least Spanglish.

El Diablo got to talking about politics. "I guess I'll take my chances *con el negro*," he said, referring to his plans to vote for President Barack Obama in the upcoming race.[22] He is very interested in politics and said he listens to National Public Radio constantly, on and off the job. He said that when Obama gave a speech on health care, it almost made him cry. "He was talking to me," he said.

Issues surrounding politics and education are recurring themes during the workday. As we were talking, I recalled a previous conversation I had with Galo on the job. One day I got into his car near Dakota Fanning's and Vanessa Hudgens's homes in Studio City and he said, "You know about Cuba, right? What's the deal with Che Guevara? Was he a killer? I don't want to learn about the motorcycle diaries, I want to know what really happened. I wear his shirts, and someone got mad at me for it once, so I don't want to feel ignorant or jump on a bandwagon I don't know about. I want to learn." Galo knew that I had done research in Cuba since I was eighteen years old, and so he wanted me to talk through Cuban history and Che Guevara while we staked out celebrities and conducted image sales.

As I sat with El Diablo talking about the presidential race, he asked me what I did, so I explained my research and that I had worked for *People* magazine. I told him Galo had been helping me out and that we had mutual friends, and he said, "He's one of the few people in the industry who is really genuine." El Diablo went on to talk about what a stand-up guy Galo is, while he did arm presses on a bench on a small walking path in the Brentwood-Palisades neighborhood, his arms mostly exposed from his short-sleeve T-shirt, showing his tattoos and muscles. He got his nickname because his fellow paps said people think he is scary. He was wearing a golf cap and sunglasses and has a thick goatee. He reminded me of my dad, both in his looks and in the way he talks. He and the other paps seemed to have become immune to the fact that the passengers in every car driving by were staring at them; the passersby either knew who they were and did not like them or looked at them as if they were wondering, "What in the world are these Latino men doing here?" The only other people on foot were in construction clothes or carrying cleaning supplies; the residents of the wealthy white neighborhood were protected behind the windows of their Bentleys, Mercedeses, and luxury SUVs as they glared at the paps.

That day I came home sweaty, dehydrated, and exhausted. I had arrived to meet Galo four hours after he got to the neighborhood, and I left four hours before he and the other paps went home. I could not have kept up for their entire eleven-hour day. But these hours are worth it since, in a good year, Galo could make over $100,000 (though at the time of my research, most paps were making around $30,000 or less). "The American Dream, right? Entrepreneurship," Galo had said to me as I left him that day, completely worn out.

The Changing Demographics of the Los Angeles Paparazzi

One of the few scholarly texts to engage with the topic of contemporary paparazzi is Kim McNamara's *Paparazzi*. In it, she references the male-dominated nature of the industry but does not reconcile the ways in which race, ethnicity, and perceived immigrant status factor into the characterization of paparazzi as "aggressive and frightening." McNamara suggests that the paparazzi boom had to do with changes in camera technology and mentions nothing of the market demands that I outline. She posits, "Up until the late 1990s, high-level photography was not an easy career choice: from the heavy cameras which required manual focus and exposure, to the inconvenience of flashes which needed to be constantly changed, to the expensive film which also required changing as well as development in darkrooms, followed by the sheer expense of distributing and syndicating the best images, it is little surprise that the field of the paparazzi was a relatively small one."[23]

None of the paparazzi I worked with had easy-to-carry equipment, as is evidenced in images throughout this book (e.g., figs. 1.1, 1.2, 1.5). They had the most up-to-date high-tech cameras, which weigh a great deal and require switching of lenses (some of which measured well over a foot long) and extensive knowledge (even if self-taught) to manipulate. This runs counter to McNamara's description, which paints the new generation of paparazzi as unskilled, echoing the problematic way they are often described in the industry. She writes, "When we see the paparazzi in action, they may often appear to be almost amateurs, holding the camera aloft without even using the viewfinder"[24] (see fig. 1.6).

McNamara's claims about the shift toward amateurism (which she describes as occurring in the late 1990s) are historically inaccurate and fail to

1.5 Paparazzi shooting celebrities at the beach, very clearly looking into their viewfinders, contrary to McNamara's assessment. Photo courtesy of Ulises Rios.

fully address the political history she lays out. She states that the late 1990s were "a point when the long-established paparazzi photographers were jostled by an influx of amateurs, immigrants and 'citizen' paparazzi seduced by the promise of big payouts for capturing exclusive images of the likes of Britney Spears. This period known in the industry as the 'gold rush,' was character-ized by spiraling prices for often unremarkable images, driven by circulation battles between major entertainment publishers, primarily Time Inc's *People Magazine* and Wenner Media's *Us Weekly*."[25] As I describe in the introduc-tion, *Us Weekly* was not a weekly magazine until 2000, before which *People* had no direct competition. McNamara does not address that the influx of "im-migrant" paparazzi she mentions, which in fact took place in the early 2000s, consisted of nonwhite immigrants and nonwhite U.S. citizens who were nec-essarily read as "foreign" and "other." The "long-established" photographers were mostly white and often European immigrants themselves, although be-cause of their race they were not read as foreign.

To elaborate on this phenomenon, McNamara cites a 2010 interview with a New York photo editor who explained, "You had all these illegal immigrants

1.6 Selena Gomez and Justin Bieber with his little sister, Jasmyn, at the beach in 2012. This image is demonstrative of the highly sophisticated, artistically framed candid shots paparazzi are known for. Photo courtesy of Galo Ramirez.

coming to LA. You could be washing dishes at a restaurant for 2 bucks an hour, or I will give you a car and a camera and you can chase celebrities around all day and get paid 1000 dollars a week even if you suck. . . . So the number of guys on the street exploded. And that's when you started seeing all this TMZ stuff, with the 'Lindsay, Lindsay, look at me,' 20 guys on the street and the pack mentality, which was bad for the industry." She also quotes one of the owners of the photo agency X17 as claiming that the Brazilian photographers they hired could not clearly communicate since English was not their first language. Another photo editor observed that the potential to make fast cash as a paparazzo was "causing this frenzy of gang members or illegal people or anybody who's trying to make a living." This is one of several references in the text (by other non-Latino paps) to paps looking like gangbangers or criminals, or to the "new" paparazzi's having "bad attitudes, bad clothes." McNamara's book, which is the only text that even engages with any understanding of the demographic shift I describe, offers no analysis or problematizing of the highly racialized language used to describe the paparazzi. Aside from noting the "consensus that there has been a shift in the paparazzi freelance labour market from professional photographers to less skilled newcomers," McNamara never addresses the problematic nature of the language used to refer to the new wave of paparazzi or its implications for the industry and broader public perceptions of paparazzi, instead merely parroting the hostility of her interviewees.[26]

Several factors contribute to animosity toward the paparazzi, including the male dominance of the profession and the symbolically violent and sexualized language associated with them. The animosity in turn reifies the gendered and racialized ways in which paparazzi are talked about publicly, by individuals and the media.

As with other forms of informal and on-the-move labor, the demographics of paparazzi are not easily researchable.[27] The paparazzi are a transient and constantly changing group of workers who are not confined to any particular workspace. Though they sometimes become highly visible via videos and photographs of "gangbangs"—the socially charged term used to reference several paparazzi photographing one celebrity—they generally seek to not be seen and are thus often hard to locate. The number of paparazzi in Los Angeles is unknown, though two hundred is often suggested as a ballpark range by the paparazzi themselves and photo agency workers. Some paps estimate that in 2000, they numbered between ten and thirty, a figure that has multiplied exponentially as the market for candid celebrity photos has grown.[28] The very nature of this unregulated, informal field dominated by freelancers and itinerant workers makes it impossible to accurately and thoroughly quantify its demographics. However, I have been able to count and observe paparazzi while in the field and make lists of paparazzi with the help of my closest informants, noting the names, backgrounds, gender, and ages of the photographers my informants know best. Based on these lists, I estimate that the present-day paparazzi in Los Angeles can be categorized roughly as follows: 60 percent Latinx (mostly Salvadoran, Mexican, Guatemalan, and Brazilian), 25 percent Asian (including Filipino, East and South Asian, and Middle Eastern), 10 percent African American, and 5 percent white/Caucasian.[29] The percentage of Latinxs includes those born in Latin America and the U.S. The percentage of undocumented paparazzi could be as high as 50, though this is an imperfect and rough estimate based mostly on unspoken understandings about the status of the photographers my informants work with; the latter emphasized that this is not something they actively discuss. The gendered nature of paparazzi work, however, is entirely clear: approximately 98 percent of paparazzi are men.[30]

Thus it is not by chance that all the interviews I conducted with paparazzi were with men.[31] Throughout the course of my research, I personally met only one paparazza—a term that I have never even heard used. She did not feel comfortable doing an interview with me or talking with me outside of my observations of her on the street. Indeed I rarely saw her, and when I did, she was often alone or with one other person and shooting less-followed celebrities (i.e., not A-list stars, who would attract a lot of attention). This gender division is not surprising given that photography is a historically male-dominated field, as is journalism.[32] In response to my curiosity about this male dominance, one pap said, "That's like asking why there aren't more women mechanics. There just aren't." Another paparazzo offered this explanation: "Women get scared, and you get a bad reputation, and women care more about that than men do. Some paps say it's more of a man's business." There is also an element of simple logistics: women generally can't urinate as easily into a bottle as men can, an invaluable skill during long days stuck in a car.

The fact that the paparazzi are almost universally men provides additional avenues for criticism and contributes to the use of bodily harm against paparazzi in a way that would not be socially acceptable if they were women; paps are often seen as thugs and gangsters who deserve the treatment they get. The fact that the paparazzi in Los Angeles are predominantly Latino men, who have historically been stereotyped as aggressive, macho, violent sexual predators, makes it convenient to demonize them and justify physical aggressiveness toward them.[33] Stereotypes like these have real-life consequences. A 2016 study by evolutionary biologists and anthropologists, focused on race, aggression, and size, found that black and Latinx men are presumed to be larger and more aggressive than their white and Asian counterparts, "despite the fact that the two groups are of equivalent average height in the U.S."[34] The language of "shooting," "giving it up," and "gangbanging" associated with paparazzi gets put into the context of men who are already seen as aggressive and violent thugs or gangsters, further degrading their public personae.

The entertainment industry, and the Hollywood-industrial complex it has helped build and sustain, is predominantly white.[35] Not only is this overrepresentation obvious in Hollywood products readily available for public consumption, like films and television programs, but those working behind the scenes of these consumable entertainment products notice and critique it. In the article by Chris Rock that I referenced in the introduction, he exposes the hierarchical racist structure in Hollywood that generally prevents Latinos from entering the industry: "Forget whether Hollywood is black enough. A better question is: Is Hollywood Mexican enough? You're in L.A., you've got to try not to hire Mexicans. . . . You're telling me no Mexicans are qualified to do anything at a studio? Really? Nothing but mop up? What are the odds that that's true? The odds are, because people are people, that there's probably a Mexican David Geffen mopping up for somebody's company right now."[36]

Social media movements like #OscarsSoWhite promulgate the black/white binary that contributes to Hollywood's inability to grasp American diversity. Relative to population representation, black actors are surprisingly proportionately represented in Hollywood roles, but every other minority group is grossly underrepresented, with Latinxs the most underrepresented relative to population. (Roughly 18 percent of the country is Latinx, but only 5 percent of Hollywood roles are played by Latinxs. It is also imperative to point out the shortcomings of existing Hollywood diversity data, which typically treat black and Latinx identities as mutually exclusive, as opposed to overlapping.)[37] Because Hollywood's dominant whiteness does not take into consideration representation that reflects the actual population, a token black actor is inserted here and there in an attempt to appease public talk of racism. #OscarsSoWhite is constructed in opposition to a theoretical #OscarsSoNotBlack, as opposed to #OscarsSoNotRepresentative OfU.S.Demographics. Celebrity response from white actors to #OscarsSo White primarily commented on black actors and did not address the lack of representation of any other minority group.[38]

We are well aware that "mass media institutions such as Hollywood are major transmitters of racist ideologies," but this fact is often relegated to discussions of on-screen representation of people of color in Hollywood—the most visible and, thus, most easy to critique.[39] The common assessments of race in Hollywood leave out every other realm of work within the Hollywood-industrial complex. We know people of color are underrepresented in film and television. We know representations of people of color far too often are derogatory. But what about the labor behind the scenes that further promotes racial hierarchies? Until recently there has never been a predominantly non-white group in any realm of the Hollywood-industrial complex. The fact that the Latino paparazzi have managed to create a toehold for themselves within Hollywood is particularly significant, despite the problematic ways in which they are positioned in the hierarchy of Hollywood and in public culture more broadly. Indeed the criticism of the paparazzi within the Hollywood-industrial complex is telling. That this group is predominantly Latino adds layers to the social framing and critique of these media producers who are so central to yet so at the margins of Hollywood.

Within this industry "there is widespread nepotism—the employment of people along family lines. This means that if your family does not have a presence in the business, you are less likely to be hired and promoted."[40] As the media scholar Kristen Warner points out, "Hollywood is an industry built around relationships, networking, internships, and apprenticeships— a classed set of practices from which people of color are systematically excluded."[41] Thus it is difficult for young Latinxs to break into the entertainment and media industries. But paparazzi work has given them an avenue, as the paparazzo Ulises "Trucha" Rios explained: "There are no requirements to be a paparazzi. Tomorrow you could decide you wanna be one. There's no, 'Who did you work for last?' Or 'Where's your résumé?' None of that."

There are no barriers to entering the business (aside from attempts by the current paparazzi to informally regulate it by either training, helping, or rejecting paps who try to enter the workforce) because paparazzi work does not take place in regulated elite spaces, like red carpets, private events, or press junkets. The recent shift in the demographics of the paparazzi demonstrates Latinx agency; it is an avenue for professional development and a way to earn a living in an otherwise inaccessible entertainment industry. I see Latinos' domination of this realm of work as an assertion of local presence. They are aware of and analyze the fact that people who look like them are not valued bodies in Hollywood, so they co-opt what they can by photographing and selling images of the white stars they can never embody.[42]

Unlike many celebrity reporters, paparazzi generally did not grow up with aspirations of being stars themselves. Many cite their working-class or poor background as shaping why they felt far removed from dreams of Hollywood. A Brazilian paparazzo named Luiz came to the U.S. as an adult and could not believe the amount of money his paparazzi friends were able to make as recent immigrants. "It was like a new opportunity," Luiz said. "It was money that we didn't know was available in the industry. When you first come [to work for x17] at that time, you would start making two thousand or three thousand dollars a month, then it went up. I heard stories about it and I would say that's baloney. I said, 'You cannot make that kind of money at any job here.' But it was real. When I started [in 2007], most of my friends were making around ten to fifteen thousand dollars per month. They don't make that anymore because the market changed, but that's what we were making." Hollywood, and the plethora of industries within it, was inaccessible to these young men before paparazzi work. Meaningful diversity is not a reality in any Hollywood-related industry; it is unfortunate, then, that the most minority-heavy part of the celebrity-industrial complex in Los Angeles is also the most hated, antagonized, criticized, and abused group within the industry. Still, the paps take pride in the fact that they have found a way to insert themselves into this lucrative economy, particularly considering the other jobs typically available to new immigrants and men of color without a college education.

In fact the paparazzi explicitly understand their line of work to be a form of migrant labor. During the course of any given workday, paps often take photos of each other on the job and hanging out after work (see fig. 1.7). Figure 1.7 is a photo that Galo took of a group of paps known as "the Home Depots." Public perception of paparazzi, their demographic makeup, and the structural realities of their work all affect the way they understand their role as laborers. The role of "the Home Depots" in the pap economy and their racialized bodies and physical appearance are bundled together in their nickname. One Latino pap explained, "We call them the Home Depots because they look like a group of guys standing outside of Home Depot looking for work." But another pap has a different explanation: "They're *like* the guys at Home Depot. They're there every day to get pictures to sell for fifty dollars, which is what they do at Home Depot. Pick me up and, for fifty dollars, I'll paint your house." Galo has photoshopped this image of the Home Depots, which he often does with his photos of both paps and celebrities (see fig. 1.8).

From the modified Home Depot logo to the text, Galo creates a commentary around the paps' stigmatized, racialized, and deprofessionalized position within the entertainment industry. While the paps in the photo are idly waiting for celebrity action, one pap is depicted saying, "Hey . . . Guat ar jor zettings [*sic*]??" (intended meaning: What are your [camera] settings?). The pap front and center jokingly has his camera upside down while he looks at the lens, almost as if acting out McNamara's inaccurate characterization of paps, and is saying, "Lemi sheq [*sic*] . . ." (intended meaning: let me check), as if looking in the lens would provide the setting information. The satirical text added to the photoshopped image of the "Home Depots" demonstrates Galo's usage of what linguist Steven Talmy has termed mock ESL, or "the mock register surrounding the widely stigmatized acquisition of English as a Second Language," in this case in relation to ESL Spanish speakers.[43] For example, the phonetic spellings of "sheq" (meaning "check") and "jor" (meaning "your") represent common stereotypes about Spanish-accented English. This image offers a sociolinguistic reinterpretation of this candid paparazzi moment—where the paps themselves were pap'd (a colloquialism they use meaning to be captured by a paparazzo). Galo's work represents the ways in which paps

1.7 **A group of paparazzi, including some nicknamed "the Home Depots."** Photo courtesy of Galo Ramirez.

1.8 **Photoshopped image of "the Home Depots."** Photo courtesy of Galo Ramirez.

1.9 Photoshopped image of a pap nicknamed Turbo Taco.

Photo courtesy of Galo Ramirez.

conceptualize their own raciolinguistic realities, and how they see themselves in relationship to other kinds of day labor, Latinx labor, and migrant labor and the neoliberal political economy more broadly.[44]

In figure 1.9 Galo has photoshopped an image of a pap known as Turbo Taco, which was taken at a pumpkin patch that Britney Spears was visiting with her child. All the paps were kicked out by security, but Turbo ran into the pumpkin patch, grabbed a wheelbarrow, and tried to blend in. It is unclear whether, in that instance, he thought he would blend in as a farmworker or as a fellow patron of the patch. Galo's addition of actual migrant farmworkers to the photo not only demonstrates how Galo interpreted his paparazzo peer in this moment but also is evocative of the invisibility and disposability of these Latinx laborers. Paparazzi are needed to produce images for media corporations, but once their presence is deemed a nuisance, they must disperse and disappear, or make themselves otherwise seemingly invisible. In this image, Turbo shape-shifts into farmworker, a laborer commonly associated with invisibility. This photoshopped art encapsulates the ways pap labor is similar to other kinds of invisible migrant labor, and the difficulty, racialization, discrimination, and fear that often accompanies the work.

It is also important to note the ways in which their role as paparazzi incorporates these men into the celebrity culture of Los Angeles. As much as they are profiled and harassed by police and security guards, their cameras also serve as protection in the rich white neighborhoods and other public spaces in which they work. Police see paps' cameras and know who they are and their reason for being in a place they otherwise would not be perceived as belonging. In fact Los Angeles police and other enforcers understand this business because they are often on photo agencies' payrolls and thus indirectly provide tips to the paps.[45] This understanding of paps' role in the celebrity media industry does not guarantee that they won't get physically assaulted or arrested, but it does provide a context and answers to people who otherwise question why these individuals are present in the spaces in which they work.

Skill, Training, and the New Paps

> Like a car, a camera is sold as a predatory weapon—one that's as automated as possible, ready to spring. . . . Manufacturers reassure their customers that taking pictures demands no skill or expert knowledge, that the machine is all-knowing, and responds to the slightest pressure of the will. It's as simple as turning the ignition or pulling the trigger. | SUSAN SONTAG | ON PHOTOGRAPHY

> This is your camera, this is your weapon. Me and my partner, we don't have room for mistakes. This isn't a game. We're out here because we have to feed our children. | SERGIO HUAPAYA | PAPARAZZO, QUOTED IN FRANK RUY'S GIVING IT UP

The demographic change in the paparazzi workforce in Los Angeles—unique to that city—correlates with an increase in rhetoric questioning their skill and professionalism.[46] A stereotype has circulated in popular media and discourse that Latinxs are lazy and uneducated.[47] The idea that unskilled immigrants dominate low-skill work and thus bid down the wage scale in local markets demonstrates that there is an assumption "that all immigration is unskilled."[48] In the case of the paparazzi, not only has the discourse about them become racialized, but it is also intertwined with a narrative about the new paparazzi's (presumed) immigrant status and their level of skill (or lack thereof) for the job.

One former pap and agency owner referred to the new group of predominantly Latino paps as "knuckle-scraping mouth breathers" who were just working as paps as an alternative to criminal activity.[49] A *Los Angeles Times* article reported, "Agencies use foreigners working on what some say are questionable visas. Photographers are hired less for their camera skills than their ability to navigate the rough-and-tumble of the celebrity chase."[50] A *New York Times* article called the new paps "hordes of untrained or corner-cutting paparazzi who are loath to lie in wait in cars for hours or days and are willing to make their presence known, even to jump out at celebrities on the street, if it means a chance for quick cash," thus giving established Los Angeles paps "a bad name."[51]

When I interviewed him in 2011, Stanley, an Anglo-American paparazzo, brought up the demographic shift and declared, "Certainly you have the unprofessionalism brought into the paparazzi field by all these guys who aren't professional. All these guys were gang members or valet parkers. Now they're carrying around cameras, so they're not *really* trained." Interestingly, Stanley himself had no formal training as a photographer. The owner of the agency AKM-GSI Media, Steven Ginsburg, an Anglo-American, worked as a bartender in Santa Monica and also had no photography training before picking up a camera and becoming a paparazzo.[52] Another pap and agency owner who had no previous training before entering the pap business as a teenager said:

> In the past, all the photographers that were working were trained. There was a certain level of a kind of pride associated with it, and that's because they were photographers who were trained as photographers, and they knew each other's work and the talent that they had. Now it's kind of like no one takes pride really, as far as being a photographer. It's more about maybe the hunt. And you know there are some good pictures being done, but a lot of the better pictures are generally done by the trained photographers. There's a lot of shit coming out because [the newer paps] are not photographers.

These ideas, coming from untrained photographers, demonstrate the ways in which appearance — racial, ethnic, presumed immigration status — dictates assumptions about skill level and about professionalism, even in the eyes of photographers who entered the business with no professional training in photography themselves (see fig. 1.10).

Some Latino photographers also complain about the untrained immigrant paparazzi, even when they themselves are untrained. Huapaya, who grew up in Los Angeles, said, "It's gotten ridiculous out here. A lot of these guys are untrained. They really have no background on photography." But he also said,

1.10 Paparazzi on the job in Los Angeles shooting outside of the *Dancing with the Stars* set in 2013. Photo courtesy of Ulises Rios.

"I'm not a high school graduate. I'm a hustler. That's what I do. Being out on the streets [as a photographer] is kind of like being on the streets when I was younger."[53]

The Brazilian pap Luiz defended the untrained photographer, calling the work "on-the-job training": "The thing is, you're practicing every day. You're shooting something every day. It's a process of learning and trying different settings. You see the results. The other thing is that when I went to see Regis [the owner of x17] he would talk to us a lot about photography. He would make suggestions about tactics to try. We learned a lot." Luiz described how the Brazilian paps changed the nature of the industry by working around the clock, demonstrating how hard they were willing to work to learn the trade.

Ultimately the rhetoric surrounding the new unskilled paps is how a group of previously untrained laborers critique their newer competition, but the threat these newer laborers pose is intertwined with racist notions surrounding immigration and fear of the economic effects of people of color on a previously predominantly white workforce.[54]

(In)Visibility and the Racialized Paparazzi

As the number of paparazzi grew and the demographics shifted, another oft-voiced complaint was that "few [paparazzi] adhere to an unwritten code of Los Angeles paparazzi—that the ideal picture is one that a celebrity does not even suspect has been taken, shot by a photographer who is neither seen nor heard."[55] The paparazzi newcomers—the Latinos and other minorities—are accused of not adhering to the industry standards related to a particular skill: stealth. Of course, this broad assumption about the new paparazzi workforce is inaccurate. For example, in October 2012 Galo—an untrained Latin American immigrant photographer—got a highly sought-after shot. The photo of Gwyneth Paltrow, Chris Martin, and their children was shot without their knowledge, using a long lens (see fig. 1.11). Celebrity media called it "the celebrity sighting equivalent of a unicorn," and it made his photo agency around $20,000 in the first week of sales.[56]

The extent to which the paps are able to remain invisible, allowing them to snap the hard-to-get shots, factors into the respect they get from peers and the amount of money they can earn (see fig. 1.12). "This is how we separate the men from the boys," Galo told me when he got the shots of Paltrow and Martin. The Salvadoran El Diablo, who, like Galo, had no formal photography training before he began working as a pap, had the same understanding of what it means to be a good pap. "Do the job the right way. Never leave your car or shoot from a bush on a long lens. Those are the [paps] who get the big scoops like Kristen Stewart," he said, referencing the paparazzi who shot the photos documenting Stewart cheating on Robert Pattinson.

Paparazzi often say their goal is to be invisible, which may be possible when they are working on a story alone. But when there are multiple paps on one story, they become highly visible and "othered" as a group of young Latinxs and Latin American immigrants in a rich, white, celebrity-heavy area. The idea of black and brown bodies, especially immigrant bodies, being socially invisible while fulfilling necessary social roles is a familiar one.[57] In the case of paparazzi work, being invisible correlates with economic empowerment; there is value in their invisibility in a way that cannot be said of other lines of

1.11 An October 26, 2012, E! Online article that features Galo's rare photograph of the Paltrow-Martin family, discreetly shot with a long lens. The headline reflects the shock that this photo could even be taken, as does the first line of the article, which notes that this sighting of the Paltrow-Martin family is like seeing a unicorn.

work, such as farm labor and custodial work. As paparazzi strive to remain invisible, their work seeks to make others (predominantly white celebrities) hypervisible. But when these paparazzi themselves are noticed and described, it is often in a negative light that promotes racist stereotypes.

In 2012 I helped organize a panel at the Getty Center called "Are We All Paparazzi Now?" A comment by one of the panelists, Carol Squiers, a curator at the International Center of Photography in New York, distilled the racially tinged negative view of contemporary paparazzi held by both elites and the public at large: "To me the whole notion of the expansion of paparazzi brings up the question of who are these people. . . . I mean some of the paparazzi, to me, look like thugs." This racialization has been transposed onto the paparazzi in L.A. as demographics have changed. Subconsciously or not, the public and art critics like Squiers are registering the different look of paps now compared to before 2005.

It is precisely because of such racially charged perceptions that media outlets prefer the paparazzi to remain nameless and faceless. Despite their reliance on paparazzi images, the media outlets do not want to be affiliated with paparazzi in any way. This notion that the paparazzi should remain invisible, nameless, and faceless is problematized by their status, particularly in Los

1.12 Galo using a long lens while perched in a tree to shoot the singer Fergie's baby shower. July 2013. Photo courtesy of Eduardo "Lalo" Pimentel.

Angeles, as Latinxs, as immigrants, and in some cases undocumented immigrants. Essentially paparazzi are marginalized because of their race, ethnicity, and doubts about their legal status in this country, and yet they are performing a task that is in demand by major corporate organizations that further marginalize them by keeping them on the outskirts of the actual production processes. At the same time, their position as outsiders of the media production process, as well as the nature of paparazzi work as an unregulated field, allows undocumented people, individuals without formal training or education, and individuals without access to elite spaces (such as red carpet or press junkets) to do this kind of work at all.

As paparazzi work itself becomes more visible, particularly through the popularity of TMZ and TMZTV, a website and television show that relies almost entirely on paparazzi images and videos for its celebrity news coverage, scholars and industry members alike have taken to referencing the "TMZ-ization" of media.[58] Yet the workers responsible for this phenomenon are invisible. TMZ was launched online in 2005 and on television in 2010; as a whole, TMZ—which presents itself as the direct link to the paps—is thought of as the face of paparazzi. But the media producers featured on the TMZ television show are not the paparazzi on the street; they are reporters inside the TMZ offices. The people on the street getting the photos are the predominantly freelance and predominantly Latino paparazzi who are the subject of this book. They create the content that drives TMZ-ization without participating in the popularization and corporatization of their work. Furthermore the paparazzi who shoot celebrities are not invited onto television shows to talk about their shots. Instead the celebrity weekly magazine reporters, who are predominantly white women, serve as intermediaries between the public and celebrities. In short, paps are not considered legitimate or presentable news sources, and I believe this is, in large part, because of gender and race.

The paparazzi of Los Angeles have become an extension of the "Latino threat"—the idea that all Latinos are immigrants uninterested in assimilating and bent on "destroying the American way of life."[59] When paparazzi photograph and supposedly torment American celebrities—who currently represent the "American way of life" better than any other contemporary cultural symbol—they threaten the core (imaginary) members of many Americans' communities.[60] The public is thus quick to attack the paparazzi, using Latino-specific slurs and insults. It is clear that the face of the Los Angeles paparazzi has been marked as Latino. Still, just as the threat paparazzi pose to celebrities is largely imaginary, so too is the threat they pose to the American economic and cultural system; on the contrary, these photographers are major cultural producers who created some of the most circulated and iconic images of the twenty-first century.

On the Job with Paps

Researching paparazzi on the job in Los Angeles took me from the beach neighborhoods to the furthest inland reaches of the city. However, it never took me to any centralized newsroom of the kind typically associated with news and media production. The British media and communications scholar Simon Cottle has pointed out that the "reconfiguration of news corporations, news production and journalistic practices" has created a need for a new wave of ethnography of news.[61] This call for new(s) ethnography determines a need to look beyond the newsroom as a center of production.[62] Karin Wahl-Jorgensen's "News Production, Ethnography, and Power" echoes Cottle's call to look beyond newsroom-centric approaches in studies of news; she explains that one key way to do this is through studies of freelance journalists like myself.[63] This also includes freelance photojournalists and paparazzi in particular, because even those on staff at a photo agency typically spend their days in the field rather than in an office. The closest thing to an office paparazzi have are their cars and the street corners where they converge.

When doing their job, paparazzi generally seek out specific celebrities the agencies are looking for, based on who is in demand by the magazines. If a pap's contacts or agency's contacts have reliable intelligence on a breaking story about a particular celebrity, that takes priority. Beyond that, a pap's ideal photo is a full body shot with great lighting, with the celebrity wearing bright clothing and no sunglasses or hat. Catching celebrities in an emotional moment—happy, sad, in love—is also important. Figure 1.13 is an example of an ideal paparazzi photo: the circumstances and setup of the shot are so good that it was likely staged. In other words, the photo's subjects dressed this way and went to this location in hopes of getting shot by the paps, or they explicitly tipped paps off and were prepared to be shot. This occurs regularly even with A-listers but is especially popular with lesser-known celebrities and reality television stars.[64]

In order to get a perfect shot, paps also need expert knowledge of their cameras, which generally comes with time on the job. Although Galo and many of his fellow paps did not have previous training in photography before

1.13 A 2011 photo of Gwen Stefani playing with her son Kingston at a park. Photo courtesy of Galo Ramirez.

entering the field, they began their work as photography was becoming digitalized and many experienced photographers were relearning how to work with the changing technology.[65] Still, different paps have different levels of expertise with their cameras. The paps Galo trained had limited photography skills when I first saw them in the field; he was teaching them basics like how to frame shots and achieve ideal lighting and focus.

When I accompanied Galo and his colleagues on the job, I often brought along my own digital camera with a zoom lens, but it paled in comparison to their high-tech oversized machines. Still, Galo took the time to help optimize the settings on my camera, altering its aperture, shutter speed, International Standards Organization, and white balance. Because I have a background in photography and documentary filmmaking, I was familiar with some of these functions, but Galo was an expert. As he checked the settings on his own camera, we waited for something to happen outside of Vanessa Hudgens's and Dakota Fanning's homes in Studio City. Hudgens had just left, but because there were about ten cars following her, Galo decided not to join in. His justification: "I won't be able to sell the photo." Though the bidding wars on celebrity photos have calmed down quite a bit, and the possibility of exclusive photos is less likely now with the abundance of paparazzi on the street, an exclusive photo is still preferred and offers greater revenue.

As we waited for action around the stars' homes, a woman drove past, looked at us, and rolled her eyes. We were parked in front of her house. "She is going to come talk her shit 'cause we're paparazzi. She wants to fuck with us. I bet she says that to all criminals. That's what I want to tell her. Like, 'Oh, do you say that to all criminals?' We're not doing anything wrong." The paparazzi know they are not well received in the neighborhoods in which they work. But Galo would still love to live in one of these celebrity-heavy neighborhoods. "I want to move to Studio City because then I would live so close [to celebrities]. If I lived over here, I would get to Hollywood so fast. I would make a left on Ventura, jump on the 101 up the street, and be in Hollywood in five minutes. If I have to go to Beverly Hills, I just take this short cut right here, come out on Mulholland, make a right, boom, make a left on Laurel Canyon. Bam. I'm done. It's perfect." As we sat waiting for one of the celebrities to return home, Galo showed me pictures he is proud of, including some of Britney Spears around the time she shaved her head. I had recommended him for the Getty Center panel on paparazzi that I helped organize, and he was gathering photos he might want to share at the event. I asked him about a female pap I had been trying to get in touch with, and it turned into a conversation about what it really *means* to be a paparazzo:

> Oh, you mean Cat Woman, who stands out on Hollywood Boulevard? She does pap work, but she's not a pap. She is out on Hollywood dressed up like Cat Woman. She's not paparazzi. Just because they do what I do doesn't make them paparazzi. There are different types in this business. She doesn't do doorsteps. She might get a few tips and go do stuff, but she's not out here with us. The things real paparazzi do to get pictures without bothering celebrities is crazy. That's what makes you paparazzi. Paparazzi used to be in your face. It means pest. But there are stealthy ones. It's supposed to be a candid moment. By definition people think of paparazzi as scum, they think of us as being all in your face. What about if I take a picture from my car and I don't bother you? Then what? I'm letting you be. I'm not bothering you. How can you be mad? I'm the guy who doesn't bother you.

The term *paparazzi* was famously coined from Paparazzo, a character in Federico Fellini's 1960 comedy-drama *La Dolce Vita*. Paparazzo was the "annoying news photographer who raced around Rome chasing celebrities along with the jaded gossip columnist. . . . Once the film came out, the photographers—who up until then had been aptly called 'assault photographers'—were thereafter known as 'paparazzi,' a relentless bunch who stalked the many movie stars and other celebrities who poured into Italy in the postwar years."[66] Although this is still the image often portrayed in paparazzi-shot videos shown on news programs, it is, as Galo explained, just one approach to paparazzi photography. Many paps instead try to stay out of the celebrities' way and be invisible.

Still, Galo recognizes that the paparazzi in Los Angeles do come into more contact with celebrities than they used to. "New York . . . is a lot less pestering. L.A. used to be like that. We would get our shot and be done. But now L.A. is more pestering because there are more guys and more competition. The last thing I want is to be on one celebrity all day like this. If I get one picture that will sell, I'm done."

As Galo explains to me his desire to remain invisible while on the job, he shows me a video of him and his former pap partner being harassed and physically assaulted by the musician Travis Barker and his friends outside a shopping mall. This is not a unique example; the violence exercised against paparazzi while on the job is a central element of their professional experience and one they want others to know about. They have had real trauma inflicted upon them through these experiences. Galo had a camera recording the entire altercation. He and his partner were attempting to shoot photos from their car in the mall parking lot, so as to not invade the personal space of Barker and his friends. In the video, one of the musician's friends walks up to the car and, as he starts to berate them, spits in Galo's face. Barker's friends then pull Galo's partner out of the driver's seat of his car and start to beat him. They slash his tires. They steal his phone. Barker's friends call the cops, and when the cops appear, they want to arrest Galo and his partner. The majority of the assault videos the paparazzi have shown me involve white men attacking men of color in public spaces. These videos are often publicly posted to social media, thus validating the inhumane treatment of paps and reiterating their perceived disposability in the industry. Galo feels the dehumanizing aspect of his work. He says that being in a car is like being in a cage. "It's like being in prison, but I know I can leave . . . but I don't." He doesn't leave because he cannot risk missing a shot.

• • •

It was a Sunday morning, August 22, 2011. I got a text message from Galo at 7:00 telling me, "J.Lo is shooting a video downtown. Streets are blocked off. Paps are here. Get down here." He wanted me to come see him in action since most of the time I had spent with him on the job had been in his car. I threw on some comfortable clothes, jumped in my car, and hopped on the 10 freeway going east, the Hollywood sign peeking out from the smog on my left, then to the 110 south, and got off at the second exit in downtown Los Angeles. Several streets were blocked off, a common occurrence in the city where so many commercials, videos, movies, and television shows are shot. In fact all of Los Angeles is part of Hollywood—all of its diverse landscapes, neighborhoods, and people have been incorporated into Hollywood imagery. I have sat with paparazzi outside movie sets in every part of the city, from South Central to the Sunset Strip in the heart of Hollywood itself, and everywhere in between. On this day downtown Los Angeles was Hollywood, as crowds of fans and photographers gathered to get a glimpse of Jennifer Lopez shooting her music video *Papi*.

When I walked up to Galo and a few other paparazzi on the corner of Spring Street and Fourth Street, they were sitting on the sidewalk with camera gear spread out around them (see fig. 1.14). There was a sign on the door of the building they sat next to: "Notice of Filming (Commercial—Standard). Production company: Island Def Jam Inc. will be filming: Cookie Love." The name was a decoy so people would not figure out that it was Lopez's video, but the paparazzi seem to always know where and when to find a celebrity. These paps had just gotten some clear shots of Lopez and her children exiting their trailer. "Did you see that [Lopez's] daughter Emme gave her flowers when she came out? I got that shot," Galo told me as he proudly showed me the images on his camera. It was already hot out and the paparazzi were wiping their foreheads. Galo wore a muscle shirt, in part to show off his physique but also because it was an August day in downtown Los Angeles, where a breeze is hard to come by.

Galo warned me that the other paps we were with that day might not want to talk about their work with me because "it's like secret society stuff." But some of the paps later told me a few of "the little secrets [they] keep"—which they made me swear not to share—making me feel I had finally reached the moment Clifford Geertz describes in his work on the Balinese cockfight of being, "quite literally, 'in.'"[67] After a few minutes of chatting and looking at their shots, we all got up and moved to the opposite side of the street, where

1.14 Galo in downtown Los Angeles near the set for the shoot for Jennifer Lopez's music video *Papi*. August 2011. Photo by the author.

the set was located. The paparazzi were met with the usual disparate and diverse reactions to their presence: pedestrians were simultaneously curious and seemingly disgusted about their work. One person walked by and yelled, "Get a life. Leave her alone!" Another, a middle-aged Latinx man in business-casual attire, stopped and peered over the shoulder of one of the paparazzi, who was reexamining his photos, to see what the photographer had shot. European tourists gathered around the paparazzi and posed next to them. One of the tourists, a woman in a brightly colored shirt with a hot pink sweater tied around her waist, a neon green mini-backpack, and a camera bag, held a zoom lens camera and placed herself directly next to the paparazzi in hopes of getting the same kinds of shots they do (while her family members took photos of her among the paparazzi). Her camera, much like mine, looked like a joke next to the giant zoom lenses of the paparazzi. Galo's lens was about one-third his height (see fig. 1.15).

Our conversation inevitably turned to Kim Kardashian's wedding to Kris

1.15 Galo resting on his lens, which is about one-third of his height. **August 2011.** Photo by the author.

Humphries, which had taken place two days earlier and had dominated not only our own work lives as celebrity media producers but also our social and consumer lives. There was a general feeling of "Kardashian exhaustion" in Los Angeles, and maybe countrywide. As a paparazzo who had to follow her every move, Galo was tired of her as well. "The Kim Kardashian wedding images sold for 1.5 million dollars to *People* magazine," Galo said. "They just had to have it. It's like the next Will and Kate [referring to Prince William and Kate Middleton]. And the wedding was basically sponsored. They are gonna sell every wedding. It's all fake. The Kardashians are bank. The brother is the only one who isn't getting love because he's a guy. He has no sex appeal. I see him at the Twenty-Four-Hour Fitness."

"Do you shoot him?" I asked.

"No. Why am I gonna shoot him? Nobody will buy those." His response highlighted the focus on women and women's bodies as well as the demand-driven nature of paparazzi work.

The paps were bored as they waited for Lopez to reemerge for the next scene, so they started spontaneously quizzing each other on celebrity kids' names, inspired by the talk about Lopez's twins, Max and Emme. They started with the "Brangelina" babies, Zahara, Knox, Vivienne, Pax, Maddox, and Shiloh, then Ben Affleck and Jennifer Garner's kids, then Britney Spears's, Gwen Stefani and Gavin Rossdale's, and the list went on. "We know all the celeb kids' names," Galo boasted. This is part of their job; just as I had to do as a reporter for *People*, they must stay on top of all the celebrity names, news, faces, and trends. They have to know who and what to be looking for at all times, and they're proud of their knowledge. There were five paparazzi on this job, all men, as usual—three Latino men and two white men. The Latinos broke off into their own group and were speaking Spanish. A white security guard started yelling at them. "Stay off this side of the street and we won't have any problems," the guard said without ever making eye contact with them, so as to reinforce their inferiority. One of the guards had made it his task to get in front of every potential shot the paparazzi could get, blocking Lopez each time. Another person working on staff at the video shoot stood with a pair of binoculars, scoping out the paparazzi, counting them, looking at where they stood. The paps said he was doing this to report back and strategize how to keep Lopez out of their view.

"Shooteando," José, one of the Latino paparazzi, said to me. "This is what we do. Exciting, huh?"

"Yeah, it is," I said. "It's really interesting." I had never met this pap before.

"They're not all nice, though. Some paps won't talk at all," Galo informed me, happy that the paparazzi we were with that day had welcomed me into their group. He sometimes worried that people wouldn't want me around, but it hadn't been an issue so far when I was with him. I was, however, dismissed by some paparazzi I approached on my own, particularly some I had been told were undocumented. When I asked, in Spanish, to talk with them and explained my research, they fled immediately. They could not be sure of my actual interest in them and could not risk explaining their stories to me.

"¿Hablas español, verdad?" (You speak Spanish, right?), José asked.

"Sí, claro" (Yes, of course), I said. He wanted an explanation. I told him my father was from Puerto Rico and that I grew up speaking Spanish with my dad's family, that I spent a lot of time in Puerto Rico and Cuba, and that I had lived in Spain for a while.

"¡Que rico! Yo estaba shooteando en Puerto Rico hace poco. Mira, te lo juro que la gente allá me trataba bien. Me encantó, de verdad" (How wonderful! I was shooting in Puerto Rico recently. Look, I tell you the people there treated me well. I truly loved it), he enthused. Naturally I smiled with pride; nothing makes me happier than people loving Puerto Rico.

"Hay, que bien. Me alegro mucho. ¿Y econtraste muchos paparazzi allá?" (That's nice. That makes me very happy. And did you find many paparazzi there?)

"No, no tanto. Unos pocos. A nosotros nos mandan allá para shootear. Mira, no puedes incluir esa info que te dije" (No, not many. Just a few. They [the agencies] send us there to shoot. Look, you cannot include the information I told you), he replied, referring to the secrets they had told me earlier.

"Sí, yo sé. No te preocupes" (Yes, I know. Don't worry). I got the feeling that he wasn't convinced I wouldn't include the secrets they mentioned until he said it in Spanish; that sealed the deal. Before that, it was just a hope that I wouldn't blow their cover. José started to show me photos he had shot the day before, which had sold well and were on People.com that morning.

"We thought about not coming back after yesterday 'cause we didn't think we could beat that, but we might," Galo said.

Security, again, started harassing them as they stood on the public street corner. The reality is that paparazzi generally stay on public property—parks, sidewalks, and streets. The celebrities they follow are protected regardless of where they are, and their security details go to great lengths to keep the paparazzi away, even when the paps are in public spaces where they have a right to be. The paparazzi have grown thick-skinned, but they are always aware of the potential for a situation to escalate into violence, so they do their best to stay calm and cooperate; the taunting they have to put up with is often humiliating, and when they are attacked, they often do not defend themselves for fear of getting blamed, arrested, or worse. They also do not want to be physically aggressive toward the staff or the celebrities whose cooperation they need in order to get their work done and make money. As a result, their bodies are constantly vulnerable.

For example, an altercation in 2012 between Justin Bieber and a paparazzo named José Osmin Hernández Durán resulted in Bieber's physically attacking the paparazzo, who did not fight back for fear of jeopardizing his livelihood. Bieber did not have that fear. Galo was present at this incident and shot pictures of the aftermath. These photos made over $25,000 for AKM-GSI within the first few weeks.[68] Apparently there is a market for photos and videos of paparazzi being assaulted. Paparazzi take these images as evidence for legal recourse, but, based on online comments about incidents like the one involving Bieber, the public sympathizes with the celebrities. Galo was disturbed that the witnesses he approached at the scene of the altercation told him that they "saw what happened" but that they would "tell the police it was the pap's fault because paps should leave Bieber alone": "They gave false information to the police, but I got that confession from them on video. There was no provocation, and Bieber got out of the car and punched the pap." One would think that Bieber's staff might be concerned that this would create bad press for him, but the fans who buy the media in which the paps' work appears are the same fans who tell paps they deserve to be punched by celebrities.

"I hope the kids go home because we are the only two that got them. The less my competition has those shots, the better," Galo declared. He told me that he never tells anyone who he is shooting because they could be informants and share that information with other paps, who could then come and scoop the story. "See that girl walking? She could be a reporter because she is walking back and forth and texting," Galo said.

A security guard approached the paps and said, "You can all be here, but we are closing this part of the street and so I have to ask you to move now. You can cross the street, but we are gonna do a shot here." The paps reluctantly stepped back; they didn't know if he was telling them the truth or just trying to get them to leave.

One pedestrian asked Galo who they were shooting, and he answered, "Jennifer Love Hewitt." He told another person who asked that it was Marc Anthony. Other passersby continued to ask for a peek at their shots. "How much does one of those cameras cost?" one man inquired. Security returned and asked the paps to move even further back. The paps and I relocated to the other side of the street. This time the security guard had a new approach. He seemed to be humbling himself because he knew that, like the paps, he was not high ranking in the entertainment industry hierarchy, or perhaps he was simply trying to get the paps to cooperate further. "Sorry, guys," he apologized. "I don't want to be a dick. I'm just doing what they tell me. I know you guys are just trying to make a buck too."

A policeman rode up on his bike and asked the security guard what he was doing. "You can't shut down both sidewalks," the cop told the guard. "If they do that I will shut the whole shoot down. You cannot stop pedestrians on both sides."

In this moment the paparazzi received validation from a police officer, and it felt good. "This is one of the only times we got the law on our side!" one of the paps declared.

The guard reopened the sidewalk that he had just pushed the paps off and said, "To be honest, man, I don't give a shit if you take pictures."

As we stood on the sidewalk, we could tell that they were going to start shooting a moving scene because Lopez got into a car that was perched on top of a trailer. Pedestrian traffic had drastically increased by this time, and people were commenting on how good Lopez looked. The shoot started, and the trailer moved forward, making it appear as though Lopez were driving the car. Dozens of men dressed in business suits chased her aggressively with flowers and teddy bears while she looked frightened and panicked. The shot is almost too ironic; the men chasing her are supposed to demonstrate how highly desired she is, her importance, her appeal. Yet when paparazzi chase her to get photographs, their behavior is ridiculed even though their interest in her is similarly representative of her importance, her desirability. In fact, as the hordes of men chased Lopez down the street as part of the shoot, the five paparazzi I was with (plus one latecomer) mirrored them from behind, chasing Lopez and the set. The image was so striking, and yet no one in the crowd of onlookers seemed to grasp the irony, the complexity, the hierarchy that played out in front of our eyes. When the scene was done shooting, the paps gathered together and compared shots. Lopez got out of the car and waved to the hordes of fans who had gathered on the street before climbing into a black SUV that drove her to a different part of the set.

I asked Galo about the pap who had arrived just before that scene was shot. "He's old school," was Galo's reply. "I got respect for him, but he probably doesn't know who I am. He owns his own thing. Eric Ford. He won't talk to you. He keeps to himself."

I approached Eric anyway. He had been working as a pap for about fifteen years and was enthusiastic about talking to me. He thought it was interesting that I was doing research on his profession and he had a lot to say about the economics of it, specifically how he used to make a good living but now was struggling. He specialized in sets, mostly TV and movies. He used to get minor jobs on sets, which was how he got insider information and access to places he otherwise wouldn't have been able to go. "We're in a time when the appetite for celeb reporting is at its highest, but photos are getting paid the least," he said. "I used to make a good living, but it's harder now. There are so many people working as paps." Later that day he sent me a link to his website, On-locationnews.com. He definitely considers his work news, as evidenced by the site's name. I walked with Eric to the other side of the set, where the other paps had migrated.

The security guards were again pushing the paparazzi around. The guards did not address the paps as people; rather, they pointed at and pushed them without talking to them directly. One of the workers on the set, a young hipster-looking white guy in a plaid shirt, yelled to Galo, "Hey, you're embarrassing that camera. That is high-tech gear and you're embarrassing it." With his comment, this worker asserted his elite status and legitimacy from within the set by criticizing the informal workers for their work documenting the celebrity to whom the on-set worker has more direct access. To this person, and to many others in the entertainment industry who are more formal fixtures of the Hollywood-industrial complex, it does not matter what kind of images these paparazzi produce; they and their images are unworthy.[69]

Yet, as always with the paparazzi, the disdain is mixed with fascination. At that same moment another pedestrian passed by and asked one of the paps, "Who are you shooting for?"

"Myself," the pap responded.

"Oh, well, I'm a photographer too. I got my master's in photography, and I live in the neighborhood. I need work, if you can help." A young woman approached and asked to see Galo's photos. A middle-aged woman dressed in a purple sari, with a bindi on her forehead, also drew near the crowds gathered around the set, hoping for a glance at the paparazzi's shots.

CHAPTER TWO

Latinos Selling Celebrity:
Economies and Ethics of
Paparazzi Work

Paparazzi seek out the types of photos wanted by media outlets, which are based on what the magazines project will sell and what kind of newsworthy stories the paps uncover. Randy Bauer, who co-owns Bauer-Griffin photo agency, says that a lot of the decision making depends on magazine editors' favorite celebrities: "It's funny how I know the [magazine] editors' pet celebrities. I know for a fact that editors at *People* magazine love Reese [Witherspoon] and they love Cameron Diaz. It's a personal choice; you're not always saying, 'Readers love that,' you're saying, 'I love that.' And you see it with all of the magazines. And I target subjects based on that too. No one ever says anything to me about it, but I see which pictures the magazines run, and when I see them leaning towards using a lot of pictures of whoever, I know that if I get those pictures, my chances of selling photos to them are higher." Bauer regularly polls editors at the weekly magazines to get current lists of the celebrities they are most interested in:

> I have a list, and it's the same list as always. You would not find it surprising in the least. Jennifer Aniston and Justin Theroux, Brangelina,

J.Lo hopefully with a new man, the Kardashians, Tom and Katie and Suri, Will and Kate, the *Twilight* kids, Pink and her daughter, anyone in a bikini. That's it. I call [the magazines] and I say, "Hey, what [do] you guys want?," so that I know what to target. You have to give the customers what they want. It's a boring list [of people], but that's what you want. Do you know how many times I've told photographers [to shoot] Jennifer Garner with the kids? It's so boring, but it's like, no, you give the customers what they want. That's a new thing — magazines used to never run the same person two weeks in a row. They'd say, "We just ran it last week. We're not going to run it this week." Now they do it all the time. Jennifer Garner with the kids, Suri, Jessica Alba, the Kardashians — it's the same pictures every week, over and over. I have tracked *In Touch* magazine, and this is the fifth week in a row they have run photos of Tori Spelling with her kids. Their editor says, "[Spelling] knows how to work the game. They give us what we want. They wear bright clothes; they have cute babies; they have smiles on their faces like they love being photographed. It's like, that's what we want and they give it to us, and they know how to play. So we put it in the magazine."

Sales to the celebrity magazines make up a majority of paparazzi photo agency sales. This, combined with the fact that other media outlets (such as *Access Hollywood*, *Extra*, and local and national newspapers and television) often build celebrity-focused stories based on what *People* or *Us Weekly* report, and the magazines generally dictate which celebrities the paparazzi target. According to one pap who has his own agency, "The weekly magazines are still my bread and butter, and that's about 75 percent of my sales. Then I'd probably say about 20 percent of sales are the blogs now for me. And then the final 5 percent are interesting new customers and TV." Since the decisions behind the photo publication and the market demand are out of the hands of the paparazzi, Galo is often frustrated at the blame they receive from celebrities, the media, and the public. "Why am I the bad guy? It's not my responsibility. I'm a photographer. I'm not the person who sits behind the desk at a magazine and decides what story to run that week. If you are gonna blame us, then blame everyone. Don't just single out the paparazzi because they're the ones who take the pictures. No, dude. I can take a million pictures, dogg, and, unless you buy them, what are they worth to me? Nothing. It's not worth anything to me. It's supply and demand."

The people and corporations making the most money from the pap business are the photo agencies and magazine owners, not the paps themselves or the magazine reporters. Many former paparazzi from the 1990s and early 2000s have gradually made their way into positions as strictly "image brokers," selling paparazzi photos from behind desks while hiring or selling photos on behalf of the next generation of paparazzi, who are now predominantly Latino.[1] In general, freelance paparazzi make between 60 and 70 percent of the proceeds of their photos. Since the freelance paparazzi do not deal with the sale of their images at all, however, it is difficult for them to know if they are getting paid based on what their photos actually make; some paparazzi trust their agencies, while others do not believe they are being compensated fairly. But paparazzi stay freelance for a few reasons. One pap who briefly tried to start his own agency quickly realized that "they are two full-time jobs and you can't do both." The only way to get the full profits from your photo sales is to deal with the business side of things alone, which for this pap proved to be impossible. Another reason is that not just anyone can sell to the magazines. In order to be seen as a legitimate company, "You have to have about five hundred thousand images for magazines to see what you have, and then they might agree to do business with you. You have to get permissions to upload images to the magazines' FTP [File Transfer Protocol—a standard for the exchange of program and data files across a network] sites," Luiz, the Brazilian pap, told me. "Otherwise you have to go through an agency."

Formal Economic Channels of the Paparazzi Business

When Galo started working on staff as a pap for Fame, he made $100 per day. Early on in this job, he took a photo that sold for $300,000; he received a $500 bonus for it. These types of sales, in which paparazzi receive less than 1 percent of the amount paid for their photos, serve as incentive for paps to work freelance. This tendency toward freelance work, however, also contributes to the informal, open-access nature of the business.

Of course, with the possibility of greater reward comes greater risk. When Galo first went freelance, he made only $700 in three months. For those three months, he and other paparazzi and reporters were camped out in front of the house of Katie Holmes and Tom Cruise twenty-four hours per day, waiting for Holmes to go into labor so they could follow her to the hospital. Galo could not leave his car or the site for food or to use the bathroom. He began to have health problems from the working conditions, and he was not making enough money to live on. This prompted him to go back to working for an agency, this time JFX, before deciding once again to go freelance.

Galo's experience is not unique; Luiz also remembered when a shot of Brad Pitt, Angelina Jolie, and their children would make $300,000. Luiz said this is why, for agencies like X17, which had greatly expanded their staff photographers rather than using mostly freelance photographers, "having us on staff was cheaper." Phoebe, a former photo editor of a celebrity weekly magazine, described this period of expansion from 2002 to 2008 as the "paparazzi boom," and a photo agency owner referred to those years as "the gold rush."

The boom was triggered by an explosion in demand for photographs by the celebrity weekly magazines. Prior to 2000, *People*, which launched in 1974, had no direct competition in the magazine market. In 2000 *Us Magazine*, which had existed since 1977 as a trade-focused bimonthly and then monthly publication, became a weekly to compete with *People*.[2] Two years later *In Touch* began publication. Then, in 2004, *Life and Style* entered the market, and the tabloid newspaper *Star* was relaunched as a magazine. The U.S. version of the British weekly celebrity magazine *OK!* was launched the next year. These new magazines created competition for content, which had not previously existed in the industry.

The expansion from one celebrity weekly magazine to six in the span of only five years created a market in which the magazines struggled to make their product distinctive. In contrast to posed red carpet photos, which are obtained by multiple photographers at any premiere or special event and typically sell for about $150, candid paparazzi shots are more unique and thus have the potential to be much more valuable. In this newly competitive environment, the ability to procure exclusive paparazzi shots became a crucial selling point for the magazines. Phoebe believes the paparazzi boom started after the first major bidding war for photos by the magazines, which was over a set of photos of Ben Affleck and Jennifer Lopez kissing in 2002. *People* purchased the photos for approximately $75,000.[3] The highly publicized nature of the bidding wars worked as an advertisement for the new demand for paparazzi photographs. Phoebe recalls that this period of increased competition coincided with the expansion of digital photography, which reduced costs not only for aspiring paparazzi but for the magazines as well, allowing them easier access to photographs: "One of the big reasons we started to see more was

(a) photographers flooded the market because it was all of a sudden really profitable, and (b) they could get us pictures by just pushing a button and putting them into our FTP. When it became easier for us to get pictures, more people were game to buy them." The boom ended in 2008, not coincidentally with the onset of the financial crisis. According to editors, paps, and agency heads I spoke to, the magazines reduced their budgets for photo acquisition and scaled back to pre-boom pricing standards for photos.

Since 2008, paps and agency heads alike say, sales have not come near the big numbers of the boom years. For example, x17 made over $3 million from a set of Britney Spears photos in 2007, including photos of the famous head-shaving incident; in 2011, $50,000 for a set of photos of Spears was considered high.[4] When I spoke with him in 2011, Luiz's last major sale was photos of Kristen Stewart and Robert Pattinson filming a movie in Brazil; the set grossed between $100,000 and $150,000, of which he received a percentage. Prices like these, however, were "not often [seen] anymore," he said. "But you can still get big numbers, it just depends on the story."

Throughout the course of my research the average paparazzi photo sold for anywhere between $50 and $4,000, though Gregory, photo agency co-owner, called $500 to $4,000 the "meat and potatoes" of his business and said 90 percent of his agency's image sales fell within that price range. In the absence of bidding wars, the standard magazine photo rates were cut at least in half since the boom. One pap explained, "It used to be standard to get fifteen hundred dollars for a quarter-page photo in *People*; now it's seven-fifty. Exclusive images that would have earned three thousand will only get me about five hundred. Back in the day, they had the exclusive rights, which today you don't really have anymore. Nobody really pays exclusive rights anymore, and the chances of getting anything exclusive are slim because there are so many more paps. Magazines only pay extra for exclusive rights if it's something really, really big *and* nobody else has it." Over the last few years, as photo agencies have merged, online media outlets have multiplied, and flat-rate image subscription services have become more common, prices of paparazzi images have continued to decline.

At the Getty Center panel, Galo was asked if the paparazzi profession was still lucrative. He responded, "In my opinion, I think it's oversaturated. . . . There's still a lot of opportunity to make a lot of money if you get the right photo, like Brad and Angelina or a Jen Aniston baby bump. [How much I can make on that kind of photo] depends on if it's exclusive, how good the photo is. The baby bump . . . it's enough money to make me sit at her house for a long time." Galo said that although the changes in the industry have made the job more challenging since paps can no longer rely on an average shot to make them thousands of dollars, the work can still be profitable, and many paps consider themselves lucky to be able to make a decent living.

To understand the changes in the market and the "oversaturation" Galo speaks of, it is significant to note how many photos are sent to the magazine offices—all of which have a similar process for receiving photos. Andrew, a photo transmission manager who has worked for multiple celebrity weekly magazines, explained to me that in ten years the number of digital photos being transmitted via the FTP sites multiplied exponentially. In 2001 around fifty thousand digital photos were received by the magazines. By 2011 that number had jumped to over eight million. Today the magazines receive about one million photos per month. The majority of these photos are paparazzi shots, and the remainder are red carpet photos. This jump in numbers isn't based solely on technological advancements; it also correlates to the number of paparazzi on the street every single day.

Many paps quickly got used to their lifestyle during the paparazzi boom, when Luiz, for example, estimated he was making $10,000 a month. He bought a home and then lost it when his yearly earnings suddenly dropped to about $30,000 in 2009. Another pap told me that his best year ever was 2008 and his worst year ever was 2009.

A major contributor to the decline in photo sales was the reduction in the number of exclusive images published (and fought over) by the magazines. As the price for images dropped based on the magazines' decision not to engage in bidding wars except under special circumstances, so too did the need for or the expectation of earning exclusive rights. Today, unlike during the boom years, multiple competing magazines often run the same images. The only way a magazine can get an exclusive is if no other pap shot a similar image, which is rare in today's market. Still, in addition to the saturation of photographers, magazines have made a strategic business decision not to pay what they used to for exclusive images, so it is difficult to tell the cause from the effect. Another factor is that paparazzi may not be as careful about protecting their potentially exclusive shots since they know they will not get the kind of money for those shots that they used to.

A related change is that freelance paparazzi, in an effort to maximize sales, will do what paps call "double dipping," when a pap gives the same photos to different agencies in the hope that the agencies will have better relationships with certain outlets than others, thus maximizing the pap's profits. Some paps believe that this practice is exacerbating oversaturation and having a detrimental effect on the market. As one agency owner put it, "At a time when the celebrity media is at its biggest and the photos are most important, the photos are the cheapest."

Beyond the magazines, photographers, and celebrities, the remaining major group in the economic system of celebrity image production is employees working within certain industries who tip off photo agencies and/or paps in exchange for regular payments. Among those who routinely get paid are individuals who work for airlines, at restaurants frequented by celebrities, or on the sets of studio productions. Airline employees who provide reliable information might receive several hundred dollars a month for it. For each day they provide basic set information on studio productions (e.g., what time celebrities will be arriving on set), studio employees generally receive $25. One agency owner said the "tipsters" do not have "formal contracts":

> But it's like, hey, we give you money every month. We send it to your bank account, and it's an ongoing relationship. We've had some of our key information suppliers for years and, you know, the funny thing is their desire to be a part of this industry. I mean, cash is cash, but it's about their desire for them to be involved. People want to be involved in this whole juggernaut of celebrity. It's their way of being involved and part of the action. Because they really get into it. You talk to some people, and they are giving you detailed specifics, like, "I know this person just had a fight with the girlfriend, so it looks like he's probably getting away to visit the family," like they really get involved personally.

Celebrities themselves are also often on agency payrolls. Not only do they tip paps off (directly or via their publicists) for the resulting publicity, but they also sometimes get paid by agencies for doing so. For example, an agency recently paid for Kim Kardashian's entire family to go on vacation under the condition that it could have free rein to shoot photos of the trip (see fig. 2.1). One agency owner said, "Basically Kim Kardashian does it all the time. She has deals with photo agencies and they pay her to do photo sets. The agencies will say, 'We're going to give you fifty thousand dollars and you're going to do pictures on the beach in a bikini. And they send a photographer. It's set up. They do the pictures. The agency pays Kim Kardashian her money, and the agency makes money off of the photos."

2.1 The Kardashian family vacation in the May 16, 2011, issue of *Us Weekly*, exemplifying the celebrity coordination of paparazzi shoots.

The Informal Economy of Paparazzi Images: Paps as Image Brokers

While the agencies serve as image brokers to the magazines, an informal economy of paparazzi images has also developed in which some paps serve as intermediary image brokers between other paps and the agencies.[5] This informal system revolves around certain freelance paps—who I will call informal paps—who avoid dealing with photo agencies by selling their photos to other freelance paps for a small, flat fee (generally about $50 a set). The brokering freelance pap then owns the photos and provides them to the agency (or agencies) he works with. He will earn the same percentage from the brokered photos that he would from his own images. This new form of pap image sales facilitates opening up the industry in a way that allows for more undocumented workers to compete in the market on their own, without having to engage in formal business channels and without having to provide any personal information. It is now an established part of the economics of paparazzi work and adds another leg to the complex "labor hierarchy" already in place in this industry.[6]

Based on interviews and observation in the field, I conclude that undocumented paps are more likely to sell in this fashion than others, as they generally attempt to avoid formal business transactions. However, undocumented paps are not the only ones informally selling their photos; some paps sell this way to avoid negotiations with the agencies or to avoid taxes. Regardless of immigration status, every pap who my closest collaborators have witnessed selling their images informally has been Latino. The informal sales are often negotiated in Spanish. Though a significant number of paps are Brazilian, they generally do not participate in this new informal realm.[7]

The sale of a video of Halle Berry becoming enraged at a paparazzo outside her daughter's school became an example of the complicated intertwining of the informal economy of paparazzi images and the ethical codes observed by the paparazzi. On May 9, 2012, I sat in Galo's gray Prius around the corner from the homes of Vanessa Hudgens and Dakota Fanning in Studio City. As a group of paps gathered around another pap's car, Galo and I went to say hello. The paps we approached were part of the group nicknamed "the Home Depots," who generally sell and circulate their photos through other paps. They were watching a video of Halle Berry. She had become irate at a pap because he went inside her daughter's school to take photos instead of remaining outside the entrance, as paps usually do.[8] This act violated the self-regulated ethical code, mainly revolving around legal restrictions, to which most paparazzi understand they are supposed to adhere. Upon seeing the video, Galo instantly made an ethical judgment: "She was right." He felt Berry had reacted appropriately. He did not approve of the paparazzo's behavior and wanted to make sure the video circulated to expose this pap's lack of adherence to ethical codes — and, of course, because he saw the potential for monetary gain. "What are you going to do with the video?" Galo asked the Home Depots. "I'll sell it to you," one of them offered (see fig. 2.2).

As the paps talked about the video, they discussed ethics, right and wrong, and whiteness — the pap who crossed the ethical line was white. The Home Depots described the events that led up to their shooting the video. "I was following Halle, and he [the paparazzo] was following Vanessa [Hudgens]. While I was waiting for Halle, he went inside of the school."

"I guarantee the video will sell," Galo told them.

"He really shouldn't have done that," they agreed.[9]

Galo, who normally does not play a part in the informal pap economy, offered $200 for the video, which the Home Depots would normally have sold for $50. They accepted the offer. Galo hoped to sell for at least ten times that

2.2 Halle Berry and daughter, Nahla, leaving Nahla's preschool in 2012. Photo courtesy of Galo Ramirez.

amount; he hadn't gotten any shots that day, so this was another way to make money. He called different agencies and organizations, attempting to sell the footage. His main agency didn't want it. Initially TMZ didn't want it either, because they thought that it made the paparazzi look bad, which they want to avoid in order to maintain their brand. x17 had already purchased another version of the video (there were about three versions circulating). Ultimately Galo was unable to sell the video as quickly as he hoped, so he returned it to the Home Depots. Since he normally does not buy from them and is well-respected by the other paps, they returned his money. Eventually they sold the video through other paps and agencies.

The informal economy of images illustrated by the circuitous path of the Berry video contributes to the inundation of photos available to the magazines, the corresponding lower cost for images, and the relative unimportance of exclusive photos today compared to during the boom. Informal paps generally do not sell their photos as exclusives since it would prohibit them from selling the photos multiple times. Sometimes they sell the same set of photos to multiple image-brokering paps, who often attempt to sell the informally acquired images through multiple photo agencies; thus both parties involved in the informal sale contribute to the flooding of the pap photo market. Yet paps like Galo place more blame on the brokering paps for taking advantage of the informal paps, who are not paid anywhere near the potential market value of their photos.

Galo believes that this cooperative informal economy is generally disruptive to the overall pap business. "They flood the market with pictures," he said. "Before, if there were three paps, there were only three agencies buying pictures. Now, if there are three guys, there could be ten agencies buying because one guy could give his [photos] to six agencies, and another guy gives it to another four, and it's like everyone has it now." Though less common, some informal paps sell their photos under the table to agencies for the same flat fees they receive from the image-brokering paps. This too disrupts the regular system of image sales because it drives down the overall prices of the images. Galo elaborates:

> Because the [informal paps] sell the pictures so cheap, those agencies can sell the pictures for cheap to get placement and it doesn't matter to them because they are already making profit because they paid fifty bucks. They turn around and sell it for five hundred. That's ninety percent profit, and it doesn't matter to them because they are making four

hundred fifty bucks. Whereas with my boss, he wants to sell pictures expensive, so everyone wins. He'll get a placement in *People* magazine, a full page. They're going to pay around six thousand dollars, depending on what story it is. That is nonnegotiable, whoever has it, because those are the prices he gets. The other places who get the pictures off of these guys, they sell them cheap—*People* magazine full page, five hundred dollars.

This informal economy of images adds another link to the chain of working relationships, creating an even more substantial labor hierarchy. It further distances the actual producer of the images from the final media products in which the images appear and ensures there is no dialogue with or acknowledgment of the informal paps, who are rendered professionally invisible in this process. Their position as informal workers—like the workers hanging out outside the Home Depot—again reinforces the notion of the invisible (Latino) immigrant worker and fully interconnects the racialization of these workers with their professional, legal, and (presumed) immigrant status.[10]

In this informal economy, the originating producer of the image that leads to the final media product has a relationship with neither the agencies that place his or her images nor the media outlets that ultimately publish them. Still, even paparazzi who sell their images formally do not receive any acknowledgment from the media outlets that rely on their images. The paparazzi perform the labor but seldom have any relationship with the actual media outlets that use their work; they are intentionally left out of the formal media production process and rendered invisible by the media outlets and organizations that demand their labor.

Bodies of Color Shooting White Bodies: The Effect of Race on Market Value

Although the paparazzi are in constant competition to sell images, they discuss sales and finances with each other frequently. It is common for them to stand around waiting for a shot together and talk about each of their biggest sales of the week, or even the shots they took that did not sell. My experience with the paps demonstrated that they are critical thinkers who actively reflect on their position within the celebrity media industry and the influence of that industry on American culture. The paparazzi are not passive media producers who haphazardly take photos and ignore the trends or circumstances under which their photos are published.

On one particular outing, I was struck by a conversation I wandered into while waiting with about eight paps outside the gates of the school Heidi Klum's children attend. (We had followed Klum's boyfriend/bodyguard to the school and planned to then follow their driver to see if they went on a group outing, which would make a good photo.) As we stood outside waiting patiently in the sweltering heat, most of the conversations going on were in Spanish. If I did not speak Spanish, I would have missed so much. While Klum's boyfriend went to pick up the kids inside the school gates, Galo and the other paps parked on the opposite side of the street. There were six cars in total, but two were already there waiting when we arrived. Cars were zooming by so fast—when I listen to the recording it sounds like we are on a freeway. Tuition at that elementary school cost about $4,000 a month, Galo estimated. The paps socialized while they waited. It was about 95 degrees, and Galo offered me a sip of some very cold water that the pap Milton had in an ice chest in his car. I declined, but he asked, "Are you sure? Está casi congelada [It's almost frozen]." I could see the ice-cold water sweating cold droplets that resembled the salty beads running down my face.

Unprompted, the paps began discussing their theories about why photos of people of color don't sell. Galo talked about taking an exclusive set of photos of Connor Cruise (Tom Cruise's son, adopted when he was married to Nicole Kidman) driving Katie Holmes's car recently and was shocked that it didn't sell. "I got Connor two times and they didn't even sell. I got him at the dog park and it was exclusive. And I got him at the carwash and it was exclusive," Galo said. "I don't waste my battery nor my camera on him anymore. Why wouldn't those photos sell? ¿Por qué es negro? [Because he is black?]"

"Sí," Halcón said confidently.

I had just caught the tail end of the conversation, so, as I walked over, Galo explained, "We have this theory that the magazines predominantly pick white people."

I said, "Yeah, it's true."

"It's fucking one hundred percent true," Galo replied, in a disappointed tone. "And it's weird that Connor Cruise doesn't sell, yet Suri Cruise sells all day," he continued. One of the paparazzi asked me what I was doing, what my interest was in all this. I explained, in Spanish, that I was writing a book about the production of these magazines and that looking at who is included in the magazines, and why it is mostly white people, is part of my research as well. He nodded approvingly.

"Unless it's Beyoncé or Alicia Keyes," Galo said. We discussed the cyclical nature of the business, and the paps deciding which photos to take based on what will sell. If they shoot people of color and those photos don't sell, they will be less likely to take more photos of those same people, or even other people of color. It comes down to simple math, simple economics: Which photos, which faces and bodies, will make them money? Photos of nonwhite celebrities have proven to earn the paparazzi less money than photos of white celebrities. Actors of color are noticeably underrepresented in Hollywood movies, and this correlates directly with their value to magazines.[11] If they are not cast, they do not receive symbolic or economic capital through promotion via media like celebrity magazines. This all contributes to an economy of celebrity bodies in which white bodies are systematically attributed more value. The racial hierarchies built into the various realms of the entertainment industry reinforce the racism at its core. Because the cycle is never broken, the hierarchy is static.

The paps began to discuss how people of color only sell when there is a big news story around them, but white people sell just for going to Starbucks. "Por lo general, los negros no se venden [In general, photos of black people don't sell]. Halle Berry porque es un poquito—" Galo stopped himself. He was going to say that Berry sells more because she's a bit lighter skinned. But he didn't. I pointed out that the magazines don't include many Latinxs either, which they initially would not admit. "Yeah, but they have *People en Español.*"

"They barely even have black people in that magazine either," Halcón said.

"Even though there are plenty of people who are Afro-Latino," I said.

"Yep."

I continued, "Jennifer Lopez is pretty much the only Latina who is in the weekly magazines regularly."

Galo chimed in, "J.Lo, Shakira. Mariah? What's Mariah? She's not black."

"Yes," I told him. "She's black and white, actually Afro-Latina."

"Oh, okay, well, that's probably why she still sells, then. But Connor Cruise will not sell. We're talking about the [son of the] richest fucking actor out there. All kinds of drama around him. I get [Connor] driving Katie Holmes's car and it's still not a story. It's like, what? I got Tom Cruise's son," Galo said.

"Well, it's not that black people never sell. But if it is not the most rich and well-known black people, then forget about it. But the Spanish-speaking artists, we don't even try to get them because las magazines no quieren pagar dinero por esas personas [the magazines don't want to pay money for those people]," Halcón said.

"So now you're not going to shoot Connor because he doesn't sell?" I asked Galo.

"No. He doesn't sell, so I won't shoot him."

"But don't you see about the cycle, though: because you take the pictures and they don't buy them, and then you guys stop taking the pictures because you can't waste your time doing that. But it's a cycle because if the material's not out there for them to buy, then it's going to be even less people in the magazines that are people of color. It's a fucked-up cycle. I understand because, like, on the reporting side, it's the same. Like, they don't take most of the interviews I do with black people, but I try to do them anyway because I don't want to not have that out there."

"Los negros todavia no son aceptados [Black people are still not accepted]," Halcón chimed in. "When I want to shoot someone, people will be like, honestly, he's black, fool. It's not going to sell."

"Yeah, but if you're talking about the most popular outlets like *People*, *Us*, they don't include many Latinos either," I said.

"Nope. Not Latinos. Not black people. And this affects the work we do because we can't keep taking photos of these people if they don't sell," Halcón said.

"And it's the same artists featured all the time," I said. "It's like ten people they always want us to report on and you guys to take photos of."

"Yes. In general it's like Jennifer Aniston, Brad Pitt, Angelina Jolie."

I reminded the paps of this fact: "Well, for example, the photos of Jennifer Lopez and Marc Anthony's twins were bought by *People*, but for less than half the price of the photos of Brad Pitt and Angelina Jolie's twins."[12]

"Exactly. And we're talking about Jennifer Lopez and Marc Anthony. We are talking about the most famous Latinos in the world. The photos of children of Latino stars are worth much less than those of white stars," Halcón said again, sounding sad.

In contrast to the paparazzi, red carpet photographers, who are predominantly white, never raised an issue about the lack of diversity among the celebrities they photograph during any of my interviews. The one black photographer I interviewed (and one of the few who regularly works red carpets) readily and immediately talked to me about his issues as a black person working mostly with white media producers in a hyperwhite space and producing images mostly of white bodies. These different levels of understanding are why diversity matters in the newsroom and on the red carpet. The correlation the photographers of color analyzed between celebrities' race and how well images of them sold is not something the outlets and agencies would address or confirm, nor even register.

"¿Debe salir el tipo, no?" (The guy should be coming out, right?), I ask. "Ya son las tres y media. Ya viene" (It's already three-thirty. He's coming). With that, the conversation ended. Everyone ran to their cars and got in line to follow the boyfriend and kids home. Maybe they would stop to get ice cream or something. That is what the paps don't want to miss: a chance at getting a shot of the family doing something in public. And to make sure they don't miss it, they have to follow them. "Celebrities are unpredictable," a paparazzi told me. They have their daily routines, but you never know exactly what they are going to do, so you have to follow them or you can't get the shot.

They wanted to make sure they were not following the wrong Escalade, so Galo yelled out, "Si tiene placas, es dos noventa" (If it has [license] plates, [it ends in] two-ninety).

"It's not him," one of the paps yelled back.

"Yo, it's hot as fuck, homie," I told Galo. I was dying of thirst and sweating like crazy.

"Big time. Let's sit in here. I gotta run the A.C. all day. It's hot as fuck," Galo replied. He switched on the radio and started rapping along with the Notorious B.I.G.: "I like the waistline / Let me hit that from behind / Which wall you wanna climb / My style genuine / Girl love you long time / I got you pinned up / With yo fuckin' limbs up / Or because you like the way my Benz was rimmed up." Galo continued until he had to get out to see if the car we were after was coming out of the school. Galo used to want to be a rapper; he still writes raps and poetry and likes to share his work and recite it whenever he has a chance. We were still in the car waiting for the bodyguard when Galo's cell phone rang; his ring tone is "Regulate" by Warren G. I could hear his conversations because they came through blue tooth, and he was fine with that. As we pulled out after the bodyguard exiting the school, other cars pulled in front of us. "That's what they do when they don't want me to be in the front. They want to push me out. But I don't need to be closer. I don't need to be behind them when I don't need to. I like to be there when it counts. When we're about to park and I know it, I like to be in the back."

Ethics in Paparazzi Work

That there are any ethical standards in paparazzi work may be surprising, particularly in light of the image of the paparazzi that has been crafted in the public imagination. In the coffee table book *Paparazzi*, which profiles the photographers and agency workers, the author highlights the fact that the shortest section of the book is the one on ethics, reinforcing the perception that there are few ethical standards in this kind of work.[13] Throughout my fieldwork with paparazzi, however, I found that while there are no written ethical codes for the job (and the same can be said for celebrity reporting), there are both spoken and unspoken rules and ethical expectations that are understood among the paparazzi. These serve to give structure to the profession and resolve issues within it. The maintenance of this ethical standard relies on the self-regulation of the paparazzi and the ways in which certain paparazzi punish their peers when they feel they have broken the rules or behaved in a way that will make the job harder for others. Generally these violations consist of making themselves overly visible or getting too close to a celebrity.

Galo, for example, prides himself on his ethics, as do his closest pap friends. "We get vilified no matter what. We're the criminals, and I understand that there are a few rotten apples. I have no control over the rotten apple. It gets tense out there when a pap doesn't do their job right, it makes you feel bad. You get the wrath of it because of someone else. I've gotten into fights [with other paps]. There are arguments." These fights take various forms. There are verbal and physical altercations, and there are also times when Galo tries to punish other paps by bombing their photos or exposing them to the media or to the celebrity they have angered.

Still, to the extent they can, the paps "take care of each other," El Diablo told me one day. When he first started he was hired by an agency to be competition for another paparazzo, and he didn't even know it. Still, that paparazzo took El Diablo under his wing and trained him. "When I didn't have money he'd be like, 'Here's sixty dollars, go fill up your car with gas.' I'd tell him I didn't have money for lunch because I hadn't gotten paid and he'd be like, 'Don't worry about it.' That's the kind of person he is, and all of these guys. That's why we're tight. They look out for each other. We're a small group, but we have each other's back."

On May 22, 2012, Galo called me. "Did you hear about that dick paparazzi who kicked Justin Timberlake's friend's car and left?" Galo wanted to help track down the pap, but he was upset because Timberlake had tweeted,

"A paparazzi can't get a photo of me so he kicks my best friend's truck door in? And they wonder why they can't get a 'fair' shake. . . . I mean, seriously. . . . Not ruining my day though. #getaREALjob."[14]

Galo said, "Now it makes me mad, it makes me feel like I'm responsible. But I told them, once I find that motherfucker !" As in this instance, the paps try to work with celebrities to help regulate paparazzi behavior and build respect, but the celebrities generally disregard the effort and further ridicule the paparazzi as a whole. Galo was as critical as Timberlake of the pap in question, but he was frustrated that these portrayals contribute to the negative narrative about paparazzi. "Sometimes I wonder what the fuck is wrong with these people," he said. "This is how we make money. Why the fuck would you do that?" Not only does he want there to be ethics within the profession, but he also wants to make sure that members of the paparazzi community keep each other in line. "This is the shit I have to deal with on a daily basis. Somebody made a mess, and I have to clean it up. See all the Facebook pics and posts I took? I'm trying to show people what's going on."

Referring to the Halle Berry incident described earlier, Galo said, "We try to follow the rules. What happened that day, one of the guys decided he would take a step further and go inside the [building], so she followed him outside and she flipped. And she had every right to be mad. But does that mean that we all do that? No. And every batch has a rotten apple. So a lot of times guys don't know the limits. They are so money motivated, so they do whatever they have to do. It's wrong. It really is. It doesn't mean we all do that."

In certain cases, celebrities themselves set the ethical codes for paparazzi, which the latter generally respect. For example, Jennifer Garner has directly communicated to the paparazzi that she does not want them coming close to her children. One pap, originally from Brazil, told me, "When [the celebrities] talk to us and they tell us what they want or don't want, we can work together. We respect that." There is no exact measurement of how close is too close, but paps now operate with the general understanding that they should keep a reasonable distance from Garner's children. Recently, when a group of paps shooting Garner and her daughter Violet at the Brentwood farmer's market saw one pap get what they thought was too close to Violet, they attempted to ruin his photos by blocking his shots and inserting themselves into his shots to make them less marketable.

I have seen similar tactics used in other situations where a celebrity or their security has made requests that a paparazzo did not respect; in such cases, other paparazzi intervene to protect the integrity of their work. This mentality is driven by a belief that they all need to operate with similar limitations so that they can conduct their work under the best and most cordial conditions possible. Galo expressed his opinion on taking pictures of children: "If the parents tell us not to, then we should respect that, and most of us do. But if there are no laws against that, media outlets are paying for the photos, and parents are not objecting, then we're not going to stop." As Galo said about shooting Garner and her daughter at the farmer's market, "It's not like we ruined their day. We stayed at a distance. We don't want celebs to look angry or unhappy. We want to be respectful."

Galo's assertion that he has to "clean up" messes lends itself to an analogy I referenced earlier, which is that in some ways paparazzi work is a service job, the janitorial work of celebrity media. And much like other low-end service work, it is rarely appreciated or respected. That they are a group of mostly marginalized people—most of them men of color, and many of them immigrants—makes them a convenient scapegoat for all that is wrong with celebrity media. Much like low-end and informal service workers, particularly Latinx immigrant workers, paparazzi often experience physical assault by the people who indirectly employ them and are not always paid what they are promised by the agencies who control their image sales.[15] But despite the hardships they face on the job and the way they are maligned in the public eye, paparazzi deliver images to the world, and some of the most well-known and most circulated contemporary American images at that. They are workers operating in the informal channels of an often highly formal media production process, within a hugely profitable corporate system, doing the dirty work for the celebrity media industry.

CHAPTER THREE

To Live and Die in L.A.:
Life, Death, and Labor in the Hollywood-Industrial Complex

T here are a number of forms of precarious and contingent labor throughout the entertainment industry and the culture industries more broadly, but few are as hated as paparazzi work.[1] This hatred has been amplified and reshaped since the racial transformation of the paparazzi workforce.

This is crystalized when we compare the industry treatment and social treatment of two tragic on-the-job deaths, the first of a white motion picture camera assistant and the second of a mixed-race paparazzo. In 2014, Sarah Jones, a white, twenty-seven-year-old camera assistant, was killed on the set of *Midnight Rider*, a biopic about the musician Gregg Allman. Under orders from the film's director, Randall Miller, the crew was shooting on a live railroad track when Jones was struck by a train and killed.

The Hollywood-industrial complex, from the top down, was rightfully horrified that this happened on the watch of a production company.[2] A candlelight walk in Jones's honor was set up alongside Sunset Boulevard in Hollywood.[3] Those in the industry described her death as "unnecessary," while popular media characterized her as an "indefatigable worker with a cheery disposition."[4] Her death led to "an industrywide reckoning on safety standards and inspired some Oscars attendees to wear black ribbons on their lapels in her memory," and a petition demanding that the Academy of Motion Picture Arts and Sciences include her in the "In Memoriam" video segment at the Oscars was signed by over sixty thousand people.[5] Various Hollywood-based organizations even made posters and shirts featuring the phrase "We are Sarah" to help raise funds for her family. The government took legal action in response to her death; in 2015 Miller pleaded guilty to involuntary manslaughter and was sentenced to two years in prison, eight years of probation, a $20,000 fine, and 360 hours of community service.[6]

This outpouring of support and assumption of responsibility by the industry starkly contrasts with its reaction to the on-the-job death of Chris Guerra, which I described in the introduction. In 2013 Guerra, who was mixed-race African American, Mexican, and white, was hit and killed by two cars while engaged in his job as a paparazzo. There was no Hollywood-wide mourning of his death, only continued ridicule by celebrities and the public. Miley Cyrus posted to Twitter in response to Chris's death, calling paparazzi "dangerous" "fools," and chastising Chris's mother for not teaching her "child not to play in the street."[7] Dashcam transcriptions show that, as the police officer who ordered Chris to his car and watched him die left the scene of Chris's death, he called Chris a "fucking idiot."

While the industry and the public did not view Chris's death in empathetic terms, his own communities did, including the paparazzi community. Friends and family placed flowers and a cross at the busy point on Sepulveda Blvd. where he was killed. Galo, Chris's pap mentor, started a FundRazr for Chris's family that raised $4,000. The paparazzi also worked together to create and sell T-shirts honoring Chris, in hopes of helping his family pay for funeral costs. Designed by a paparazzo named Mario, the shirts featured a cartoon-like depiction of Chris holding a camera with the phrase "Shooting Stars in the Sky." As paps sold these T-shirts via social media and on the streets while working, one friend of Galo's with a close connection to the actor Charlie Sheen persuaded Sheen to donate to the cause. Sheen wrote a $12,000 personal check to Chris's mother to help with funeral costs.[8] This was the only act of support that Chris received from an industry insider.

Both Sarah Jones and Chris Guerra were precarious media laborers whose freelance work formed part of the fabric of the Hollywood-industrial complex. However, the industry and public deemed Jones's death an unnecessary tragedy, which drew massive support, while Chris's death never received official support from the entertainment industry, and the public ridiculed the deceased photographer and paparazzi more broadly. It is impossible to make sense of the disparate treatment of similarly positioned laborers, who were even close in age, without looking at the broader context in which these two operated.

Race explains some of the obvious discrepancies. Jones was described in media reports as a hard worker and a good person. There was an institutional and public desire to honor her. In contrast, Chris was framed as someone who had no future and no value. His death could have been treated as another needless death of a young man of color at the hands of police, but instead the social stigma around paparazzi work, the power of the state and its law enforcement, and celebrity and public reaction placed the blame on Chris himself. Discourse around his death suggested he should not have been trying to take Justin Bieber's photo, and that Chris was an idiot for following the officer's directions to cross the street and return to his car. It was never acknowledged that Chris was a person of color being yelled at by an armed police officer, and that Chris may have reasonably believed that failure to obey the officer's actions, regardless of how unsafe crossing the street was, could have endangered his life anyway. In contrast to the criminal conviction of Jones's director, no one was disciplined as a result of Chris's death. The driver of the second car that hit Chris never stopped, but the police made no attempt to track down this hit-and-run perpetrator. Chris's belongings were left scattered across this busy part of Sepulveda Blvd., including his California Republic hat, one of his gray tennis shoes, pieces of his camera, and his memory cards filled with photos of celebrities.

The work of Jennifer Suchland on economies of violence can help us begin to understand the divergent ways these two Hollywood deaths were treated. Not all precarious labor necessarily accompanies "economies of violence." *Precarity* can encompass a wide variety of forms of labor, each of which might experience different types of hazards. The behind-the-camera film work that Jones engaged in is not associated with economies of violence; hence the uproar from the entertainment industry in response to her death. On the other hand, paparazzi work is seen as violent and aggressive, and the men of color who perform that work are generally presumed to be violent and aggressive as well (or *thugs*, in the terminology discussed in chapter 1). In response, it has become customary for celebrities, security, police officers, and others to act violently toward paparazzi without fear of punishment (because there often is none).

In the context of her analysis of sex trafficking, Suchland asks, "Why is the violence of trafficking so visible and the violence of precarious labor not, and why has the affective power of representing trafficking not translated into heightened criticism of the market or economic policy?"[9] To demonstrate the parallel economies of precarious labor in which violence and power are also profoundly present, I could similarly ask, Why is the perceived violence of paparazzi work so visible and the violence of the precarious labor of paparazzi work not, and why has the affective power of representing celebrities as victims of paparazzi aggression not translated into heightened criticism of the market or economic policy? Instead the paparazzi are legally and informally targeted, while the larger economic structure of corporate media and the Hollywood-industrial complex, and the paparazzi's role within that system, goes unseen and unchallenged.

Raciontologies and Social Death in the Killing of Chris Guerra

In this institutional context, the racialized precarity of Chris's death can be understood through the framework of *raciontologies*—the fundamentally racialized grounding of various states of being—which Jonathan Rosa and I have previously conceptualized.[10] In our theorization of raciontologies, Rosa and I explore the ways in which institutional contexts and processes, such as racialized labor (trans)formations, function as sites or vehicles for the reproduction of white supremacy. Our work addresses not only how institutions structure actions but also the raciontologies through which institutions become endowed with the capacity to act in their own right as profilers, and, in this case, killers free from any responsibility, prosecution, or guilt. This view of institutions as actors in, rather than simply sites of or vehicles for, the reproduction of white supremacy represents a raciontological perspective that attends to the central role that race plays in constituting modern subjects and objects in relation to particular states of being.

Chris was the victim of institutional racism and, more specifically, racial profiling. Whereas racial profiling is often understood as a problem involving discriminatory behavior at the individual level, there are institutionalized processes that shape profiling. Similarly, when institutional racism and white supremacy are enacted, it is often presupposed that these acts can be carried out only by white racists. This supposition assists in relinquishing institutional culpability and recentering the focus on interpersonal interaction and embodiment. Narratives focused on interpersonal, as opposed to institutional, racism prevent us from understanding cases such as the death of Freddie Gray, who was killed by three black police officers. A raciontological perspective suggests that the *institutional* position of officers in such cases, regardless of their race or interpersonal prejudice, allowed them to enact white supremacy as agents of the state. (Thus, simply diversifying an institution such as the criminal justice system cannot eliminate racism or the broader raciontological realities through which it is enacted and reproduced.)

Similarly complex racial politics were at play in Chris's death. The officer who policed Chris to death was black. Chris's mother, Vicky Guerra, told me, "It wasn't a race thing. It was a black officer. And Chris looked white. I'm black and people don't always see me as black. It was a class thing. Nobody cares about this because Chris was poor." However, she did draw attention to the racialization of Chris' speech: "I'm from Oakland, and Chris talked like that. If you talked to him, I think Chris sounded Hispanic or ethnic." Although the police report classified Chris as Caucasian, there are many ways in which it is evident that race was read into this situation, including the racialization of the paparazzi generally, Chris's Hispanic last name, and the coded racialized language used in the police report, including a note stating, "The man was wearing dark clothing and a hoodie."[11] Following his death, the media circulated photos of Chris looking stern, wearing a cap backward and/or a hoodie, paralleling the kinds of imagery on social media during the time the hashtag #IfTheyGunnedMeDown was trending, which showed images of youth of color picking their toughest-looking pictures that might be misused in attempts to justify their (hypothetical) killing.[12]

The death of Chris Guerra reflects the limitations of understanding race, racial profiling, and institutional racism exclusively in relation to the body; Guerra's body could be racially identified in different ways, but in this particular encounter, he inhabited a racialized structural position that rendered him disposable. As John Márquez argues in his theorization of a racial state of expendability, examples like these serve as reminders "of how expendability is not derived from the perceptions and/or consent of white people and is also not reducible to corporeal signifiers of racial difference."[13] The importance of not limiting one's analysis of race to perceived bodily features is underscored by Barnor Hesse's "colonial constitution of race thesis," which holds that "race is not in the eye of the beholder or on the body of the objectified" but is instead "an inherited western, modern-colonial practice of violence, assemblage, superordination, exploitation, and segregation . . . demarcating the colonial rule of Europe over non-Europe."[14] For Hesse, race must be understood as a historically situated, institutionalized process that creates the conditions of possibility for perceptions of bodies and the consequences thereof.

While Mrs. Guerra's opinion that her son's killing was not race-related could reflect a rejection of the intersectional politics of race, ethnicity, class, and gender, it could also be interpreted as an attempt to emphasize her child's efforts toward upward socioeconomic mobility. Race was not something that Mrs. Guerra, her husband, Juan Guerra, or their son could control. However, they understood class as a variable that Chris was trying to improve. She explained that Chris was doing paparazzi work for the money, but "being a paparazzi wasn't going to be a full-time forever job. Eventually he wanted to go back and do his own business. He had his own landscaping business before. He wanted to maybe open up a pizza place." Her understanding of Chris reflects that he was simply attempting to fulfill the American Dream, trying to pull himself up by his paparazzi bootstraps to improve his life. In her theorization of social death and accompanying attempts to humanize those who are not seen as human, Lisa Cacho notes that tropes of the American Dream and bootstraps narratives are commonly invoked in attempts to render racialized populations worthy of empathy.[15] However, Cacho suggests that such efforts run up against racialized populations' fundamental disposability. During a dialogue in which Mrs. Guerra and I collectively processed and mourned the circumstances that led to Chris's death, she considered a logic similar to that of Cacho after I pointed to Chris's potential racialization and how it might have affected the way he was policed:

> It never occurred to me how Chris looked. He usually didn't wear a hoodie on shoots, but it was January and cold. He had a baseball cap under the hood also. The more I pictured what he must have looked like, the more I agree with you, and it makes even more sense that this officer thought Chris was a Hispanic nobody from the "hood," similar to Trayvon [Martin], who was perceived as trouble as he was just innocently walking home from the store.[16] But I do think it was a power trip and rage also. So I think we are both right. But I don't think I would have ever seen that his race and appearance would have had anything to do with it unless you brought it up again. I really think you hit the nail on the head with it must have been a coping mechanism when first presented with the race scenario because that double hurts if that makes

sense. Almost like he had no chance to survive even if the cop didn't lose his temper because he thought Chris was just a lowly Mexican. And that was why he never helped him in any way and had so much hate for him even after he was hit.

Mrs. Guerra's sentiment echoes Cacho's analysis of the interplay between individual characteristics and institutional processes in her theorization of everyday life for people of color, specifically African American and Latinx people: "We learn that the 'facts' of people's behaviors have little significance for determining whose deaths are tragic and whose deaths are deserved." Even if in interpersonal encounters it was possible for Chris to be perceived as white, his racialized reality left him in a state of being "permanently criminalized," "ineligible for personhood," and thus experiencing social death.[17]

Cultivating Public Disdain: Celebrities' Strategic Use of Paparazzi

> Photo shoot fresh, looking like wealth / I'm 'bout to call the paparazzi on myself. | **JAY-Z** | "OTIS," WATCH THE THRONE, 2011

> Till I get flashed by the paparazzi / Damn, these niggas got me / I hate these niggas more than the Nazis. | **KANYE WEST** | "FLASHING LIGHTS," GRADUATION, 2007

Paparazzi are routinely hated and framed as a nuisance by those within the industry, especially by celebrities themselves. For example, in 2008 Brad Pitt told NBC's *Today* show about the paparazzi, "Let me be very blunt: I hate them. I hate these people. I don't understand . . . that they do that for a living."[18] Plenty of other celebrities have shared similar sentiments. Mila Kunis has called paparazzi work "bullying."[19] In the documentary $ellebrity, Jennifer Aniston accuses paparazzi of keeping her in "false imprisonment."[20] But despite celebrities' disparagement, the presence of paparazzi around a celebrity signifies importance. "In our contemporary world everything seeks to be made visible, and visibility conveys price and power."[21] There is a great irony, and perhaps hypocrisy, in that reality celebrities complain about the presence of the paps, but their presence, and the resulting images, provide the celebrity with power and capital and help promote the celebrity's career.

The lyrics that open this section encapsulate this tension experienced by

3.1 Vitamin Water billboard on Lincoln Blvd. in Santa Monica, CA.
September 2011. Photo by the author.

celebrities like Jay-Z and Kanye West who want to utilize paparazzi labor for promotion while simultaneously hating them. The actor Adrian Grenier reconciled this contradiction at the Getty Center panel by explaining that celebrities' hatred of the paparazzi doesn't stem from an invasion of privacy but rather the issue of control over the monetization of the celebrity's image. "Your media attention is an avenue to making money. Big studios know that. They've controlled it for years. Celebrities utilize it to make a living and they do quite well, and they like it when they're controlling it. And now what's happened with modern technology and point-and-shoot cameras is that suddenly everybody has an ability to make a couple bucks off the game. So they don't like that so much."

The presence of paparazzi in fact represents a particular kind of status in Hollywood. Shortly after I returned to Los Angeles to begin my fieldwork in 2010, I noticed a billboard on Lincoln Blvd. near Venice Beach. Advertising Vitamin Water Zero Glow were the words "Attract the Paparazzi" (see fig. 3.1). This billboard illustrates that the appearance of paparazzi signifies an individual's importance, and is something to aspire to (an aspiration that can be achieved, it suggests, through the consumption of this particular product). The status conveyed by paparazzi is further evidenced by the existence of services such as Famous for a Day, in which customers can pay to have a team of "paparazzi" follow them during a night out (see figs. 3.2–3.3).[22] Higher priced packages even include a bodyguard to "keep those pesky paparazzi from invading your personal space."

If the presence of paparazzi conveys status on their subject, annoyance at the paparazzi conveys even more. For example, some hotels and condominiums in the Los Angeles area advertise that they are "paparazzi-proof," something only those who are important enough to have paparazzi follow them would care about (see fig. 3.4). This is part of what makes real celebrities: not only having paparazzi following them and making them noticeable, but having it happen so often that it is an inconvenience. Celebrities who act like they love the attention will be seen as vain. They hire bodyguards and create other modes of protection to further promote this image. Are you really an important celebrity if you don't have a bodyguard to keep those pesky paparazzi from invading your personal space? But even those celebrities who genuinely do not like paparazzi following them have agents, managers, and PR reps who are paid by the celebrity to strategize media placement, and those people will tip off the paparazzi when it is lucrative to do so.

Despite pandering to the media and, by extension, the public, regarding their disdain for paps, celebrities do have dynamic and collaborative relationships with them. Chris Guerra had such a relationship with Jennifer Garner, the same actor who testified before the California State Assembly requesting special protection from the paparazzi. Celebrities know when and how to be shot; photographs are often staged; and the very presence of paparazzi is strategically used to signify the importance of the celebrity. The perception of fame involves, in part, the illusion that those who are famous do not want to be followed by paparazzi. Thus most celebrities do not want the public to know about their cooperation with the paparazzi.

In this way, the red carpet creates a strategic space in which to recognize and validate the sociocultural significance of the reporter-celebrity and photographer-celebrity interaction, which, by extension, invalidates and creates sociocultural tension around paparazzi-celebrity interactions. The nature (or illusion) of nonregulated pap-celebrity interaction creates the space for paps to be seen as the enemy working against celebrity desires, triggering celebrity empathy. Thus celebrities' performance of animosity toward paparazzi, regardless of their level of collaboration with them, furthers the perception of the sociocultural problem of paparazzi. The popular section in *Us Weekly* "Stars: They're Just Like Us," which features paparazzi shots of celeb-

3.2 Famous for a Day home page.

3.3 Famous for a Day: "Fake Paparazzi, Real Glamour."

3.4 Advertisement for the Fairmont Hotel in Santa Monica, CA. Image courtesy of Fairmont Hotels.

rities engaged in everyday activities, is part of this intentional mediatizing of celebrity empathy. If stars are just like us, we can be just like stars and thus should empathize with them, aspire to be like them, and believe that we already live similar lives. After all, some of those stars are former reality stars, like Carrie Underwood and Elisabeth Hasselbeck, who really were just like us before becoming famous on reality television show competitions. Celebrity empathy demonstrates how media can strategically cultivate affinity with certain people while strategically denying it to others.

The case described in chapter 1, of José Osmin Hernández Durán, the paparazzo who was assaulted by Justin Bieber outside a shopping center in 2012, is a prime example of how celebrity empathy has meaningful consequences.[23] As previously mentioned, Galo was disturbed that the witnesses at the scene told him that they "saw what happened" but that they would "tell the police it was the paparazzi's fault because he deserved it" and that the paps "should leave Bieber alone." Even Bieber's lawyer Howard Weitzman treated the situation as a joke. The entirety of Weitzman's statement in response to media inquiry about Durán's lawsuit against Bieber was "Seriously?"[24] The message was clear: Why should Weitzman, or anyone for that matter, care about the well-being of a paparazzo, even in a case where his client is being accused of assault? Durán did not fight back against Bieber for fear of losing his job and livelihood. Bieber did not have that fear. Still, to the non-paparazzi witnesses and to Bieber's attorney, Bieber was the victim.

Those celebrities willing to admit that paparazzi serve an important role within the Hollywood-industrial complex generally treat paps cordially, and on a day-to-day basis there is a functional work dynamic between them. At a red carpet event in 2011, Selma Blair told me, "I'm just a regular actor trying to get a job. You're an ass if you complain about it. I'm just gonna say that one day they will provide a scrapbook for me and that's kind of how I want to look at it, like, 'Look, there's a picture of me and Daddy. There's me and baby.' So it's nice, and the guys, when you talk to them, they're all pretty nice. They just try to be a nice part of my day. I learn their names, say, 'Hi.'"[25] Earlier that year, on Blair's birthday, Galo said, "We gave her flowers. She was so happy she hugged us" (see fig. 3.5). Some celebrities (or their public relations teams) even prearrange photos for paps based on the needs of media outlets and celebrities. For example, in 2011, after a bout of rumors suggesting Will Smith and Jada Pinkett Smith had broken up, a shot of them together was set up by the celebrities and their camps, in coordination with pap agencies, to dispel the rumors. While celebrities generally present themselves as anti-paparazzi,

3.5 Selma Blair after paparazzi brought her flowers on her birthday in 2011. Photo courtesy of Galo Ramirez.

when they need their services they are very cooperative. In this case, the paps had been tipped off in advance that Smith and Pinkett Smith would be at a certain location (see fig. 3.6). Paps who photographed the manufactured moment said Smith was pleasant with them, made sure they all got their shots, and then they all moved on. In these moments the celebrities need and want the paparazzi.

For those celebrities who do not acknowledge the important role of paparazzi within the industry, however, the paps are everything that is wrong with being famous. For example, in a 2012 interview with *Glamour* magazine, Mila Kunis discussed her views on the paparazzi in depth. The article began, "It's a beautiful day in Manhattan, but inside the Tribeca Grand Hotel, Mila Kunis is feeling claustrophobic. She'd love to go biking or walking or something—*anything*—but paparazzi are camped outside both of the hotel's exists. 'I will try to enjoy it from inside looking out,' says the actress, in town to shoot the film *Blood Ties* with Clive Owen and dressed down in jeans, a black tank top, and a comfy black sweater." The article paints Kunis as held captive by the prospect of having her photo taken. Then the interview gets more specific. The interviewer asks, "You felt uncomfortable with the paparazzi?" and Kunis responds, "Yes. I still am. I know this sounds obnoxious, but drinking coffee outside, I haven't done in my twenties, ever. A couple months ago I finally sat outside in Los Angeles for lunch with my girlfriend Lisa, who is the mother

3.6 People.com feature of Will Smith and Jada Pinkett Smith after paps had been tipped off in advance that the couple would pose for photos to help put "rumors to rest"—as the caption notes—that their marriage was in trouble. 2011.

Star Tracks: Wednesday, August 24, 2011

By **People Staff** · August 24, 2011 04:00 PM

...   ←   ▦ View All   →

2 of 18

SHOPPING SET

Time to put those rumors to rest! Will Smith and wife Jada Pinkett Smith look very much together while on a Wednesday afternoon shopping trip in L.A.

PHOTO: KMAX/X17ONLINE

---

of my god kid. It was the most beautiful day. I don't want the fear of being photographed to prevent me from doing things that I enjoy."[26] The magazines need the paparazzi to be the bad guys of celebrity media, solely responsible for the lack of privacy faced by today's stars, so that the magazines can position themselves on the side of celebrities, furthering their relationships with the stars they cover. Of course *Glamour* surrounded this article about Kunis's criticism of the paparazzi with photographs of the actress—photographs that were taken by paparazzi and purchased by the magazine.

In a nation where celebrities are role models whom their fans dream are "just like us," it is no wonder that the public's opinion of paparazzi is so closely aligned with that of celebrities. Criticism of the paparazzi starts with celebrities themselves, and those celebrities' fans emulate the hatred displayed by their idols.

Violence and Gender Dynamics in Paparazzi Work

The camera/gun does not kill, so the ominous metaphor seems to be a bluff—like a man's fantasy of having a gun, knife, or tool between his legs. Still, there is something predatory in the act of taking a picture. To photograph people is to violate them, by seeing them as they have never seen themselves, by having knowledge of them that they can never have; it turns people into objects that can be symbolically possessed. | **SUSAN SONTAG** | *ON PHOTOGRAPHY*

Working with the paparazzi to create memorable shots is called "giving it up," a sexualized metaphor that neatly captures the masculine-feminine romantic dynamic of need and reluctance that characterizes the relationship between celebrity photographers and their subjects. | **DAVID SAMUELS** | "SHOOTING BRITNEY," *ATLANTIC MONTHLY*

"I'm working on a film set," read the text that Ulises Rios sent me. Of course, Ulises wasn't literally *on* the film set; he was attempting to shoot it from the outside, but he and other paparazzi understand their role to be part of the Hollywood media production process. To Ulises and other paparazzi, their role on the outskirt of the set, and the subsequent photos, are critical to the promotion of the film and the celebrities in the film. This, of course, is contrary to the peripheral position in which most people in the industry view the paparazzi.

Ulises told me the street address where he was parked; it was in South Central, just a few blocks from where my family lived when I was born. In all my years as a celebrity reporter, no red carpet had ever been set up in this part of town. It was one of those moments when I realized how Hollywood affects Los Angeles in every corner of the city, even those areas furthest removed geographically and socioeconomically. I arrived near the set at about 1:00 p.m.; Ulises had been waiting since 6:00 a.m. to try to get a shot of Jake Gyllenhaal dressed in a police uniform for his role in *End of Watch*. As I walked toward Ulises's black Expedition a tall, sizable man in jeans and a black T-shirt emerged from the oversized car. "Well, this is my office," he said, pointing to his car, and gave me a friendly hug. We got into the car, where we would spend the next several hours waiting patiently for the shot. There was a lot of time to kill, and I quickly understood that Ulises wanted my company as much as I wanted to learn from him. I should have offered to bring him food since the paparazzo can't leave his car for fear of losing the shot. Since waiting inside the car outside a celebrity's house is what paparazzi call "doorstepping," I thought to myself, "Maybe we can call this setstepping?"

The symbolic violence inherent in the act of photographing another — especially shooting a subject without consent and with a long telephoto lens — has been analyzed before.[27] Not only is the paparazzi-celebrity interaction rife with this symbolism, but much of the slang used to describe these encounters reinforces the symbolic violence and infuses it with a sexual component. Along with the use of *giving it up*, mentioned by David Samuels in the epigraph, *gangbanging* is commonly used to describe a situation in which several paparazzi are attempting to shoot one celebrity.[28]

It's unclear whether this use of *gangbang* originated from within or outside of the paparazzi themselves, but paps have appropriated the term. Of course such terms, which evoke both street gang violence and group sexual assault, only enhance the public's perception that paparazzi are violent, angry, and dangerous.[29] The particular gang history of Los Angeles makes this term resonate especially strongly in this city.[30] But when I asked Ulises about using the term, he said, "We're already so hated. I don't give a fuck." His repose exemplified the informality I feel when talking with the paparazzi: it reminds me of talking to my brother, and starkly contrasts the general formality of speaking with editors and reporters.

On this occasion, the focus of the shoot was a male celebrity. A majority of the time, the goal is to shoot women celebrities because of the profitability of images of the female body.[31] The predominantly male paparazzi do hope for, and even rely on, the possibility of women celebrities "giving it up" to ensure that they can get profitable shots.[32] According to paps, the gangbang approach is generally used when there is a big story (e.g., Lindsay Lohan at the courthouse) or when there is a current news story attached to the person (e.g., shots of Kristen Stewart after the photos uncovering her affair were released). But in other cases, the gangbang approach is used simply to get celebrities coming in and out of Los Angeles International Airport. It isn't an intentional or premeditated attack, as the term implies, but a circumstance in which several paparazzi are aware of the whereabouts of a celebrity of whom they are all seeking shots (see fig. 3.7). Because there are many people at gangbangs and they are usually in very public spaces, these types of shoots are thus the ones that generally get publicized and shape the way people perceive paparazzi. However, in my experience, gangbangs are in fact anticlimactic. They do not last more than a few minutes (generally the amount of time it takes a celebrity to walk between the car and his or her destination), and the photographers are generally trying to cooperate with each other and the celebrity.

As we sat waiting for Gyllenhaal, Ulises showed me videos depicting violence toward paparazzi. He had been accosted and had his car vandalized by Jesse James, Sandra Bullock's ex-husband, and was in the middle of a lawsuit with him over the incident. James had smashed his window, slashed his tires, and attempted to physically assault Ulises. The case had already garnered coverage in local news media.[33] Ulises also showed me a video of the British singer Cheryl Cole's friends spitting on him through his car window. Ulises

3.7 **This image of Taylor Swift from 2012 is an example of a gang-bang.** Photo courtesy of Galo Ramirez.

Honeymoon's Over? Busted *Bachelor* Paparazzi Prepare to Take on Jason and Molly

by GINA SERPE | Mon., Mar. 1, 2010 1:08 PM

3.8 Photo of paparazzo Eric Brogmus being assaulted outside of the wedding for the show *The Bachelor* in 2010. The paparazzo Maximiliano Lopez Jr. was also assaulted.

stays in his car as much as possible; his goal is to not bother celebrities and their entourages, but in both of these instances they approached him. He has a camera mounted on the inside of his car, so both incidents were documented.

I was appalled at what I saw, but there was more. He showed me a video that the photo agency x17 posted of several paparazzi being harassed and assaulted outside of the 2010 *Bachelor* wedding between Jason Mesnick and Molly Malaney.[34] Ulises said the publicist for the television show had contacted photo agencies to let them know the location of the wedding and asked them to send photographers. When the paparazzi arrived, they were harassed. Latino paparazzi Eric Brogmus, twenty-two, and Maximiliano Lopez Jr., twenty-eight, were detained by security guards in a public park and then arrested by Los Angeles County sheriff's deputies on suspicion of misdemeanor battery and unlawful blocking of a sidewalk (see fig. 3.8).[35] In the video, as the security guards push the paps, Brogmus says, "I'm calling the police because you're pushing me." As he attempts to make a call on his cell phone, one security guard tackles him to the ground.

Another pap, standing in the background, says, "You can't grab him." While the security guard tells Brogmus, "You're under arrest" (the guard was not a law enforcement officer), Ulises can be heard yelling, "Get your knee off of his head, bro," referring to the painful position the guard has over Brog-mus. "He's a photographer. He's not an assassin or a killer. This is a public trail. There are signs everywhere saying this is a public trail."[36] Brogmus's and Lopez's racialization, including the stereotypically Latin American–accented English in which Brogmus spoke to the security guard, led to comments about the video like this on X17's website: "Literally [paparazzi are] the scum of the Earth. Why are they always Latinos? Are they even citizens? Maybe they should show their green card so they can be deported." This comment is indicative of the ways in which the paparazzi are both racially and linguis-tically profiled. "Whereas 'racial profiling' is based on visual cues that result in the confirmation or speculation of the racial background of an individual . . . 'linguistic profiling' is based upon auditory cues that may include racial identification."[37] As I've explored throughout the book and this chapter, the racialization of the paparazzi and the raciontological nature of their experi-ence is multifaceted.[38] Indeed at least one of the security guards in this case was Latino, but that did not prevent the paparazzi from suffering as a result of their racialized positionality.

Though ABC, the network responsible for *The Bachelor* and the wedding, denied any fault, they did air parts of the attack on the wedding special. The network and the program were able to use imagery of their security fighting off paparazzi as signifiers of the importance and drama of this manufactured media event. E!, a media corporation whose online content and television pro-gramming rely heavily on paparazzi images, published a news article about the incident portraying the paparazzi as the problem. The article declared that the paparazzi nearly "ruined" the wedding in their attempt to "scoop next week's ABC special," despite also highlighting that the wedding was "held on pub-lic property" and that the photographers were shooting from a distance on a "nearby trail." Written to cultivate and preserve celebrity empathy, the article claims that the paparazzi's "camera-wielding pals" "edited down" a video in attempts to portray the impossibility of "the paps as the real victims."[39] The language regarding the paparazzi's supposed attempt to "scoop" the wedding, despite the fact that they were called to the set by the show's publicist, under-scores the monetized nature of fabricated hate toward the paparazzi. The con-cern over the potential scoop is because of how it might affect ABC's ratings, which translate to profit. As Sara Ahmed trenchantly observes, "Hate is eco-nomic."[40] Celebrities are often happy to cooperate with paparazzi when it makes them money, but are protective over their image when it has the poten-tial to hurt their income.

3.9 Jennifer Aniston waving to paparazzi while showing off her bottle of Smart Water, for which she is a spokesperson. Photo courtesy of BackGrid.

The *symbolic* violence of paparazzi work contrasts with the *actual* physical violence experienced regularly by the paparazzi on the job. While Jennifer Aniston claims that the paparazzi keep her in a state of "false imprisonment," a lawsuit brought by Lopez and Brogmus against Disney/ABC Television Group and other defendants included an actual legal claim for false imprisonment.[41]

An important factor affecting how celebrities react to the violent symbolism of paparazzi photography is consent—whether or not the celebrities or their camps specifically request paps to take photographs. As I have shown, there are many circumstances in which celebrity publicists, and sometimes celebrities themselves, collaborate with the paparazzi. Aniston, for example, was photographed in 2013 smiling and waving to paparazzi while showcasing a bottle of Smart Water, a company that pays her to be seen promoting the item (see fig. 3.9). In Donald Trump's 2004 book *How to Get Rich* he states that whenever he plays on one of his golf courses, he wears a hat with "a big TRUMP logo on it" so that paparazzi photos offer him "an automatic promotion."[42] Celebrities also contract paparazzi and use them directly for financial gain. As described earlier, the Kardashians are known to sell photo agencies the exclusive rights to photograph family vacations in order to guarantee both coverage and control over the coverage. For example, in 2011 Splash news obtained exclusive rights to shoot the family on their vacation in Bora Bora, and the photos made clear both the staged nature of the images as well as perceived unencumbered access given to the paparazzo sent by Splash.[43]

As Gyllenhaal was a no-show and it was getting late, Ulises got a tip that Cheryl Cole was going to be coming into LAX, so we headed there for what turned out to be my first gangbang. When we arrived, Ulises greeted the other paps on the scene. They were all men—one Mexican (Ulises), two Salvadorans, one Guatemalan, three Brazilians, and one white man. Only Spanish was spoken among the Spanish speakers, only Portuguese among the Brazilians, and the lone English-only speaker was left standing and observing. The paparazzi spread out, a few stationed at different exit points.

Standing outside one of the exits, Ulises informed me that airline reservations workers often receive money from the largest agencies in exchange for tips about which celebrities they can expect to see come through LAX. The airport provides a unique opportunity for such tips because, unlike at hotels and restaurants, celebrities are legally required to book their air travel under their real names. Individuals who provide these tips are paid up to $5,000 per month in exchange for a continual stream of information on celebrity travel reservations. As we wait, the paps take test shots of each other and of me to get the lighting and settings right. "I think she might not even come out the terminal she landed in," Ulises said. "They might take her to another terminal, and she will leave through there and we will be standing here like fucking idiots." A few moments later Ulises and I heard a commotion and ran downstairs. Cheryl Cole was exiting through baggage claim and, suddenly, what had been a small group of paparazzi swelled to about twenty-five men with camera bags and oversized lenses all over the place. I got lost in the swarm of paps and passengers, but I could see one pap ahead of me whom I recognized. His black leather biker jacket that says "paparazzy," a spelling error that became his trademark, made him hard to miss.

Once Cole got in her car, things died down and I reunited with Ulises. He was headed straight for his car to edit and post his photos to his agency's site. "We used to not have to upload immediately. We used to be able to wait until Monday. But now we have to do it immediately. We put info with the photo too. We do reporting. The goal is to get things up quickly, so we do a basic crop,

3.10 A paparazzo editing images in the parking lot at LAX after shooting a celebrity who had just arrived. Photo by the author.

adjust the brightness, sharpness, and color, then we post it," he explained as he edited and posted. Several other paparazzi had their computers on top of their cars and were cropping and sending photos furiously (see fig. 3.10). I was tired and had only ridden along with Ulises for half of his workday. Ulises works seven days a week. On this day he worked from 6:00 a.m. until 10:00 p.m. He was ready to go home to his wife and two young children.

Anti-Paparazzi Laws

Rather than work to protect paparazzi from the violence they routinely face, California has spent the past decade enacting legislation that criminalizes the profession. Over the past ten years, the legislature has passed a number of laws specifically designed to punish paparazzi. The office of Assembly Speaker Karen Bass (who was later elected to the U.S. Congress) contacted a lobbying group called the Paparazzi Reform Initiative in May 2009 with a request for assistance in passing new paparazzi-reform legislation. The result was AB 524, which was signed into law by Governor Arnold Schwarzenegger in October 2009 and imposes penalties from $5,000 to $50,000 on those who purchase a photograph taken illegally. Thus the penalties are directed at the media outlets that purchase photos taken by paparazzi who break a law during the act of capturing it. Subsequent laws did not follow this example of enforcing reform at the level of the corporate media.

Another anti-paparazzi law, SB 606, was passed in 2013, under which photographing a person's child "because of that person's employment" became punishable by up to one year in prison. SB 606 states explicitly that "the act of transmitting, publishing, or broadcasting a recording of the image or voice of a child does not constitute a violation of this section." In other words, unlike the earlier AB 524, it exempts corporate media outlets from any punishment for publishing the very pictures that could now land a photographer in prison. Additional anti-paparazzi laws passed in 2014 impose harsher penalties for traffic violations if the driver was pursuing a photograph and prevent paparazzi from using drones to photograph celebrities. Many of the laws prescribe fines and jail time for paparazzi while explicitly permitting media outlets to purchase and publish the resulting illegally taken photos. In addition, a number of the new laws, including SB 606, contain civil enforcement provisions, under which aggrieved celebrities are granted the right to file lawsuits directly against paparazzi. Thus the laws not only criminalize paparazzi labor but also grant celebrities power to police the paps. Rather than attempting to change the practices of celebrity media production from the top down, these reform efforts place legal restrictions on the laborers who carry out a form of work that is demanded by corporate media outlets and a voraciously consuming public.

Even though SB 606 exempted media outlets from punishment, in 2014 *People*'s then executive editor, Jess Cagle, published a letter following passage of the law entitled, "Why PEOPLE Does Not Support Paparazzi Who Target Celebs' Kids." In the letter, Cagle clarified the types of photos of celebrity children that *People* would and would not publish: "Of course, we still run a lot of sanctioned photos—like exclusive baby pictures taken with the cooperation of celebrity parents, and photos of stars posing with their kids at events (like a red carpet) where they're expecting and willing to be photographed. But we have no interest in running kids' photos taken under duress. Of course, there may be rare exceptions based on the newsworthiness of photos. And there's always the tough balancing act we face when dealing with stars who exploit their children one day, and complain about loss of privacy the next."[44] There is a tension between the "newsworthiness" caveat cited by Cagle and the anti-paparazzi laws themselves, which are predicated on paparazzi not being journalists and therefore not protected by the First Amendment. If *People* will now publish only "newsworthy" photos of celebrity children, but paparazzi are not journalists because they are not documenting news, how can paparazzi photos possibly meet this standard? In essence, Cagle's letter indicates that paparazzi are to be seen as journalists documenting *real* news only when *People* or other media outlets say they are. This is lip service to save face with celebrities without actually changing the practices of corporate media. Blame is once again laid on the paparazzi for taking "un-newsworthy" shots of celebrities' children, which creates the illusion that the paparazzi are the only ones violating a moral code. In fact market forces within the field of large-scale cultural production and the economic capital that these photos can yield for the media corporations are what truly determine which photos are sought after by paparazzi and ultimately published.

The details of these anti-paparazzi laws were shaped and promoted by a lobbying organization called the Paparazzi Reform Initiative. An article built around an interview with the initiative's founder, Sean Burke, proclaims, "Whilst ambitious in philosophy and approach, Sean has proven to himself, the entire Paparazzi + celebrity obsessed industry and the MPAA (Motion Picture Association of America) Board that his ideation and unstoppable self-belief is more than capable of making pertinent change in our society, *benefitting all those that count most*."[45] This sentence—a summation of many of the points outlined by Burke himself in the interview—illuminates the very clear demarcation of the scales of personhood that are part of the Hollywood-industrial complex. In this common conceptualization of the industry, the paparazzi do not count at all; they exist strictly to be policed and regulated, not unlike other Latinx bodies, and bodies of color more generally. Burke and his organization have formed around the idea that celebrities—or those *People* magazine might consider *people*—are the persons that count most. This book grapples with the dynamic relationships that exist to create and sell this notion of mass personhood (celebrity), the social beings who "count most." At a time when public debate over the institutionalized mattering of lives, and the ways in which race factors prominently in degrees of mattering or counting, it is important to interrogate the scales of personhood that purport to identify those who "count the most."

The Paparazzi Reform Initiative has been supported in its lobbying efforts by some of Hollywood's biggest stars. In August 2013 both Halle Berry and Jennifer Garner testified before the California State Assembly in support of the anti-paparazzi laws. Media called Garner's tearful testimony "harrowing," as she declared, "Large, aggressive men swarm us. . . . I don't want a gang of shouting, arguing, law-breaking photographers to camp out everywhere we are."[46] Her testimony took place the same year that Chris Guerra was killed on the job and José Osmin Hernández Durán filed his lawsuit against Justin Bieber for assault. While paparazzi are physically accosted and even subject to death on the job, celebrities believe they must be granted particular legal protection from them. There is a jarring contrast between the disregard for the protection of the racialized paparazzi and the formalized opportunity for Garner to voice her concerns about them in gendered and racialized terms in front of the California State Assembly.[47]

Following in Garner's footsteps, the actress Kristen Bell spoke to media outlets in support of SB 606. In these interviews she deployed the term *pedorazzi* to describe the men who photograph her children, insinuating that nonconsensual pictures of her children are akin to their sexual molestation. Yet in spite of this rhetoric, many celebrities continue to actively communicate with paps, arrange photo shoots, and use the paparazzi as a tool to facilitate media coverage. This raises the question of whether the anti-paparazzi movement is truly about privacy or about the degree to which celebrities are able to exert monetary and brand control over their images. While many top celebrities have received six-figure deals for the first photos of their baby, Kristen Bell and husband Dax Shepard did not. Instead a paparazzo took and sold the first photos of their child, preventing them from being able to negotiate an exclusive first photo series with a magazine. The paparazzi speculate that this contributed to Bell's anger toward them and her promotion of what she dubbed the "pedorazzi" law.[48] This strategic attempt by a public figure to reassert control over her ability to monetize her image and the image of her child resonates with the characterization of the *Bachelor* incident as the paparazzi ruining the wedding by attempting to "scoop" the broadcast.

The incidents of violence against paparazzi described here, and the reaction against paparazzi by media institutions and the state, exemplify the current moment in the United States, in which the lives of people of color and the lives of immigrants and perceived immigrants are under attack. Latin American immigrants have been construed by the president as "bad hombres," murderers, and drug dealers. There are parallels in the way Garner refers to the paps as a "gang" of "law-breakers." They are Latino men, and Latino men are continually construed as "bad" and "large, aggressive men," as Garner describes, as well as foreign "others" who do not belong. The treatment of the paparazzi by law enforcement, security guards, celebrities, bystanders, and online commenters throughout this book, and this chapter in particular, demonstrates how, as the linguistic anthropologist Bonnie Urciuoli says, "Racialized people are typified as human matter out of place: dirty [and] dangerous."[49]

Media Rituals of Hate

Performed hatred of the paparazzi in order to signify social status and engender empathy is a ritual practiced often in contemporary celebrity media. Media rituals are "formalized actions organized around key media-related categories and boundaries, whose performance frames, or suggests a connection with, wider media-related values."[50] Building on Sara Ahmed's conceptualizations of affective economies—and economies of hate, in particular—I want to address what I call *media rituals of hate*, which are grounded in raciontological realities and function as an extension of social death.[51] In *Racism, Sexism and the Media*, Clint Wilson, Felix Gutierrez, and Lena Chao explore various phases in the history of news media coverage. The "threatening," "confrontation," and "stereotypical selection" phases, which are still in practice, revolve around portraying nonwhite people as threatening to white people through various forms of fear tactics, promoting social hate. Their analysis illuminates the intentionality behind the media's institutional practices intended to shape collective emotion or, in other words, to strategically stimulate affective economies. Demonstrating the raciontological realities of media as institutional actors that participate in the maintenance and reproduction of white supremacy, the authors recount what became the most iconic coverage of Hurricane Katrina, wherein "reportage of White journalists included a racially biased Associated Press photo caption that described a Black person who rummaged through the flooded debris for food as 'looting' while the same activity was captioned in an Agence France-Presse image of a White survivor as 'finding' food."[52] This racist and dichotomist media representation exemplifies the central role that media play in the creation and circulation of affective economies, and as a space where there is a *ritualization* around the promotion of hatred.[53]

The way the Hollywood-industrial complex and the media in general treated Sarah Jones's death compared to Chris Guerra's death parallels the divergent representation of white and black people in New Orleans after Hurricane Katrina. Jones and Chris were both media laborers with varying levels of precarity, and both were following instructions they were given by institutional forces—the Hollywood-industrial complex and, in Chris's case, also law enforcement. These factors led to their equally tragic deaths. And yet Jones's death was universally recognized as a tragedy, while Chris's death was not. The ritual of hating paparazzi practiced by the media (the same media who purchase and circulate paparazzi images), celebrities, and the general public does not end when a paparazzo dies. Instead, the state of social death Chris occupied prior to his actual physical death merely amplified the preexisting hatred for him, for his life, and for his work. It is particularly important to note how the paparazzi's physical, legal, and social constraints deeply contrast with the capacity for movement and socioeconomic value of the media they produce. Posthumously, images Chris had taken of mostly rich, white celebrities continue to circulate and generate profits for the agency that purchased the rights to his images. Even upon his death, and as photos he produced continued to be sold and consumed across the globe, Chris was seen as an idiot or as a problem, as opposed to a legitimate cultural producer like Jones.

Ahmed uses the concept of affective economies precisely to demonstrate "how hate works by sticking 'figures of hate' together, transforming them into a common threat," and "how the language of hate affects those who are designated as objects of hate."[54] The paparazzi of Los Angeles are an embodiment of this transformation—their profession has historically been denigrated, Latinxs are treated as a threat and as criminalized "illegal" humans, whether undocumented or not, and men of color (black and/or Latinx men in particular) are often presumed to be dangerous thugs.[55] These specific hatreds accumulate to form the particular way the paparazzi are disparaged today. Ahmed's work also explores how hate works on and through bodies, and Chris's experience exemplifies the ways hate is strategically and institutionally projected onto particular bodies with deathly consequences.[56] It was clear from the dashcam transcript that hatred of paparazzi, and the raciontological layers that shaped this institutionalized and ritualized hatred, was involved in his death. My ethnography and analysis of paparazzi demonstrate how the hate they experience contributes to their state of social death and the constraints they feel around their own ability to shift institutional and public vitriol directed at them, since they are keenly aware that they are "already hated." In the wake of Chris's death, institutionalized collective hate took the form of a ritual the media has produced—a ritual of hating paparazzi, encouraged by celebrities and the media that rely on paparazzi images.

• • •

On January 5, 2020, just a few days after the seventh anniversary of his death, the following tweet was posted from the Twitter account for Chris run by his family: "I had a dream too, then I was TOLD by a cop . . . to get back to my car and hit by a car and ran over by a second car which was a hit and run because I was a Mexican/black mixed race paparazzi. I was just doing my job and my life was taken."[57] Chris's family continues searching in vain for answers from the criminal justice system that was involved in Chris's death, and support from the Hollywood-industrial complex that benefited from the media Chris's labor produced. When institutions are incapable of admitting or even articulating the racially grounded realities that guide their policies and practices, we must conceptualize and name these realities ourselves. This is how we make sense of our own lived experiences and those of our communities. The theory of raciontologies and conceptualization of media rituals of hate become possibilities, offerings, tools to begin to help parse through the painful racialized and institutional hierarchies that shape both our lives and our deaths, and led to Chris's tragic killing in particular.

Reporting on the Stars

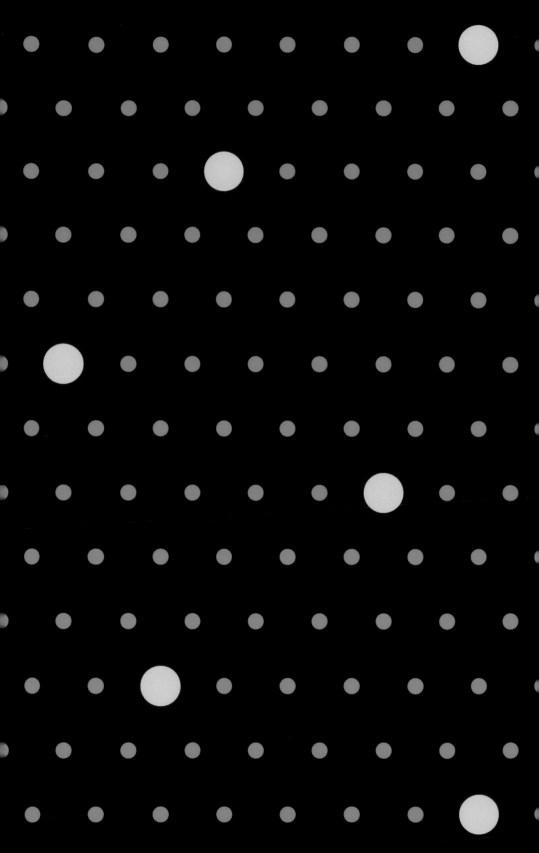

CHAPTER FOUR

Red Carpet Rituals:
Positionality and Power in a Surveilled Space

At its mythical best, entertainment reporting involves dressing up for parties, receiving messengered envelopes with Governors Ball tickets, and schmoozing celebs over a glass of champagne. While red carpet reporting has its perks, it does not always live up to that fantasy. | **KWALA MANDEL** | FORMER *PEOPLE* REPORTER, "SECRETS FROM RED-CARPET REPORTERS," 2012

I don't get to go to the Oscars, I get to stand on the Oscars red carpet and scream at people like I'm an idiot. | **ASHLEY** | CELEBRITY REPORTER, 2012 INTERVIEW WITH AUTHOR

The red carpet as an event is a strange concept at the center of what it means to be in the industry (see fig. 4.1). In Hollywood a designer boutique has not officially opened, a film has not premiered, an award show has not begun, until a red carpet procession occurs in its honor. Despite an increase in the circulation of photos in celebrity weekly magazines portraying

4.1 Red carpet for the premiere of *The Fighter* at TCL Chinese Theatre in Hollywood (formerly Grauman's Chinese Theatre and later Mann's Chinese Theatre). This red carpet takes up the entire westbound lane of Hollywood Blvd., between Highland and La Brea. The eastbound lane of the same block was occupied by the red carpet for the premiere of *The Tempest*, which took place at the El Capitan Theatre across the street. **December 6, 2010.** Photo by the author.

stars as being "just like us," the magazines still publish photos of red carpet events in every issue. These events are icons of what it means to be a celebrity, and magazines use these photos to show that celebrities remain part of an elite group with access to this elite space, regardless of how "like us" they may be. Red carpet events and their infrastructure are among the most visible elements of the cultural fabric that makes the industry cohere.

The red carpet is, in fact, a ritual of the industry—a symbolic set of performative actions by particular actors. In the era of a reality television president and celebrities becoming ever more central and relevant to American culture, reporters and photographers are the messengers who link consumers to the celebrities. It is the media producer's job to make sure all details about the celebrities are recorded and shared, to make the celebrities look good, and to perform their own form of worship on the red carpet in front of the celebrities' guardians—their publicists and managers.

This chapter explores the framework of the red carpet ritual with a focus on the media producers who are critical to its success. It draws on ethnographic fieldwork on the red carpet and interviews conducted with reporters, photographers, celebrities, publicists, and fans in Los Angeles, and with reporters and editors of celebrity weekly magazines in New York and Los Angeles from 2010 to 2012, as well as my earlier experience as a red carpet reporter beginning in 2004. I examine the figures involved in the ritual and break down its significance, from obtaining permission to enter the carpet to the barricading of the reporters; how the order of media outlets is determined; the gender dynamics at play on the red carpet; the strategic arrival and presentation of the celebrities; the various kinds of negotiations that take place on the red carpet; and the spectacle, from the lights to the fans, that surrounds this ritualistic event. I aim to put the reporters and photographers in action and in conversation with each other as I describe the red carpet, and my own experience as a red carpet reporter weighs heavily in this chapter. I also address the presence of fans and the politics of positionality on the red carpet.

To understand the ritualistic nature of the red carpet, it is helpful to examine the red carpet as an example of what the media scholar Nick Couldry calls a media ritual: "formalized actions organized around key media-related categories and boundaries, whose performance frames, or suggests a connection with, wider media-related values."[1] Instead of writing these rituals off as contrivances, as Daniel Boorstin famously did his 1961 *The Image: A Guide to Pseudo-Events in America*, I consider these events as serious ceremonious processes with sociocultural ramifications. As Stephen, a red carpet videographer, told me, the red carpet is "a ritual. You stand in these lights. You talk to each person for one to three minutes in a pre-scripted fashion and everyone thinks they're really getting to know you. It's always been this way. It's a tradition." Media rituals help naturalize and legitimate order and the distinction between categories.[2] The red carpet is only a cheap piece of polyester fabric, yet it is imbued with the symbolic power of exclusivity that gives those who walk, strut, and pose on it a power that those beyond the barricades, watching and cheering at the processional, do not possess.

The history of the red carpet is quite complicated. There has been no comprehensive research on the precise roots and developments of the tradition, although the historian Amy Henderson has provided a brief overview of its origins. She found that the earliest reference to walking a red carpet is in the Greek tragedy *Agamemnon* of 458 BC, when Clytemnestra welcomes the king and invites him to walk a "crimson path" to his house.[3] A connotation of wealth and prestige has been attached to the red carpet in the United States since the nineteenth century. President James Monroe walked down a red carpet that stretched from the boat that brought him to the Prospect Hill Plantation, where he was hosted in 1819.[4] Passengers walked a red carpet to embark and disembark from the luxury train the *20th Century Limited*, which ran between New York and Chicago, from 1902 to 1968; scholars trace the expression *red carpet treatment* to this instance.[5] Even today many airlines signify their "priority" lane, reserved for first-class customers, with a red carpet. Upon exiting Air Force One, the president of the United States walks down a red carpet that lines the path from the jet to the airport entrance.

The first Hollywood red carpet event was the opening of Sid Grauman's Egyptian Theatre in 1922. The first use of the red carpet at the Oscars was not until 1961, eight years after it was first broadcast but five years before it was first broadcast in color, which made the carpet a major component of the spectacle.[6] While the Oscars may be the iconic red carpet event, the carpet is a frequent element of the day-to-day culture of celebrity reporting in Los Angeles.

Although there is a long history of relating celebrities to gods by calling them idols or icons and describing fandom as worship, the red carpet ritual is a secular event.[7] As Mary Douglas points out, secular ritual is at least as prevalent as sacred ritual in contemporary society.[8] A. R. Radcliffe-Brown saw rituals and ceremonies as a means by which both individuals and society maintain social cohesion and a sense of organization.[9] My analysis reveals how the ritual of the red carpet contributes to the development of social understandings of celebrity culture. Furthermore the experience of all of the various players in the red carpet ritual contributes to a sense of community within Hollywood and celebrity culture, as "collectively performing rituals fosters a communal spirit, part of something larger than self."[10] The red carpet ritual truly is a collective performative ritual, and I take a processual approach to exploring its complexities.

Gaining Entry into an Elite Space

June 8, 2011: a different night, the same setup. The day before, I had received an email from the event assigner at *People*. She sent me the tip sheet for the event, the valet parking pass, the contact info for the event publicist, and a few specific questions for certain celebrities who were scheduled to attend. The tip sheet is a list of celebrities expected to attend the event. The press "call time"—the time the individuals coordinating the event request media arrival—was 6:30 p.m., close to the event's 7:00 p.m. start time. For bigger events, like awards ceremonies, call time may be several hours before celebrities begin arriving.

I pulled up to the w Hotel in West Hollywood, a trendy and stereotypically "Hollywood" space on Hollywood Blvd., for the Forbes Celebrity 100 Event: The Entrepreneur behind the Icon. The event honored a Real Housewife of New York, Bethenny Frankel, and the Kardashian sisters for their entrepreneurial work. I arrived in my 1999 Toyota Celica, which I call "Old Faithful," with "wash-me's" written in the coat of dust and dirt that covered it. The valet attendant accepted the pass I presented when he asked if I was there for the event, but on some level I shared his distrust. Did I belong there? No matter how many I attended, I was always cognizant of the elite nature of these events, and of my conditional access to them.

Ashley, who has worked for multiple celebrity weekly magazines, described the feeling that inequality creates:

> You're interviewing these people who have so much money and they get so much stuff for free and they talk about things you can't relate to. I remember, I don't even know who the star was at this point, but it was some midlevel TV person, who [said], "Oh my god, we had the best vacation in France. The only way to go is with renting a villa, getting a chef, and just hanging out there for a month. That's the only way to really get to know it." I remember thinking in my head, "I guess I'm never going to really get to know France." Like, I'm just never going to have that experience because I'm pretty sure I'm never going to be able to afford a villa, a chef, and a month off.

Most reporters I worked with on this project come from middle- or upper-middle-class families, and there is still an immense differentiation between their lifestyle and that of the celebrities they interview. Still, the pressure to look a certain way on the red carpet can drive reporters to push their financial limits to play the part. Ashley said:

You watch all these girls get ready for awards season and they're girls that are making three hundred fifty dollars on this event. But you had to buy a two-hundred-dollar dress. Then you start to believe the bullshit that they're selling, like, "Well I can't wear this dress again, I have to get something else! I look like crap, I have to lose ten pounds! I should go on a cleanse!" All these things go through your head, like, "I should get a haircut. I definitely need to get my nails done." And then all of a sudden you realize, I just spent all the money I made today. So I definitely think you need to realize you are reporting on these people, but you aren't these people. There is a natural jealousy that occurs, especially when you're interviewing people where you're like, "You're dumb. You happened to be born with the right dad. You're not a good actress, and yet you're getting all these roles."

Before taking my spot on the red carpet, I always experience a sense of both irritation and anxiety, knowing that I will have to be fake, pretend to know celebrities I have never seen before, and schmooze the public relations people. The work is repetitive and often uncomfortable. Sarah, a weekly magazine reporter who had worked in the industry for over five years when I interviewed her, depicted the extremes of this pretense very early one morning in the journal she offered to keep for me: "My feet hurt so badly right now I feel like I can't walk. I'm hungry, I'm tired, and I doubt I'll even be able to sleep. I will have to write more tomorrow, but I am completely delirious. This is the effect of the 24-hour news cycle." She had started work at 3:00 p.m. and wrote in her journal of her exhaustion after getting home past 5:00 a.m. after covering a post–Golden Globes party. She had eaten and drunk very little in the course of this fourteen-hour shift.

In the same entry, Sarah reflected, "It actually isn't fun after a while." She likely had arrived at the event she covered with some level of excitement. I know that I always arrived at events where I was reporting with some eagerness, even before I chose to research and reflect on this culture through an anthropological lens. If originally anthropologists studied isolated cultures and tribes, the world of celebrities and reporters in Hollywood, and particularly the ritual of the red carpet event, is a perfect example of a very contained culture and tribe that engage in ritualistic and regulated practices on a regular basis. And over the years I had become a part of this culture and tribe, as a participant in the red carpet ritual.

I walked up to the media check-in desk and gave them my name and affiliation: "Vanessa Díaz for *People* magazine." Immediately the "Do-not-waste-my-time" expression on the junior public relations representative transitioned to an overzealous smile. "Hi, Vanessa! We're so happy you could make it. Here is the updated tip sheet. Your spot is marked on the carpet. Let me know if you need anything." *People* is highly regarded and generally liked by those doing PR for an event. They recognize that even the presence of a *People* reporter is no guarantee of coverage, and they want *People* to cover their event. I walked over to my spot, the white lights shining down on the bright red carpet and illuminating the step-and-repeat banner, which boasts names and logos of the evening's sponsors; a gobo of the Forbes logo danced across the carpet.[11] In the lineup of media outlets, *People* was the first print media outlet following the still photographers and the television camera crews.

My spot on the carpet is not random. Media members know where they stand, literally and figuratively (see fig. 4.2). The lineup always begins with an open space for the red carpet photographers, followed by network and cable television programs, followed by major news outlets (such as Reuters and the Associated Press); sometimes *People* magazine is before some news outlets and camera crews, but, more often than not, it is the first of the celebrity-focused print media. The marker is often a piece of paper taped to the carpet, or the concrete next to it, that says the name of the media outlet. At one event, the order began with *Entertainment Tonight*, followed by E! *News*, CNN, AP, *People*, and Fox News, followed by the remaining weekly magazines and other online sources. The pieces of paper on the ground that dictate our physical placement have come to represent our identity—we are the media outlet; the organizers of the event do not care about our individual names.

The order of media outlets on the carpet matters for several reasons. First and foremost, celebrities are increasingly less likely to stop and talk the further down the carpet they get, since their patience decreases as they go. Many of the media outlets will ask similar questions (Who are you dating? What is your workout and diet regimen?), and the quality of answers also decreases as celebrities continue down the carpet; they give shorter answers to questions they have already answered multiple times. By the time celebrities get to the end of the carpet, if they are still answering questions, the publicist is usually grouping interviews, which leads to generic answers that are not based on personal interactions and conversation.

There is always room for negotiation on a red carpet placement, depending on the outlet a reporter is working for. When the arrangement changes, it is usually because an outlet had made an agreement with the PR people planning

4.2 At the Alma Awards in Santa Monica, CA, on September 11, 2011. The reporter for *Just Jared* stands on the sheet of paper labeled with her outlet's name. To her left is *People en Español* and to her right is *People*. Photo by the author.

the event, such as promising to put the event in the magazine or tacitly agreeing to publish something specific if they receive a better spot. Sometimes the reporter is a friend of the PR person doing the carpet lineup. There are various ways of handling this kind of negotiation. Jasmine, a freelance red carpet reporter for a weekly celebrity magazine, said, "I had an instance in which a reporter threw a serious tantrum when my outlet was placed on the carpet ahead of hers. She literally yelled and stomped her feet." As a *People* reporter, I knew that the PR people doing the event wanted my magazine to be happy because it has the largest readership of any of the celebrity-focused magazines. In fact I have been able to negotiate a better spot on the carpet when I have asked for one because the event publicists do not want to upset *People*.

At many large premieres and formal events metal barricades separate the path the celebrities walk from the concrete where the reporters stand. Reporters are smashed in with dozens of other people in a few feet of space; the barricades are hooked together, and once they're in, they can't get out until the end of the event, even to go to the bathroom. If they are not at their spot punctually, the six inches that were once reserved for them become absorbed by a camera person who was not given enough room for their equipment in the first place.

I look down the carpet for familiar faces and see some of my other reporter friends—all women. Based on data I gathered over the course of my fieldwork, including statistics from over fifty red carpet events, I conclude that approximately 75 percent of the reporters on the red carpet are women. The majority of reporters, regardless of gender, are between twenty-five and thirty-five, with some as young as twenty and as old as forty-five. The gender breakdown of the photographers is almost exactly the inverse, at approximately 85 percent men and 15 percent women. Virtually all of the reporters and photographers except for me were white, which is typical except at "ethnic" events (e.g., Alma Awards, BET events, NAACP Awards), to which I was disproportionately sent. Joy, a former *People* writer, shared a similar experience: "When I got to *People*, I was the only black girl. Also, there weren't any black editors. There was no one. And so when I first got there, there were the BET Awards, and the Soul Train Awards, certain events I was *always* sent to."

While we wait, reporters chat about our latest concerns with work, who we "care about" that night (i.e., who our magazines have interest in), and take goofy photos, which we then post to our social media accounts. Social media has become a way for celebrity reporters to connect online but also to let the other reporters know where we are, that we are still getting work, and essentially to assert that we are continually on the radar of the outlets we freelance for. This is a competitive industry, and all freelance reporters are potential threats to each other's jobs. Some reporters use social media to show off who they have interviewed recently, while others use it as a place to show how "red carpet ready" they looked for a show.

The reporters generally know each other fairly well, particularly those from the same kind of outlets. One reporter who appears at many events is notorious for moving up and down the red carpet line filming other people's interviews without permission and then posting them on YouTube. Reporters from weekly magazines increasingly jump into interviews other reporters are conducting, fearful they may not get time with that celebrity. Other reporters would stand behind me to hear what I was asking, trying to poach my inter-

4.3 A weekly magazine reporter researches celebrities and transcribes interviews on the red carpet while waiting for additional celebrities to arrive. July 23, 2011. Photo by the author.

views. But this is uncommon between reporters who are friends. Some friends huddle together, then tell the publicist that they will do the interview together, which the publicist and celebrity both see as a valuable time-saver. They share transcribing duties and then send the reports to each other to speed up the filing process (see fig. 4.3). This decreases the possibility of developing individual or exclusive stories that an outlet can break. Group interviews can also happen because a publicist insists on them.

While some red carpet reporters simply arrive with a list of questions from an assigning editor, many spend hours reading up on the latest news for each celebrity listed on the tip sheet for the event and come up with their own questions to complement those required by their outlet. Jasmine said that before events the most important questions for her to know about the celebrities set to attend are "Did they have a baby recently? Are they dating anybody? What have they been in? Do they have any connections to anyone? What are they working on right now?" The work continues after events as well. Sylvia, a free-lance reporter who previously worked on staff for multiple celebrity weekly magazines, spends at least eight hours working for every event:

> When you're a freelancer too you've got to justify your job on every assignment. I think that puts that hunger and desire into reporters. I pick three things that stand out the most, and then I take it a step farther and I create headlines for each one so it can get the editor thinking, "Hey that's a great headline, let's make a story out of it." I love coming up with a clever headline. I love pitching it and seeing it run. I like being useful. Isn't that what we all want in life? We want to be useful.

Even after over a decade of covering red carpet events, Sylvia still gets an "adrenaline rush": "It's the thrill of the chase. I think it's fun. There are worse jobs to have than talking to celebrities, even if it's silly stuff."

As I reviewed the tip sheet for the Forbes Celebrity 100 event, I saw that most of the celebrities listed were reality television stars. The public may believe that every red carpet event is filled with A-list celebrities like Angelina Jolie and Brad Pitt, but, in truth, most individuals attending even many of the most exclusive celebrity events are reality television stars and lesser-known actors. The tip sheet also revealed that, atypically, multiple people of color were scheduled to attend. Among them was the African American actress Regina King, whom many reporters ignored as she made her way down the red carpet. She quickened her pace once she observed this, but I stopped her. "Do you want to talk to brown people too?" she asked me, both seriously and sarcastically. I was the only reporter who talked to her and the other black women walking the carpet that night.

This was not the first time a celebrity of color had referenced the racial imbalance in celebrity reporting in an interview with me. As recounted in the introduction, an interviewee at my first red carpet event—the VH1 Hip Hop Honors awards—referred to *People* as "*White People* magazine." The *New York Daily News* used the same epithet ten years later, after *People* fired their only black editor.[12] The relationship between the race and ethnicity of reporters, interviewees, and the publications' target demographic is layered. Nonwhite reporters are well aware that we are often the ones to interview celebrities of color and to attend the "ethnic" events. Racial politics are a major factor in celebrity culture, red carpet rituals, and entertainment journalism, and without firsthand accounts it is difficult to understand what these politics look like on the inside. As my interaction with Regina King suggests, people of color in Hollywood are comfortable addressing this issue, but white people often ignore it.

King's question put Hollywood's racial hierarchy front and center in our conversation. She has worked in the industry for years, but she was still clearly uncomfortable with the racialization of the red carpet space. Another significant aspect of the interaction I had with her was that it did not involve a publicist mediating our conversation. It is not clear to me why she did not have her personal publicist or manager with her that evening, as the other black women attending that night did. Normally one of the event publicists walks with a celebrity whose publicist or manager is absent. This strongly suggests the publicists did not think reporters would want to talk to her.

Publicists typically assess, censor, and set parameters on their clients' interviews. A guest I once brought to a red carpet event described the PR rep as a "babysitter." Indeed Samantha, a staff writer and reporter for a weekly celebrity magazine who has also been a freelancer, explained that publicists make it difficult to have a natural conversation: "There's [always] a publicist tapping your elbow as you're holding your recorder and you're like, 'You've got to be kidding me, this is the second question. Give me a break.'" Thus it is unsurprising that my conversation with King at the Forbes event was far more natural than those I have with publicists looking on. Our mutual acknowledgment of the highly racialized nature of the event may also have played a role. But still I found myself wondering, "Did we really have a moment—a real connection? How much is planned performance? Are we both performing?" We were both prescribed to some extent. The red carpet is a highly regulated space in any case, and of course our conversation took place in public. As Samantha points out, people are not "themselves on the red carpet because they're aware of how they look. They're also looking around their shoulder."

By the end of the red carpet for the Forbes event, it was clear that, as usual, many of the celebrities listed on the tip sheet would not actually attend. Event planners include on the list any celebrities who were invited and did not tell the event that they were *not* coming. The names on the list are intended to entice and guarantee media coverage, but in reality those names are often just a tease.

Walking the Carpet

The ritual of the red carpet centers on the display and worship of celebrities. The reporters, photographers, and video camera crews arrive early and check in with the leaders of the ceremony—the event publicists. The media outlets are lined up so that the celebrities feel properly worshipped and attended to as they arrive. The barricade—typically a waist-high divider with metal bars—separates the media producers from the celebrities. We are crammed together and look and feel like animals at a zoo, but it is, in fact, the other side of the barricade that is on display.

As the first celebrity arrives, the media representatives in attendance quickly turn as they hear the photographers screaming the name of the celebrity who is posing: "Jennifer, over here!" "Jennifer, can I get you to look right here!" "Jennifer, let me see that smile!" "Jennifer, one more for me!" I can make out those few phrases, but most of the yelling is indecipherable because all of the photographers are yelling at once, and there may be as many as fifty of them. Celebrities generally oblige and look clearly into the cameras of as many photographers as possible, alternating between serious faces and smiles. They also change angles to show off their outfits—over-the-shoulder-looks to show the intricate details of the back of a dress, and front-facing shots to more fully display the complete outfit, accessories and all.

A red carpet photographer named Liam, who works exclusively for one agency, told me he always has earplugs with him for such events. Yet he noted, "For some reason nobody screams at Samuel L. Jackson. Everybody is quiet. I guess they are afraid of being called a MF. Sometimes when women are pregnant, like when Natalie Portman was pregnant, everybody was quiet. Some publicists, beforehand, they say to keep it calm because they don't like to be yelled at." He noted that the celebrity publicists are a major obstacle to good photographs, and that photographers get louder in their attempts to get a good shot with the most famous celebrities. Despite the sometimes aggressive nature of the red carpet photographers, the hierarchy between them and paparazzi remains intact. A red carpet reporter named Ron explains, "It is still a controlled situation and it's by invite and clearance." The surveilled and exclusive nature of the red carpet contributes to its legitimacy and, conversely, the illegitimacy of the paparazzi.

Given the screaming of the "photogs," it always amazes me that many of the celebrities who pose patiently on the red carpet are the same who claim

4.4 Bethenny Frankel doing obligatory poses for the cameras on the red carpet at the Forbes Celebrity 100 event on June 8, 2011. Photo by the author.

to feel threatened by paparazzi who, at the very least, do not create the same amount of audible chaos. The photographers take photos of every person who walks the red carpet, and they yell out for a name if they are unfamiliar with the celebrity. (The publicist usually stands near the photographers and repeatedly says and spells the names of lesser-known celebrities while the photographers jot down the information.)

Celebrities stop to talk to reporters from the various media outlets, while fans outside of the barricades snap photos (see fig. 4.4). I regularly worked as one of these red carpet reporters, a term used in the industry to reference journalists who predominantly report on red carpet events. Print media red carpet reporters typically work freelance, though this has changed since I completed my research, as many weekly magazines and other celebrity-focused media outlets have simply asked more red carpet reporting of their staff writers and reporters and have cut back on freelance budgets. Broadcast red carpet reporters are typically regular anchors on the television channels and programs they work for. Not coincidentally, in the typical red carpet lineup, television outlets always go first, for screen is considered more important than print. A video of a celebrity snubbing a television reporter can make that celebrity look unrelatable or unfriendly, while print reporters write only about the celebrities who stop to talk to them. Now, however, some online outlets for celebrity magazines include video, so reporters doing video for People.com, for example, get much more attention than a *People* reporter who does not have a camera crew.

Despite the frequent portrayal of celebrities' annoyance with the media, that is a luxury afforded to only the most famous. Reporters often do not recognize a celebrity who has had only a minor part on a recent show or movie, or who has been on a new reality television show and is walking the carpet hoping to make it into the magazines. Publicists who have prestigious clients attending an event will often bring along a lesser-known client and essentially barter with reporters: interview the newcomer, and you'll get more time with the A-lister. New clients thus get practice doing interviews and feeling comfortable in this highly surveilled and regulated space, boosting their confidence and sense of importance.

Celebrities and their publicists handle interviews by following a standard formula, and the celebrity's level of fame can be demonstrated by the way they handle the media. When a celebrity is C- or D-list, the publicist generally pitches the client to the media in advance to avoid humiliation, as Regina King nearly suffered. "You don't have to talk to her, but, if you don't mind, it would be helpful," the publicist might tell me. I say, "No problem," and try to make the interviewee feel important. I can always ask them about the clothing they are wearing, what brought them out, and what projects they are working on. Before I had a smartphone, I would just wing it and research the interviewees afterward, hoping to uncover some connection they might have to a big movie or other upcoming project. Since the advent of the smartphone, I often use it for on-the-spot research, which enhances my questions. There's always a chance the person will become more famous down the line and remember that we spoke before he or she was big, but this seldom pays off the way reporters might hope.

I missed such an opportunity when Paris Hilton introduced me to Kim Kardashian at a red carpet event in Hollywood in 2005, back when she was a member of Hilton's entourage and before the discovery and release of her sex tape. I spoke to Hilton on a regular basis at various events at that time, and she was acting as her own publicist as well as Kim's. "This is my friend Kim," she said. "You should ask her some questions." I could have talked to Kim on the red carpet all night if I wanted to, but I really had nothing much to ask her. At an event six years later, her publicist told me that Kim would be answering no more than one question. She had transitioned from being unknown to an A-list celebrity.

Most celebrities fall between the extremes of giving all the time in the world to a red carpet reporter and answering only one question. But the very top A-list celebrities often opt to skip the red carpet altogether, even the photo op, and enter events through a back entrance, unless they are promoting something specific or the event is a major awards show. All celebrities have the option to bypass the red carpet. This, of course, poses a problem for those expected to produce reporting on celebrities, especially on A-list celebrities. It can also lead to speculative reporting that, while not fully acknowledged by every media outlet, is very common. Sarah recalled one instance when she was not able to get any time with Sandra Bullock at an event, and her editor at a weekly magazine pressed her for details that she did not have. She feared she would lose her job if she didn't turn in a detailed file, so she sent in this report:

> Sandy showed up around 8p. She walked down the red carpet with Kevin Huvane (her publicist). Though she was rushed into the event quickly, surrounded by event reps, she did stop to pose for photos on the red carpet and seemed in very good spirits. She laughed and smiled while she posed in her gold dress and looked like she was having fun getting photos taken. (Tried to get her fashion ID, but nobody had it at the event, Just Jared says it was AllSaints). She looked really amazing and, though she didn't stop to talk to anyone on the carpet, she did smile as she walked past reporters and seemed to be in a very upbeat mood.

This is the kind of speculative reporting that inevitably gets written up when a highly sought-after celebrity bypasses interviews. Another common tactic is to get a quote describing how the star "seemed" at the event from a bystander or attendee—often the reporter's guest or a fellow reporter. While the ethics of this will be explored in a later chapter, from the perspective of the reporter, this is no different from using material from a "man on the street" style of interview, which is a cornerstone of journalism.

When celebrities do stop to answer questions, there are ritualistic rules of timing. Regardless of whether one is talking to a celebrity for five minutes or only thirty seconds, an element of the surveilled nature of this space is the signal that publicists give when they want the reporter to know they have had enough time with their client (see fig. 4.5). When I am interviewing a celebrity, even if we seem to be in a mutually enjoyable conversation, the publicist will often subtly tap my forearm, usually twice with the index and middle fin-

ger. Depending on the demeanor of the publicist, who usually stands to the left of me while the celebrity is slightly to the right, this signal tells me that I need to either simply allow the celebrity to finish answering the question before bidding adieu, or I can try to quickly get in one more question before the publicist whisks the interviewee away. Some publicists simply cut things off with, "Okay, thank you," before guiding the celebrity to the next interview. The red carpet is a ritual of display, in which the celebrities can be gazed upon and admired, photographed, and worshipped, as they carefully craft, under the supervision and surveillance of their hired publicists, the image they wish to portray of themselves. The reporters similarly get to craft the ways they want to portray celebrities, depending on the information they get (or sometimes do not get) from the celebrities themselves. It is a highly regulated space, and one that is emblematic of American celebrity culture.

The Not-So-Glamorous Side of the Red Carpet

> I don't like red carpet reporting because it's an art. I'm not good at it, for
> starters. People who do it well, I'm always impressed that somebody can ask
> and interview a subject. Wait, you got this on the red carpet? You got to ask

them six questions? Oh my God, how did you keep their attention for that long? | **SAMANTHA** | A WRITER FOR A CELEBRITY WEEKLY MAGAZINE, 2011 INTERVIEW WITH THE AUTHOR

In my research with celebrity reporters, they often complained that magazines required them to ask questions that are either inane, such as the celebrity's favorite color, or invasive. One reporter from a weekly magazine shared that she felt "ridiculous asking questions like 'Who do you like on dancing with the stars?' It's embarrassing." On the red carpet at a Grammy after-party in 2011, I observed as another reporter looked through a list of questions her magazine had given her and tried to decide which ones to ask: "Well, let's see here . . . how about . . . what's your go-to pair of shoes or how many pairs of shoes do you have?" Another reporter at the event had to ask each celebrity, "Bieber fever: On a scale from one to ten, how bad do you have it?" These kinds of questions often lead reporters to preface their questions with, "I'm so sorry, my editors told me I had to ask." Many reporters would love to talk to Angelina Jolie about her humanitarian work, but instead they have to ask her how long it took her to get ready for the event or about the current state of her relationship with Brad Pitt.

Journalists who cover celebrities have to push for news. Thus, in the pursuit of breaking stories, they often try to find clever ways to get personal information. One strategy is to reference stories that are already in the media to try to position the reporter as being separate from the rest of the media—and on the side of the celebrity: "There's been a lot of media speculation on [a current event]. What do you think about that?" For example, when there were rumors that Mariah Carey was pregnant, one reporter set herself up in opposition, asking Carey's husband, Nick Cannon, "There's lots of talk in the media right now that you and Mariah are expecting. How do those rumors make you feel? Do you want to clear them up? How do you stay supportive of your wife through all of this? Is it hard to deal with media speculation?" The goal was to get inside information without offending the celebrity.

But sometimes when news is on the line, reporters have to offend. For example, just a few days after Justin Timberlake's breakup with Cameron Diaz, I had to work a movie premiere he attended and was very specifically instructed to ask him how things were between them. I had only a brief window of opportunity as part of a group interview to ask the question; there was no time to finesse it. It was humiliating, but I knew I had to do it, and I was not surprised that he was annoyed and walked away without answering.

Invasive questions can cause problems when celebrities are reluctant to divulge details of their private lives, but also when celebrities are looking to monetize their personal information themselves rather than give it to reporters for free. For example, one reporter shared with me her thoughts on the following exchange she had with Kim Kardashian:

REPORTER: Have you decided if you want to be a summer, winter, or fall bride? What time of year are you thinking?

KARDASHIAN: I do know, but we're not going to reveal that. I'm going to try to keep it as private as we can.

The reporter reflected, "Bullshit answers. This is what we get. She means private from everyone but the cameras that will film it." Keeping personal details of their lives a secret in the immediate future means the celebrities have information to sell, whether as an exclusive to a magazine or via other media channels. In Kardashian's case, she was making sure she had new information to reveal on her reality show. She did not literally mean she wanted to keep the information private; she wanted to maximize the benefit for herself when she revealed it.

In addition to the sometimes awkward interview process, other aspects of red carpet reporting are less than glamorous. While it's true that there are some times when red carpet reporters are afforded some of the same luxuries as celebrities, like extravagant gift bags and tickets to sit inside the Oscars, those are rare. In reality it is a job that involves standing outside for hours, often in the cold (since most events are at night), knowing that the most famous celebrities may not show or may not talk to reporters. If reporters are lucky enough to be brought inside after the carpet closes, they must act like stalkers, tracking the celebrities' every move.

Some reporters like to post to Twitter or Instagram about hanging out with celebrities at a party, so that their friends and family will see their work as glamorous, when in reality they were working, trying to get a glimpse of the celebrities and make notes of everything they are doing. There is rarely interpersonal interaction between reporters and celebrities inside the events or award ceremonies, and when there is, publicists coordinate every aspect of it. It is the reporter's job to not bother the celebrities, but to just observe them.

Reporters often talk about celebrities treating them negatively. Stephanie, a longtime freelance red carpet reporter for a celebrity weekly magazine, once asked an actor how he was doing, and he replied, "How about I give you a big can of shut the fuck up," and walked away. A male celebrity violently pushed

Amber, a staff writer for a celebrity weekly magazine, against the wall at a party for a major award ceremony after she asked him for an interview.

Some media relations representatives decide that the barricades should apply to reporters at an event as well as on the red carpet. I once stood outside in the cold for six hours before being led to a balcony above the event, where the reporters were allowed to watch from above as seated guests below ate a lavish five-course meal. Our position gave us the opportunity to take note of what the guests were being served and who was sitting with whom, and thus it made sense to stay to report on our observations, uncomfortable as the situation may have been.

Of course, I understand why reporters don't usually post to social media messages like, "Standing around outside of Tom Cruise's house hoping to catch him on his way out with Suri" or "Standing behind a barricade on the red carpet getting snubbed by every celebrity who walks by me."

Reporters as Celebrities?

After the PR reps closed the red carpet at the Forbes Celebrity 100 event, I was escorted inside. I never ask to take photos with celebrities at events I am covering for the magazine, but I noticed a reporter who was giddy after obtaining a selfie with Bethenny Frankel. Being a reporter does not mean we are jaded about celebrity, and some of the reporters I work with have even been approached about starring in their own reality television shows. While I do not agree with the well-known designer who told me that merely reporting for *People* made me "a celebrity in [my] own right," many celebrity reporters desire fame. The rise of Mario Lavandeira, aka Perez Hilton, has given some celebrity reporters hope. However, Hilton did not start reporting on celebrity gossip to be a journalist; he started reporting bits and pieces of information on celebrities and making fun of them on his website *in order to* turn into a personality.

As I stood on the carpet at the premiere for the *Glee* 3D movie at Regency Village Theatre in Westwood, waiting for the stars to arrive, I found myself next to Hilton for the first time in a long while. He was on the red carpet being filmed interviewing celebrities (see fig. 4.6). I had seen him at an event months earlier and asked if he would let me interview him for my research. His publicist and I exchanged many emails, but I never got a definitive answer. I reminded him about my research and that I had been seeking an interview

4.6 Perez Hilton interviewing Kathy Griffin at the *Glee 3D* movie premiere at Regency Village Theatre in Westwood on August 6, 2011. Photo by the author.

with him. Suddenly he said, "Well, why don't we just do the interview now?" So I turned my recorder to him and started asking him questions about how he marketed himself and what his goals were when he got into the industry. At the end of the interview, the person who had been filming us handed me a waiver requiring use of the footage of my interview for a reality show he was shooting called *Sleeping with Perez*. The footage ended up showing me interviewing Perez as if he were a celebrity walking the red carpet when, in fact, he was there in his capacity as a reporter. All of the teen and twenty-something actors walking the carpet that night stopped to talk to him and told him they were huge fans of his.

Hedda Hopper's legacy demonstrates that if someone fails to make it in Hollywood as an actor, there are other options, including reporting. Her mediocre acting career led her to develop a well-known celebrity gossip column in the 1930s. More recently Mario Lopez, best known for his role as Slater on *Saved by the Bell*, became an anchor for the entertainment news show *Extra*, and Lycia Naff acted in *Total Recall* before becoming a staff reporter for *People* and eventually rising to prominence for her reporting on the Bill Cosby rape cases. Perez Hilton presents an alternative approach: start as a reporter and blogger, *then* become a celebrity.

Sandra, a former staff and freelance reporter for multiple weekly celebrity magazines, believes many reporters want to become celebrities. She called them "star fuckers"—reporters who think their job will give them access to celebrity themselves. Sometimes it happens. A former *Star* reporter, Kate Major, while covering a story about a former reality television star, Jon Gosselin (of *Jon and Kate Plus Eight*), "fell for him," and *Star* magazine featured an article about her in its July 2009 issue.[13] After the two broke up, Major went on to date Lindsay Lohan's father, with whom she had a highly publicized and tumultuous relationship.[14] Thus the lines between celebrity reporters and celebrities can be crossed by a rare few.

We Are Not Paparazzi: Red Carpet and Event Photographers

The celebrity reporters make up only half of the media presence on the red carpet; the front of the lineup is the domain of the red carpet photographer (see fig. 4.7). According to several I spoke with, there are about thirty regulars at nearly all Hollywood events. (Of course, for larger events and awards

4.7 Red carpet photographers shoot Kerry Washington at the 2011 VH1 Do Something Awards in Hollywood. Photo by the author.

ceremonies there can be many more.) Much like paparazzi, most red carpet and event photographers are freelance but work for one agency in particular, though some are on staff. They work hard. Liam, the photographer I focus on in this section, calculated that in fifteen months he collectively took 500,000 images at the events he covered. This is not the number of images he sent to magazines, but rather how many times he took a photo. Liam himself is amazed by the quantity of images he takes, and also by the instantaneous distribution of photos through the agencies:

> When we shoot an event like a movie premiere, all this stuff goes worldwide within a matter of hours, sometimes minutes. Our cameras actually have radio devices, and some of them you can do a tether. You can run a wire from the camera to a device in the briefcase, which is a wireless device, and they can have an editor clone the images that you're shooting. So if I'm shooting you, I have an editor in the office that's linked up to my camera, pulling the images from that thing, and photoshopping. That's why red-carpet images are up so fast. That's amazing to me.

Placement works differently for photographers than it does for reporters. Red carpet photographers represent agencies that do not necessarily have the same clout as outlets and thus do not have established place settings on the carpet. The photographers have therefore taken it upon themselves to create their own process for order on the carpet, a "first come, first served" policy. Those who want a prime position establish they were at the location at a particular time by presenting a receipt with a time stamp from a nearby business, such as a Starbucks. Liam explains: "Photographer number one starts the list of photographers, and then as the day goes on it grows. You have to stay an hour or so at the location and wait until the next photographer shows up. He is number two. Then if there is any discrepancy later on, no, I've got my receipt right here." It took a while for Liam to find out about this rule, and it affected his ability to get the shots he needed. "I didn't realize that was a rule until I kept showing up to premieres and I'm like, 'I'm getting here an hour early, why can't I get a good spot?' Then someone told me."

As new photographers join the ranks, they have to go through the growing pains Liam faced: "When there is a photographer nobody knows, the other photographers give them hell. We call it initiation. It happened to me. There is one photographer whose name I won't say, but she is sort of known for hazing. You have to be initiated. . . . You get hazed for about an hour. It depends on how you react. People determine if they like you or not. If they like you, you're good. If they don't like you, they will rip you apart." Photographers also share a distinct collegiality; they trust one another to keep an eye on thousands of dollars' worth of equipment when they leave to get coffee or dinner. But since the recession the competitiveness in the business has led to a change at work. Liam said, "It's been aggressive since day one. But it became more aggressive when the sales dropped. So what happened was, people aren't making as much money as they were. I definitely noticed the change. I remember talking to my editor about it. People are getting really, really aggressive. The magazines aren't paying what they used to, so people have to work harder. They have to get more eye contact." This can contribute to the level of yelling heard on the red carpet.

An important tactic of red carpet and event photography is *seeding*, when a designer has paid a publicist to distribute a product to celebrity clientele, and the publicist will ask a photographer or a photo agency to take close-up shots of the item. "When you see a close-up photo of a purse in a magazine, that was a seeding job." The publicist usually requests the photos for a particular publication, although photos with fashion products can sell well even without such requests. This is similar to set-up paparazzi shots, in which a publicist tells an agency to send a photographer to a certain place at a certain time to shoot a certain celebrity. For example, if Mercedes-Benz wants to get their new car promoted, a celebrity will be paid to be at a gas station at a certain time to be seen putting gas in the car. The paparazzi will focus on the logo to make sure they get the shot the company needs.

While Liam acknowledged that seeding is similar to set-up paparazzi shots, he said, "We're not paparazzi. There's a distinction, and we want that known and clear. We just feel like paparazzi work is dirty work. It's not ethical at times, which I've seen firsthand." But he also admitted that pap work is "definitely" harder. "I hung out with one of my paparazzi friends one day just to see," he told me. "I can't do it. The waiting. You're waiting, and if you have to go to the restroom, there is no restroom." The way red carpet and event photographers have to work with celebrities also affects their ability to cross into the paparazzi world, even if they wanted to. Liam said:

> I know a lot of celebrities, and the moment they catch me out on the street it's going to mess up my other work because of the agency that I work for. We're known for doing inside party shots. We take somebody like Nicole Richie or a number of celebrities. And Sophia Bush or Angie Harmon—people who I know. I have a rapport with these people. I show up to the party and they know I'm going to get great fashion. But the moment they see me out on the street chasing them or whatever, it's done. My rapport is done with them. Raven-Symoné lives somewhere in my neighborhood. She was in Whole Foods the other day with a knit hat on her head, a T-shirt, and pajama bottoms. If I were paparazzi and I had my camera in the car I could have lit her up in the grocery store or coming out of the grocery store. I know if I want to shoot Raven, I know she sees me when I see her—I don't know her personally but we've talked—and that would ruin our relationship.

Liam feels particularly recognizable because he is "always the only [black photographer] on the red carpet." When he covers the events inside, he is often the only person of color in the room. He keeps his focus on producing the best work he can, despite feelings of isolation. He does, however, suspect that some PR companies have refused to work with him because of his race, and he has found that some "have a really nasty attitude." There are pronounced racial politics happening on both sides of the camera, in all realms of celebrity media production. This chapter began by exploring these politics, and the chapters that follow will continue to address the way forms of difference affect the labor of my collaborators at every stage of their work.

CHAPTER FIVE

Where Reporting Happens:
Precarious Spaces and the Exploitation of Women Reporters

Throughout the years I spent as a celebrity reporter, in addition to traditional red carpet events, I worked in classrooms, restaurants, nightclubs, dive bars, shopping malls, even sitting in my car outside of celebrities' homes. In this chapter I explore some of these divergent workspaces. As Samantha, a white woman in her forties on the staff of a celebrity weekly magazine, said, "I don't think of the office as a newsroom. The office, to me, is a time suck. In my world, I find that when I go visit people at the studio, that to me is more like my newsroom, because I feel like I'm on site, I'm in my element, I'm in the TV world. That to me is more a meeting place where I'm gathering news and processing it. I don't view the office in that way at all."[1]

The historian Robert Snyder situates our "contemporary fascination with celebrity . . . in journalistic practices and cultural transformations that emerged in the first half of the twentieth century."[2] These celebrity-focused journalistic practices were pioneered by reporters such as Louella Parsons, Hedda Hopper, and Mike Connolly, who dished Hollywood gossip across the country, allowing readers to feel that they knew what was going on in Hollywood and making them hungry for more. Parsons wrote a syndicated newspaper column from 1913 to 1965, Hopper for the *Los Angeles Times* from 1938 to 1966, and Connolly for the *Hollywood Reporter* from 1951 to 1966. These columnists were a cornerstone of the Hollywood-industrial complex. Parsons was not the first to write about film stars or celebrities, "but by writing a daily column exclusively devoted to motion pictures and by extending the existing celebrity journalism tradition to film stars, Louella pioneered a new journalistic format and started a new chapter in the history of American celebrity." The approaches to celebrity reporting off the red carpet have not changed substantially since those early days. Parsons "sneaked into theaters attended by stage and screen stars, loitered for hours in the lobby of Blackstone Hotel, a popular hangout for actors, and eavesdropped in bathrooms."[3] As a reporter in the twenty-first century, when not on the red carpet, I found myself often engaged in similar behavior in order to obtain information. This is what was expected, even of a *People* reporter.

I have already mentioned that the majority of the celebrity reporters in Los Angeles are women. This chapter provides a deeper analysis of the reasons for this discrepancy as well as some of the gender politics that emerge from this reality. The dominance of women in this particular part of Hollywood has been casually acknowledged within the industry but not critically examined, much like the predominance of Latino men working as paparazzi. Women (particularly white women) have dominated the celebrity reporting world at least since my first days in the offices of *People* magazine, although men generally outnumber women among editors. During the course of my research, I found that participants had observed this gender disparity but had not given it much thought. My data demonstrate that women celebrity journalists are highly sexualized in their positions—by straight male celebrities and also by being on display on the red carpet in the service of celebrities. Editors encourage reporters to use their sexuality (a presumed heterosexuality), both to relate to celebrity women on the basis of sharing common "women's issues" and to obtain information from male celebrities. Particularly when the reporter is a woman and the celebrity is a heterosexual man, these gender dynamics create a complex tension around power.[4]

Editors' encouragement of reporters to use their sexuality was cited by many women reporters as a reason why the field of celebrity reporting is dominated by women. However, the male reporters I spoke with believe that a reason for the woman-heavy demographic is because it is more socially acceptable for women to ask the types of questions the magazines want answered. As a freelance celebrity weekly reporter named Ron said, "It's weird for me to go out there and ask somebody intimate questions about their body. It's an odd thing for a man to do to a woman in a conversational, chatty way; on a red carpet it's basically a total stranger." Ron, a white man in his forties, is keenly aware of the fact that most of the people he works with are women. "Here in L.A. the weekly magazine offices are really dominated by women, at *People* in particular. I think it's the nature. I'm a straight man. I can talk to a girl about her dress and her makeup and her diet and her pregnancy; I can do it. I'm not comfortable doing it, I never have been, but I don't particularly care. It's a skill that I've had to develop. It's not easy. Women can ask that kind of stuff. It's a [platonic] girlfriend kind of vibe." In fact, Ron says, women have a definite "edge" over men in the celebrity reporting world when it comes to interviewing both men and women.

> With women it's because you go into a ladies room and you run into a total stranger and you might ask them, "Oh my gosh! That dress is so cute. Where did you get it? Your makeup looks great. Where do you get your hair cut?" You chitchat, put on lipstick, look in the mirror and you might have that experience in a ladies room anywhere in L.A. Men don't do that. Men don't talk to each other in those kinds of situations unless they are very, very friendly guys. We don't care about where you got your hair cut or where you got your pants. We genuinely don't.

While these notions do reflect the experiences of some women reporters, the calculation of these benefits is, again, based on a stereotypically heteronormative notion of what women and men bring to the table as celebrity journalists.

Sandra, a Latina reporter in her twenties who had worked as an intern, a freelance reporter, and a staff reporter for various celebrity weekly magazines, shared her perspective on how gender affects celebrity interviews:

> I think it is easier for women to do the job of a celebrity reporter because it's a very slippery slope that you have to navigate in the celebrity world. I'm not talking red carpet or anything because I think when it comes to red carpet celebrity journalism, I think a man and a woman reporter are on an equal playing field. I'm talking more about the reporter that has to go get the scoop. I think it's just a little easier for women. I think women can use—I don't want to say "themselves" because that sounds so wrong. In my experience the people who I have tried to report on or the people who I have dealt with are mostly men. This is just common sense. Who is a man most likely going to open up to, a man or a woman? Obviously

a woman. I think that is why it's maybe a little bit easier for women in that sense. I think women can get a little flirty, they can be friendly or whatever the case may be, and you will most likely get a story. I'm not saying go sleep with your source or whatever, but men are more likely to open up to women.

Sandra's response underscores the squarely heteronormative attitudes that are promoted within the context of celebrity media production. And while Sandra said it was not expected that she would sleep with sources, Amber, a white woman in her thirties on staff at a celebrity weekly magazine, said, "I know other people at other magazines have been told specifically to make out with sources, to sleep with sources, and to lead sources on. Whatever you need to do to get the story. Everything is acceptable and encouraged." Sandra's opinions have been shaped by her own success using the tactics she described. Her editors instructed her to

use my woman-ness to flirt with a guy, to get closer to celebrities, to get scoops. I was being told flat out to flirt with people. "Be nice to them. Be friendly. Act like a fan. Act kind of dumb." They didn't tell me flat out to act like a bimbo, but they did tell me to act a little looser. And I'm not really that person. I felt very exploited. I did not appreciate it, not at all, and, in that respect, it's not something that I would do again and since I've had those experiences I've lived and I've learned. I've grown as a woman, and I don't think I would ever do that. A story isn't more valuable than me and my self-worth, and I would not do it again. When you're young and you're hungry and your editors are asking you for it, you want to succeed, you want to freelance more and, so, sure.

Similarly, at age twenty, a former celebrity weekly magazine intern named Brittany was assigned to cover a pre-Oscar party; while she was there, she approached a television star, of whom she was a fan, to introduce herself and request an interview. "He started to rub my back and try to talk to me romantically. He was very physical with me, and I did not know how to handle it. I was just an intern and I did not know what the magazine would say if I told them. I was new."

The precarity of young women in Hollywood has been brought to the forefront recently, via the #MeToo movement and accusations against powerful Hollywood figures like Harvey Weinstein. Power is abused across many different contexts and industries to exploit the young, the impressionable, the vulnerable; in this case, it is used to manipulate the precarious laborers of celebrity media production. In fact the slippery slope in celebrity reporting that Sandra mentions left her at the center of controversy:

> Sometimes you become the story. I had that happen to me. I had another weekly [magazine] write about me. I was the other girl. I don't even remember which reporter it was, but it was when an actress was cheating on her husband, they were about to get divorced, and I was there trying to follow her husband. He and I were spotted in the car. There was either a reporter there or that reporter somehow got the information from another source that he was there talking with a girl and they referred to me as "the A-lister lookalike." I was saying, "Oh my gosh! I became the story." They wrote about me. I still have the magazine. My friends laughed about it. I haven't done that type of reporting in years, but when I did it, it made me really uncomfortable. Personally I'm a very honest person and I don't like to lie. At that time I did kind of have to label myself as a college student or I just graduated and I didn't know what I was doing. I had my guilty conscious telling me, "This isn't okay." It made me very unsettled. It gave me a lot of anxiety.

Despite her feeling uncomfortable with these types of situations, Sandra continued this line of work for several years. After several experiences where she felt her gender and sexuality were exploited for the magazine, she said, "I had that internal talk with myself of 'What the f'? I thought, 'This isn't what I went to journalism school for. This isn't what I was being taught in my lecture or anything we ever talked about in my journalism class.' It was a very eye-opening experience, but I would say that is the nature of the beast. I don't mean to talk down upon it, but women can be exploited in this field definitely. I think they have to be aware of what is happening and not let it happen to them." The ethics of celebrity journalism are not well-defined; in fact several reporters I spoke with asserted that there are *no* ethics in celebrity journalism. This contrasts with the less-regulated field of paparazzi work, which, as I explored in earlier chapters *does* have self-enforced ethical codes.

Despite accusations that paparazzi lack ethics, including by the magazines that use their images, the celebrity weekly magazines also use women to get in with the predominantly male paparazzi.[5] Christy, a former *People* intern, said:

> *People* has a regular freelance reporter whose only job for the magazine is to tag along with paparazzi on everything. I mean anything and every-

thing, but they will never put that person on staff because their whole goal is to keep them not connected to them legally so they can go ahead and use any of that material and call it a source or call it whatever—however they want to frame it so that legally they are not actually tied to that person. Literally she does all of her reporting with paparazzi. And, of course, they choose a pretty girl who can go and flirt with the paparazzi and get more information.

Thus reporters are in a precarious situation at nearly every turn in their work. In terms of sexual exploitation and harassment on the job, one of the most disturbing, though not entirely unique, stories was that of Natasha Stoynoff, which I introduced at the beginning of this book.

In July 2011 Natasha agreed to meet me at the Gramercy Park Hotel for an interview. It had been a few years since we had seen each other, but we had a special connection. During my senior year of college at New York University I was an intern at the magazine's New York bureau, where she was a star reporter. My barren cubicle was right outside of her office, which was adorned with photos of her and the celebrities she covered regularly, some of whom she had written books with. She would often give me tips on interviewing celebrities, and that day at Gramercy Park Hotel she told me a story that I never imagined would have the meaning and ramifications that it does today.

Natasha had not changed at all—her long blonde hair was as thick and flowing as ever. Tall and sturdy, she still carried herself with a humble yet palpable strength and confidence. She still called me "Glitter Girl," the nickname she and our former boss, Liz McNeil, then chief of the New York bureau, had given me during my days as an intern because of my habit of wearing glitter eyeliner. As we sank into our plush green velvet chairs in the dimly lit room, the air conditioning blasting to cool us from the sticky New York summer, we picked up where we left off. As a reporting intern, I had needed her guidance, and I needed her now to guide me as I gathered research for this project.

We discussed the question of ethics in celebrity reporting, and she shared with me that she was sexually assaulted on the job by Donald Trump. "[My superior] asked if I wanted to press charges. And I'm like, 'No.' I just thought, this guy felt so big," she confessed. In 2012, in a follow-up interview, we talked more about why she had not done anything in response to Trump's assault. She explained that she questioned whether it was her fault, if she had done something to deserve it. She characterized it as being like a "classic rape victim" narrative. "I sort of blamed myself. . . . And that's why I didn't do anything about it." She expressed very deep regret for not doing more at the time, although based on the accusations that have come out since, it does not seem that Trump will ever experience any repercussions for his actions. Natasha said:

> What I regret was not being strong with him in the moment. Like punching him or slapping him or something. And saying "Get away from me, you fucking asshole." Because at the moment I couldn't get in touch with my anger. I was kind of shocked. And for me, it took me a while for me to get in touch with, "You son of a bitch, how could you do that?" And by then it's too late to act in the moment. The only thing I really regret is me not putting him in his place properly, in a better way. I mean I pushed him away and all that kind of stuff. But five minutes later I continued the interview with him and Melania. And they talk about how happy they are, this and that. You know, I really wish I would have gotten up and left. And then I would have to explain why, to my editor. And that's what I wish I would have done. Not that they could have done anything, but for my own power.

People has covered Trump for many years and thus contributed to his fame through their consistent coverage of *The Apprentice* and Trump's personal and financial life.[6] Nonetheless, from October 12, 2016 — when *People* published Natasha's first public account of the assault — until the election, the magazine had the courage to condemn Trump and support their employee.[7]

In fact, after the initial People.com story about Natasha had run its course, *People* published follow-up stories both online and in the magazine going into further detail, including Natasha's response to Trump's denial of the accusations and testimony from others corroborating her story.[8] Just four days before the election, People.com featured a video of *People*'s then managing editor Jess Cagle interviewing Natasha, asking her to respond to offensive comments Trump made about her after her accusations went public.[9] Both Cagle and Larry Hackett, who was managing editor when Natasha was assaulted, publicly expressed their support for her. In a statement about why they printed the story, Cagle noted, "Ms. Stoynoff is a remarkable, ethical, honest and patriotic woman, and she has shared her story of being physically attacked by Donald Trump in 2005 because she felt it was her duty to make the public aware. To assign any other motive is a disgusting, pathetic attempt to victimize her again. We stand steadfastly by her."[10] The statement was accompanied by a video of senior editor Charlotte Triggs explaining Natasha's story with great empathy, noting that it was a "terrible thing that happened to her." Triggs also made appearances on multiple television shows to tell Natasha's story. On November 4 several of *People* magazine's staff posted photos of themselves with Natasha on Facebook with such captions as "Team Natasha Stoynoff."

The day after Trump's election, however, Triggs authored a story on People. com entitled "My Front-Row Seat to History: PEOPLE Senior Editor Charlotte Triggs Watches Trump Win the Presidency," featuring a photo of her and the president-elect smiling together. *People* followed up with more lighthearted Trump family coverage, such as "27 Photos of Ivanka Trump and Her Family That Are Way Too Cute," "Melania Trump's First Lady Style: See Her Best Moments on the Campaign Trail," and a piece about the election titled "He's Hired!"[11] In response to backlash over this complimentary coverage, *People* issued a statement on November 10: "Donald Trump's win is a history-making news event that warranted the cover of the magazine. The story is not a celebration or an endorsement and we continue to stand by Natasha Stoynoff."[12] But the claim that Trump's election was being covered as a news event and that the coverage was "not a celebration" willfully ignores the posture of these puff pieces. This flattering coverage suggested that *People* cared little about sexual assault, even when the victim was their own employee who was assaulted on the job.

By attempting to make Trump cutesy and consumable again, *People* cast doubt on the claim that they would not have published Stoynoff's story in 2005 if they had known of the assault at the time. The former magazine editor said in no uncertain terms that he would have "killed the story that Stoynoff had gone to Palm Beach to report."[13] In a conversation I had with Natasha in the wake of this controversy, she said she had the impression that the current editors felt the same way. But the claim that, had they only known then what they know now they would not have published the story of Trump's marital bliss, was belied by the magazine's laudatory coverage of Trump and his family at the time.

As Cagle so emphatically pointed out, Natasha did not have any ulterior motive for revealing her assault. But what about *People's* motive? Cagle admitted in an interview that "Natasha was not, frankly, eager to tell this story." Cagle, on the other hand, said, "I was thrilled to run it." Why? Their about-face gives the distressing impression that it was all to bait clicks and to sell issues, exploiting their own employee's assault for profit. The *People* staff are not novices—they know what will draw in readers. Once the story was fully monetized and Trump was elevated to the presidency, the magazine wasted no time in wringing sales out of adoring coverage of her assaulter. As one former *People* writer presciently predicted on Facebook following Trump's victory, "They will get cozy with Melania and highlight her fashion. They will have our annual fawning Presidential Christmas interview. They will admire all things Ivanka. These things will not change."

Informal Workspaces

The work of celebrity reporters takes place in many spaces beyond the red carpet. It is often in these less formal spaces that their working conditions can become the most precarious, as exemplified by Natasha's experience interviewing Trump in his hotel. Another workplace for the celebrity reporter is inside the venue once the formal processional component of a red carpet event is finished. Expectations of reporters vary depending on the type of event. At major award shows, hundreds of reporters line up for a chance to interview celebrities, but only a few might be brought inside the show. Award shows are the rarest of the red carpet ritual, since there are only a few of them every year, compared to the hundreds of other Hollywood red carpet events. At galas and benefits, the red carpet is generally followed by an informal cocktail hour, and then a more formal program. At a movie premiere, the formal red carpet is followed by the film screening, which is generally followed by a reception or after-party. At a designer boutique opening or any other kind of party, the red carpet is followed by a more informal program. In my experience as a freelancer for *People*, access to red carpet events was often expected, whereas for my colleagues working for less prestigious magazines, the chances of going inside were more remote. On the red carpet, reporters often discuss if they have access inside the event or not, which, in essence, becomes about flexing industry power.

At any red carpet event where inside access is provided to a reporter, the reporting does not end when the processional ends; in fact reporters may do more reporting inside events than on the carpet. This is particularly true when celebrities skip the red carpet and the only way of reporting on them is to find them inside the venue. Reporters have to be particularly vigilant about observing celebrities associated with a current newsworthy conflict, or if they have a new significant other with them, had a recent breakup, or are pregnant.

I spoke to Susan, a celebrity weekly magazine intern covering a red carpet event for the first time. At this particular event, there was one celebrity who was in the middle of a highly publicized scandal, and all the reporters in attendance were under instruction to monitor his behavior as closely as possible. Susan told me how she felt while doing the kind of observation-based reporting required of her inside the event:

> I felt really stealthy. I really felt like a spy, strategizing where I could be to look less awkward by myself. I went to the bar and sipped on my drink. Luckily I found him right away and he was right next to the bar. I was by myself so I wasn't looking to talk to anyone. There were people there, so I didn't want to be there, but for a while I was by the table where you could sign up for the raffle and, from time to time, I would be on my phone typing notes. Then I moved to the table and I was almost scared he was going to look and see me looking at him. I had adrenaline going. [The editors] asked me to write down anything, and I was trying to find things to write that were relevant. I focused on how he was behaving, what kind of mood he seemed to be in, that sort of thing. Some of the things I know the magazine wanted me to report on seemed irrelevant to me, like what he was drinking. How is that relevant? But his emotions, who he was talking to, how he was interacting with his date—that all seemed very relevant to me.

This is a typical description of the kind of work reporters have to do once inside red carpet events, particularly when there are specific celebrities they need to focus on. Celebrity reporters are concerned with what celebrities are eating and drinking, whom they are talking to, and what kind of mood they are in. These details contribute to the ways celebrity personas are shaped by the media. Inside red carpet events is a critical professional space for reporters precisely because it provides intimate details to contribute to the crafting of these celebrity images.

On the red carpet, reporters are generally behind the barricades, wearing a press badge, holding the tape recorder, and asking questions. Their role and their physical positioning are clearly defined. Inside an event, however, journalists are less conspicuous, so celebrities do not always know they are being observed. While paparazzi are typically conceptualized as the most invasive producers of celebrity media, reporters can be equally invasive, but in less obvious ways, since they record their observations on their cell phone's Note app rather than a camera. In addition to the ways that race, gender, and class shape paparazzi's access to particular spaces, the large camera equipment they must carry prevents them from being able to report in discreet ways that are more available to celebrity reporters.

Classroom

A somewhat unique informal space where I spent time reporting was the college campus. I was originally hired by *People* magazine as an intern when I was a senior at New York University. This was the same year that Mary-Kate and Ashley Olsen enrolled at NYU. Because the college requires school identification to enter any campus buildings, my position as a student provided me the possibility of reporting on the Olsen twins. From the time I began my internship, one of my responsibilities included reporting on how they were as students and where in Manhattan were their favorite spots to hang out. By asking around and taking note of the very obvious bodyguards who accompanied them, I quickly came to know, at least roughly, when they were on campus. Thus much of my work happened on campus (and at their favorite nightclubs and lounges) rather than at an event or in the office. And I was not the only reporter in this position. I quickly came to know the other magazine reporters who would use similar tactics to report on the twins. They too were NYU students who had been hired by other celebrity weekly magazines to engage in work similar to my own, and we would often sit next to each other near the Olsens' classrooms. One of my first items published on People.com was this small bit of reporting on Mary-Kate Olsen, "Mary-Kate's Classroom Chitchat," on November 18, 2004: "The first student to arrive for a freshman writing seminar at New York University on Monday was none other than Mary-Kate Olsen, who showed up 15 minutes early wearing baggy gray Nike sweat pants and holding a Starbucks cup. Olsen sat on the floor outside the classroom, and smiled at her classmates as they arrived. When everyone started filing into the classroom, Olsen, still sipping her Starbucks and chatting with a fellow classmate, picked up her notebook and lime green leather handbag and followed suit." This type of informal observational work is customary in celebrity reporting and in other even more personal venues.

Hospitals

When it comes to celebrity journalism, there are few, if any, places reporters will not go to get the job done (or, at the very least, will be asked by their outlet to go). One of the most difficult spaces in which celebrity reporters must work is a hospital. Ron told me about one occasion when he was asked to report at a hospital under precarious circumstances:

> When Owen Wilson tried to commit suicide, I was pressured by one of the celebrity weekly magazines to monitor the situation. I had interviewed Owen and his brother I don't know how many times. What's going to happen in a waiting room in a hospital? I don't know, but I went in and I babysat. I sat there and I'm like just waiting for somebody to recognize me because it's not like I've always done undercover. I've done a lot of sit-down interviews. I was in Hawaii for a film festival with the Wilson brothers for a week. So my attitude was, "I don't want to do this." I hated it. Nothing bad happened. I sat there with another reporter who was talking incessantly about everyday stuff for work, and I'm like, "Dude? Aren't we supposed to be low-profile here?" I was stunned. Of course people are worried about a sick family member so they probably didn't notice, but still, it's a weird experience.

Hospitals are a place where freelance reporters are forced disproportionately to put their careers at risk. Because they do not work on staff, they do not have the same leverage or any guarantee about their next project. Thus, when they are asked by a publication to cover something they are uncomfortable with, their sense of empowerment quickly dissipates. Ron said he "hated" his experience but knew that he needed to accept it to keep up his relationship with the publication. At hospitals it is not only sad news that must be reported on. When a pregnant celebrity is close to a due date, reporters are tasked with waiting at hospitals to glean information about the birth. In addition, reporters are often asked to wait outside the homes of A-list pregnant celebrities, to be ready to follow when they head to the hospital.

Reporters Doorstepping

Samantha, who had worked on staff and as a freelance reporter for multiple celebrity weekly magazines throughout her career, shared her uncomfortable experience as a freelancer monitoring the pregnancy of Katie Holmes:

> Tom Cruise and Katie were expecting, and we were all expected to do shifts sitting outside Tom's house. We were instructed to follow any of the cars that left the house. Even my boss was doing shifts, so I thought, if she's going to suck it up and do it, then I'll do one. And I was getting

paid. So it's easy money. But it's a little bit freaky. So I showed up. I think my shift was five a.m. to noon, so it was dark when I got there. I felt so dirty after sitting outside of there. Tom Cruise's mother had left the house around ten a.m. and I had to follow her. And I remember calling one of the people that was on weekend duty. And I said, "So here's where we're headed." "Oh, she's probably headed to the Scientology center. You don't have to follow her. Yeah, that's where she's going. Turn around. Go back." I didn't pick up any more shifts. I can't do this. This is weird. And when I got to the Scientology center, somebody took a picture of me and my car, and it just felt weird. The magazine was like, "Oh yeah, did they take a picture?" And everyone thought it was funny. I thought, no, this is weird. I don't want to do this. It felt dangerous to me. It felt sneaky. The rationale that we were told was, "If you don't do it, somebody else will. The other weekly magazines would do this. We don't want to lose out on the story." It just felt gross to me.

Joy, a former celebrity weekly magazine reporter, had a similar experience outside of Cruise's home:

We were all hands on deck for Tom [Cruise] and Katie [Holmes], when the baby was due. And that was scary. The family was sending decoy cars because they knew reporters and paparazzi were at the house. We would have to chase after cars. . . . I was going down the 405 freeway following a decoy Mini Cooper. I didn't know it was a decoy. I had my boss on the phone, I was going ninety miles an hour, and he was like, "Do not let them out of your sight." Ninety miles an hour on the 405. I thought, "You ain't got to pay my ticket, you ain't going to bail me out. You ain't going to buy me a car." I did not want to do it, but I just didn't want to be the one on the team not pulling my weight, and I didn't want to mess the whole thing up and have the entire magazine looking at me saying, "You could have gotten it, but you weren't willing to go to that next level." Even sitting outside of Tom and Katie's house was seedy to me. Those neighbors would see us and would come over and take our license plate numbers. Me going on high-speed chases to follow this chick is not all right with me. There were times when I got out of it. There were times when I said, "I'm not okay with it."

During this period Joy was on staff at one of the weekly magazines, thus illustrating that while freelance reporters are more frequently asked to do grunt work, staff reporters do it as well. This practice of "doorstepping" is a common tactic for paparazzi. When reporters must do it for the magazines, they conceptualize it as a "seedy" practice, despite the fact that the magazines (and other media outlets) routinely rely on photos captured from doorstepping. Paparazzi know they are being watched and judged constantly by those in the neighborhoods where they doorstep; they accept it as part of the stigma of their work. The reporters are mostly shielded from the kinds of discrimination paparazzi experience, but when they find themselves exposed to the same kind of surveillance and judgment, they find it scary and "gross."

There are certain tasks that a magazine would never send a staff reporter to do for fear of legal repercussions. As with paparazzi, media outlets want the work paparazzi produce, but they do not want to be formally associated with them. Freelance reporters get used to doing the riskier work so that the publication is insulated; if something goes awry, the magazine can blame it on an independently contracted freelancer. In 2005 a freelance reporter, Jeff Weiss, was arrested outside of Brad Pitt's Santa Barbara home while on assignment for *People*. *People* would have received no public relations consequences whatsoever, except for the fact that "sheriff's deputies escorted Weiss back to his car and found a copy of an e-mail between Weiss and an associate bureau chief for People's Los Angeles bureau."[14] In a rare turn of events, *People* was implicated as part of this controversy. Still, the *Los Angeles Times* article about the incident referred to Weiss as "some kind of a scout or forward guy," minimizing the significance of freelance celebrity reporters to the industry.

Sandra, who worked as an intern, freelance reporter, and staff reporter at various weeklies, shared her experience and the tactics she used while reporting outside of Reese Witherspoon's home:

> One of my first freelancing jobs was when Reese Witherspoon had her second baby, Deacon. I had to sit outside of her house and wait for the nanny to leave. Somehow I was magically going to talk to the nanny. Well, I magically stopped her vehicle, got out of my vehicle, stopped hers, I waved her down, she rolled down her window, and I just said, "Oh my gosh! Hi! It's so good to see you." I was pretending like I knew her. She was kind of looking at me like, "Who is this woman? I don't know you." I was trying to be a neighbor and I said, "Oh, I heard Reese had her baby. How is she doing?" She started feeling more comfortable and said, "Oh she is doing great. She's at the house." I said, "Who does the baby look like? Her? Ryan?" She said, "The baby looks just like her father."

That was the quote right there. It was just as simple as that. It's something that is not that hard to do, but there is a certain *je ne sais quoi* kind of way that you have to go about it. These scenarios are just a different kind of reporting than set-up interviews where everything is orchestrated and everything is arranged for that interview. Just going up to someone and speaking to them, you have no idea how they are going to react. You have no idea if they are going to tell you to fuck off and they are going to walk away. You just have to kind of go into it and hope for the best and hope that you will get a quote that will get you a good bonus or something. I detested the work, but I did it.

Sandra explained that she especially felt she had to do this kind of work because she had to keep the magazine interested in her. She was not alone in this sentiment. One of Joy's first assignments was to go to Britney Spears's home in a gated community:

The nursery was under construction for her second baby, and the magazine didn't know if it was a boy or girl. My boss wanted me to find out what the color of the room was, so we could figure out the gender. I lied to get into the clubhouse where she lived. I said I was going to a meeting at the top, because I had friends who lived there, and I knew there was a community center situation. So I lied and said that. Then I went to Britney's. I had scaled the walls to see if I could find out what the room looked like. I'd asked one of the architects. Had looked in her mailbox. I mean, stuff that's illegal. But here I am, twenty-two or twenty-three years old. And my boss told me "Don't come back until you know the damn color of the room." I didn't feel comfortable, but I was trying to get a job.

Despite the fact that reporters often engage in similar tactics to paparazzi, the position of paparazzi still remains at the very bottom of the industry hierarchy. Because of their race, gender, class, and education paparazzi would not have had access to the NYU buildings where I reported on the Olsen twins, would not have been able to get through the gated community where Britney Spears lived, would not have had a sit-down interview with Donald Trump at his estate. There are not incidents of reporters being beaten or killed on the job, as there are of paparazzi, but the predominantly women reporters are still put in precarious situations, exposing them to potential arrest, sexual assault, and other forms of exploitation.

Restaurants

While restaurant and nightlife reporting is no longer treated as a vital part of celebrity reporting, as it was in the previous decade, many reporters I interviewed spoke of the level of seriousness with which this kind of informal reporting was treated during those years.[15] Reporters were asked to dine at celebrity-frequented restaurants in hopes of spotting one (or more) stars and gleaning information. Sometimes celebrities' camps would tip off the magazines about their clients' whereabouts specifically so that the client would get coverage.[16] Just as paparazzi are treated as nuisances even though their tips often come from celebrities and their camps, the so-called tabloids are similarly tipped off to generate media coverage.

The following is one of Sarah's files from a night of restaurant reporting when the magazine she reported for was tipped off by Cameron Diaz's camp:

> On Thursday, Nov. 17, 2005, at 7:45pm Cameron Diaz and an older man and woman (couple, possibly her parents) dined at Il Sole in Hollywood. The actress dished about friendships and her recent time in Europe. "When we got to Italy after Paris, we were speaking French, when we got to London after Germany, we were speaking German. We just got the languages all crossed up," she explained to her friends, after Diaz said "merci" to the waitress at the Italian restaurant and then corrected herself by saying "grazie." Diaz ordered lamb chops, but couldn't finish them. "I'd love this to go," Diaz told the waitress. "I'm taking this home for Justin [Timberlake]," she said to her friends. For dessert, the group ordered a plate of cookies. Before leaving, Diaz asked the waitress, "Can you pack another macaron to go?" She stashed the cookie in the bag with leftovers for Timberlake. As the group got up to leave the table, Diaz grabbed a chocolate cookie off of the plate and said, "If you're not going to eat it, I am," and took a bite of the cookie. Diaz paid for the dinner.

While this kind of reporting may seem trivial, it is precisely the kind of information used to manufacture a celebrity persona. Cameron Diaz often portrays fun-loving characters, as in *There's Something about Mary* and her famous dance scene to "Baby Got Back" in *Charlie's Angels*. Obtaining details that show her as the sweet, fun-loving girl next door she plays in the movies satiates the consumers of this material, helping fans feel more "in the know" about what a celebrity is *really* like. Sarah's reporting offers a glimpse of Diaz as a thoughtful, considerate girlfriend and a world traveler who attempts to blend into local culture, which are the kinds of details fans and publicists live for. Similarly intimate, though usually not quite as endearing, information on celebrities is also gathered from reporting at nightclubs.

Inside the Clubs

> Part of what we cover is where celebrities are and what celebrities do, and the nightlife stuff is part of that. While it might be an unofficial thing, it's a great glimpse into their lives. | **MEGAN** | STAFF REPORTER FOR A CELEBRITY WEEKLY, 2009 INTERVIEW WITH THE AUTHOR

> When I was a club reporter I definitely felt like a stalker. | **JASMINE** | FREELANCE WEEKLY REPORTER, 2011 INTERVIEW WITH THE AUTHOR

Much like coverage of the restaurant scene, coverage of Hollywood nightlife was once a major component of celebrity reporting, but there is no longer much money pumped into producing such content. More typical today is that specific tips about where a celebrity partied and with whom are passed down to media outlets from third parties. However, there was a period during which the magazines sent reporters to all of the most exclusive clubs in Hollywood and New York where celebrities were regulars. While PR reps for celebrities may not always show reporters the most respect on the red carpet, PR reps for nightclubs showed a great deal of appreciation for reporters, who provided a whole new level of exposure for the clubs. Reporting that began neutrally describing the name of the club a celebrity had attended and the brand of alcohol he or she consumed quickly grew into a carefully orchestrated dance of product placement and brand-name-dropping, as alcohol and nightclub reps competed to make sure their products were associated with celebrities in the pages of the weekly magazines. Once a reporter gave a significant amount of coverage to a club, the PR reps for that club often welcomed them in with reserved booths, free alcohol, and other VIP treatment.

Significantly, however, the level of racial discrimination in Hollywood did not stop on the red carpet. Jasmine, an African American weekly magazine freelance reporter in her twenties, described her humiliation during routine stops at Hollywood clubs. In a 2011 interview she told me, "I would show up at my regular spots that I covered. The bouncers knew me really well. They were often black too. When they would keep me waiting to get in, we would start talking and they disclosed to me that they were only able to let in a certain number of black people at a time. That's why I would have to wait while they let others in. They would say, 'I know it's fucked up, but that's how it is.'" While the red carpet is a white space because of the continued white dominance of Hollywood actors and reporters, the club environment too created a space of contemporary segregation practices. Jasmine said, "I can't say I was shocked at how racist clubs were. I'm going to say *racist* because they really are, still to this day. The hot-spot clubs, they have a quota. I developed friendships with the bouncers and they would tell me they have quotas at the club of how many black people—black people specifically. I hated it. Who wants to go to a place that doesn't want you there because you're black? But you know, I was getting paid to do it, so I had to look at it that way."

Joy, also African American, witnessed not only the racial politics of night-life reporting but also the politics of gender and other elements of physical appearance:

> When you're doing club reporting, you're at the club and you're try-ing to get in, [the magazine] is not going to send someone that they don't think can actually mesh and meld into the club, especially when you have relationships with the owners and they're calling the next day saying, "Okay, who was the ugly girl sitting in the corner stalking Paris Hilton the entire night? It was obvious it was your reporter. Don't do that again." Or sometimes we would hear, "Was that you guys? Does anybody else know an overweight chick?" That [overweight] person wouldn't be let go, they would just be reworked into another situation; some people just wouldn't be brought out for those sorts of things. But there were always reports back from club owners or whoever our PR contact was at the club. It was either, "Your person came late" or "They were drinking too much" or "They didn't look right"—there were always things that came back. You always want to blend in. You want to look like you're actually supposed to be there, so you need to look a certain way. You need to dress a certain way. But if you're the only chick in there that weighs more than one hundred fifty pounds, you're standing out. I don't care who you are, everyone's going to know. There were people respon-sible for helping us get our reporters in at clubs.

As I explore further in chapter 6, the beauty and body standards for women are such that what is classified as overweight by Joy and other celebrity report-ers in Hollywood may not be the same classification others have.

Women who did club reporting regularly were also subject to potentially dangerous situations. While engaged in nightlife reporting myself, on multiple instances when I went on my own because I could not find anyone to accompany me, I was solicited as a prostitute. Jasmine had similar experiences, on top of the anxieties inherent in nightclub reporting assignments:

> People think you're a prostitute because you're in a club by yourself. It's weird for you to be in a club by yourself, so people would ask, "Why are you here by yourself?" Also it's really dark in a club. Sometimes celebrities are deep in the cut somewhere and you may not see them. And if you miss a celebrity, it's a problem. That can be very stressful because you're always on the lookout the whole night, you can't relax for a second because if you miss that person or you miss something they did and a reporter from another magazine was there and they caught it, you can get in a lot of trouble. The magazines compete with each other and they do not want to lose any information to a competitor.

Beyond these problematic gender and racial dynamics in club reporting, ethical lines were also questionable. To get a celebrity scoop during nightlife reporting, no tactic was unreasonable. Joy recounted her feelings about spying on celebrities in the bathroom and attempting to catch them in illegal activity: "I'm not a club person, so being sent out for club watch to me is seedy. The idea of sitting in a corner at Hyde and all these other clubs waiting to see if somebody's doing cocaine in the bathroom, and following somebody into the bathroom, that is seedy to me. But that is what we were supposed to do."

The following is an excerpt from a file submitted by Sarah when she covered nightlife in Hollywood. The file is from October 2005, during the peak of nightlife reporting:

> At about 1:30a.m., Kristen Cavalleri of "Laguna Beach" showed up with friends and joined the [Paris] Hilton booth. While "Hey Mickey" was playing, Hilton sat in the booth with her legs completely straddled as [Stavros] Niarchos [Hilton's then boyfriend] pushed his pelvis into her. And while Niarchos and Hilton spent a majority of the time grinding and making out, during DMX's "Ruff Riders' Anthem," the couple stood atop the booth hugging and caressing each other's arms for the duration of the song. Hilton went right back to dancing when N.E.R.D.'s "Lapdance" came on. During and right after the song, she gave Niarchos a bit of a lap dance, turning around to face him and then grinding on him, as he put his hands up her dress. During one of the last songs of the night,

Kelly Clarkson's "Since You've Been Gone," Hilton went wild, flailing her arms, jumping on the booth, and singing. Right after this song, at about 2:15 am, Hilton, [Kristen] Stewart [Rod Stewart's daughter], and Bijou Phillips took a bathroom trip (turned gossip session) before the club closed.

While this kind of information is still considered invaluable for the manufacturing of celebrity images, it is not printed as frequently anymore. To save money, the magazines cut down nightlife reporting budgets and, more recently, have cut down on freelance reporter budgets generally. Celebrity nightlife is still reported on, but the reporters have been largely cut out of the process. Now public relations representatives for celebrities, alcohol brands, and nightlife venues send blurbs directly to the magazines with information about who attended which club, whom they were with, why they were there, what they were drinking, and what designer(s) they were wearing.

Reporting While Black

In previous chapters I addressed the pervasive "possessive investment in whiteness" and white supremacy across the Hollywood-industrial complex.[17] The systematic exclusion of people of color in the Hollywood studio system coincides with similar practices in the publications that exist to serve that system. One has only to attend a single Hollywood event to see that this is the case. Melissa, a white Los Angeles–based freelancer in her twenties who reports for various entertainment-focused publications, said, "I am assigned to cover BET after-parties every year, and every year I imagine people are wondering, 'Doesn't that outlet have any black reporters?' The answer is no. I have been on red carpets for BET events where there are no black reporters." At various points during my time working for *People* in New York, I was the only person of color reporting out of that bureau and thus was sent to cover the "ethnic" events. Similarly, during my time in Los Angeles I was often called on to cover "ethnic" events when one of the few staff members of color was not available.

In rare instances, *People* has published articles focused on the lack of diversity in Hollywood. In 1996 the magazine published a multipage spread entitled "Hollywood Blackout: The Film Industry Says All the Right Things, but Its Continued Exclusion of African-Americans Is a National Disgrace" (fig. 5.1). Expressing a rare and reflexive voice not found in the magazine today, *People*

Marcia Clark: A new life & a rock'n'roll beau

MARCH 18, 1996

People weekly

Farewell to Minnie Pearl

HOLLYWOOD BLACKOUT

The film industry says all the right things, but its continued exclusion of African-Americans is a national disgrace

The 166 nominees at this month's Oscars include only one black and none of the stars at right

$2.59

ANGELA BASSETT

DENZEL WASHINGTON

LAURENCE FISHBURNE

WHITNEY HOUSTON

offered a critical evaluation of Hollywood and took a long-term and ethno-graphic approach to studying the situation:

> With the academy awards two weeks away, we are taking an intensive look this week at one side of Hollywood rarely exposed to bright lights: racial discrimination. "The exclusion of minorities from the film industry is one of Hollywood's dirty little secrets," says senior writer Pam Lambert, who wrote our cover story. "Despite the stars all of us can name, once you get behind the scenes, blacks remain the invisible men and women." Four months ago a team of PEOPLE correspondents in Los Angeles began interviewing black and white actors, actresses and film-makers about racism in Hollywood. Our first reporting came from national correspondent Lois Armstrong, who in 21 years with PEOPLE had already interviewed such prominent black stars as LeVar Burton, Billy Dee Williams, Danny Glover and Blair Underwood. Then staff corre-spondents Karen Brailsford, Betty Cortina, Johnny Dodd, Lynda Wright and Paula Yoo called 130 sources and gathered more than 60 interviews. . . . "The fact that you can still name the people [blacks in various jobs] illustrates the problem," says John Mack, president of the Urban League's Los Angeles chapter. "The continuing reality is that if you're an African American, it's still a good ol' boys club." Within that fraternity, studio executives, producers and superagents make handshake deals on the beach at Malibu or after backyard barbecues in Bel Air. And if blacks are shut out of the socializing, then they're also cut out of the wheel-ing and dealing that takes place. Such was the case last month at a small dinner party at the Malibu home of record and movie mogul David Gef-fen. The dozen or so guests who shared caviar, roast duckling and small talk with visiting President Bill Clinton—among them co–Dream Works SKG founders Steven Spielberg and Jeffrey Katzenberg—were exclusively white, and exclusively male.[18]

In 2001 "Hollywood Blackout, the Sequel" appeared in the magazine and echoed the sentiments expressed in the 1996 article, with some very minor improvements described in terms of percentages of representation.[19] Perhaps the most significant section from the 1996 article was *People*'s critical evalua-tion of issues of diversity within its own publication:

> Those of us in the print media have an equal responsibility to report accurately on American life and also to reflect it. Twenty-two percent of

PEOPLE's editorial staff of 255 is composed of minorities and 13 percent is African-American, but they represent only 7 percent of our managers. A staff lacking in diversity is at risk of losing vitality and responsiveness to the social mosaic that surrounds it, and stories like this one vividly remind us just how complex that mosaic can be. "We're never profiled unless the issue is race," black filmmaker Reginald Hudlin told correspondent Karen Brailsford. At PEOPLE, we plan to make it our challenge to change that.[20]

It seems that *People* said all the right things in 1996 and 2001, but the celebrity weekly magazines have been slow to make advances in the ensuing years. When Tatsha Robertson was hired by *People* in 2010, she was the only black senior editor in its history. She was fired in 2014 and subsequently filed a lawsuit against the magazine, claiming it fostered a racially discriminatory workplace. She alleged, "Every day, millions of readers pick up a *People* Magazine, open its glossy cover filled with celebrity photographs, and flip through its pages containing sensational human interest stories. Little do these readers know, behind the cover and pages of *People* Magazine, is a discriminatory organization run entirely by White people who intentionally focus the magazine on stories involving White people and White celebrities." Despite *People*'s 2001 assertion that they would develop a diverse staff and their mission to more inclusively report on black people, the lawsuit also points out, "In total since 2010, only 14 out of 265 covers have been focused on African-American individuals."[21] Robertson's lawsuit spoke volumes about the sentiments of racial hierarchy felt by reporters of color.[22] To provide an in-depth perspective on this issue, the extended quote that follows allows Joy to share, in her own words, some of her experiences as one of the few African Americans on her magazine's staff.

> When I got to the magazine, I was the only black girl. Prior to that, there had only been three women who were black in the L.A. office. So there was a void. Also, there weren't any black editors. It was just a known thing. There was no one. And so when I first got there, there were certain events, like the BET Awards and the Soul Train Awards, and it was automatically me who would be assigned to cover those. It seemed exciting because of course I wanted to sit down and do an interview with [rapper] TI, so of course I pitched that idea. So it came from both sides: the magazine was looking to us to have information, and we were look-

ing to them to include black people on the pages. It was something I always felt was super important—to open the magazine and make sure there were brown faces in there.

Then it got to the point where it was all I was doing. At some point I was like, "That sort of sucks." It felt like I could *only* do black stuff. But then, it definitely hit me—no one else knows this shit, so I would rather do that than have someone handle it who doesn't get it at all. I saw it as a beat, just like style and fashion was a beat at the magazine, just like television was a beat, just like anything else, but it was something that I excelled at, that I happen to know about. And I think in those sort of situations, you can either take it as a negative thing like, "Oh, they're trying to keep me down. I only get the black stories," or you can take it as a positive thing like, "I'm the only one who knows this industry, and because I was the only one at the Soul Train Awards from the magazine, I was the only one who saw Chris Brown and Rihanna walk down the carpet so I know what's going on," or "I was the only one who had sources in the black community." And, especially when it came to sources, my role was vital because you're not talking about the same group of producers as white Hollywood. You're not talking about the same casting directors or agents or managers. You're just not. And so everyone else is like, "I can call Brad and Angelina's publicist." Well, it's not the same publicist . . . the players were different. A lot of these African American talents, they had the publicists they started out with, they had the manager they started out with, and then when they got big enough, the mainstream agencies started calling. So that was all fine, but I knew all the players before then, and that was a nice thing. So it was great to be able to say, "Let me call so-and-so's stylist just to see what we can get." Or someone's hair stylist. Well, they're not going to the Ken Paves and the mainstream celebrity stylists; they don't do black hair. You've got to know those people. It became a beneficial thing, and it became a youthful, alternate route that a lot of people just didn't have.

So, like I said, a lot of people could see it as pigeonholing, and some people told me to beware. But I thought of it as getting a leg up on the competition. I don't want to be fighting with the other reporters for the television and young Hollywood beat. There's no need. And I say sometimes at weeklies in particular, there tends to be this focus on what's hot and who's being photographed right now. And we're all doubling up on the same damn people. It's not to say that it's not important, but then what happens when an Eddie and Mel B situation happens? What happens when TI gets arrested and you don't know anybody? Or Whitney and Bobby—the magazines don't know any of those players. And then everyone is scrambling like, "Oh shit!" And it's all because we had six people covering Nicole Richie and Paris Hilton. So I found my focus to be super beneficial and a feather in my cap because I could always pipe up and because I knew what was going on with the black blogs. Everyone else was reading *Pink Is the New Blog* and *Perez Hilton* and TMZ and all that, but I was reading the black blogs like *Concrete Loop, Bossip*, and *The Young, Black, and Fabulous*. These were not even on the magazine's radar. But what happens when Kanye [West] gets up on stage at an award ceremony and does something to Taylor Swift, and everyone's like, "So what's Kanye really doing right now?" Or "Who's Amber Rose?"

I remember distinctly having a conversation when Amber Rose first popped on the scene, and someone was like, "She's not black." I looked at them like, "She's black." And everyone's like, "No. I hear she's Italian and Filipino." I said, "Physical features betray you. She is black. Trust me." I called my girl who is a friend of hers, and she was like, "Oh no, she's Cape Verdean, which is black." So anyone who's from Boston knows Cape Verdean. And it's not like I'm trying to be racist, but you know a Latino walking down the street. Just like there's gay-dar, we know who's what. You can just tell. Somethin' ain't right in the water. I know this woman is not Italian and Filipino. I just felt empowered to speak up in meetings and be that authority because it wasn't there otherwise. And there weren't that many black people at the magazine at all. And yes, I did find it empowering.

I think people recognized that I was black and I was proud of it. And they knew that they came to me for certain things, and they always did it in a respectful way. I had one instance where I felt that a reporter got a story assigned to her that she should not have—I pitched it, it should not have gone to her. And I piped up and said, "Look. Something is not right. This is not making any sense." I felt that there were some things that were said that were a little racially motivated. I said something to one of my bosses and he took me out to lunch and was like, "Let's talk about it. I'm your human resources representative." I told him the situation, and he said, "I don't even see how that's racial." And I said, "It's not for you to see. It's how I feel. You're not black. I'm not a man, so I can't assume what you feel." In some instances, it was hard. You definitely had to bite your tongue, but that's in any workplace.

But you saw other people using their backgrounds to their advantage as well. One of the few Latinas on the red carpet I knew, if Penelope [Cruz] is walking down the carpet or Javier [Bardem] is walking down the carpet, she would yell out something in Spanish, and they see her and they know and you can work it to your advantage. As long as your co-workers don't get out of hand abusing it, and they're like automatically, "You take the Negro story." No. Let me speak up and be the one who wants to take that story. But don't get upset if I somehow don't know the inner workings of Nigerian community. That's not me. I'm not Nigerian. So, you have to watch it. Just because it's out there doesn't mean it's safe. You have to watch how your race is utilized in the news world, and every situation has to be watched. Whatever image you have in the workplace, you have to sort of watch, I think, especially when you do what we do, because it can be used and packed in so many different ways on a daily basis, you really have to watch out for it and make sure you're the only one in control of it. I said it's a gift and a curse. It's a great thing if you use it as that. It works for certain people. At some weeklies, their writers are really sexy and they use that to get close to the paparazzi or whatever the situation is. "You use what you got to get what you want," which is one of my favorite quotes from *The Players Club*. But you have to watch out for it because sometimes it does bite you in the butt.

As I explored in the previous chapter, reporters of color are often funneled into doing "ethnic" events and following celebrities of color. In her story, Joy offers an interpretation of this as a positive, even an empowering aspect of her job. For her, covering black celebrities was a niche she could fill that white reporters were not willing or able to. Her experience in a corporate magazine office highlights the significance of the role of people of color in media. While the celebrity weekly magazines are notoriously devoid of people of color, having someone like Joy ensured a certain level of representation and inclusion in the magazine she worked for, or, at the very least, ensured there was someone advocating for that inclusion inside the corporate space.

Despite her positive spin on racial and ethnic pigeonholing of reportage, Joy's acknowledgment of the limitations placed on very few reporters of color might be best understood as an extension of what Michel-Rolph Trouillot refers to as the "savage slot," the small space carved out for representation of the non-Western other.[23] And as Richard Dyer has pointed out, "'Other' people are raced, white people 'are just people,'" and "there is no more powerful position than that of being 'just human.' The claim to power is the claim to speak for the commonality of humanity. Raced people can't do that—they can only speak for their race."[24] That reporters of color have to fight for space in the industry and for space to cover stories that are not perceived by the magazine as coinciding with the identity of the reporters of color is not surprising since "precarity [is] a historical state of being for marginalized men and women in the entertainment industries."[25]

Ethics in Celebrity Journalism

From the days of Hollywood's earliest reporters, Louella Parsons, Hedda Hopper, and Mike Connolly, ethical codes of celebrity journalism have historically been and remain unclear.[26] Loitering in hotels and outside of celebrity homes, eavesdropping in bathrooms—celebrity reporters are often in compromising and stressful situations that can lead to the revelation of extremely confidential celebrity news.[27] These unclear ethical lines are the livelihood of celebrity reporting, and have been for decades. The reporting under a twenty-four-hour news cycle with exponentially more forms of media is on a level incomparable to the reporting during Hollywood's golden years. Reporters today are not necessarily happy with the lengths to which they must go for their work, but every day is a test of their individual ethics and limits.

Ron found his experience reporting in a hospital educational: "I'm being pressured to do it so I'm going to test myself and see if I like it or hate it. I know I went in predisposed to hate it. See if it totally blows up in my face and the magazine's face to prove, 'Don't ask me to do this crap' and to just know what that experience is like so that I have it. It was absurd for me. It's why I don't do it anymore." Sandra felt similarly about her experiences outside of celebrities' homes: "I certainly detested sitting outside of people's homes because it's just not normal. It's a little creepy to be sitting outside of someone's house, and it always made me really uncomfortable, but starting out at the magazine as an intern, I felt that that was what I had to do. I was paying my dues and I didn't really have an option."

One of the first questions I asked reporters during an interview was, "Do you think there are any clear-cut ethics in celebrity reporting?" The response I received was a nearly unanimous no. When I asked Sandra if she was given any training or presented with any particular ethical codes of the magazines she worked for, she replied, "No. I cannot recall ever having any of those conversations with any of the magazines that I worked for." Sylvia, a freelance and former staff weekly magazine reporter, did not have any issues with this state of affairs: "Even the things that should be bothersome, at the time weren't because I get to say I did it for the magazine. Just sitting in the car outside of Tom Cruise's house waiting for Katie to come out—I had never done a stakeout. We were totally in our legal limits. We weren't doing anything wrong. There was nothing immoral or unethical. I should look back on that and go, 'God! I can't believe I did that,' but I thought it was kind of exciting and fun and I don't feel like I did anything wrong." Joy had a different perspective on ethics at the magazine she worked for: "A lot went unsaid. You just sort of had to figure it out and use your own moral compass for a lot of things. But again, if you didn't have your moral standing or you just didn't give two shits, you could go above and beyond." With a shorter news cycle, fewer (if any) fact-checkers at the magazines, and young and aggressive colleagues, some reporters believed their peers were fabricating material for the sake of a story. Joy said, "Somebody would call and say, 'We need a source to say x. This hole is missing in the story.' And somehow, on a Monday, in one hour, this one reporter somehow had a source that said the exact thing that was needed. Something's not right. And that was happening time and time again. I'm not saying that she was lying every time. I think she definitely has well-placed sources. However, there isn't really a check-and-balance system for sources. There just isn't." This emphasizes the real power that celebrity reporters have to shape the ways in which we understand individual celebrities. They are not simply recounting objective observations of news but are actively (and perhaps overactively) crafting stories that affect our understanding of these public figures.

A veteran reporter who has worked for *People, Us Weekly*, and *Life and Style* told me, "There are certain standards media outlets say they adhere to, but they will completely bend the rules if something too appetizing and potentially profitable comes along. If a bathroom attendant overhears something, should that go to a magazine? To report on those things is tempting. Most of the weekly [magazines] in particular will fall to temptation. They don't think they're going to suffer for it and they know that they will profit. And I think it's a problem." The inverse situation is true as well: magazines will refrain from publishing certain information if they believe they will profit from that restraint. Reporters are conflicted about the way the information they uncover is withheld and manipulated by publications to maintain leverage in celebrity relationships. For example, Richard, a former *OK!* reporter, discussed the coverage of Mary-Kate Olsen's supposed treatment for anorexia: "She was treated at Cirque Lodge, which is known to be a place for substance abuse, where Lindsay [Lohan] was treated. But [the magazines] didn't give you the real name of where she was treated, even though they know, because they want to keep celebrities on their sides. They cover things up—then when it broke the magazines ignored it to play it safe; they are trying to guarantee future story. We don't question ethics when we're covering for celebrities."

For these reasons, I see the ethics of reporting as being equally complex as the ethics of the largely unregulated field of paparazzi work. While celebrity reporters operate more formally and are treated with more respect, they often find themselves in similarly ethically compromising situations. Furthermore, one line of critique lodged against the paparazzi is that they have no formal training and that this should somehow invalidate their ability to produce celebrity media content. Yet reporters often have no training or guidelines before jumping into reporting. All but one reporter I worked with in my research had a college degree, but many had not studied journalism. And they received no training to be a celebrity reporter other than the on-the-job variety. Just like paparazzi learn on their feet how to work a camera, celebrity reporters hone their craft on the job.

Crafting the Media
& the Sociocultural
Consequences

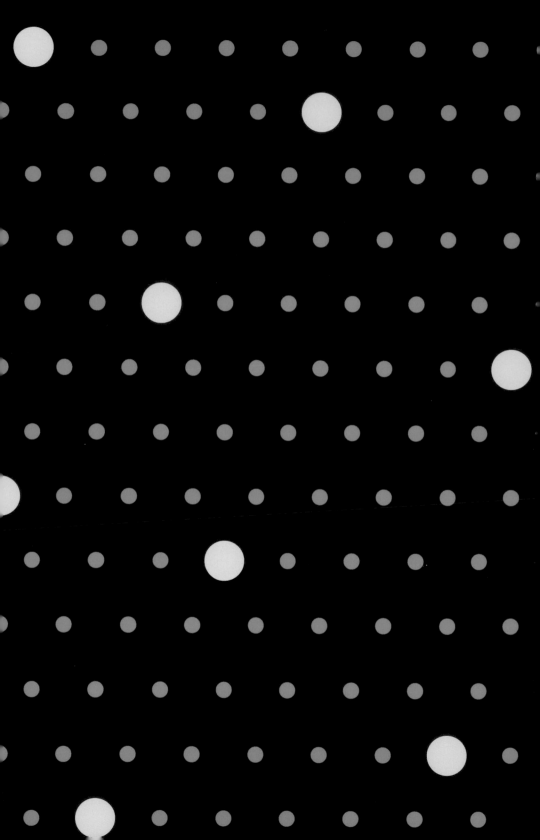

CHAPTER SIX

Body Teams, Baby Bumps, Beauty Standards

For those who can afford it, the body is fully customizable and adaptable, whether through tattoos, piercings, branding, liposuction, or cosmetic surgery. And although identity is considered conterminous with lifestyle, a commodity to be purchased, dominant ideology promotes looking young and beautiful ("californication") as a way of being healthy, successful, and morally right. | **STEVEN VAN WOLPUTTE** | ANTHROPOLOGIST, "HANG ON TO YOUR SELF"

It's a miracle we don't all have eating disorders. Because even if I stopped covering this stuff, the rest of the industry is still doing it. Everyone has a personal responsibility, media producers, celebrities, managers, trainers. | **KENDRA** | *US WEEKLY* PHOTO EDITOR, 2012 INTERVIEW WITH AUTHOR

Women's beauty and appearance have been a focus in celebrity weekly magazines since *People* began in 1974. The early issues, however, left the beauty product promotion to the companies that purchased advertising space. There were, for example, plenty of Oil of Olay ads about how to look younger. Now the publications themselves tell readers what to do to appear younger, get thinner, or look cooler, and the companies that used to pay for advertisements instead work with the celebrities and publications to place their products more discreetly. To understand how celebrity media coverage of women's bodies is produced requires more than just content analysis. In this chapter I combine historical analysis of the media texts themselves with ethnographic data on the processes of production to consider the kinds of discourse and decision-making processes that go into developing magazine coverage of women's bodies. While I draw on the experiences of various reporters, photographers, and editors, my focus is on two key collaborators, Jackie and Kendra. Jackie, a blunt and outgoing woman in her twenties from Los Angeles, was a former *People* reporter and member of the magazine's "body team"—those reporters (and an editor) focused on covering celebrity weight loss and weight gain. She worked in the Los Angeles and New York offices of the magazine at various points in her career. Kendra, a woman in her thirties from New York, is an *Us Weekly* photo editor who had previously worked as a photo editor for other celebrity weekly magazines and also had experience working in television. She initially got into the industry as a women's studies major, interested in media effects on young women's bodies. Jackie's and Kendra's reflections on their work provide context and background for understanding media motivations and ethical quandaries faced by the women selecting photos and developing stories about celebrity women's bodies.

A 1986 issue of *People* featured the cover story "New Year's Resolution: Shape Up! New Machines, New Regimes, Diet Dos and Don'ts from Dozens of Celebs." In subsequent years, similar covers appeared to mark the new year. The January 13, 1992, cover boasted the caption "Who's Winning, Who's Sinning: Diet Wars. You Think You've Got a Weight Battle? Celebs like Oprah Winfrey, Dolly Parton and Jack Nicholson Have Problems That Are Off the Scale. Here's the Latest Skinny on Hollywood's Heavy Hitters."[1]

At the time, Oprah Winfrey was one of the most regularly covered people of color in *People*, much of the coverage focusing on her weight rather than on her relationships or accomplishments. As Kendra points out, celebrity weekly coverage of Winfrey vacillated between "Oprah big, Oprah small." The magazine issues focused on Winfrey's body were "very wrapped up in identity issues. Was she trying to be thin to appeal to a whiter audience, because that's what they wanted to see on TV?" This focus on weight became a regular feature of the early January issue. The January 10, 1994, issue of *People* was a near

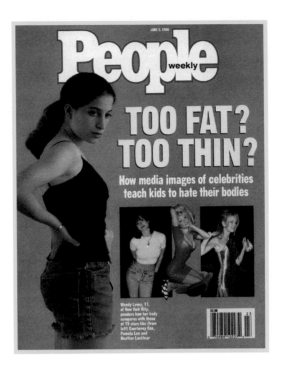

6.1 *People*'s June 3, 1996, cover.

carbon copy of two years prior: "Diet Winners and Sinners of the Year: Here's the Skinny on Who Got Fat, Who Got Fit, and How They Did It."[2] The early January weight-loss issue has shifted over the years and now features non-celebrities in the "Half Their Size" issue, making it even more explicitly about the "average" person. *People* is not alone in their yearly diet coverage. "Everyone does [an issue] around New Year's because of diets and New Year's resolutions. And then there's one right before the summer starts," Kendra said.

While their New Year's issues featured diet secrets from the stars, other issues of the magazine raised concerns about the role of media in shaping perceptions of women's bodies. A September 20, 1993, issue also focused on weight: "Skin and Bones: Supermodel Kate Moss is the ultrathin symbol of the underfed waif look. Is a dangerous message being sent to weight-obsessed teens? (Big girls don't cry: Jeans model Anna Nicole Smith is sexy and successful—at 155 pounds)." Their January 22, 1996, cover, "How the Stars Fight Fat: Celeb Tips on Eating Smart, Feeling Great and Losing 5 Pounds Fast," was a stark contrast to their June 3, 1996, cover: "Too Fat? Too Thin? How Media Images of Celebrities Teach Kids to Hate Their Bodies" (see fig. 6.1).[3] The cover image, as well as the article, makes it clear that their use of the word *kids* references young women specifically. This back and forth between conversations on body size and questions about how those conversations affected readers fed an endless cycle of diet-focused issues that always sold well.

Despite the reference to "media" on the June 3, 1996, cover, that issue does not engage with or even refer to content from *People* itself. It is a regular tactic, even in my own reporting, to use "the media" as a generic "othering" that positions the media producer using the phrase (and their media outlet, by extension) as separate from "the media" to which they refer. Thus it puts the onus on "the media" that does not include, in this case, *People*, despite their regular coverage of the very issue they say teaches "kids to hate their bodies." Still, even if the magazine does not acknowledge its own role in this problem, at least covering the issue shows some critical reflection on the media production process (not unlike their coverage of race issues mentioned in chapter 5). It was coverage like this that led Kendra to pursue a paid internship in the 1990s at a magazine aimed at teen girls while she was working on her senior honors thesis, which focused on "messages the media send to young women": "That's something that still interests me a lot. It's why I really love working at celebrity weeklies more than I liked working in mainstream television because the magazines are really geared towards female readers. And I am the demographic." In fact Kendra and other women at the magazine identify as the magazine's audience. "Very often the editors will call me and say, would you be interested in reading a story about so and so? And that's kind of how we make a judgment. We go around the office and poll the ladies that work here. We are their readers and we have to put ourselves in their shoes."

Because of the circulation and demographics of the celebrity weekly magazine, this medium's potential influence must be taken seriously. Based on their print magazine sales alone (i.e., not including website hits), the celebrity weekly magazines I examine in this book collectively reach well over 100 million consumers each week, with *People* and *Us Weekly* making up roughly 80 percent of that share. Of those consumers, 70 to 84 percent are women, mostly between the ages of eighteen and forty-nine. There are variations in median income across publications, and there are few data readily available on race, but the magazines are clearly reaching a significant proportion of the population.[4] The magazines aim to make readers feel socially connected to celebrities (with whom the magazines deem their readers "obsessed") and to provide "readers with the hacks, hints and honest how-to's so they can look [as] flawless as their favorite Hollywood star."[5] Getting readers to feel connected with and to emulate celebrity is a central mission. The majority of the weekly magazine reporters are also women. Thus the focus on women's bodies becomes a factor that affects not only the consumer but also the producer in complex ways. Jackie pointed out that there were no men on the body team, which she thought was a good thing. "The insight is really about the women. The women are the ones being profiled. The women are the ones reading."

The focus on weight loss and weight gain was evident from early in *People* magazine's history and set a precedent for the magazines that emerged as competitors. The trend has continued through today for all of the celebrity weekly magazines and their websites. *People*'s focus on the body culminated in the formation of the "body team" at the magazine in 2006. While *People* is the only celebrity weekly magazine that openly discusses the fact that they have a body team, each of the celebrity weekly magazines has similar teams and pays close attention to celebrity bodies, as evidenced by their coverage.[6] *Star*, for example, has an editor who specializes in diet, even if they do not have a diet team. This increased specialization on the body has, of course, affected the market for photos as the need for body-focused images is more explicit than ever. The paparazzo Luiz Pimentel said that the photos of women celebrities in swimsuits and showing obvious pregnancy progress are among his "most valuable photos." With the exception of major weight-loss cover shoots for magazines like *Us Weekly* and *People*, most photos of celebrities in bathing suits or other revealing images are paparazzi shots. In my first interview with Kendra, we sat in the *Us Weekly* office where she selected the photos that would appear in the opening pages of the magazine, including the "Stars: They're Just Like Us!" section. We sat surrounded by printouts of almost exclusively paparazzi images, which were also displayed on wall monitors. Jackie explained that, prior to body team meetings, team members had to scour paparazzi images and come prepared with commentary on celebrity bodies:

> In body watch it's like, "Oh my God, did you see those pictures of so and so?" And we'd all bring pictures. You've already done your photo research. You've already chose through the freelancer files. You bring those pictures, and you're like, "Something about her face looks fuller now. Didn't she reportedly have an eating disorder back in the day? Maybe she was back on it?" Or "Oh my gosh, her cankles are ridiculous." That sort of thing. And a lot of us felt bad about that situation, simply because we're a roomful of women deciding on how other women will feel about these women. It was a very disgusting thing. But at the same point, we were really one of the highest grossing groups, in terms of dollar signs, in

terms of sales on newsstands. Body covers sell more than any other cover of the magazine unless it's Princess Diana or Brangelina. We sell. So we are also actively looking for the paparazzi photos to fulfill this need. But we needed a body-focused team because the numbers were there, time and time again. We gauged the need because we saw how well issues were selling. We saw how much pickup we were getting from other outlets. The PR was really a great litmus test. Seeing how many requests we were getting for those images. Seeing how many requests we were getting for the cover or for me to be on TV. That was very popular. And we also read readers' letters. *People* magazine's letters team would send us letters. The reader letters had a big impact on the content. Middle America women wanted to know how everybody lost weight. And because they were watching *Biggest Loser*, they were watching all these shows about how really hard it was to do this, they knew wheatgrass shots and jogging with my friends in Runyon Canyon ain't gonna do it. They wanted to see people being truthful, but also they were seeing these issues in *National Enquirer* and everywhere else, and you couldn't just say, "That's a doctored photo," because it wasn't. And some celebrities were starting to become, as far as the public discourse, really open about it.

Complementing Jackie's perspective, Kendra confirmed that not only were body issues at *Us Weekly* strong sellers, but body-focused paparazzi shots were specifically a selling point:

These are paparazzi images. These are not shoots. These are not someone being retouched within an inch of life. This is what they actually look like. I can enlarge and blow it up and see every grain and morsel on them. That has a certain power. It's real. I think a lot of people can look at other magazines and say, "That's not really what they look like. They've been retouched." When you have a page like that [points to a photo of Angelina Jolie], no, they actually look like that — and they're even thinner if you see them in person. They are tiny, so tiny.

Kendra's experience of the discourse around the body at *Us Weekly* also coincided with Jackie's at *People*:

If I'm sitting there with another photo editor and an art person, we'll be like, "We saw so-and-so. That's not a flattering dress on her. Can you believe those cankles?" We say things that you would say if you saw a picture on Facebook of your friends somewhere. It's the same sort of reaction. When I see pictures of celebrities, I feel emotionally the same way I do when I see pictures of my friends, which is really weird, because it's just my job. It's my reality. When you look at these people as much as we do, we notice everything about them. We're covering all aspects of their life. And we all talk about and we'll say, "Oh, she was really thin, and when she was in a relationship she was this way, and she's not anymore." You sort of get to know people. Some [celebrities] just look amazing all the time. We don't go around tearing people down. It would make me feel uncomfortable as a women's studies major and a woman myself to say, "Oh she's so fat," because they're not. They're beautiful, famous, and successful people.

Kendra might not print commentary on women's bodies that she finds offensive, but those bodies are still discussed in production spaces. It's clear that reporters and editors have moral quandaries about the work they are doing but accept it as part of their job. Kendra said that her experience at *Us Weekly* was not different from her earlier experiences at other celebrity weeklies in terms of what body components were focused on. "They look at their boobs, they look at their butt, they look to see if their thighs are nice and their stomach is flat. How's your hair? Skin, nails. It's the whole package. Always the whole package."

The focus on body also affects the way reporters assess celebrities on red carpets. As a reporter, I noticed that, following the formation of the body team, editors increasingly expected that we would keep an eye on certain celebrities for weight gain or loss and report this back to the magazine. It also affected the discourse among reporters at celebrity events. At one event after a young singer approached the red carpet for interviews, Lena, a freelancer for a celebrity weekly, told me, "I feel bad for her, she is just not pretty. Her hair and her nose, it's just not cute." At a January 5, 2011, event for Cover Girl, a weekly magazine reporter named Ariel commented that the actress Jennifer Lowndes should not have been wearing a tight leather dress: "I can't believe I'm saying this, I know she has an amazing body, but only certain people can wear that, and I can't believe she wore that." This critical assessment of women's bodies by other women is part of what celebrity reporters do: view, assess, and judge celebrity bodies, particularly women celebrities.

While body teams are generally made up of full-time staff members, the predominantly freelance red carpet reporters bring back answers to the questions crafted by the body team.[7] "We are all responsible members of this bigger project, even if we aren't on the 'team,' all of us are supposed to have eyes peeled, etc.," said Christy, a former *People* intern and freelance reporter. "Many of the questions we have to ask are body and diet questions that are designated specifically for women. The magazine would instruct us to 'ask young, style-watchy celebs about what their go-to diet is around award season, what their fitness routine is'—this is a constant. We are always to be on the lookout for people post-baby, for big weight loss. Even the events themselves are set up around looking at the women's bodies in revealing outfits. The men wear suits that cover them up, while the women have to pose to the front, side, and back, so that we can see their boobs, their butt, their waist." Jackie confirmed that much of the material that leads to body-focused stories begins on the red carpet:

> At red carpet events, certainly looking at women's stomachs, searching for a baby bump, or searching for any bump even if it was just that her dress was too tight, these were important things to keep an eye on. And we would get a lot of these tips from the carpet. Someone would see someone looking a little different, thinner, thicker, and this information would trickle down and turn into a story. And there was real crafting as to how to talk about or how to ask a celebrity about looking thicker. Like, "How do you stay in love with your body?" or "What do you love about your body?" Different ways to get celebrities to say, "Yes, I've gained some weight" or "Yes I've been going to yoga." Celebrities used to be open on the carpet about details about their lives too. Like they would say, "Yes, I'm going to this specific yoga studio five times week." But then five paparazzi would be standing outside of that studio. So now the celebrities don't say where they're going or where they work out. And if you notice in the publications, the captions always say, "Nicole Richie working out." But it never says where because now the paparazzi don't want other people to know where they are getting those shots because they are valuable. And those paparazzi are doing a lot of that reporting too. They are some of the best reporters. And there has also been a change to the crafting or changes in how celebrities are prepped by their managers and press agents, PR people. Because they tell them how to say things, what not to say, et cetera.

Jackie was among the few celebrity reporters in all of my research to acknowledge the reporting contributions of the paparazzi and the magazines' reliance on paparazzi images and reporting.

While the body teams solidified and validated a specific place within the magazines for this kind of gendered judgment of bodies, the work of watching bodies was required of everyone affiliated with the magazines. "Ridiculing other women's bodies was the hardest part of my job, and I was definitely not the only one who felt this way," Jackie said. "There were times when we would leave body watch meetings and say 'I cannot believe we are talking about this.' Or I would talk to other team members, or someone would sit in on a meeting for body watch and be so surprised as to what we talked about and how we had to talk about people." This critical assessment of women's bodies leads to media content that critiques women's bodies, which leads to social circulation of media discourse focused on the ridicule of women's bodies.[8] Yet while reporters like Jackie and editors like Kendra had their reservations about the weeklies' focus on the body, they also saw value in it and felt good about some of the coverage that resulted. Kendra said that their focus on the body would "sometimes shock" the team:

> We had a picture once of Helen Mirren in a bathing suit and we almost fell off our chairs. She looked amazing, so we ran that picture in Hot Pics. Besides Body After Baby, we've also done things on diets or people that are vegetarians and have retained muscle mass while training. Stuff like that is useful and is of service to the reader. People look up to celebrities. And these people are living healthy lifestyles and really making an effort to keep themselves fit. Some people quit doing drugs because Demi Lovato got clean. People do a lot of things because they're inspired by celebrities. So I think that, if drinking green juice is one of them, it's not a bad thing.

Jackie similarly said that the reporters at times felt fulfilled by the kind of work they did:

> When we first kicked body watch off, no other magazines were doing body coverage. The *National Enquirer* and *Star* would do, "Guess whose cellulite this is." But not in the same way, where you're talking about how all these celebrities lost weight on Jenny Craig, or, oh my gosh, you didn't know so-and-so had an eating disorder and now she's like that. There were stories that made us feel really good. Tyra Banks, Jennifer Hudson, Valerie Bertinelli. There were a lot of stories that made up for the "so-and-so lost fifty pounds," "so-and-so gained fifteen pounds."

Bikini Bodies

A May 29, 2009, *New York Times* article made public the fact that *People* magazine has a "body editor," which is essentially an editor dedicated to monitoring celebrity bodies. The body editor heads up the body team. While drastic male weight gain or loss may get mentioned in celebrity weekly magazines, the focus is mostly on women. *People* magazine's then managing editor Larry Hackett explained, "'[The body editor is] the one who alerted me that Valerie Bertinelli was offering to pose for us in a bikini.' Mr. Hackett wasn't sure a teenage star from a 1970s sitcom would sell, until he saw the photos. 'She looked fantastic.'"[9] While there were no men on the body team, Jackie made clear that "the highest up editors like Larry Hackett were very much weighing in on the big stuff." The April 6, 2009, Bertinelli cover with the title "Valerie Bertinelli Lost 50 Lbs. Bikini Body at 48!" was the second-best-selling *People* cover that year. An excerpt from the article portrays a self-conscious Bertinelli:

> Bertinelli tried to summon up a pep talk, telling herself, "What am I so afraid of? Come on — it's just a bathing suit!" And yet as any woman knows, those innocent-looking strips of Lycra can be a terrifying sight — especially for someone just shy of her 49th birthday (April 23), who only two years ago tipped the scales at 172 lbs. — more than 40 lbs. over her goal weight for her 5'4" frame. But after whittling herself down to 132 lbs. in about 9 months on Jenny Craig (for whom she serves as a company spokeswoman), Bertinelli, who had last worn a bikini when she was 20, was ready for a new challenge.
>
> During what she calls the bikini "homestretch" — the last three weeks — she trimmed her daily caloric intake from 1,700 to around 1,200, and gave up her regular "splurge" glass of champagne. "It was crunch time," she says, "like getting ready for your class reunion!" The result? Bertinelli dropped another 9 lbs. to get down to 123. (She says she hopes to "settle in" at 125, and that she has drawn a "stake in the ground" at 132 lbs., meaning she hopes to never let herself get above that number again.)[10]

Following up on the 2009 cover story, in 2012 a People.com article proclaimed, "Three years after she first donned the itsy-bitsy green bikini on a cover of PEOPLE, Valerie Bertinelli is ready to break it out again. 'The green bikini is in my drawer just waiting for me to put it back on,' the *Hot in Cleve-*

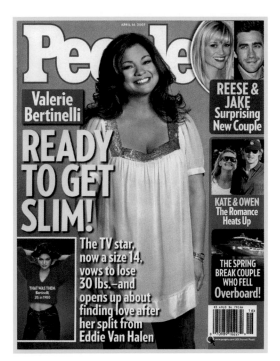

6.2 April 16, 2007, *People* cover with Valerie Bertinelli. The headline "Ready to Get Slim!" primes readers for her weight loss to come.

land star, 52, said at Thursday's American Heart Association's Wall Street Run & Heart Walk in New York. 'When these 5 lbs. come off, then I will put that back on.'"[11]

Strategically, however, an April 2007 *People* cover told readers Bertinelli was "ready to get slim," and the cover story showed a photo of the actress with the quote "I know what you're thinking—I'm fat" next to it (fig. 6.2). This created the beginning of a dialogue about her weight that would guarantee follow-up stories. The article opens by describing how her house is filled with Jenny Craig goods, priming the audience for her weight loss. "'Every single piece of food in the house is Jenny Craig,' laments the high school sopho-more and guitarist [Bertinelli's sixteen-year-old son, Wolfie], surveying the airy kitchen in the family's Studio City, Calif., home, which is now brimming with prepackaged food from the weight loss program."[12] During the course of my research, several reporters across the weekly magazines openly discussed the fact that celebrities use weight loss as a way to gain endorsements and pro-motion through magazine covers. The endless cycle of weight gain and loss has proven lucrative for the celebrity weekly magazines both through issue sales and corporate relationships. Jackie shared, "We had great relationships with the diet companies. Weight Watchers, Jenny Craig. Whoever their new person was, they were going to break it with us. . . . Every diet company wanted us."

The April 2007 article explained that Bertinelli planned to lose thirty pounds and drop from a size 14 to a size 8 within six months: "Going public with her goal 'is the motivation I need,' she says. 'I need to do this in front of millions of people so I can't mess up. It is freeing because I can say it first: I know what you're thinking—I'm fat.'" Thus the article at once promotes Jenny Craig, announces a drastic weight-loss plan, and actively uses public scrutiny as motivation. "'I was a Hollywood hermit.' Also, she adds, 'I didn't like going up for interviews because I didn't want to hear how fat I am,'" the article continues, underscoring that her only reason for stepping back into the spotlight is because she is going to lose weight. Her story encourages women to hide when they gain weight and step out in a bikini when they lose weight.[13] *People's* coverage of the weight-loss plan, as well as the eventual bikini-body reveal, validates Bertinelli's approach. Hollywood industries more broadly also responded positively: the 2009 bikini cover story truly did relaunch her dormant career. She dropped the weight just as she was cast in the sitcom *Hot in Cleveland* and a few years later she joined the Food Network, starting as a guest judge for various shows and then becoming the host of *Valerie's Home Cooking*.

The actress Kirstie Alley was the focus of similarly cyclical coverage in *People* just a few years earlier, beginning with an August 2004 story in which she proclaimed that she was fat and happy, followed by a December 2004 story in which she declared that she would lose weight using the Jenny Craig program, followed by a series of other covers and articles chronicling her subsequent weight loss.[14] By September 2005 Alley was "slimmer and wiser" (see figs. 6.3–6.7).[15]

Jackie described the invasive and abrasive nature of the body team's reporting:

> [I was] responsible for keeping in touch with and negotiating with all the major trainers out here, figuring out all of the diet trends, but also paying attention to the pictures every single day. Who looked bigger? Who didn't? And our conversations in meetings were very raw. "She has cankles. She has back fat. What the hell is up with her stomach?" Those were the conversations, and you had to get adjusted to that. I think that really started and kicked off in a major way bringing a lot of money in

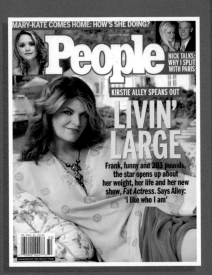

MARY-KATE COMES HOME: HOW'S SHE DOING?

People

NICK TALKS: WHY I SPLIT WITH PARIS

KIRSTIE ALLEY SPEAKS OUT

LIVIN' LARGE

Frank, funny and 203 pounds, the star opens up about her weight, her life and her new show, *Fat Actress*. Says Alley: 'I like who I am'

People

KIRSTIE ALLEY

'I HAD FUN GETTING FAT. NOW IT'S TIME TO LOSE THE WEIGHT'

The star of *Fat Actress* talks about her wild new show and her big decision to start a diet

OPRAH How Her Giveaways Work

GEORGE CLOONEY His Life, His Love & *Ocean's Twelve*

PRINCE WILLIAM Talks About His Future

6.3–6.7
Covers of *People* magazine focused on Kirstie Alley's weight.

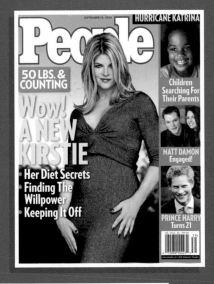

HURRICANE KATRINA

People

50 LBS. & COUNTING

Wow! A NEW KIRSTIE

- Her Diet Secrets
- Finding The Willpower
- Keeping It Off

Children Searching For Their Parents

MATT DAMON Engaged!

PRINCE HARRY Turns 21

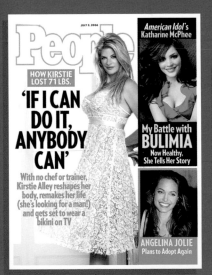

JULY 5, 2004

People

HOW KIRSTIE LOST 71 LBS.

'IF I CAN DO IT, ANYBODY CAN'

With no chef or trainer, Kirstie Alley reshapes her body, remakes her life (she's looking for a man!) and gets set to wear a bikini on TV

American Idol's Katharine McPhee

My Battle with BULIMIA Now Healthy. She Tells Her Story

ANGELINA JOLIE Plans to Adopt Again

ELIZABETH EDWARDS MY CHEATING HUSBAND

People

KIRSTIE ALLEY WEIGHT SAGA

YES, I GAINED 83 LBS!

SEXY & SLIM IN 2005

All about the 'blame, shame and regret' and her vow to get back into even better shape

FARRAH'S FINAL FIGHT LOVED ONES SPEAK

with Kirstie Alley. And then you had Valerie Bertinelli. But because *they* gave such raw quotes, you were going after that every time. You couldn't just have someone say, "I work out three time a week. I watch what I eat." Hell no. That wasn't enough. There was such a big push. Like if someone says, "You know, cardio is what makes me so thin." No it doesn't, Tara Reid, you're skinny because of cocaine. So let's address that. My interview with one actress was unbelievable because it was when she had all the cellulite on the back of her thighs and she swore that she didn't really look like that. So we did a shoot out on the beach here. I had her turn around. We interviewed and I said, "What do you eat? What do you do?" That's a very different interview style than some of our other reporters who say to talk to celebrities like they are your friends. I only had so much time. You had to get in there and ask the really tough questions. "Do you have an eating disorder? What is it? What's the issue? How many times do you work out? Do you feel fat? You talk about doing some post-baby workouts, but really, how many calories were you consuming? What was the trick?" That kind of stuff. And pushing. The interview style changed because you automatically assumed everybody was lying. Because they were so good at it already. So in the teams, because you had these big stories on Kirstie Alley, Valerie Bertinelli, and Jennifer Hudson, it's like the ante got upped, and you saw the ante getting upped in the TV realm. Finding the pictures was also a big challenge. Your before picture had to be the saddest possible picture. It had to be the most and the least appealing photos.

Just a few months after the April 2007 Bertinelli cover, both Alley and Bertinelli appeared on the cover of *People* for a "tell-all" about keeping off the weight.[16] A few years later yet another follow-up was published in which it was revealed that Bertinelli had gained back some of the weight and was ready to lose it again and to put the bikini back on.[17] Similarly Alley's weight continued to garner her press coverage for years beyond her initial 2004 cover. In 2009 Alley declared, "I've let myself go," after gaining back more weight than she had lost on Jenny Craig.[18] Former *People* editor Hackett "found multigenerational, multicover appeal to roller-coaster weight sagas like Ms. Alley's. 'It's like Kirstie's out there again,' he said. 'She's like family—we have traveled this road with Kirstie.'"[19] The emotional investments in celebrities' personal lives, which Hackett admits are deliberately facilitated by the magazine, are foundational to the imaginary social relationships with media figures that I previously explored.[20] The body team was constructed to exploit this particular facet of the emotional investment, and the reporters create the content to ensure that these strategies are successful. As Jackie explained, "Our coverage wasn't just, 'Oh, we have a girl in a tight top and jeans.' We had a bikini on Kirstie Alley. We had a bikini on Valerie Bertinelli, who everyone loved. It pulled in all the best things that people loved about *People* magazine—the nostalgia, the fact that these actors had been in our homes forever. That's what it was drawing on."

In April 2014 the weight gain-and-loss cycle came back full circle when Alley announced that she would once again be a Jenny Craig spokesperson and, once again, received coverage in *People*.[21] That same month Bertinelli was covered on People.com and said, regarding her minor weight gain, "We all need to give each other a break—especially women. . . . Let's leave each other alone."[22] Bertinelli's sentiment is certainly appreciated—there is no question that there is too much pressure for women at every age to conform to certain physical expectations. However, if she wants everyone to be given a break, then taking responsibility for the false hope and unreasonable expectation of getting down to 123 pounds and posing in a bikini at age forty-nine might be a good place to start. The celebrity back-and-forth between being superhuman and "just like us" rears its head in these situations in which celebrities do not acknowledge that they are being paid to consume and promote diet food and that they have the money for full-time personal training and an overall healthy lifestyle. Despite these advantages, they want to strategically use weight gain to make themselves seem more relatable and to continue getting paid by diet sponsors like Jenny Craig.

The focus in celebrity weekly magazines on the drastic weight gain and weight loss of celebrities did not begin with Alley or Bertinelli. For example, the September 29, 1997, issue of *People* had the following headline on the cover: "Who Says Size Counts! So what if they aren't size 6? Healthy, wealthy, and unabashed, they're proudly proving big is beautiful too." Pictured on the cover were Oprah Winfrey, Rosie O'Donnell, Delta Burke, Wynona Judd, and the plus-size model Emme. Inside the magazine other "big" celebrities were featured as well, including the Wilson Phillips singer Carnie Wilson, who declared her happiness with her size. Yet just a few years later, on January 15, 2001, *People* published an issue with the cover headline "Half Her Size! Seventeen months after stomach-reducing surgery, singer Carnie Wilson has dropped 150 lbs. and 20 dress sizes. 'I can't believe it's me in that tiny body!'" (see fig. 6.8). The popularity of this issue prompted the reoccurring "Half Their Size"

6.8 *People* magazine cover of January 15, 2001, featuring Carnie Wilson.

issue, which now includes non-celebrities on the cover along with their triumphant diet stories. *Us Weekly* took inspiration from *People* and has published similar covers, such as their May 2007 cover featuring Ricki Lake with the headline "Half My Size! From Size 24 to 4 without Surgery!" (see fig. 6.9). Kendra noted that the Wilson cover was the beginning of the "iconic" cover trend in which those who lose weight pose swimming inside of their now far-too-large pants.

The symbiotic role of the media producers and celebrities is critical to the creation of these stories. While Alley may have been ridiculed for being overweight, she was hardly in the spotlight when she did the first *People* cover about her size. She had not been acting regularly, and consumers may not have had any interest in her had she not been ready and willing to begin a conversation about her weight, which then led to future opportunities for sponsorship (by Jenny Craig) and promotion (by magazines like *People*). At the 2011 Cover Girl event I discussed earlier, the actress and singer Raven-Symoné arrived looking noticeably thinner than usual. Despite the fact that she had been "combatting body critics" and claimed she was happy with her "thick and fabulous" body, she advertised her capitulation to societal pressure by assert-

6.9 *Us Weekly* cover of Ricki Lake. May 21, 2007.

ing, "I thought I looked fabulous before and nobody else did."[23] Similarly Tyra Banks was featured in a strapless bathing suit on the January 24, 2007, cover of *People* sarcastically asking, "You Call This Fat?" The cover stated her weight as 161 pounds (see fig. 6.10). Here is an excerpt from the article:

> On her hit show *America's Next Top Model*, Tyra Banks has always stressed the importance of body confidence—but it still hurt when tabloids ran an unflattering photo of her in a bathing suit under headlines that screamed, "America's Next Top Waddle" and "Tyra Porkchop." Now, for the first time in an exclusive interview with PEOPLE, Banks, 33, is publicly discussing her much-buzzed-about weight gain. "I get so much mail from young girls who say, 'I look up to you, you're not as skinny as everyone else, I think you're beautiful,'" she says. "So when they say that my body is 'ugly' and 'disgusting,' what does that make those girls feel like?"[24]

After having asserted in this 2007 article that she was happy with her body, on September 21, 2009, *People* featured an article covering Banks's thirty-pound weight loss. "But Banks took pains to reassure fans in an Aug. 9 Twitter post-

6.10 *People* magazine cover of Tyra Banks. February 5, 2007.

ing, 'My butt is still juicy and round'—albeit small enough to fit into a sample size 2 Rachel Roy dress at the Aug. 30 Daytime Emmy Awards."[25] There is an uncomfortable and confusing discursive conversation between media and celebrities about expectations of women's bodies that, as *People* pointed out back in the 1990s, has real effects on those who consume this media.

While Banks was portrayed as looking great at 161 pounds, the former teen actress Melissa Joan Hart was featured on a June 8, 2009, *People* cover in a bikini and weighing 113 pounds: "How I Lost 42 Lbs! A 'horrifying' photo (above) led the *Sabrina* star, 33, to take control. 'I realized I don't have to be heavy just because I have kids'" (see fig. 6.11). Next to the shot of the bikini-clad actress is the "horrifying" "before" photo and a note that she weighed 151 pounds at the time. None of these articles explains what a healthy weight is, based on height and body type.

Kendra illuminated the fact that the fickle magazine narratives presenting celebrities as too fat and then too thin remain cornerstones for celebrity week-lies. During an interview in 2012 she said, "I think we did a Hot Hollywood beat a couple of months ago with photos of Lindsay Lohan and Nicole Richie on the beach with the words 'scary skinny.' We may have even had a cover on

6.11 Weight loss–focused cover of *People* featuring Melissa Joan Hart. June 8, 2009.

'Are They Too Thin?' Or 'Has Hollywood Gone Too Far?' One of those kinds of covers." She references "those kinds of covers" because they are a recurring trope. For example, *Us Weekly*'s May 30, 2005, cover features Richie and Lohan with the headline "Extreme Diets: How Lindsay & Nicole Got Skinny—but Have They Gone Too Far?" Similarly, *OK!*'s September 5, 2011, cover showcased Gwyneth Paltrow, Angelina Jolie, and LeAnn Rimes under the headline "Hollywood's Most Extreme Diets" (see fig. 6.12). A 2010 UsWeekly.com special, "Scary Skinny Bikini Bods," featured paparazzi photos of Kelly Ripa, Lindsay Lohan, and many others at the beach.[26] *Life and Style*'s cover was headlined "Obsessed with Being Skinny" on October 10, 2011, and "Desperate to Be Skinny" on both August 8 and December 12, 2011 (see figs. 6.13 and 6.14).

Kendra pointed to *Us Weekly* coverage of Janet Jackson that sent a different message: "Remember when Janet Jackson was heavy and she was in that Paddington Bear–looking hat and coat, and everyone was like, 'Oh my God, she's heavy again!' And we ran photos of that. Then she lost weight and then she was on our [June 5, 2006] cover. We inset that photo of her in the hat, put it next to her showing off her weight loss, and it's a source of accomplishment.' The 2006 cover story featured the headline, "How I Got Thin: 60 Pounds in

6.12 *OK!* magazine's "Hollywood's Most Extreme Diets." September 5, 2011.

4 Months!" (see fig. 6.15). In 2017 *Us Weekly*'s website featured coverage of Jackson's seventy-pound post-baby weight loss at the age of fifty-one.[27]

This editorial vacillation has existed and thrived across the weekly magazines and over time. The October 18, 1999, issue of *People* featured the cover headline "How Thin Is Too Thin? Hollywood rewards a new and shockingly skinny shape, but health experts warn that the trend has gone too far." But the next year the magazine featured a number of sensational cover headlines about body image: June 12, 2000: "Diet Wars! Low Carb? No Fat? What's Dangerous? What's Not? Celebs Take Sides in the Food Fight"; September 4, 2000: "Special Report: Searching for the Perfect Body: How do women really feel about their shapes? And whose bodies do they admire most and least? A surprising PEOPLE poll"; October 30, 2000: "Special Report: Dying to Be Thin"; October 21, 2002: "Sexy at Any Size: Can we get real? Fed up with the pressure to look perfect, celebs get more confident living large, lean or in-between." This diet- and body-focused coverage is a prime example of the manufacturing of celebrity carried out by weekly magazine staff while relying on the paparazzi's photographic evidence. The moments of (real or perceived) weight

6.13–6.14 Covers of *Life and Style* critique celebrities' bodies as too thin. Both covers also emphasize the concern of . . .

. . . the male partners: Tom (Cruise) is "worried" and Brad (Pitt) "begs . . . Angelina to stop starving herself."

6.15 *Us Weekly* cover of June 5, 2006, featuring Janet Jackson.

loss and weight gain are used to make celebrities relatable to others who might struggle with weight and to promote sales; the expanded focus on body coverage came from repeated high sales of magazines with body-focused covers. But this coverage continues to put the women reporters in the position of ridiculing women celebrities' bodies for predominantly women readers.

Pregnancy: Body after Baby

Back in the day you would wait until [new celebrity mothers] got to where they wanted to be, and then you would approach them for a [body] story. Now you approach her as she is on a gurney [going] into the delivery room or you're approaching before. If you can't get the baby pictures, then you should get the body after baby. . . . [It's] the home run if you can get [both]. | JACKIE | FORMER MEMBER OF *PEOPLE*'S BODY TEAM

We're all motivated in this capitalist society to make money. And really at the end of the day, the magazines are motivated for eyeballs and viewership because that's what pays the bills. I think if you would get viewership on baby bump or a little bit of chunk, you'd probably run it because that's paying your bills and paying to keep the magazine alive or keeping the website going, and paying the paparazzi, so let's not pretend that that's not the real motivation. That is the motivation. | **ADRIAN GRENIER** | ACTOR, AT THE GETTY CENTER EVENT "ARE WE ALL PAPARAZZI NOW?," MAY 12, 2012

When I asked Kendra what "newsworthy" meant in the context of her job, she told me, "If a celebrity's body looks fantastic and she just had a baby two weeks ago, that would be newsworthy to *Us Weekly*." Thus it is no surprise that one of the most popular angles for stories focused on celebrities' bodies is the "body after baby" story. An example is an *Us Weekly* cover featuring Trista Sutter, the original *Bachelorette*, in a bikini holding her baby, with the headline, "How I Got My Body Back." This headline, similar to many of those featured on other celebrity weekly magazine covers, suggests that women should aspire to return their body to the way it was before pregnancy. This is not possible for many women, but celebrities have the money to lose the weight and are likely to get large endorsements from diet companies for doing so. Celebrities can also earn money by mentioning trainers' names in the publications. The body-after-baby stories are ultimately centered around marketing products and weight-loss plans.

"The relationship between celebrities and the news media is never more symbiotic than during the arrival of a new baby." As this *New York Times* article points out, "Magazines get a boost to their newsstand sales, reality TV shows get a new plotline and the expectant parents often get lucrative paydays."[28] While celebrities can get six-figure cover deals for the first photos of their baby, that part of the celebrity pregnancy deal is all celebratory. After the first baby shots, celebrity mothers often milk their pregnancy for additional coverage while simultaneously contributing to the unrealistic expectations for women's bodies.

The first body-after-baby story in *People* was published on February 10, 2003, and featured profiles on several celebrities, including Uma Thurman, Sarah Jessica Parker, Brandy, Holly Robinson Peete, Cindy Crawford, Anne Heche, Julianne Moore, Elizabeth Hurley, and Cynthia Nixon. The article included details about their diet and exercise regimes. "For Hollywood's new moms, snapping back into red carpet shape is a business imperative — one that doesn't come cheap. Hurley dropped 53 lbs. with the help of a nutritionist and private Pilates instructor; other stars turn to custom weight-training workouts or yoga. And a pro to do the cooking can't hurt (anything to keep Uma Thurman away from M&Ms). Read on for the weight-loss secrets of nine red-hot mamas."[29] That the regimes outlined in the article are out of reach for the average reader is obvious. Letters from readers in response to this first article express a combination of praise and frustration with the coverage. It is clear, however, that, whether positive or negative, the body story generated interest. Tara Kearney from Washington wrote, "I'm six months pregnant, and after reading your cover story I don't know whether to be inspired or depressed by how quickly the celebrity moms profiled got their bodies back. Could you ask them to loan me their personal trainer? I'll need to be in shape to impress the other moms at the play group." Trish Jordan from Hawaii said, "Your staff has sunk to a new low with your cover about celebrities who quickly regained their figures after giving birth. As if new mothers today don't suffer enough societal pressures to be übermoms, now you venerate those of us who managed to fit back into our pre-pregnancy clothes in record time. It's not a contest!"[30] The pressure Jordan speaks of is felt not only by the readers but by those who work on staff at the magazine as well.

Amber, a longtime staff reporter for a celebrity weekly magazine, lamented the position she was often put in by hounding post-pregnancy women for body covers. After a pop star gave birth, Amber was tasked with calling her rep to ask if she would be willing to do a special spread on her post-baby body. "A senior male editor saw a photo of her just a few days after she gave birth. And he asked, 'Did you see her? Oh my gosh we have to do a body after baby.' I knew it was too soon. I'm a mother. The editor was not considering that it takes three weeks for the uterus to go back to its normal size. But this is what the magazine wanted. When I talked to the rep, I apologized, but said I had to ask." When Amber asked editors if they could wait to do the post-baby stories until a year after the baby was born, they would say, "That's too late." The desire of the magazines to show these women's bodies rebounding within just a few weeks after giving birth fuels the culture of unrealistic expectations.

The emphasis on "body after baby" developed quickly. In just one issue in 2005, *People* featured multiple articles on the topic. The November 7, 2005, issue featured Denise Richards, Britney Spears, Victoria Beckham, and several others.[31] The articles embody the synergy identified by Jackie in her description of the body team practices, which included cooperation between celebrities, magazines, trainers, and diet companies. One of the November 7 articles is entitled "Losing It Fast: They're Breaking Speed Records, but Celeb Moms Like Denise Richards Know That Getting Back in Shape after Baby—Whether

6.16 The November 28, 2005, issue of *People* featuring yet another "body-after-baby" spread, this time on Heidi Klum.

It's the First or Fourth—Takes Sweat and Sacrifice." The article explains that Richards "threw herself" back into exercising as soon as she got approval from her doctor. "'I'm not going to lie and say, 'The pounds just came off,' she says. 'There's definitely pressure in Hollywood to be thin, but even if I didn't have to work, I would still want to lose the weight.'" She worked with the celebrity trainer Garret Warren four to six times a week and did not have to cook for herself: "Richards has her own portion-controlled meals delivered by nutritionist Carrie Wiatt's Diet Designs."[32]

An issue of *People* later that same month featured yet another body-after-baby spread, this time about the model Heidi Klum. "Heidi's Secret: From the Maternity Ward to Lingerie Model in Two Months? Here's How Heidi Klum Did It" shows a photo of the new mom walking the Victoria's Secret Angels runway show, where "she wore little more than a bra and thong studded with tiny lights and Swarovski crystals" (see fig. 6.16). The article outlines Klum's "few advantages": "Genetics, for one. Another: some time off. A third: the ability to get top New York City trainer David Kirsch, 45, to fly out to her Los Angeles home (he arrived Oct. 13). So, yes, her situation is far, far from that of a typical new mom. Still . . . eight weeks?" Her workouts included "the

David Kirsch jiggle test," Kirsch says. "If it jiggles, it ain't good."[33] The September 1, 2008, issue of *People* featured the article "Jessica Alba Body after Baby: Now She's Pregnant, Now She's Hot! Here's How the Famously Fit Actress Got Red Carpet Ready in Record Time." The title insinuates that pregnant women are unattractive, as Alba was only "hot" after her pregnancy was over and she got "fit" again. This article too emphasizes celebrities' relationships with trainers: "Now Alba's trainer Ramona Braganza reveals how Alba dropped 25 lbs. so fast" by following "Braganza's 321 Baby Bulge Be Gone program."[34] Such articles give very specific and intimate details about celebrities' lives, make it clear that ordinary people cannot follow the regimens celebrities follow, and provide product placement for high-end trainers' brands.

Prior to the announcement that Jessica Simpson had been hired as a Weight Watchers spokesperson, Stacey, a celebrity weekly magazine writer, told me in an early 2012 interview, "I have a theory that Jessica Simpson got so big during pregnancy because she has a deal with Weight Watchers and so she wanted to get big so she could get paid more." Just as Stacey predicted, Simpson began mentioning her desire to get fit immediately after giving birth, and soon thereafter it was announced that she had signed on as a Weight Watchers spokesperson.[35]

Subsequently Kendra explained that *Us Weekly*'s coverage of women's bodies is "very careful." "I don't need to say, 'Oh my God, look at how big Jessica Simpson is pregnant,' because I'm just running a photo and I can just write, 'She's eight month's pregnant.' And someone else can say, 'Oh my goodness, that's a big baby.' Or 'She got really big.' It's not for me to pass judgment or say anything about [her weight]. I just have to run the photo." Kendra acknowledges that the photo will elicit an intense response from readers because of how big Simpson looks, without the need to comment specifically on her size. "She's already signed a multimillion-dollar contract [with Weight Watchers]. So the more weight she gains, the more amazing the transformation is going to be. If I were her and I was getting paid to lose weight, I would—and you know you're going to have to diet the second that kid comes out, and train and kill yourself—I would be eating the house. I'd be eating a whole house," Kendra laughed.

It was reported that Simpson made between three and four million dollars through her contract with Weight Watchers.[36] In a Weight Watchers ad released later in 2012, Simpson declares, "I'm Jessica Simpson and, yes, I'm doing Weight Watchers. There is a lot of pressure to lose weight, but I'm not a supermodel. I'm just Jessica trying to eat real food in the real world and I really just want to be healthy for my daughter, so I knew Weight Watchers was the only way to go. It's working. I'm on my way and it feels amazing. Really, I just want to be a better version of myself. Join for free, you'll see. Weight Watchers, because it works."[37] Comments posted below the video of the ad online demonstrate the consumer's understanding of Simpson's position as a pitchwoman and frustration with the boons of celebrity life. One viewer commented, "Only in America can you get paid for fattening yourself up. And even then, ONLY if you're a celebrity." Another wrote, "Eat like a nasty pig, get paid 4 million bucks. WTF America?"

Perhaps no celebrity has received the kind of ridicule during pregnancy that Kim Kardashian faced. Kendra said, "Kim Kardashian being the focus of body stuff is good and bad. Because she's not a skinny, skinny girl." Kendra's perspective is that bodies like Kardashian's might lead to acceptance of more diverse body types. Echoing the *People* cover featuring Tyra Banks in a bathing suit with the headline "You Call This Fat?," the May 20, 2013, *Us Weekly* article featured a photo of a pregnant Kardashian with the same headline (see figs. 6.17–6.18). Part of the reason Kardashian is so popular is because she is easy to hate. We know she became famous, at least initially, for something many people would not be proud of: the public release of a sex tape. Still, she lets us into her life through her various television programs and online presence. We feel we really know her. Then, when she gains weight or goes on a date with a rich European man who paid half a million dollars for her to attend an opera with him, we can all react in disgust and not feel guilty about it.[38] We never respected her to begin with. However, this attention also allows her to continue to build her fame, advance her career, and grow increasingly rich.

At a red carpet event, I asked the comedian Melissa Rivers what she saw as the Kardashians' real contribution to entertainment. She answered, "They make people happy. What does it matter? Isn't entertainment just about entertaining people in one way or another? They make people happy." That happiness may not be so straightforward, however. The anthropologists Lara Descartes and Conrad Kottak suggest that part of Americans' media obsession is to validate themselves by noting "Bad things happen to people unlike me." The consumer might think, I'm glad I'm not a young celebrity like Britney Spears; the pressure she is under from stardom is contributing to her failed marriage, her mental breakdown, her hospitalization, her separation from her children.[39] But this does not take into account the envy that many fans and

6.17–6.18 *Us Weekly* covers featuring Kim Kardashian. The May 20, 2013, cover showing a pregnant Kardashian is used to defend her pregnant body but also to prime readers for the weight loss to come. Much like *People*'s cyclical diet and post-baby coverage, *Us Weekly*'s December 23, 2013, issue features . . .

. . . Kardashian with the headline, "My Body Is Back! No Gimmicks, No Surgery! Kim slams the fat bullies and gets her sweet revenge." This coverage has the effect of validating the notion that she needed to lose weight, even if the May coverage of her pregnant body was supposed to challenge that presumption.

consumers feel toward celebrity, particularly mothers struggling to lose baby weight and who cannot afford a private chef and trainer to help them reach their goals.

Responses to Weight Criticism and Body Patrolling

People's body team is certainly not the only feature of the weekly magazines that contributes to the constant assessment and ridicule of women's bodies while conveying intimate details and knowledge about celebrities' weight, personal issues, diet, and workout plans. While *Us Weekly* may not have a body team, they have dedicated much time to the evaluation of women's bodies. In fact their website features a section labeled "BODY," which is home to all their body-focused articles, including a regularly featured photo essay called "Body Evolution" (with some variations, like "Hot Body Evolution" and "Post-Baby Body Evolution"). Readers can click through several photos of (almost entirely) women celebrities at their heaviest, thinnest, and most pregnant, while reading the commentary. Kate Middleton, Jessica Simpson, Snooki, Reese Witherspoon, Blake Lively, Beyoncé, and Kim, Kourtney, and Khloe Kardashian have all been profiled in this section. The focus on the body is meant to create interest and dialogue, whether from a place of envy or disgust. With the exception of a magazine like *Star*, which publishes covers that blatantly attack celebrity bodies (e.g., their annual "Best and Worst Beach Bodies" issue is particularly harsh; see fig. 6.19), the celebrity weekly magazines tend to use careful language that nods to weight gain without explicitly calling the celebrity fat or heavy. They use the tactic of quoting others (e.g., "The tabloids have said . . .") or using rhetorical phrasing (e.g., the Tyra Banks cover asks, "You call this fat?").

As an example, I will examine *Us Weekly*'s coverage of the "body evolution" of the singer Christina Aguilera, beginning in 1999 (see fig. 6.20). The photo essay comments on such aspects as her "toned tummy," "toned, tanned body," "abs and ample cleavage," "lean legs," and "tiny waist," and later her "svelte post-baby body." This complimentary coverage continues until 2010, when they begin to highlight a change in her shape. "After her performance at the American Music Awards in L.A., Aguilera was bullied for putting on a few pounds." They do not say *who* bullied her, while they themselves are pointing to her weight gain. The 2011 photo features the caption "*The Voice* mentor was subjected to intense scrutiny for her ill-fitting Herve Leger dress at the

6.19 *Star* magazine's "Best and Worst Beach Bodies" issue of March 6, 2012.

American Music Awards in L.A." Again she was scrutinized, but by whom? The celebrity magazines refuse to acknowledge that they (and other similar publications) are the ones doing the scrutinizing. Finally, the photo essay is rounded out by a compliment on her weight loss): "Aguilera revealed a more fit figure while taping *The Tonight Show with Jay Leno* in Burbank, Calif."[40] These photos and commentary are particularly problematic in ignoring the fact that Aguilera's "evolution" from 1999 to 2012 consists of her growth from a teenage girl to a thirty-one-year-old mother.

Just a few months after the *Us Weekly* "body evolution" feature on Aguilera, *People* wrote carefully about the singer's figure.[41] The image of Aguilera featured in the front section called "Star Tracks" was accompanied by the suggestive caption "Curve Appeal: Christina Aguilera flaunts her figure before announcing the nominations for the American Music Awards. 'I embrace my body,' says Aguilera. 'I embrace everything about myself.'" The use of the word *curve*, which can be seen as a positive descriptor, is used strategically by the magazines to suggest thicker or heavier bodies, which for celebrities is generally a negative attribute. In the Star Tracks section of its May 5, 2012, issue,

6.20 *Us Weekly's* "Body Evolution" feature on their website.

Inside image: Us | News Stylish Entertainment Royals Moms Food Wellness Pets Video More ▾ | CELEBRITY BODY | **Christina Aguilera's Body Evolution** | By Us Weekly Staff December 18, 2014

People ran a photo of the teen star Demi Lovato, who was struggling with drug abuse and an eating disorder, with the caption, "While on her world tour, Demi Lovato took a break to hit the beach with friends—and show off her curves in a bikini." Lovato appears very thin, but the magazine still refers to her "curves." Similarly *People* included a photo of Lady Gaga in their November 19, 2012, Star Tracks section, shortly after there had been much media attention on her weight gain. The caption is "Poolside Laugh: San Juan, Nov. 2: Flaunting her curves during a break from her Born This Way Ball tour, Lady Gaga relaxes poolside with one of her album's producers, DJ White Shadow." This is a highly unflattering photo in which no "curves" are visible; the mention of curves is simply to allude to the fact that she does not look as skinny as she once did. The image was placed next to a photo of the actress Rumer Willis looking extremely thin with a caption stating that she "turns heads."[42] On November 7, 2012, *People's* web edition of Star Tracks featured a similar photo of Lady Gaga in a bathing suit with the caption "Curves Ahead: Lady Gaga flaunts her fuller figure" (see fig. 6.21). Weeks earlier, on October 8, 2012, the cover of *People* featured a small photo with the caption "Lady Gaga: How She Hides Those Extra 25 Lbs!" The article explained that Gaga was "showing off her fuller figure. . . . Online bullies quickly called her 'gargantua' and 'a fat little monster.'"[43] By using unidentified "online bullies" as the mouthpiece for

PEOPLE.COM ⟩ CELEBRITY

Star Tracks: Wednesday, November 7, 2012

The singer shows off her bikini bod while greeting fans in Rio de Janeiro, Brazil. Plus: Kim Kardashian, President & Michelle Obama, Hilary Duff and more

By **People Staff**   November 07, 2012 05:00 PM

···   ⊞ View All   →

1 of 17

CURVES AHEAD

Lady Gaga flaunts her fuller figure while catching some rays Wednesday in Rio de Janeiro, Brazil, where the Born This Way singer, who recently pledged $1 million for Hurricane Sandy relief, greeted fans from a rooftop pool.

PHOTO: AKM-GSI

6.21 People.com image of Lady Gaga, indicating she has a "fuller figure." November 7, 2012.

LADY GAGA

She Gained 25 lbs....

THE CONFIDENT POP STAR ISN'T APOLOGIZING FOR HER CURVIER FIGURE—BUT IT'S HARD TO SEE UNDER HER OUTRAGEOUS CLOTHES

Lady Gaga often wows the world with her wild outfits, but now she's making headlines for what's going on *under* her clothes. On Sept. 19 photos surfaced of the Grammy winner, 26, showing off a fuller figure during her concert in Amsterdam. Online bullies quickly called her "gargantua" and "a fat little monster." Back in August, Gaga—who has publicly spoken of suffering from eating disorders in the past—admitted in a radio interview she was dieting because she'd gained, "like, 25 lbs." from dining at her father's restaurant. "I was eating pasta and pizza. . . . It was great!" (According to her onetime trainer Harley Pasternak, she used to fuel up on quinoa and lentils.) "And you know," she added...

2009   NOW

WITH A LARGE BAG

WITH AN A-LINE SKIRT

WITH A WEDDING DRESS

WITH AVANT GARDE FASHION

WITH A FLORAL BURKA

...And Hid It 6 Ways!

WITH DISTRACTING HEADGEAR

6.22 An October 8, 2012, *People* article highlighting Lady Gaga's weight.

6.23 *Us Weekly*'s "Body Evolution" photo essay on Khloe Kardashian.

insulting comments, the magazine is able to repeat the comments while ostensibly distancing itself from them (see fig. 6.22).

Us Weekly's "body evolution" photo essay on Khloe Kardashian employs similar tactics to describe her changing body. The essay starts out with praise, calling her "the queen of body evolution" and suggesting she is "inspiring fans and helping to spread a healthy message" (see fig. 6.23). But then *Us* begins parroting the ridicule Khloe faces as the "fat" Kardashian. The caption for a 2007 photo reads, "When Khloe Kardashian and her family let viewers into their household for a new E! reality show in 2007, the 'tough skinned' Kardashian had no idea how mean some viewers and online critics would be—instantly billing her as 'the fat sister.'"[44] Kendra points out that *Us Weekly* focuses on Khloe's body because, "her weight struggle has been documented on the show," so "people feel connected to what these women go through." A 2008 photo in the series refers to her showing off her "curves," with the caption "Emotional Eating: Kardashian showed off her curves in an emerald green dress in 2008, but admits that her weight was always a battle. 'As a girl, you have baby fat,' she explained. During her parents' divorce in 1991, she said, 'My brother [Rob] and I were always heavy. They gave us food to keep us company. All we did was eat crap.'" Again *Us* is able to criticize her weight in a way that does not directly implicate them. The photos starting in 2009 are the beginning of the yo-yo commenting, as the captions range year to year commenting on her weight loss and gain. A 2009 caption says, "Slimming Down: Debuting a slimmer figure in a tight purple frock in 2009, Kardashian revealed she did it by using the weight loss program QuickTrim (all three Kardashian sisters were spokeswomen for the product). 'QuickTrim is seriously amazing and I swear it works!!!' she wrote in a blogpost." This caption is an opportunity to see how the magazines and celebrities work with diet companies.

Now that the specific diet information has been shared, the magazine moves on to focus on her exercise program. "Making Progress: Taking a break from QuickTrim, Kardashian stepped out in 2011 with a more toned bod, largely due to upping her exercise regimen—doing 30 minutes of cardio daily, boxing, hiking, and even using a sauna suit to work out. 'It's like a trash bag that makes you sweat,' she told Us at the time. Her goal? To be bikini ready! 'Most girls in their 20s get to be in bikinis around their friends,' she explained. 'I was never that girl.'" The phrasing of this last caption insinuates that weight loss is always the goal: because she has a "more toned body," she has made "progress." This phrasing and this coverage contribute directly to the concerns Jackie had about the effects of body team work, as well as the concerns of the earlier *People* magazine issues that raised the question of "how media images of celebrities teach kids to hate their bodies." The takeaway is that if you are not losing weight, you are not making progress. By 2012, according to *Us*, "Kardashian was feeling sexy enough to flaunt her curves in a leg-bearing red dress—haters be damned. 'I'm a size 6/8,' she told Us Weekly in the past. 'If I weren't in Hollywood world, no one would ever say I was fat.'" Again the term *curves* is used as a substitute for *fat*, despite Kardashian's assertion that she is only a size 6/8, and the anonymous "haters" give the magazine permission to address her weight. For the final photo, the magazine once again confirms that thinner is better: "Rocking Body: Stepping out on May 22, 2013 in a red-and-white striped dress, the 5 ft. 10 in. star was looking better than ever, showing off her 20-pound weight loss."[45]

Us Weekly's website similarly featured a photo special entitled "We're Tired of the Fat Jokes!" It featured images and quotes from several celebrities who have apparently been called "fat"—by whom, *Us* does not disclose, but all are celebrities who have been featured in the magazine. Here are a few examples of the quotes featured: "Kelly Clarkson: 'For seven years it's been happening. It's like, "OK cool, the fat joke,"' she said earlier this year. 'I don't think artists are ever the ones who have the problem with their weight, it is other people'"; "Jennifer Love Hewitt: 'A size 2 is not fat!' she seethed on her blog after critics mocked Web photos of her in a bikini in 2007." Much like Tyra Banks's

January 2007 cover of *People*, a bikini-clad Love Hewitt was featured on the December 17, 2007, cover with the caption "Stop calling me fat!" The magazines are in an ironic and hypocritical position as they simultaneously replicate the critiques of celebrity bodies while also providing a space for them to denounce those same critiques.

Doing Damage to Themselves: The Effects of Body Coverage on Those Who Produce It

How women's bodies are portrayed in these magazines has real ramifications for the women consuming the images as well as for the women producing them. Nicole shared her experience working on the body team and how it affected her personally: "I saw myself becoming a different person while I was on the body team. When we were discussing women's bodies, people would say things like, 'Why are we even talking about her, she is too fat.' And we were talking about people who are size eight. I felt like I started to obsess over my own body. I started to feel like I needed to lose weight."

Jackie shared similar perspectives on the potential damage the body team could do to its members:

> It was definitely difficult because you can't be a thick chick, or forget thick—you can't be a chick with body issues in that room. You just can't. It's hard to sit there and talk about it every day, and talk about that. And you feel the pressure. Like I'm naturally a relatively skinny chick. I was skinnier than this when I first started. When I first started I was a hundred fifteen pounds. I'm currently a hundred thirty-five. But I know when I started to get to that point, I take Hydroxycut. A lot of people say it's not FDA approved. A lot of people call me on it. My editor used to get on me about it. She's like, "Why are you taking that shit? I can tell you're on it right now because you're so hyper." "I know. Just get me some more water. I have to fit into this dress." It was a joke, but if someone really did have an issue, it's not the safest place to be. But there was never a concern, like, "Are you girls okay?" You were in charge of that. If it was too much and you felt like this is not what I really want to be doing, then you had a private conversation with your editor. But I think being out here in L.A., because you see celebrities on a regular basis, you're used to small. You had to remember that you have a bias, just by being here and being

around people who are skinny. So when someone says, "Oh, I'm five-seven and a hundred fifteen pounds," to the rest of the world that's small, whereas to me that's sort of average. But it's not average to anyone else.

While Kendra never attempted to conform to the kind of bodily expectations her magazine promoted, she did admit, "The detrimental part is to my own self-image":

> I know what goes on behind scenes, what they have to do to—the crazy diets and stuff. I don't want to live a life of eating greens and grilled chicken breasts. It sounds like torture! No rice? Are you kidding me? Nothing but tea and maybe a cracker? Not even. It's juice cleansing or stuff like that. I did my little senior thesis in sociology and women's studies on whether teen magazines push a negative body-type image on young girls. And the answer was yes then, and the answer is still yes. Of course they do. Of course we do. Someone like Adele, who is amazingly beautiful, is great, but they're only buying photos of her in magazines like from her navel up. Where's my full body shots of Adele laid out like Scarlett Johansson in *Vanity Fair* with Tom Ford and nothing but a little sheet around her? They'll never do that. She would never do that.

The reporters and editors of the weekly magazines are critically reflective of their positions and they understand both their potential power and the limits of that power. As Kendra pointed out, she could stop doing this work, but the industry would still be there. Their logic is not entirely different from how the paparazzi talk about their own work. The paparazzi, reporters, and editors like Kendra reflect critically on ethical questions about the work they do, but as Galo said about his work as a paparazzo, "It could be a good job or a bad job, but it's my job." Kendra feels that, as a women's study major, as a woman, and as someone who has not conformed to the body expectations her magazine promotes, she has a more grounded perspective on women that helps balance the decisions at the magazine. Conversely, Nicole eventually asked to be removed from the body team due to the effect it was having on her own body image.

In a more drastic move, as her profile at the magazine, and specifically on the body team, rose, Jackie found herself in a moral and existential crisis. "I thought, 'Damn, this is what we are putting out there?' It was true, but it was always the most gripping of the truth. It was never the soft and easy version. So I didn't think about the little girl in Tallahassee who was reading this, per se. But more so I would think, 'Damn, that's kind of cold.' And I'm the person doing this work, but that to me isn't what's most important. So is it really what I want to be doing?" Her critical reflections eventually led Jackie to leave the field of celebrity reporting entirely. The magazines' treatment of women's bodies has a real impact not just on consumers but on the media producers themselves—especially the women specifically tasked with creating the content that scrutinizes and critiques women's bodies.

CHAPTER SEVEN

"Brad and Angelina:
And Now . . . Brangelina!":
The Cultural Economy of (White)
Heterosexual Love

Babies and weddings in particular are the most popular things that we showcase. We care about children of all of our friends and family, and the thing about celebrities is you feel like they're friends and family, even though you don't know them. | **IAN DREW** | *US WEEKLY* ENTERTAINMENT DIRECTOR, ABC *NIGHTLINE*, 2013

Melissa was the founder, owner, and administrator of the website StrictlyRobsten.com, which chronicled the relationship between actors Kristen Stewart and Robert Pattinson of the *Twilight* movies (who shared both an on-screen and an off-screen romance). On July 25, 2012, Melissa posted in response to the news that Stewart had cheated on Pattinson, "Sadness and hurt is all what the Robsten community is feeling right now. Tears are streaking down my face as I post this, but I presume it was only inevitable, although I thought Rob & Kristen would grow old together." While there are varying degrees of intimacy and imaginary social relationships that fans develop with celebrities, Melissa's level of dedication to and interest in "Robsten"—the combined celebrity couple name for Pattinson and Stewart— was particularly remarkable. Through her site, she served in certain ways as a spokesperson for what she refers to as "the Robsten community." In an interview she elaborated on the personal impact that Robsten's breakup had on her:

> When I first heard the news, it made me extremely sad and depressed. I noticed myself going through the stages of depression, denial, sadness, anger, et cetera. . . . Initially upon hearing about the scandal, I was in complete shock. Normally, tabloids come up with these stories and never really have proof that they even happened, but the fact that *Us Weekly* had picture proof of the incident sent me into tears. I wouldn't say that the reason for my tears was the fact that Kristen cheated on Rob; it's the fact that I had spent COUNTLESS times defending the girl, saying that she's a genuine person and a terrific role model for young women. . . . In hindsight, my emotions got the best of me during that time. Thankfully, it's made me realize that I shouldn't be so invested in these people I have no real contact with.

Melissa was not alone in her emotional reaction. *People* magazine's coverage of the scandal included a special section entitled "Tough Times for Twihards."[1] Included were a photo and quotes from a British "Twihard," Emma Clark, who, upon learning of the scandal, posted a video on YouTube during which she cried and pleaded for others to "leave [Rob and Kristen] alone" (see fig. 7.1).[2] Clark's video garnered over two million hits in a matter of days, and *People* deemed her newsworthy. In the age of digital and social media, the imaginary social relationships and level of investment fans have in stars are enhanced, promoted, and rewarded by the print media, which need fans to be invested in celebrities in order to have a consumer for their product.

In line with what psychologists call *parasocial relationships*, the anthropologist John Caughey uses the term *imaginary social relationship* to account for a relationship individuals develop with people they do not know or with fictional characters played by actors.[3] While most of the relationships between fans and celebrities remain imaginary and one-sided, there have certainly been shifts in this dynamic since the development of social media. There is now an opportunity for celebrities and fans to interact, so more direct connections can be formed. For example, Kim Kardashian uses her Twitter account to acknowledge and stimulate "the online community based upon her

Tough Times for Twihards

Faster than you can say "trampire," fans reacted passionately to the scandal. Tweeted one Twihard: "Now when I watch the last movie, all I'm going to be thinking of is how Bella cheated on Edward." Emma Clark, a British fan whose "Nutty Madam" YouTube video lamenting the betrayal has scored more than 2 million hits, says, "I feel bad for them all," noting that fans have long memories: "He will always be Rob Pattinson who got cheated on by Kristen Stewart and vice versa."

Clark pleaded with viewers to "leave [Rob and Kristen] alone."

7.1 Coverage of the viral "Twihard" video featured in the August 13, 2012, issue of *People*.

by consistently directing attention to fans that curate online pages devoted to her and her family, singularly naming individual fans, and applauding other family members' forays into social media."[4] At a Hollywood event the actress Sophia Bush told me, "[I use Twitter for] charity and social change. It's a place of dialogue for me. That was my intention when I started it. To have a dialogue. Some of us that follow each other, some of the people who follow me, we don't know each other. But we have dialogue about why we feel the way we do. It's a really incredible thing." Of course thousands of people are reading the tweets, so it is much more than an intimate exchange between two people. The overarching goal of celebrities on social media is to make consumers and fans *feel* as if they are developing a more intimate relationship with the celebrities they follow. The exchanges are public and intended for widespread consumption, all while conveying an illusion of intimacy that ultimately helps the celebrity sustain their fan base. Kardashian's fans are invested in her, and her tweets make them feel like close friends. Fans watch her show on television and feel as if they know the innermost details of her life; that compounded with following her on Twitter makes them feel as if she is a part of their lives in a real and intimate way.

How have we arrived at this place in which imaginary social relationships exist between fans and celebrities? If we look to the questions and approaches celebrity journalists use to craft their stories, it becomes clear how these kinds of imaginary social relationships develop and sustain interest. The coverage offered by celebrity weekly magazines is intended to foster the kind of intimate relationships fans perceive themselves as having with celebrities. Many tactics employed by the magazines are intended to make readers feel connected to the subject of the coverage, such as the in-depth focus on celebrities' intimate relationships and coverage of celebrities' workout and diet regimens. The reporters ask celebrities what they like to wear, beauty products they like to use, food they like to eat, places they like to travel to, and items they like to purchase. Consumers can then incorporate those very things into their own lives and feel more like their favorite stars. There is a desire to experience *how* particular famous people live and what particular famous people do. The celebrity weekly magazines, celebrities, and social media provide access to the information that facilitates the feeling of closeness and level of investment that consumers have in individual celebrities.

"Robsten" is just one of many celebrity couplings that have been heavily promoted by the weekly magazines in recent years. The tactic of celebrity couple name combining reached a contemporary turning point in 2005, with *People* magazine's coining of "Brangelina," a blend of the first names of the celebrity couple Brad Pitt and Angelina Jolie. It made its debut in *People* on May 9, 2005, while I was an intern and reporter for the New York bureau of the magazine.[5] The name was created by then editor Larry Hackett (who later became the managing editor), and fueled a multipage spread of the couple in that issue (see fig. 7.2). This spread was anchored by paparazzi photographs of the new couple rumored to have cost about $500,000, which was a mere fraction of what the magazine would later pay for exclusive photos of Brangelina's children. I remember the mock-ups pasted along the edges of the cubicles on the thirtieth floor of the Time Inc. building, near Rockefeller Center. At the time I didn't realize that this Brangelina spread would become legendary, would stimulate a continuing trend, and would announce a term that is still referenced today by celebrity reporters.[6]

Coining *Brangelina* did not just affect celebrity media producers; it popularized a new naming practice among the general public and impacted contemporary meanings of celebrity. With the popularity of *Brangelina*, a new standard was set in which celebrity couples linguistically merged into one, and the term grew to represent several social meanings. While *Brangelina* was not the first combined celebrity couple name, it led to the practice becoming

Brad & Angelina

AND NOW... BRANGELINA!

There's no denying it. Pitt and Jolie have a romantic rendezvous in Africa

7.2 The original Brangelina spread in *People*, May 9, 2005.

7.3 The Jolie-Pitt family in New Orleans on March 24, 2011. From the left is daughter Zahara, son Pax, son Maddox (only his arm is visible; he is holding Pax's hand), and daughter Shiloh; behind Shiloh is Jolie, holding twin daughter Vivienne, and Pitt holding twin son Knox. Photo courtesy of Galo Ramirez.

commonplace in celebrity media newsrooms and sparked a race among celebrity magazines to come up with the next catchy couple portmanteau. One former *People* magazine reporter, Nora, told me, "The name Brangelina represented a shift in celebrity culture and in celebrity reporting. Saying 'Tom Cruise and Katie Holmes,' for example, was no longer enough. We needed something short and catchy. The popularity of Brangelina reflected our celebrity-focused society. It was not necessarily about them as a couple. It was what they represented—a new level of celebrity" (see fig. 7.3). *Brangelina* has thus taken on several other meanings in American popular culture; the term is its own cultural entity and carries both symbolic and real capital. In addition, the process of bestowing a nickname on the couple promotes a sense of intimacy between consumers and celebrities, because nicknaming is a practice normally reserved for those intimate with a person.

The combining of celebrity couples' names by media outlets and its subsequent adoption by consumers is indicative of the power of social circulation of media, the potential impact of current social norms on media marketing tactics, and the public appetite for mediated intimacy with celebrities. Through the example of *Brangelina*, I explore these assertions by examining the conditions under which combined celebrity couple names emerged, the social meanings that have been attributed to *Brangelina* (e.g., how it evolved from a noun representing the couple to an adjective), and the various social media platforms through which consumers have decoded and adopted the practice of blending the names of individuals. The anthropologist Grant McCracken suggests that the "meanings" celebrities come to represent are derived "from the roles they assume in their television, movie, military, athletic, and other careers"; I suggest that these meanings are also derived from the framing of the stars by the celebrity news media industry, including through linguistic marketing tactics such as name combining, which fundamentally shift the identities of individual celebrities.[7] Finally, I explore the ways that the blending of celebrity couples' names has largely been an exclusionary practice that predominantly promotes white heteronormativity.

The History of Celebrity Couple Name Blending

Celebrity uni-names, bundled names, combined names, name meshing, name blends, portmanteaus—there is no agreed-upon name for this trend, but combining the first or last names of celebrity couples has proven to have sustained momentum in popular media and popular culture in the early twenty-first century.[8] *Brangelina* began as a celebrity magazine's marketing tool and turned into a common newsroom name, a name used by the general public, a term used by celebrities themselves, and a practice the public uses in their everyday lives. But *Brangelina* was not the beginning of the name-blending trend.

The film historian Michael Williams has traced the trend to the 1920s, when the fan press referred to John Gilbert and Greta Garbo as "Gilbo."[9] Referring to their business rather than their personal life, Desi Arnaz and Lucille Ball gave their production company the name Desilu in 1950. In 1980 John Lennon and Yoko Ono trademarked Lenono Music as the name of their music publishing company. The name Billary, for Bill and Hillary Clinton, was popular on talk radio in the 1990s, during Clinton's first years in the White House, but it never caught on in the mainstream media. In terms of contemporary popular culture, in late 2002 or early 2003 the celebrities Jennifer Lopez and Ben Affleck begin dating and the term *Bennifer* was coined.[10] *Bennifer* was common in the media until the couple's breakup in early 2004. Scott Huver, a Hollywood-based reporter who has worked for *Us Weekly, People*, and several other major celebrity-focused media outlets, told me, "There was a clever bit of inspiration in *Bennifer*, the first celeb-couple portmanteau to really hit the zeitgeist hard, and I think it became a fun game for writers, editors, bloggers and their readers to play whenever a new couple surfaced." *People* last used the term *Bennifer* in 2005.[11] That May, the magazine launched *Brangelina. Tom-Kat*, for the actors Tom Cruise and Katie Holmes, came shortly thereafter, and the trend snowballed from there. Over the next decade the trend was often applied to younger couples, like Zack Efron and Vanessa Hudgens, *Zanessa*, Leonardo DiCaprio and Blake Lively, *DiLively*, and the reality television stars Spencer Pratt and Heidi Montag, *Speidi*.[12] More recently there is *Kimye*, combining the names of the reality television star Kim Kardashian and the music producer and rapper Kanye West (see fig. 7.4).[13]

Graeme Turner suggests that "we can map the precise moment a public figure becomes a celebrity. It occurs at the point at which media interest in their activities is transferred from reporting on their public role . . . to investigating the details of their private lives."[14] The name change for couples like Brangelina is fully representative of media interest in the personal lives of the celebrities *as a couple*. As a celebrity reporter, I know that the priority in covering celebrities always centers on their love lives: it is a general rule that, in an interview with a celebrity, the more personal information a reporter can

7.4 Kim Kardashian and Kanye West on July 11, 2012, in Los Angeles.

Photo courtesy of Galo Ramirez.

get, the better. This is a strategy that has persisted since the popular celebrity gossip columns of Hedda Hopper and Louella Parsons in the first half of the twentieth century.[15] By providing details about a celebrity's love life, media producers encourage consumers to feel invested in that celebrity. A celebrity in a relationship guarantees additional news—an engagement, a baby, marriage, divorce, cheating, or a breakup—that will continue to feed a consumer's already developed appetite. Many consumers become invested and take sides as the relationship progresses or unravels, as in the case of Jennifer Aniston and Brad Pitt (who left Aniston for Jolie); their breakup led to the creation of websites and T-shirts and other paraphernalia that allowed individuals to declare themselves members of "Team Aniston" or "Team Jolie."[16] As a couple, Pitt and Aniston missed the blended-name trend, but just as the end of their relationship led to Brangelina, a new relationship provides a space for a celebrity to be redefined. Accordingly, it has become increasingly commonplace for popular media outlets to blend celebrities' names in order to formally remake them into a new, marketable entity.[17]

"As silly as it sounds, this new tendency to make up single names for two people, like 'Bennifer' (Ben Affleck and Jennifer Lopez) and 'TomKat' (Tom Cruise and Katie Holmes), is an insightful idea," commented Robert Thompson, director of the Centre for the Study of Popular Television at Syracuse University. "'Brangelina' has more cultural equity than their two star parts."[18] Brad Pitt was old news; Brad Pitt dating Angelina Jolie was new news and thus was of more cultural relevance to consumers and more monetary value to media outlets.

I have previously explored the pressure on celebrity weekly magazines to stand out in a competitive market at the very time *Brangelina* was first published by *People*.[19] From 1974 to 2000 *People* had no direct competition in the magazine market, when *Us Magazine* relaunched as a weekly.[20] *In Touch, Life and Style, Star*, and *OK!* entered the celebrity weekly magazine market in the subsequent five years, generating competition for content that had not previously existed in the industry. The expansion from one celebrity weekly magazine to six in the span of only five years created a market in which the magazines struggled to make their product distinctive. During that time, using new and catchy tactics like combined names was a way to draw and maintain readership. Huver said, "The celebrity naming trend was fun and familiar-feeling at a time when celebrity gossip was reaching an all-time zenith, and it made for catchy cover blurbs and headlines and actually effectively 'branded' some of these celebrity romances for public consumption." Being the first to publish an issue with a name like Brangelina on the cover set *People* apart in an increasingly saturated market.

The Effects of Blended Names
on Identity and Public Perception

Whether formal or informal, name changes have effects on identity and public perception of identity and thus have powerful social meaning.[21] Graeme Turner argues that the "whole structure of celebrity is built on the construction of the individuated personality."[22] Along with Turner, Frances Bonner and P. David Marshall see celebrities as "brand names as well as cultural icons or identities; they operate as marketing tools as well as sites where the agency of the audience is clearly evident; and they represent the achievement of individualism."[23] The practice of combining celebrity couple names illustrates a trend toward the construction of couples, rather than individuals, as icons and marketing tools. As Nora told me, "[Blended couple names] add more publicity to them as a couple because it makes for a cuter headline, and it makes for people talking about it. You're in the know if you say 'Bennifer' instead of 'Ben and Jen.' It causes more buzz. Any word or phrase that is creative helps promote that thing, be it a film or a couple or a product. It's advertising. It's a hook that people attach onto." From the media's perspective, there are clear marketing benefits. There are implications for the celebrities who form the couple as well.

They were Brad and Angelina, and *now* they're Brangelina.[24] Given the significance of names on individual identity, the bestowing of a blended name upon a celebrity couple by the media may feel like a violation to the celebrities it affects. Perhaps this is why Pitt and Jolie eventually told *People* magazine editors that they would not cooperate if the name Brangelina was used. A former *People* reporter named Seth told me, "Angelina Jolie gave the ultimatum that she would not cooperate with any photos or stories unless we agreed to stop using that combo-name. Clearly having her give the magazine a first look at things like baby photos was more important than a silly name that had been co-opted by all of the other celebrity weeklies anyway." Since Jolie worked almost exclusively with *People*, they granted her request.

Despite Pitt and Jolie's rejection of the name Brangelina, it took on a life of its own and its multiple meanings cannot be erased from popular culture. Other magazines did not stop using the name, and more blended celebrity couples' names were created. Perhaps most important, the circulation of the name online by fans and bloggers continued. Modern celebrity couple name blending is a distinct practice from earlier cases, in which the celebrities themselves were exercising their agency rather than the media. *Desilu* and *Lenono* signified the joint ownership of companies by celebrities who were partners in both business and marriage. By contrast, modern combined names are bestowed by the media upon pairs of celebrities when they merely begin dating, and signify the media's validation of a pair as an "official" couple regardless of the way the individuals define their own relationship.

The anthropologist Richard Alford writes, "A name change is a constant reminder that an identity change has occurred. . . . Most people identify so strongly with their names that a name change almost inevitably affects their sense of self." While Alford's study of naming practices shows that, in various cultures, names are known to change soon after birth, at marriage, or at the death of a relative, they are not known to change at arbitrary points in relationships.[25] *Brangelina* and *TomKat* were coined by the media before children were conceived or adopted and before marriage. In fact Pitt and Jolie had symbolically become one through the name Brangelina nearly a decade prior to becoming one in marriage in 2014. The Associated Press's breaking news on the wedding quipped, "The celebrity press and 'Brangelina' fans alike had been consumed with the matrimonial mystery."[26] However, as the former *People* reporter Mark Dagostino told me, it was precisely because they were already Brangelina that, to celebrity reporters (and presumably fans), "the wedding seemed like a non-event. They'd long proven themselves to be a real couple." The use of celebrity couple names is a way for the magazines to suggest who is in fact a "real couple" in a time when committed relationships are not soon signified by marriage (see fig. 7.5).

In bestowing the names Brangelina and TomKat upon the couples they represented, the magazines furthered one of their primary goals: making celebrities relatable to consumers. This goal is evidenced by the first section of every *People* issue, called "Star Tracks," in which celebrities are shown doing everyday things like picking pumpkins for Halloween with their kids or grocery shopping—things that many American families do. The first section of *Us Weekly* is entitled "Stars: They're Just Like Us!" It displays photos similar to those in Star Tracks, reflecting how "the iconography of celebrity photography has begun to move away from the contrived gloss of 'the ideal' towards the more mundane territory of 'the real.'"[27] Positioning celebrities as "normal" people has been a strategy of media producers since at least the 1940s, as relayed in Hortense Powdermaker's 1950 ethnography *Hollywood: The Dream Factory*. This "production" of "authenticity," how stars *really* are, is at the core of successfully marketing celebrities; consumers crave "para-social interaction" with celebrities, to feel that they can emulate celebrity behavior.[28] To

7.5 Just a few months before their wedding, Angelina Jolie and Brad Pitt are pictured with daughter Zahara at LAX on June 14, 2014.

Photo courtesy of Eduardo "Lalo" Pimentel.

be successful, celebrities need to be relatable, and that must include their personal lives.[29]

The celebrity couple name-blending trend is another way for celebrity magazines to prove that stars are "just like us" in reflecting the changing trends in marriage and marriage practice. Couples in the U.S. are increasingly living together without getting married. According to the 2010 U.S. Bureau of the Census, the number of "cohabiting" couples—defined as two unmarried people of opposite sex living together—tripled from 1970 to 1980, nearly doubled from 1980 to 1990, nearly doubled again from 1990 to 2000, and continued to rise from 2000 to 2010.[30] Census Bureau data also confirm that young people are continuing to delay marriage.[31] Considering that *People*'s demographic is primarily women ages eighteen to thirty-four, it is fitting that the magazine has worked toward increasing the social acceptability of unmarried couples.[32] The blending of couples' names reflects this new generation and, by so doing, connects the audience of celebrity magazines to the stars they are observing, idolizing, and/or emulating.

The use of blended names has real effects, not just on media production but also on public discourse. For instance, I did not take my husband's last name when I got married. Friends have taken to calling us *Benessa*—a combination of my husband's name, Ben, and my name, Vanessa. Even before we were married, friends and family called us by this nickname. I took the use of *Benessa* as a marker that, in the eyes of our friends and family, we had become an "official," if unmarried, couple, just like Brangelina. In the article "Reel to Real" the anthropologist Shalini Shankar discusses how popular media affects language use, particularly of youth.[33] In the same way, the target audience of celebrity weekly magazines might be prompted to incorporate the practice of combining names into their own language practices if it is relevant to their reality (e.g., if they are cohabiting).

"In most societies, many individuals informally receive nicknames from their intimates," not from strangers at magazines.[34] Because nicknames are generally demonstrative of a close relationship between the speaker and the subject, their use by the media and public is a concrete example of the imaginary social relationships between consumers and celebrities.[35] The celebrity media intentionally cultivates these imaginary relationships. Nora told me, "When you put together a name like [Brangelina], we are saying that we are *intimate* with them, that we know them well enough to give them a nickname." Bonnie Fuller, a former managing editor of both *Star* and *Us Weekly*, echoed the point: "[Media consumers] want to have a nickname for the couples because they feel as if they are part of the stars' extended group of family and friends."[36] Huver explained that this manufactured intimacy encourages consumers to want to follow the couple further, presumably through the continued purchase of celebrity magazines: "[Brangelina] made the story of two rich, gorgeous, and desirable celebrities feel weirdly intimate to the outside world. And in some ways, I think it also personalized them in a way that downplayed the scandalous nature of their union—despite the notorious circumstances of how they got together, the public seemed to want to root for them to work out as a couple." The closer and more intimate consumers feel to celebrities, the more likely they are to invest in the magazines, which aid in the maintenance of these imaginary, parasocial relationships. In this way, the combining of a celebrity couple's name is symbolic language capital that can be translated into actual capital for the celebrity industry.

Brangelina: Object, Icon, Commodity

In *High Visibility* the marketing and communications scholars Irving Rein, Philip Kotler, and Martin Stoller discuss the significance of a celebrity's name on his or her marketability, writing, "A celebrity is a person whose name has attention-getting, interest-riveting, and profit-generating value."[37] If celebrities themselves are commodities, their name is an important part of that commodity, as it can be imbued with meanings that reinforce the celebrity's brand identity.[38] Thus it is critical to consider the name as a particular kind of property and capital.[39] "In practice, the individual star has a highly identifiable, even iconic, physical image, a specific history for the circulation of this image, and accrues psychological and semiotic depth over time."[40] The combined name *Brangelina* creates a shift from the iconicized individual star to the couple, so that now it is difficult, if not impossible, to talk only about Brad Pitt without also talking about Angelina Jolie and vice versa.

The uni-name, however, accrues more than just linguistic, symbolic, and cultural value; it also accrues *actual* financial value. "While they are cultural workers and are paid for their labor, celebrities are also 'property': that is, they are a financial asset to those who stand to gain from their commercialization."[41] If we consider language and celebrity as property, the language that is used in discourse on celebrity is both property and a commodity. There is linguistic and material significance to the combining of Pitt's and Jolie's names. "As the asset appreciates—as the celebrity's fame spreads—so does its earning capacity."[42]

Peter, a paparazzi photographer I worked with, told me that his "biggest [sale] ever was the first pictures of Brad Pitt and Angelina Jolie, and that was on [the set of] *Mr. and Mrs. Smith*. So that was a hundred fifty thousand dollars spread out over six months because sales kept coming in." The photos were shot in 2004, and Peter was still earning royalties from them as of 2012. As the public continued to be exposed to Brangelina and established an increased perception of intimacy with the couple, the value of all things Brangelina increased. U.S. rights to photos of Brangelina's first biological child, daughter Shiloh, were sold to Getty Images and then to *People* for a reported

7.6 The August 18, 2008, cover of *People* magazine features the most expensive celebrity baby photos in magazine history.

$4 million in 2008. For the first photos of "the Brangelina twins," *People* and the British tabloid *Hello!* paid $14 million for "joint rights to publish the most expensive celebrity pictures ever sold" (see fig. 7.6). This was "more than double the $6 million People paid for Jennifer Lopez's twins on a March cover, according to Forbes."[43] The celebrity status of Jennifer Lopez is on par with that of Pitt and Jolie as individuals, but she cannot compete with Brangelina. Part of the disparity in the monetary value of the photos is due to the linguistic and symbolic capital that the marketing of the combined name Brangelina has yielded.[44] The June 19, 2006, *People* magazine issue with photos of Brangelina and baby Shiloh sold 2.2 million copies, and the August 18, 2008, *People* magazine issue with the photos of the Brangelina twins sold 2.6 million copies.[45] The issue with the twins was the magazine's "biggest seller in seven years, and is the fourth highest newsstand seller in the magazine's 35-year history."[46] Would the baby pictures be as marketable if they merely depicted Pitt and Jolie's babies rather than "the Brangelina Twins"?[47]

As I elaborated in chapter 4, a prominent piece of the California anti-paparazzi legislative movement was a law banning the commercial photographing of children because of the profession of their parent. The point of this law was not to maintain the privacy of the celebrity children but to control the monetizing of those children. Control over the images of celebrity children has become more prominent as celebrity children have become more lucrative and featured more often in the weekly magazines. Brangelina's decision to market their children's photos in the manner they did was the beginning of a shift in the kind of agency and monetizing of celebrity family imagery.[48]

Brangelina have strategically utilized the position of their family within the Hollywood-industrial complex. For example, as part of my research, I asked several paparazzi to carry GoPro cameras while on the job and to share their footage with me. Footage that Galo took in New Orleans while shooting Jolie and her children demonstrates the systematic collaboration that happens between celebrities and paparazzi in order to create value for both parties. During this encounter in New Orleans, Jolie and her children had a bodyguard walking in front of them. The guard was there to protect them, but he did so in a way that ensured no one, including himself, interfered with the shots that paparazzi were getting of the family. Photographers were allowed to get as many uninterrupted shots of the family walking down the street as they wanted. Unlike the popular image of a swarm of paparazzi, here there was no direct contact and no aggression. All of the players in this economy played their roles in the machine that generates celebrity content. In the bidding war over images of their twins and in everyday encounters like the one Galo captured in New Orleans, Pitt and Jolie strategized to reap the benefits of public demand.

Among celebrity media producers, the buying power of Brangelina remained strong for the duration of their relationship, even when other major moments in A-list celebrity life took center stage in the media. For example, in March 2012, while I was doorstepping with Galo outside of Sandra Bullock's home, he told me, "Ever since she had that kid, she is like the biggest thing. Well, Brad and Angie are always [the biggest thing], but she's like number two." Though Bullock had just added a child to her family and was earning more as an actress than Jolie, she was still not able to unseat Brangelina as the most valuable celebrity commodity.[49] The strategic marketing and validation of the love between Pitt and Jolie underscores the social and financial power of the constructed celebrity couple.

The Evolution of Brangelina: Meanings and Uses

The use of *Brangelina*—first by *People* magazine, then by other media, then by celebrities themselves and the general public—is an example of what the linguistic anthropologist Debra Spitulnik describes as social circulation: "Social circulation of media discourse provides a clear and forceful demonstration of how media audiences play an active role in the interpretation and appropriation of media texts and messages."[50] While *People* may have intended only for *Brangelina* to refer to Pitt and Jolie, the couple, the term has taken on myriad meanings through a variety of media audiences.

Brangelina also refers to everything that this couple embodied, such as cohabitation, glamour, fame, and a globe-trotting lifestyle. Individual names are bound to certain qualities and ideas, and blended names expand on this binding.[51] *Brangelina* refers to a couple, a family, celebrities, and fame. It also refers to marketability, extravagance, and beauty. A November 13, 2008, MSNBC segment featured the *Us Weekly* editor Albert Lee referring to President Barack Obama and his wife, Michelle, as the "new Brangelina":

> MSNBC ANCHOR: It used to be that if you wanted to sell magazines, you'd put Angelina Jolie and Brad Pitt on the cover.

> US WEEKLY EDITOR: I mean, the Obamas are like the new Brangelina. You know? That's why we keep putting them on the cover, you know, week after week. And we did sell over a million copies with the last issue. Everything else on the newsstands just feels totally irrelevant right now. People want to learn more about this family.[52]

Lee is indexing the celebrity status of the Obamas by equating the marketability of Brangelina to the marketability of the Obamas. He is not referring to Brangelina in the sense of an extravagant, unwed couple adopting and having babies; rather he is referencing the celebrity status and public importance of Brangelina and relating that aspect of the couple to the Obamas.

Even other celebrities are using these terms to create new forms and meanings for use in everyday interactions. In a People.com article on the wedding anniversary of the actors Jerry O'Connell and Rebecca Romijn, O'Connell says, "I wish I had something sexy and all Brangelina to tell you where we're going to go flying. But it's really just going to be my in-laws crowding us."[53] Since Brangelina were known for their jet-setting travel, O'Connell has taken *Brangelina* to mean extravagant traveling, spontaneity, or something "sexy."[54]

Brangelina has come to index glamour, fame, extravagant travel, and sexiness, and it has done so explicitly through the portmanteau of the celebrity couple rather than the individual names Brad Pitt and Angelina Jolie. This challenges the prevailing celebrity studies scholarship that argues celebrity is the apotheosis of neoliberal individualism.[55] *Brangelina* shows that meanings of celebrity are now also being defined through constructions of couples as celebrity entities in their own right, with unique names that develop their own meanings.

An important implication of *Brangelina* is how the practice of celebrity couple name making has impacted the consumer on a more personal level. "Fame can be understood to be the 'glue' that holds the cultural centre together and which offers the alienated and anomic forms of para-social relations . . . a part of a material culture that they can invest in and which 'invests' in them."[56] Such investment in consumers was demonstrated by a People.com poll that asked website visitors to vote on their favorite combined celebrity couple name; through that poll, *People* could learn which couples to focus on in order to please the consumers.[57] Similarly, *USA Today*'s "Celebrity Couple Name Maker" database that accompanies an online article on celebrity couple names gives consumers something in return for reading and visiting the site.[58] If they are interested in Brangelina and other celebrity couples, they can become part of the naming practice themselves; thus the consumer is rewarded for consuming. It is also significant that the user-generated site wikiHow has a page titled "How to Make Your Celebrity Couple Names."[59] Separately from the *USA Today* database, *consumers* have created instructions on how to develop their own celebrity couple names. *Brangelina* was fed to media consumers by *People* as simply a combination of the names Brad Pitt and Angelina Jolie to index their relationship. The consumer, from other media producers and celebrities to the general public, has owned the term *Brangelina* and redefined it in several ways. The creation of the wikiHow page shows the completion of the cycle of agency from media producers to media consumers.

Where Are Pellen, Mennifer, and Jayoncé? The Marginalization of Celebrity Couples of Color and LGBTQ Celebrity Couples

In her 2004 book *The Cultural Politics of Emotion*, Sara Ahmed explores how invoking love can be an exclusionary practice. What kind of love do we recognize, validate, and brand for consumption? What kind do we ignore and invalidate? How media producers decide which celebrity couples get their names combined demonstrates the ways in which recognizing certain people's love is an exclusionary practice. Nonwhite and LGBTQ celebrities are largely left out of the name combining. I encountered numerous justifications for this, including the aesthetics of the sound and appearance of a blended name and assumptions about which celebrity couples evoke emotion in readers. Brian, a freelance reporter for *People*, said, "The ones that do land seem to be those that have a frenetic amount of attention surrounding their personal lives alongside their tremendous fame, and I think the name combo also simply needs to be fun to say or put in print."

It is no secret that the celebrity weekly magazines focus primarily on white celebrities. As the token Latina in the New York bureau at that time, I was particularly sensitive to how little people of color and other minorities were represented in *People*. As an intern and developing reporter, I wanted to know how it was decided, and who decides, which celebrities get their names combined. Was it simply a representation of those celebrities who are thought to evoke "strong emotions" in the consumers?[60] Why are nonwhite and LGBTQ celebrities so often left out of the name combining? To take one example, Lindsay Lohan and Samantha Ronson were not given a name when they were a couple, despite the media's constant interest in Lohan during those years and the potential catchiness of "Lohnson." The October 13, 2008, issue of *OK!* magazine featured a cover story and four-page spread about Lohan and Ronson next to a shorter Brangelina-focused article, but no attempt was made to combine their names.[61] The article proclaimed that Lohan and Ronson had been together for months, which is more than could be said of Pitt and Jolie at the time the name Brangelina was coined. It is difficult not to interpret the magazine's clear interest yet tangible difference in its attempt to market the couple as connected to their queerness. From my perspective, as someone who works in the industry, this practice reinforces wider social hierarchies even in the celebrity world. Portia de Rossi and Ellen DeGeneres were featured on the cover of *People* for their 2008 wedding, but they were never given a combined name. Pellen could have worked well.[62]

One same-sex couple name that gained limited traction among consumers is Larry Stylinson, the name One Direction fans gave to a fictional romance between group members Louis Tomlinson and Harry Styles. This is the most widely used example of a combined name for a gay couple, yet not only is the couple fictional, but the name is sometimes used by fans as a way to demean the boy band members.

Like queer celebrity couples, celebrity couples of color are noticeably less present in the name-combining trend. There has yet to be a popularized blended name for a couple wherein both individuals are racial minorities. Michelle and Barack Obama may have been called "the next Brangelina," but they have not been given a combined name by the press. Other examples of couples who, based on their popularity alone, seem natural choices for a blended name are Beyoncé and Jay-Z and the former couple Jennifer Lopez and Marc Anthony. When Jennifer Lopez was with Ben Affleck, they were termed Bennifer. But when she was with Marc Anthony, they were never "Mennifer." On the other hand, Ben Affleck and Jennifer Garner became Bennifer 2.0 and then Garfleck. When Lopez was in a couple with a white man, she was marketed with a combined name, but when she was with another Latino, they were never given such a name, even though her former partner was given one immediately. This fact exemplifies structural prejudice within the celebrity media industry and celebrity culture. The difference cannot be attributed to the celebrity status of the individual members of the couples, since Beyoncé and Jay-Z, for example, are longtime A-List celebrities in the U.S. and are inarguably as famous as if not more famous than Ben Affleck, Jennifer Garner, and Katie Holmes (especially Garner pre-Garfleck and Holmes pre-TomKat).

To date, *Kimye* (for Kim Kardashian and Kanye West) is the only combined name commonly used in the mainstream celebrity press that includes an African American. Previously the only people of color included in a highly publicized name were women, Jennifer Lopez and Vanessa Hudgens.[63] In the case of the Kardashians—especially Kim, who launched her family's entertainment career from an (allegedly) accidentally leaked sex tape—their entire celebrity is built around access (or the illusion of access) to the intimate moments of their everyday lives. As Alice Leppert explores, the Kardashian family has reaped profits as a result of the promotion of their romantic relationships; perhaps they are invested in the circulation of the intimacy implicit in blended names to an even greater degree than Pitt, Jolie, and other celebrity couples referenced here.[64] While the inclusion of people of color in blended celebrity couple names is significant regardless of the circumstances, the structure of the name itself is also significant; perhaps not coincidentally, Kimye and Khlomar (for Khloe Kardashian and Lamar Odom) are two of very few combined names anchored in the woman's name.

Many of the media producers I spoke with had not considered the demographics of the celebrity couples who received combined names. Brian admitted, "Honestly, it only now registered to me that, as a celebrity super-couple, Beyoncé and Jay-Z never landed a portmanteau. There seem to be plenty of fun combos to experiment with. They certainly fit the bill of both being uber-famous." Throughout my ethnographic research, my suggestion that celebrity name combining has been an exclusionary practice promoting white heteronormativity has been met with reasonable skepticism by other reporters and editors in the celebrity media industry.[65] Those who disagree with my proposal have suggested that perhaps the couples I am pointing out simply do not have good-sounding possibilities for combined names; after all, marketability has to do with catchiness. However, based on my experience in the industry and my observations of how decisions are made in celebrity media production, I do not believe the many examples I provide to be a mere coincidence, nor is it adequate to attribute the discrepancy to the pleasant sound of some of the combined names that have been heavily promoted. My suggestion of *Mennifer*, for example, echoes *Bennifer*, with the exception of one consonant. *Pellen* (Ellen DeGeneres and Portia de Rossi), *Mirack* (Michelle and Barack Obama), and *Jayoncé* (Jay-Z and Beyoncé Knowles-Carter) seem to flow better than *Garfleck*, for example. And, of course, which names sound appealing is subjective and grounded in racialized and ethnocentric biases.

I attribute the discrepancy in representation not to the aesthetics of the potential combined name or the level of fame of the individuals, but to conservative decisions made by celebrity media producers (reporters and editors alike) based on what they think will sell to the imagined consumer, whom they generally presume to be white "mainstream" couples. In 1950 Hortense Powdermaker wrote, "Hollywood people live more or less normal family lives, and it is the current studio policy to do everything possible to publicize this. Publicity and fan magazines have been concentrating on pictures of 'normal' family life."[66] Note the emphasis on the word *normal*, which, when combined with *family life*, tends to reference the status quo white American nuclear family. In my experience, not much has changed since Powdermaker's research; the only difference is that the magazines seek this angle on their own, without the aid of studios. This can explain the restriction of combined names to largely white celebrities and heteronormative couples.

Perhaps this presumption is not surprising, given the lack of diversity in celebrity media newsrooms, and in the Hollywood-industrial complex more broadly. My earlier discussion of the firing of former *People* editor Tatsha Robertson as well as perspectives from other reporters of color underscores this issue. When we conceptualize diversity problems in Hollywood, it must be understood as a holistic problem. When so-called diversity is present in the industry (e.g., the tokenized paparazzi or *People* editor Robertson), how are they treated within the context of Hollywood-industrial complex? What power are they given, and who ultimately wields the power, to determine whom the media chooses to manufacture into celebrities? It is not accidental that, while small steps are made to diversify Hollywood, the celebrities manufactured by the Hollywood-industrial complex are predominantly white and heterosexual.

As Halle Berry stated in her 2002 Academy Award acceptance speech for Best Actress, women of color have remained "nameless."[67] So too, literally, have celebrity couples of color—at least as far as the magazines are concerned. However, although the magazines have ignored couples of color when bestowing combined names, consumer use of the practice has been more inclusive. On various sites for independent and ethnic media, blogs, and on social media, one can find combined names for couples of color.[68] On Instagram alone there are over 275,000 instances of #jayonce, giving the kind of validity and intimacy to couples like Jayoncé who have been strategically excluded from this effective marketing tactic.

RIP Brangelina?

Pitt and Jolie filed for divorce on September 19, 2016. As with the Robsten story that opened this chapter, there was an intense emotional reaction from the media and the public. Mainstream media sources like CNN featured articles with headlines like "RIP Brangelina: 2006–2016," demonstrating the sadness and sense of loss for this couple as an entity.[69] Their breakup was treated as the loss of two people, a dual mourning. The end of their relationship marked the end of the emotional development that people had taken on for them as a couple and as a family, which had been nurtured over the course of a decade. It emphasized the significance of the marketing tactic and the effectiveness that is Brangelina. Even in reporting the break in this relationship, media did not separate the names.[70]

A broad range of media consumers have transformed *Brangelina* into much more than *People* editors ever intended or imagined. *Brangelina* first represented the informal, even speculative union of two people. It came to represent the blending of all things associated with those two people as a couple. Consumers at once consumed and produced their own meanings of Brangelina. Media depictions that resulted from Brangelina's surveillance provided fodder that led to the ever-evolving meanings that Brangelina embodied. This phenomenon represents the dynamic relationship between media and consumer: the media provided images and meanings of Brangelina for the consumer, and the consumer created, molded, and redefined what those images and meanings were. This process challenges the assertions of popular culture and celebrity studies scholars who argue that celebrity is built around individualism. Brangelina does not override the individuality of Pitt and Jolie as celebrities, but is its own entity carrying its own shared meanings and value, thus complicating the ways we understand the construction of celebrity in contemporary culture. Just as Brangelina began before the marriage of Pitt and Jolie (or even confirmation that they were a couple), the cultural and linguistic significance of Brangelina make it so that, despite their divorce, the meanings of Brangelina live on after their marriage.

CONCLUSION

Reconsidering News and Gossip in the Trump Era

On August 20, 2011, I found my car in desperate need of a wash, so I headed to the neighborhood hand car wash. In Los Angeles there are car washes every few blocks, and on any given day crowds of people linger, waiting for their cars to be hand-washed by mostly Latino men (known as *carwasheros*), who generally rely on tips to earn a living. On this particular day all the patrons were crammed inside the small convenience store that was attached to the car wash. They were crowded around the store's television, which was broadcasting part of Kim Kardashian's wedding to then NBA player Kris Humphries. This moment was not unique to Los Angeles. The televised two-part wedding special on E!, titled *Kim Kardashian's Fairytale Wedding*, garnered 4.2 million viewers.[1]

My mind instantly went to the only other time I saw people crowded around a television in public. In Manhattan on the morning of September 11, 2001, I found myself in a crowd of pedestrians outside of an electronics store on 14th Street near Union Square, trying to get a glimpse of what was happening on the store's display of television sets. Almost exactly ten years later I was in a crowd of people watching Kim Kardashian's wedding on television nearly as intently as on that terrible day. This experience in the car wash was emblematic of the rise of celebrity culture as a form of escapism in a post-9/11 context; it also illuminated the attention people pay to entertainment news today. As I argued in the introduction, any distinction between entertainment and news media at this point in American culture is simply a function of a public imaginary—that there *should* be a difference between "hard news" and "entertainment news."

A former Google employee told me that the "Google news" tab did not originally include stories from the celebrity weekly magazines, but it eventually began to include them as celebrity news became more popular. Celebrity journalists grapple with decisions about what news is, and whether it includes celebrity stories. The notion that celebrity journalism is not news in the traditional perspective has affected celebrity journalists' feelings about their work. They are often conflicted about their role as producers of media that many of them believe is diluting news, journalism, and the depth of American culture. Broadly, celebrity journalists acknowledge that celebrity news is incorporated into all forms of news media, but they experience their own work as less significant than hard news.

When I asked celebrity reporters about their understanding of themselves as journalists and news media producers, I received the following responses:

> JASMINE: "I consider myself an entertainment journalist. Sometimes it does feel silly for me to even call myself a journalist when I'm doing entertainment stuff."

> RON: "Celebrity reporting can feel stupid. When something really serious happens—something major newsy—it always makes everybody kind of look at, 'Britney Spears got married again.' It's like, 'That's not news; that's crap. We need to care about this disaster.' Well, we don't always care. It really is a global village. The conversations that people have at home are like, 'Did you know my hairdresser is fucking my pharmacist?' It's just on a mega level about famous people or political people."

> SAMANTHA: "I had trouble with stories like Lindsay Lohan going to jail and Britney Spears shaving her head being a lead news story. I still do. I think it indulged that bad behavior. Charlie Sheen [at one point] was everywhere: *Dateline* did an hour special, *20/20* did an hour special. Everybody wanted to have their hand in the pot to attract more viewers, more readers. And that, to me, wasn't news."

> SANDRA: "I think anything that pertains to a famous person could be titled as news. Is it news? Is it substantial? Is it something that is really

going to benefit our society? Is it going to benefit us by reading this crap? Not really, but you know what, people read it. I think it's all about what people feed into. As long as people keep reading these stories and keep looking at these pictures, I mean it is news; it is news because that's what people make it to be. . . . CNN was the leading evening news, and here they are struggling, so why not throw a couple of pieces in about celebrity breakdowns and Charlie Sheen? Why not have him on *Piers Morgan* to get the ratings up or get more exposure? They have to cave into what society is demanding. It is supply and demand; basic economics."

JOY: "During my time at the magazine, celebrity news and hard news started converging. When the first story on the *Today Show* is on Britney Spears, you know what's happening. They report it and they say 'the tabloids,' but they're reporting it. There was a definite convergence because everyone wants to know what was happening. Brad and Angelina and the kids was top-rated news on *Good Morning America* and the *Today Show*. . . . Even CNN now has entertainment coverage. And CNN covers the red carpets and they're doing all that stuff too. I could be on a red carpet next to CNN and AP. They are there too. Celebrity news has gone mainstream. The big events like the Oscars have always been mainstream news, but a lot of the hard news outlets are covering the smaller stuff in a frequency that I just didn't expect."

SYLVIA: "Celebrity has become so big that when CNN is covering breakups and stuff, unfortunately, that is news. Everyone has to serve their audience and that's what sells. . . . News is anything that your readers or viewers are interested in, that's all it is. We could fight it as much as we want, but nothing is going to change. . . . So what is news is whatever your readers are going to turn the channel on or buy that magazine for."

KENDRA: "When someone says, 'I work on the news,' I don't think of *Us Weekly* magazine. I think of Brian Williams, and the nightly news. I used to really beat myself up and say, 'Oh God, I went to journalism school. I should be working on important, serious things. What am I really contributing? What am I really doing?' But you know what? Pop culture for me has always been something that I loved. It's important. It matters. It keeps us all employed."

STACEY: "I think generally people think of celebrity news as its own sort of category for sure. However, CNN you know has celebrity news on their website every day. I mean, Prince William and Kate Middleton getting married was news. And the magazine websites have changed what news is as well. Before, news had to be like a major life event to warrant space in a magazine and carry through, and now it doesn't have to be. It can just be something very small because you're not competing against anything for space in the magazines since the website can include everything. . . . So news now, I think it is something that can be defined as whatever's happening from like minute to minute in a celebrity's personal life, whereas before I think it would have to be something more consequential."

The celebrity journalists say they feel "silly" or "stupid" covering celebrity news, yet they acknowledge that the stories they report on are increasingly covered by outlets that are considered hard news. The journalists largely blame the news media's growing celebrity focus on the desires of consumers, ratings, and advertisers. They emphatically state that media content is consumer-driven. If a more inclusive notion of hard news were popularized, there might be a shift from the judgmental and classist discussions that emerge from the discourse presented here about readers not wanting or being interested in real news. An increased sociocultural understanding and awareness around the reasons for this desire in consumers—like escapism and desire for community—could perhaps shift the onus for the increased focus on celebrity news from the consumer to issues like the economy, politics, and international affairs.

But as the media producers themselves express, they want to provide the material that consumers desire. Ridiculed for his work as a paparazzo by both audience members and fellow panelists at the 2012 Getty Center event I've previously mentioned, the paparazzo Galo Ramirez responded by saying, "I'm giving the audience what they want. So if it's bullshit they want, it's bullshit I'll give them. It's very simple." The actor Adrian Grenier offered support for Galo's position:

I'd like to just defend that bullshit for a second because life can't all be about elevated thinking and transcendence. Sometimes you just gotta live and have a little fun. It's like the equivalent of going to a dinner party just for sustenance, just to eat for sustenance. You go for all the frills. And sometimes the frills aren't that lofty, sometimes it's just a basic joke or just little banter, so let's not just let the tabloid be the scapegoat for all of us who have to take ultimate responsibility about what experiences we want to consume. You choose.

Why do today's consumers desire so strongly to consume celebrity media? Aside from its potential for escapism, Ron pointed to another reason. He compared celebrity news to traditional localized gossip about the neighborhood pharmacist and hairdresser. In today's increasingly crowded, urban, and transient society, we have fewer and fewer acquaintances in common with others in our communities. The people we do have in common are celebrities. Thus discussion of celebrities serves the function of gossip on a mass scale.

This point was brought home to me while I was staying at a bed-and-breakfast about an hour outside of New York City, when I sat at breakfast with a group of people I had just met. At first, the conversation around the table was stilted and awkward, but within five minutes this group of strangers was engaged in an intense dialogue that lasted more than an hour. The conversation centered on their opinions about specific celebrities and their personal (or imagined) connections to celebrities.

A guest in her forties named Sarah brought up a story about Lady Gaga that had recently been covered in the news: "Did you see what Lady Gaga wore to her sister's graduation? The beekeeper hat? And then did you see what she wore to the Mets game? The Mets hate her now. I hate her too. She's too much. Why does she want to draw so much attention to herself?"

"Well, you know, my friend's friend's boyfriend is her hair stylist," another guest chimed in. "He has to be there for her all the time. He basically is her. I mean he has to work so hard and they pay him a ton of money."

"Yeah, my son's friend's friend went to high school with her and she was really normal," Sarah said.

"I heard that she was just a hippy. Totally normal. But she told this friend's friend that she was going to be a superstar. I guess she knew. A lot of people say that, but they don't always become famous."

"Did you see the video with her and Beyoncé?" asked Cassandra, a twenty-something secretary at a New York law firm. "I mean, what was that all about? It's just a PR thing. It's fake. And what about Lindsay Lohan? I'm tired of these celebrities getting special treatment. She should just be in jail. Oh, and I can't stand Miley Cyrus." Cassandra expressed her strong opinions about people she has never seen in person. "You know who I love? Sandra."

"Who?" One of the guests asked.

"Sandra Bullock," Cassandra clarified. "I love her. It's crazy how the adoption came at the exact right time when she had nothing. Right, now she has the kid, she got rid of him [ex-husband Jesse James]. I feel so bad for her, she seemed so happy. I felt really bad. To be honest, I never understood the attraction to him. She's so girl-next-door. So vulnerable. I feel bad for her that she's subjected to these headlines. Let her live her life without being turned into this pathetic character."

In this gossip session, strangers shared ideas and opinions about celebrities and their feelings of intimacy toward them, calling them by their first name and having genuine emotional reactions about them. Celebrities become a shared part of the lives of many people they do not know, like the women discussing celebrities here, at a bed-and-breakfast in New York.

In her work on celebrity-focused media, Anne Helen Petersen declared that the celebrity weekly magazines accomplished the transition of "gossip" into "news."[2] Gossip is broadly considered news about someone's personal life. Thus gossip and news are often intertwined both informally through conversation and formally through news media.[3] But what of gossip on a mass scale? When public figures are gossiped about, does it still serve the role of gossip that the sociologist and ethnographer Jörg Bergmann posited—that the news to be communicated as gossip "is always 'news-for-a-social-unity'"?[4] Through the imaginary social relationships cultivated by celebrity media, celebrities become common ground for strangers to discuss, perhaps contributing to a new social unity in a postmodern state. American celebrities are now globally known citizens of an imagined (global) community. They are our common ground, our connection, our community.

While some of the celebrity reporters I interviewed expressed embarrassment that they covered celebrity news rather than hard news, the respect and prestige afforded to hard news reporters has undergone a dramatic shift recently. Donald Trump, the first reality star president, has fomented hatred of mainstream news media outlets like CNN and NBC News by relating to White House and national reporters in ways that mirror how celebrities often relate to celebrity media producers, especially paparazzi. "Trump's team likes to say the celebrity media training has served him well in politics."[5] He understands how to use the media to generate interest, such as when he revealed his Supreme Court nominee *Apprentice*-style on prime-time television. Yet he constantly performs anger toward the very media who gave his candidacy, and now his presidency, nonstop coverage. He disparages them as "fake news" and "dishonest." This behavior mirrors the way celebrities rely on paparazzi shots for promotion while simultaneously performing hatred toward them. For Trump, it is directly carried over from his career as a celebrity. In his book *How to Get Rich*, he wrote, "If I happen to be outside, I'm probably on one of my golf courses, where I protect my hair from overexposure by wearing a golf hat. It's also a way to avoid the paparazzi. Plus the hat always has a big TRUMP logo on it—it's an automatic promotion."[6] Trump references wanting to avoid the paparazzi while in the very next sentence revealing how he uses them to promote his own brand—a celebrity tactic I explored in depth in chapter 4.

While Trump has used celebrity media strategically to build his brand, he has also exploited, humiliated, and assaulted celebrity reporters. Since becoming president, he has continued this belligerent behavior in White House press conferences and other media events. Trump has kicked out, verbally bullied, and even banned news reporters and media outlets from his press conferences. His ire has been directed at the corporate media entities themselves, as well as individual media laborers. For example, in 2015 Trump had Univision's Jorge Ramos symbolically deported from a press conference while yelling at him, "Go back to Univision," another way of telling the Mexican American reporter to go back to Mexico.[7] This kind of racialization and racialized discrimination is closely linked to the treatment of Latino paparazzi I exposed in earlier chapters. A 2016 *Dallas Morning News* op-ed titled "Trump Can't Treat Press Like Paparazzi" pointed to Trump's problematic approach with the political media: "Trump may see these reporters as an extension of the paparazzi that hounded him when he was a reality television promoter and real estate mogul. They aren't. The press pool isn't about staking out celebrities."[8] The article insinuates that, unlike political reporters, paparazzi *are* and *should be* treated as problems. Trump has drawn no distinction between the celebrity news and hard news outlets that have followed him at various stages of his career. While using them for self-promotion, he has treated the political press with the same disdain that he showed to celebrity media producers—including Natasha Stoynoff.

Just as I began this book with a discussion of Natasha Stoynoff and Chris Guerra, I want to return to these two media producers as I end this book. They embody the level of precarity that celebrity media producers endure in their daily lives. As they manufacture celebrity and sustain the Hollywood-industrial complex, they face life-threatening and life-altering predicaments.

Since coming forward with her story, Natasha has continued to endure intense harassment from Trump supporters. She has had to see the face of her assailant everywhere she turns and has to live with the fact that he is the most powerful person in this country. And now that she has found her voice and her strength, she has begun advocating for survivors of sexual assault. From 2017 to 2018 Natasha partnered with *People* magazine to write the series "Women Speak Out: Powerful Stories from Survivors of Sexual Assault," through which she brought to light the stories of several women. In 2019 she cowrote a segment of a *Vagina Monologues*–esque production about seven women who accused Trump of sexual assault titled *The Pussy Grabber Plays*. The play recounts her encounter with Trump in an empowered fashion, expressing the anger she told me that she couldn't express in the moment.[9]

Similarly, Chris's mother, Vicky, has continued to fight for justice for her son. Whenever I speak about Chris in my work, I try to record videos and share these with Chris's family; I discuss his life and why he mattered, and these become moments of memorializing Chris for his loved ones. His family provided me with the images and evidence related to his death, and they hope that sharing this information will bring some awareness to the mistreatment of paparazzi more broadly. There is an entire conglomeration of media outlets aimed at not just humanizing but fostering deep and personal empathy for celebrities, often by dehumanizing those who manufacture celebrity. While the official police record sees Chris as responsible for his own passing, I instead see the kinds of public discourse, racialization, and cultural idolization of celebrities I have explored in this book as creating the circumstances and the vulnerabilities that led to his death.

Throughout this book I have aimed to show how the structural hierarchies that affect the content of media also affect the way this popular media is produced and how we view and critique that production. I have grappled with the complex juxtaposition between the agency media producers have to sell celebrity and their acutely gendered and racialized precarity within the Hollywood-industrial complex. It is my hope that this book has provided a better understanding of the reporters' and paparazzi's work, lives, and struggles, as well as how their lives and struggles impact the media they produce, which is enjoyed by millions of consumers every day.

APPENDIX

Interview Sources

This is a list of all interviewees quoted in the book. It is not an exhaustive list of every individual interviewed throughout the course of my research. Those individuals listed by their first and last name are either public figures or requested use of their real names. In cases where only a first name is listed, these are pseudonyms to protect the anonymity of my collaborators, per their request. All information about individuals listed here is based on their status at the time of my first interview with them. Any identifying information used was approved by the interviewee. It should also be noted that no staff reporter worked for more than one celebrity weekly magazine at the same time; this is against the policy of the magazines, as they are direct competitors.

AMANDA: Amanda is a white woman in her early twenties. She is a freelancer for a celebrity weekly magazine.

AMBER: Amber is a white woman in her thirties with a bachelor's degree. She is on staff at a celebrity weekly magazine.

ASHLEY: Ashley is a white woman in her thirties. She worked for multiple celebrity weekly magazines, both on staff and as a freelancer, and currently freelances for one of the celebrity weekly magazines focused on in this book. Prior to her work for the celebrity weekly magazines, she had worked for several other media outlets focused on entertainment.

BRIAN: Brian is a white man who does freelance reporting for *People*.

BRITTANY: Brittany is a white woman in her twenties who worked as an intern for one of the celebrity weeklies.

CHRISTY: Christy is a woman in her twenties who was an intern at *People*.

EDUARDO "LALO" PIMENTEL: Lalo is a Latino man who works as a paparazzo in Los Angeles.

GALO RAMIREZ: Galo is an immigrant from El Salvador who came to Los Angeles as a child, fleeing the civil war in his home country. He works as a paparazzo.

GREGORY: Gregory is a photographer and co-owner of a major photo agency in Los Angeles.

HALCÓN: Halcón is a Latino immigrant man who works as a paparazzo in Los Angeles.

HECTOR CAMPOS: Hector is a Latino man who works as a paparazzo in Los Angeles.

JACKIE: Jackie worked on staff at *People* magazine as part of the "body team," a group of staff members dedicated to documenting stories about celebrity bodies.

JASMINE: Jasmine is an African American woman in her late twenties who is a freelance reporter for a celebrity weekly magazine. She has a master's degree in journalism.

JOY: Joy is an African American woman in her late twenties with a bachelor's degree. She worked on staff as a reporter for a celebrity weekly magazine.

KENDRA: Kendra is a photo editor for *Us Weekly*.

KHLOE KARDASHIAN: Khloe is a reality television star and member of the Kardashian family.

LIAM: Liam is an African American man who works as a red carpet photographer.

LUIZ PIMENTEL: Luiz is a Brazilian immigrant who moved to the U.S. to pursue work as a paparazzo in Los Angeles.

MARK DAGOSTINO: Mark is a former staff writer at *People* and the author of numerous books, including the *New York Times* best-seller *Outside the Ring* (2009), which he cowrote with Hulk Hogan.

MEGAN: Megan is a white woman in her late twenties. She worked as both a staff reporter and a freelance reporter for multiple celebrity weekly magazines. She currently is on staff at a celebrity weekly.

MELISSA: Melissa is a white woman in her twenties with a bachelor's degree. She works freelance for various celebrity-focused publications in Hollywood.

MELISSA FROST: Melissa is a blogger who focuses on Kristen Stewart and Robert Pattinson. She is one of the founders of the website StrictlyRobsten.com.

MELISSA RIVERS: Melissa is an actress and the daughter of famed comedian Joan Rivers.

MIRANDA: Miranda is a woman who worked on staff for a celebrity weekly magazine for over a decade.

NICOLE: Nicole is a woman who worked on staff at *People* magazine as part of their "body team."

PHIL: Phil is a white man who worked for *People* magazine both on staff and as a freelancer for several years.

PHOEBE: Phoebe is a woman who worked as a photo editor for a celebrity weekly magazine.

RANDY BAUER: Randy is a photographer and co-owner of the photo agency Bauer-Griffin. He started out working as a photographer for the famed paparazzo Ron Galella in New York before relocating to Los Angeles.

REGINA KING: Regina is an African American actress.

RON: Ron is a white man in his forties who has freelanced for several of the celebrity weekly magazines throughout his career. He currently freelances for one of the celebrity weeklies.

SAM: Sam is a white man who works as a red carpet photographer.

SAMANTHA: Samantha is a journalist with a bachelor's degree who has worked as a freelance reporter for multiple celebrity weeklies during her career. She is currently on staff at a celebrity weekly magazine.

SANDRA: Sandra is a Latina woman in her late twenties. Throughout her career she has worked as an intern, freelance reporter, and staff reporter for multiple celebrity weekly magazines.

SARAH: Sarah is a woman in her twenties who worked as a freelance reporter for a celebrity weekly magazine.

SCOTT HUVER: Scott has been reporting in Hollywood for over a decade. He has written for Hollywood.com, Myhollywood.com, *In Touch, Life and Style, Us Weekly,* and *People,* and is the author of the book *Rodeo Drive* (2001).

SEAN: Sean is a white man in his forties. He has worked for *People* magazine as a news and human interest reporter for many years.

SOPHIA BUSH: Sophia is an actress.

STACEY: Stacey is a white woman in her late twenties with a bachelor's degree. She worked as a freelance reporter and on staff at a celebrity weekly magazine.

STANLEY: Stanley is a white man who works as a paparazzo in Los Angeles.

STEPHANIE: Stephanie is a white woman in her late thirties. She has worked on staff and as a freelance reporter for numerous celebrity-focused publications. She currently freelances for a celebrity weekly magazine.

STEVEN: Steven is a white man in his fifties who has worked as a red carpet videographer on and off for two decades.

SUSAN: Susan is an intern for a celebrity weekly magazine.

SYLVIA: Sylvia is a white woman in her thirties who worked for several different weeklies, both as a staff reporter and as a freelancer. Prior to her work as a celebrity weekly magazine reporter, she had worked for E!, *Entertainment Weekly,*

Teen People, *Cosmo Girl*, and several other entertainment-focused publications. She currently freelances for a celebrity weekly.

ULISES "TRUCHA" RIOS: Ulises was born in the U.S. of Mexican descent. He works as a paparazzo, as well as photographing weddings and quinceañeras. He specializes in photography of Mexican musicians and has also produced videos about low-riding cars in Los Angeles.

VICKY GUERRA: Vicky is the mother of deceased paparazzo Chris Guerra.

NOTES

Introduction

1 Velasco, State of California; Walton, State of California.

2 Walton, State of California.

3 Miley Cyrus, Twitter post, January 1, 2013 (9:13 p.m.), https://twitter.com/miley cyrus/status/286354541828530177; January 1, 2013 (9:24 p.m.), https://twitter.com /mileycyrus/status/286357265429180416; January 1, 2013 (9:25 p.m.), https:// twitter.com/MileyCyrus/status/28635748043397761.

4 Hayley Marlar, Twitter post, January 1, 2013 (11:01 p.m.), https://twitter.com /haleymarlar/status/286354774390108160.

5 Nicolini, "Celebrity Photographer Killed."

6 Miley Cyrus, Twitter post, January 1, 2013 (11:01 p.m.), https://twitter.com /MileyCyrus/status/286381648663166976.

7 Finn, "Miley Cyrus."

8 Halbfinger and Weiner, "Eye vs. Eye: Inside the Photo Wars"; Pearson, "'Britney Beat'"; Winton and Alanez, "Paparazzi Flash New Audacity"; "Photographers Sue!"

9 This interview was completed with an understanding of anonymity, which is standard practice in ethnographic methodology. After going public with her story in 2016, Natasha asked me to refer to her by her real name since the story had become public information.

10 Stoynoff, "Physically Attacked."

11 Stoynoff and Lipton, "Happy Anniversary."

12 Fahrenthold, "Trump Recorded."

13 Stoynoff, "Physically Attacked."

14 Bird, *For Enquiring Minds*; Caughey, *Imaginary Social Worlds*; Caughey, "Gina as Steven."

15 Braudy, *The Frenzy of Renown*.

16 "Survey of Teens."

17 Ulhs and Greenfield, "The Value of Fame."

18 Martin, *Haunted*.

19 For example, Yuen, *Reel Inequality*; Hunt, Ramón, and Price, "Hollywood Diversity Report"; Hunt and Ramón, "Hollywood Diversity Report"; Hunt, Ramón, and Tran, "Hollywood Diversity Report"; Hunt, Ramón, and Tran, "Hollywood Diversity Report 2019"; Hunt et al., "Hollywood Diversity Report: Setting the Record Straight"; Hunt et al., "Hollywood Diversity Report 2018: Five Years."

20 Rock, "Chris Rock." The same issue of *Hollywood Reporter* featured its annual "actor roundtable," which consisted of six white men (Galloway, "Benedict Cumberbatch"). Its "actress roundtable" two weeks later was seven white women (Belloni, "Reese Witherspoon"). The fact that the roundtable reflects the publication's prediction of who will get Oscar nominations only calls attention to the scope of the problem Rock described.

    Throughout the book I use the term *Latinx* or *Latina/o/x* as a gender nonbinary/gender-inclusive alternative to *Latina* and *Latino* to refer to U.S.-based persons of Latin American descent. I use *Latino* or *Latina* in direct quotations and when referring specifically to individuals or groups who identify as Latino(s) or Latina(s) and not as Latinx(s).

21 Caldwell, *Production Culture*; Caldwell, "Both Sides"; Mayer, *Below the Line*; Mears, *Pricing Beauty*.

22 Caldwell, *Production Culture*.

23 Ortner, "Access," 4.

24 Peterson, "Getting to the Story."

25 Behar, *An Island*; Gwaltney, "On Going Home Again"; Jones, "Towards a Native Anthropology."

26 Clark, "Journalism," 50.

27 For example, Gans, *Deciding*; Tuchman, *Making News*; Cottle, "New(s) Times," 22.

28 A "legitimate vision of the social world": Bourdieu, "The Political Field," 40. For "very few case studies," see Cottle, "New(s) Times," 27–28.

29 Beltrán and Fojas, *Mixed Race Hollywood*, 2; Shohat and Stam, *Unthinking Eurocentrism*.

30 Powdermaker's works include *After Freedom*, *Hollywood*, *Copper Town*, and *Stranger and Friend*.

31 Powdermaker, *After Freedom*, *Hollywood*, and *Copper Town*.

32 Askew, "Introduction," 3; see also Askew, "Striking Samburu"; Cherneff, "The Legacy"; Silverman, "American Anthropology."

33 For example, Askew, "Striking Samburu"; Martin, *Haunted*; Ortner, "Studying Sideways"; Ortner, "Access"; Ortner, *Not Hollywood*.

34 Davis, *City of Quartz*, 104.

35 Davis, *City of Quartz*, 104; Rodriguez, *Los Angeles Now*.

36 Webb, *Happy Birthday*, ix, 1, 19.

37 Webb, *Happy Birthday*; see also Caughey and Caughey, *Los Angeles*, 255; Cherneff, "The Legacy," 434.

38 Webb, *Happy Birthday*, ix.

39 Webb, *Happy Birthday*, 26.

40 Webb, *Happy Birthday*, 49; Barbas, *The First Lady*; Ponce de Leon, *Self-Exposure*.

41 Webb, *Happy Birthday*, 145; see also Barbas, *The First Lady*; Biskind, *Seeing Is Believing*, 3; Boggs and Pollard, *The Hollywood War Machine*, 3; Holley, *Mike Connolly*, 3.

42 Webb, *Happy Birthday*, 169.

43 Webb, *Happy Birthday*, 193.

44 Powdermaker, *Hollywood*, 36; see also Boggs and Pollard, *The Hollywood War Machine*.

45 Beltrán and Fojas, *Mixed Race Hollywood*, 2; see also Askew, "Striking Samburu"; Biskind, *Seeing Is Believing*; Blum, *Flesh Wounds*; Mazur, "U.S. Trends"; Powdermaker, *Hollywood*; Shohat and Stam, *Unthinking Eurocentrism*; Silverman, "American Anthropology"; Sutton and Wogan, *Hollywood Blockbusters*; Traube, "Secrets"; Ulysse, "Avatar."

46 Blum, *Flesh Wounds*; Descartes and Kottak, *Media*.

47 For example, Tabibian, "On the Hollywood Industrial Complex."

48 Orth, *The Importance*, 19–20.

49 Ledbetter, *Unwarranted Influence*.

50 Herwitz, *The Star*, 18.

51 Alsultany, *Arabs and Muslims*.

52 Petit, "Revealed."

53 Triggs, "My Front-Row Seat."

54 *People* Staff, "27 Photos"; PeopleStyle, "Melania Trump's First Lady Style"; Triggs, "He's Hired!"

55 Kuczynski, "Striking Back."

56 Fuerbringer, "PEOPLE," 1–2.

57 Fuerbringer, "PEOPLE," 1–2.

58 Sternheimer, *Celebrity Culture*, xiii.

59 Anderson, *Imagined Communities*.

60 Ganti, *Bollywood*.

61 For celebrity journalism: Petersen, "The Gossip Industry"; Ponce de Leon, *Self-Exposure*; Slide, *Inside*. For the Hollywood studio system: Davis, *The Glamour Factory*. For celebrity and fame: Braudy, *The Frenzy of Renown*; Herwitz, *The Star*; Ferris and Harris, *Stargazing*; Rojek, *Celebrity*; Rojek, *Fame Attack*; Ward, *Gods*. For contemporary textual analysis of celebrity magazines: McDonnell, *Reading*. For Hollywood media products: Bucholtz, "Race"; Bucholtz and Lopez, "Performing Blackness"; Meek, "And the Injun."

62 Herman and Chomsky, *Manufacturing Consent*; Powdermaker, *Hollywood*.

63 Orth, *The Importance of Being Famous*.

64 Dávila, *Latinos, Inc.*

65 Bird, "Introduction"; Boellstorff, *Coming of Age.*

66 Askew, "Striking Samburu."

67 Randolph, "Pap Smear"; Randolph, "Stalking the Paparazzi."

68 Regarding change wrought by the internet: Cottle, "New(s) Times"; "Ethnography"; Wahl-Jorgensen, "News Production." The term *virtual ethnography* borrows from Behar, "Believing"; Boellstorff, *Coming of Age*; Constable, *Romance.*

69 Spinney, "A Chance."

70 Caldwell, *Production Culture*, 2.

71 Cox, *Shapeshifters*; Bonilla, *Non-Sovereign Futures*, xvii; Rappaport, "Anthropological Collaborations," 27.

72 Trouillot, *Global Transformations*; Bonilla, *Non-Sovereign Futures.*

73 Cox, "Afterword."

74 For example, David, "Self for Sale"; Ganti, *Producing Bollywood*; Ganti, "The Value"; Hasty, *The Press*; Hasty, "Journalism"; Martin, *Haunted*; Ortner, *Not Hollywood*; Peterson, "Getting to the Story"; Peterson, *Anthropology*; Powdermaker, *Hollywood.*

75 Hopper, *The Whole Truth.*

76 Peterson, "Getting to the Story."

77 Rosa and Díaz, "Raciontologies."

Chapter One. *Shooteando*

1 Discover Los Angeles, "The Guide to Spotting a Celebrity in LA."

2 I use the terms *pap* and *paparazzi* interchangeably. *Pap* is the informal term used by paparazzi, and others in the entertainment industry, to refer to paparazzi photographers.

3 Herwitz, *The Star as Icon*, 130; Jordan, "Ellen and Portia's Wedding!"; Riding, "Public Likes"; Squiers, "Class Struggle."

4 The October 15, 2012, issue is examined. The first twenty-five pages featured twenty paparazzi shots and only ten non-paparazzi shots. Overall the magazine had 29 percent paparazzi photos, 19 percent red carpet photos, 24 percent photos shot specifically for the magazine, and 26 percent promotional photos from television studios, movie studios, or record labels.

5 Ortner, "Access."

6 Gürsel, "The Image Industry," "U.S. Newsworld," and "The Politics."

7 Loomis, "Paparazzi."

8 "Crashes and Deception."

9 Paparazzi rely on their sources for confidential tips on where to find celebrities, so they do not want to expose their sources or celebrity addresses or share their tips with others who may pass that information on to the competition.

10 Howe, *Paparazzi*, 37.

11 *Doorstepping* is the paparazzi technique of parking near a celebrity's home and waiting as many hours as necessary to spot the celebrity, or any newsworthy individuals, entering or exiting the home.

12 For more on El Salvador's civil war, see Byrne, *El Salvador's Civil War*, and Wood, *Insurgent Collective Action*.

13 A *follow* is when a paparazzi follows a celebrity in his or her car.

14 Fame Pictures, Inc. was one of a few prominent photo agencies that specialize in paparazzi photo sales. In 2012 they merged with another former major photo agency, Flynet, to become FameFlynet. In 2016 FameFlynet merged with two other major photo agencies, Xposure and AKM-GSI, to form BackGrid. Other major photo agencies selling paparazzi photos in the U.S. include x17, Splash News, and Bauer-Griffin. There are several smaller agencies as well.

15 Balassone and Piccalo, "Lohan's Car Hit"; Winton and Alanez, "Paparazzi Flash New Audacity"; Halbfinger and Weiner, "As Paparazzi Push Harder."

16 Winton, "Paparazzo Will Not Face Charges."

17 Hennessy-Fiske, "UCLA to Pay."

18 The agency AKM formed in 2009, while GSI formed in 2007. The two agencies merged in 2012. AKM's owner, Alex Kantif, and GSI's owner, Steve Ginsburg, jointly owned AKM-GSI until 2016, when they merged with FameFlynet and Xposure to form BackGrid. This interview with Galo is from the time when AKM-GSI existed.

19 To avoid confusion with Galo, I refer to Gallo by the English translation of his nickname in the text.

20 Pearson, "'Britney Beat'"; see also Halbfinger and Weiner, "As Paparazzi Push Harder" and "Eye vs. Eye"; Howe, *Paparazzi*; Winton and Alanez, "Paparazzi Flash New Audacity"; Ruy, *Giving It Up*.

21 Buch, *Inequalities of Aging*; Garcia, *Latino Politics*, 156, 184.

22 This literally means "with the black man."

23 McNamara, *Paparazzi*, 1, 5.

24 McNamara, *Paparazzi*, 5.

25 McNamara, *Paparazzi*, 12–13.

26 McNamara, *Paparazzi*, 31, 30, 42, 60, 42.

27 Soto Laveaga, *Jungle Laboratories*, 260.

28 Halbfinger and Weiner, "Eye vs. Eye"; Winton and Alanez, "Paparazzi Flash New Audacity"; Sanschagrin, "Paparazzi Success Secrets."

29 This is based on a sample of approximately one-fourth of the paparazzi working in Los Angeles today.

30 To my knowledge, there are no transgender people working as paparazzi. I also did not meet any openly gay or queer paparazzi.

31 Howe, *Paparazzi*, 43.

32 For photography as a historically male-dominated field, see Rudisill, Joseph, and

Palmquist, *Photographers*, 34. For journalism as a historically male-dominated field, see Chambers, Steiner, and Fleming, *Women and Journalism*, and Pedelty, *War Stories*.

33 Aparicio, *Listening to Salsa*, 157; Carroll, *American Masculinities*, 263–66; Delgado and Stefancic, *Critical Race Theory*; Larson, *Media and Minorities*, 60; Parada, "The Mestizo Refuses"; Sutherland and Felty, *Cinematic Sociology*.

34 Holbrook, Fessler, and Navarrete, "Looming Large," 74.

35 Hughes, "The Real Scandal."

36 Rock, "Chris Rock Pens Blistering Essay," 56.

37 Hunt et al., "Hollywood Diversity Report: Setting the Record Straight," 25; see also Smith et al., "Inequality in 1,100"; Hunt, Ramón, and Price, "Hollywood Diversity Report"; Hunt and Ramón, "Hollywood Diversity Report"; Hunt, Ramón, and Tran, "Hollywood Diversity Report"; Hunt, Ramón, and Tran, "Hollywood Diversity Report 2019"; Hunt et al., "Hollywood Diversity Report 2018."

38 Yuen, *Reel Inequality*, 2.

39 Yuen, *Reel Inequality*, 7.

40 Valdivia, *Latina*, 49.

41 Warner, "Strategies," 177; see also Caldwell, *Production Culture*; Hunt, "Race in the Writers' Room"; Hunt et al., "Hollywood Diversity Report: Setting the Record Straight"; Powdermaker, *Hollywood*; Yuen, *Reel Inequality*.

42 As an example, in the October 1, 2012, issue of *People*—the weekly celebrity magazine with the most diverse representation—there were five times as many photos of white celebrities as of celebrities of color.

43 "Mock ESL": Talmy, "Achieving Distinction." "The mock register": Mendoza-Denton, "Norteño and Sureño Gangs," 147. Thank you to Norma Mendoza-Denton for pointing to the usage of mock ESL in this image following my lecture at UCLA's Culture, Power, and Social Change speaker series in the spring of 2016.

44 "Raciolinguistics": Rosa, *Looking Like a Language*, 6.

45 Winton and Alanez, "Paparazzi Flash New Audacity."

46 Doing research in New York, I found that while there was a diverse group of paparazzi, most were from Eastern Europe.

47 Andersen and Taylor, *Sociology*, 249; Baugh, *Latino American Cinema*, 259; Petty and Wegener, "Attitude Change," 379.

48 For information about bidding down the wage scale in local markets: Espenshade, "Immigrants," 128. For the quote "that all immigration is unskilled": Dustmann and Glitz, *Immigration*, 17.

49 Pearson, "'Britney Beat.'"

50 Winton and Alanez, "Paparazzi Flash New Audacity."

51 Halbfinger and Weiner, "Eye vs. Eye."

52 Howe, *Paparazzi*.

53 Huapaya quotes from Ruy, *Giving It Up*.

54 Kaplan, *The Myth*, 76; Chavez, *The Latino Threat*.

55 Halbfinger and Weiner, "Eye vs. Eye."

56 Serpe, "Gwyneth Paltrow."

57 Harzig and Lee, *The Social Construction*, 240; McDonald and Sampson, *Immigration*, 63.

58 Huver, "R. J. Williams"; Swanbrow, "Presidential Campaigns."

59 Chavez, *The Latino Threat*, 2; see also Valdivia, *Latina*, 1.

60 Anderson, *Imagined Communities*.

61 Cottle, "New(s) Times," 20.

62 Cottle, "Ethnography," 8; see also Cottle, "New(s) Times."

63 Wahl-Jorgensen, "News Production," 30; see also Cottle, "Ethnography," 8–9.

64 Montag and Pratt, *How to Be Famous*.

65 Gürsel, "The Politics."

66 Squiers, "Class Struggle," 278.

67 Geertz, "Deep Play," 416.

68 This figure is the amount of money the agency made. Galo would receive about a 70 percent cut of those sales, to be split with his pap partner.

69 Orth, *The Importance of Being Famous*.

Chapter Two. Latinos Selling Celebrity

1   Gürsel, "The Image Industry," "U.S. Newsworld," and "The Politics."

2   Kuczynski, "Striking Back."

3   Carr, "Paparazzi Cash In."

4   Lambert, "The Kristen Stewart Mess."

5   Gürsel, "The Politics."

6   Soto Laveaga, *Jungle Laboratories*, 140.

7   The majority of Brazilian paps work on staff for x17 or are freelance and sell their photos directly through agencies.

8   "Halle Berry Puts Paparazzi on Trial."

9   This and other dialogue in Spanish was translated from Spanish to English by the author.

10 McDonald and Sampson, *Immigration*, 63.

11 Rock, "Chris Rock Pens Blistering Essay."

12 For more on this, see chapter 7 of this book.

13 Howe, *Paparazzi*, 148.

14 Justin Timberlake, Twitter post, May 22, 2012 (1:52 p.m.), https://twitter.com/jtimberlake/status/205038514482577408, May 22, 2012 (1:54 p.m.), https://twitter.com/jtimberlake/status/205038957359153152.

15 Valenzuela, *On the Corner*.

Chapter Three. To Live and Die in L.A.

1   For the entertainment industry: Curtin and Sanson, *Precarious Creativity*. For the culture industries more broadly: Mears, *Pricing Beauty*.

2   Cieply, "Death Raises Questions"; Curtin and Sanson, *Precarious Creativity*, 3–4; Johnson, "A Train."

3   Cieply, "Death Raises Questions."

4   "Unnecessary": Cieply, "Death Raises Questions." "Indefatigable worker with a cheery disposition": Johnson, "A Train."

5   "An industrywide reckoning": Johnson, "A Train"; a petition: Brzeski, "Oscars."

6   Lewis, "'Midnight Rider.'"

7   Miley Cyrus, Twitter post, January 1, 2013 (9:13 p.m.), https://twitter.com/miley cyrus/status/286354541828530177, January 1, 2013 (9:24 p.m.), https://twitter.com /mileycyrus/status/286357265429180416, January 1, 2013 (9:25 p.m.), https:// twitter.com/MileyCyrus/status/286357480433397761.

8   "Charlie Sheen Cuts $12K Check."

9   Suchland, *Economies of Violence*, 16.

10   Rosa and Díaz, "Raciontologies." This section borrows largely from this article, where the term *raciontologies*, and the relationship between race and ontologies, is explored in more depth. Relatedly, in her work on practitioners of the African diasporic religion Santería, Aisha Beliso-De Jesús discusses the notion of racial-ized—and specifically "blackened"—ontologies to address the embodied racial-izing experiences of Santería practitioners, regardless of their racial identification ("Santería Copresence," 508; *Electric Santería*, 7, 31). While Beliso-De Jesús speaks to a set of unique realities that encompass these particular forms of racialized ontologies, her conceptualization is a natural precursor to raciontologies.

11   Walton, State of California, 18.

12   Bonilla and Rosa, "#Ferguson."

13   Márquez, "Latinos as the 'Living Dead,'" 498. Referencing recent extrajudicial killings in which the names of U.S. Border Patrol agents who killed people have been kept confidential by the state, Márquez asserts that "the namelessness of the agent reflects how he is transformed from a person who killed into a mechanism of the sovereign state, programmed to perform a duty that has been normalized as routine, just, and necessary" (492).

14   Hesse, "Counter-Racial Formation Theory," viii.

15   Cacho, *Social Death*. This sentence and the following borrow directly from the analysis in Rosa and Díaz, "Raciontologies."

16   Trayvon Martin was a fifteen-year-old who was killed by George Zimmerman in Martin's neighborhood in 2012. Zimmerman was acquitted of charges in 2013.

17   Cacho, *Social Death*, 151, 6–7.

18   Associated Press, "Brad Pitt Says He Hates Paparazzi."

19   "Mila Kunis," 126.

20 Mazur, *$ellebrity*.

21 Herwitz, *The Star as Icon*, 39.

22 Famous for a Day home page, https://famousforaday.co/Home.html.

23 Bieber settled the case in 2016 for an undisclosed amount; see Associated Press, "Justin Bieber Settles Lawsuit."

24 Stallworth, "Justin Bieber Sued."

25 Díaz and Leon, "Selma Blair."

26 "Mila Kunis," 124.

27 Sontag, *On Photography*.

28 Ruy, *Giving It Up*.

29 Sanders, *Gangbangs and Drive-Bys*.

30 Vigil, *The Projects*.

31 Herwitz, *The Star as Icon*; McDonnell, "Just Like Us" and *Reading Celebrity Gossip Magazines*.

32 Ruy, *Giving It Up*; Samuels, "Shooting Britney."

33 D'Zurilla, "Jesse James."

34 "Photographers Sue!"

35 Blankstein, "Paparazzi Arrested"; Divito, "'Bachelor' Wedding Paparazzi"; Serpe, "Honeymoon's Over?"

36 "Photographers Sue!"

37 Baugh, "Linguistic Profiling," 158.

38 Rosa and Díaz, "Raciontologies."

39 Serpe, "Honeymoon's Over?"

40 Ahmed, "Affective Economies," 119.

41 "Paps Sue."

42 Trump and McIver, *How to Get Rich*, 179.

43 Littlejohn, "Why Wait for the Honeymoon!"

44 Cagle, "Editor's Letter."

45 "Sean Burke," my emphasis.

46 O'Connor, "Jennifer Garner's Harrowing Anti-Paparazzi Testimony."

47 Guerra, Gilbert, and Vizireanu, "Paparazzi Data Brief."

48 "Kristen Bell Targets People Magazine."

49 Urciuoli, *Exposing Prejudice*, 15.

50 Couldry, *Media Rituals*, 29.

51 Ahmed, *The Cultural Politics of Emotion* and "Affective Economies"; Rosa and Díaz, "Raciontologies"; Cacho, *Social Death*.

52 Wilson, Gutierrez, and Chao, *Racism, Sexism, and the Media*, 130–36, 132.

53 Mankekar, *Unsettling India*, 45; Ahmed, *The Cultural Politics of Emotion* and "Affective Economies."

54 Ahmed, *The Cultural Politics of Emotion*, 15.

55 For Latinxs: Chavez, *The Latino Threat*. For men of color: Holbrook, Fessler, and Navarrete, "Looming Large."

56 Ahmed, *The Cultural Politics of Emotion*, 49.

57 Chantel Guerra Brown, Twitter post, January 5, 2020 (11:26 p.m.), https://twitter
    .com/ChrisPaPinOff/status/1214085812490342402.

Chapter Four. Red Carpet Rituals

1 Couldry, *Media Rituals*, 29.

2 Couldry, *Media Rituals*, 27, 38. For perspective on mediated *religious* rituals, see
   Beliso-De Jesús, "Santería Copresence."

3 Henderson, "What Is the Origin?"; Grene and Lattimore, *Greek Tragedies*, 34; see
   also Cryer, *Curious English Words*, 300.

4 McAlister, *Wooden Ships*, 25.

5 For a description of the *20th Century Limited*: Cryer, *Curious English Words*, 300.
   For more on the phrase *red carpet treatment*: Wolmar, *Blood*, 283.

6 Mansky and Walker, "Oscars Red Carpet"; Henderson, "What Is the Origin?";
   Osborne, *80 Years*.

7 For example, Boyd, *Christ*; Braudy, *The Frenzy*; Kobal, *Gods and Goddesses*;
   Laderman, *Sacred Matters*; Lawrence, *The Cult*; Ward, *Gods Behaving Badly*.

8 Douglas, *Purity and Danger*, 68, qtd. in Couldry, *Media Rituals*, 23.

9 Radcliffe-Brown, *The Social Anthropology*, 99.

10 Turner, "Ritual Symbolism," 94.

11 A step-and-repeat banner generally lines the back of the red carpet. Celebrities
    pose in front of this banner, which displays logos associated with the event, in-
    cluding the name of the event and its corporate sponsors. A gobo is a template
    that is placed in front of a lighting source to control the shape that is emitted.
    Gobos are very common at red carpet events, which often have multiple corpo-
    rate sponsors who want their brands projected on and around the carpet as much
    as possible.

12 Gregorian, "Fired Black Editor."

13 Marikar, "Michael Lohan."

14 "Michael Lohan Marries."

Chapter Five. Where Reporting Happens

1 I include identifiers like race, gender, the publication a reporter worked for, and
   other details only when these identifiers will not reveal the identity of my collaborators. When the information is omitted, it is done to maintain anonymity.

2 Snyder, "American Journalism," 440.

3 Barbas, *The First Lady*, 44, 55.

4   As in all realms of dominant culture, in celebrity reporting heterosexuality is problematically presumed unless otherwise stated.

5   For example, Cagle, "Editor's Letter."

6   Stoynoff, "Donald Trump Weds"; Pearl, "'Poor Donald!'"

7   See the introduction to this book; Stoynoff, "Physically Attacked."

8   Adams, "The Inside Story"; Mizoguchi, "Former PEOPLE Writer."

9   Cagle, "The Natasha Stoynoff Interview."

10 Cagle, "PEOPLE Editor in Chief"; Hackett, "I Edited the People Writer."

11 *People* Staff, "27 Photos"; PeopleStyle, "Melania Trump's First Lady Style"; Triggs, "He's Hired!"

12 Melas, "People Magazine." See also Díaz, "Donald Trump." *People* has gradually removed some of the stories mentioned here from their website and has altered the headlines of other stories to be less celebratory.

13 Hackett, "I Edited the People Writer."

14 Morin, "Man Is Cited."

15 As I explored in earlier chapters, paparazzi images became increasingly valuable in the mid-2000s as celebrity weekly magazines multiplied and struggled to create unique products. In a similar vein, the magazines put tremendous effort into reporting celebrity nightlife news during that period in an attempt to offer unique insider material.

16 *Camp* is an industry term used to refer to a celebrity's staff or team that is responsible for his or her career. For most celebrities, this includes a publicist, agent, and manager.

17 Lipsitz, *The Possessive Investment in Whiteness*.

18 Lambert, "Hollywood Blackout."

19 Miller, "Hollywood Blackout, the Sequel."

20 Lambert, "Hollywood Blackout."

21 "Complaint," 1. The case settled out of court in 2016.

22 Gregorian, "Fired Black Editor"; "Complaint."

23 Trouillot, *Global Transformations*, 9–28.

24 Dyer, *White*, 1–2.

25 Warner, "Strategies," 172.

26 Barbas, *The First Lady*; Gamson, *Claims to Fame*; Holley, *Mike Connolly*; Ponce de Leon, *Self-Exposure*.

27 Barbas, *The First Lady*, 55.

Chapter Six. Body Teams, Baby Bumps

1   Rosen et al., "Who's Winning, Who's Sinning."

2   *People* Staff, "Diet Winners."

3 Schneider et al., "Too Fat?"

4 *People* 2019 Media Kit; *Star* 2019 Media Kit; *Us Weekly* 2019 Media Kit; *OK!* USA 2019 Media Kit; *In Touch* 2020 Media Kit; *In Touch, Life and Style*, and *Closer* 2018 Media Kit.

5 For making people feel socially closer to celebrities: *People* Media 2019 Kit. For "celebrity obsessed": *In Touch* 2020 Media Kit. For providing "readers with the hacks": *In Touch, Life and Style*, and *Closer* 2018 Media Kit.

6 Winerip, "People Magazine."

7 While *People* is the only magazine to officially state they have a "body team," the other magazines have equivalents (masked with names like health, fitness, diet, or beauty teams). So, for the purposes of this chapter, I refer to these collectively as "body teams."

8 Spitulnik, "The Social Circulation."

9 Winerip, "People Magazine."

10 Leonard, "'I Can't Believe.'"

11 Strohm, "Valerie Bertinelli."

12 Sheff-Cahan and Tauber, "I Know."

13 Sheff-Cahan and Tauber, "I Know."

14 Tauber and Cagle, "Big Star."

15 Adato, "Slimmer."

16 Harrington, M., "Confessions."

17 Strohm, "Valerie Bertinelli."

18 Leonard, "Kirstie Alley."

19 Winerip, "People Magazine."

20 Caughey, "Gina as Steven."

21 Hamm, "Kirstie Alley."

22 *People* Staff, "Valerie Bertinelli on Gaining Weight."

23 "Thick and Fabulous": Tauber, "Raven Takes Flight." "Combatting body critics": Pham, "Raven-Symoné." "I thought I looked fabulous": Shira, "Raven Symoné."

24 Keith, "Tyra Banks."

25 Keith, "Why Tyra Lost 30 Lbs."

26 *Us Weekly* Staff, "Celebrity Body."

27 Gibson, "Janet Jackson."

28 Bernstein, "The Baby Bump."

29 Espinoza et al., "Mother Figures."

30 "Mailbag."

31 Adato and Jordan, "They're Breaking Speed Records"; Sóuter and Wong, "Body after One Baby."

32 Adato and Jordan, "They're Breaking Speed Records."

33 Adato, "Heidi's Secret."

34 Keith, "Now She's Pregnant."

35 "Scoop: Jessica Simpson's Slim-Down."

36 Fox, "Weight Watchers"; Johnson, "Jessica Simpson."

37 Weight Watchers ad, YouTube, accessed April 5, 2013, http://www.youtube.com
    /watch?v=gjIZPftTjbg.

38 D'Zurilla, "Jesse James."

39 Descartes and Kottak, *Media and Middle Class Moms*, 149, 154.

40 *Us Weekly* Staff, "Christina Aguilera's Body Evolution."

41 "Star Tracks: Curve Appeal," 11.

42 "Star Tracks: Poolside Laugh," 16.

43 O'Donnell and Pham, "Lady Gaga," 109.

44 *Us Weekly* Staff, "Khloe Kardashian's Body Evolution."

45 *Us Weekly* Staff, "Khloe Kardashian's Body Evolution."

Chapter Seven. *"And Now . . . Brangelina!"*

1   Tauber et al., "Kristen's Shocking Betrayal." *Twihard* is a nickname that *Twilight*
    fans adopted. In fact fans coined several different names and classifications to
    demonstrate their allegiances to different celebrities from *Twilight*. For example,
    there were the "Robsteners," who supported Robsten being together, and the
    "Nonstens," who were anti-Robsten. This illustrates the depth of investment and
    level of self-identification Twihards had to the personal lives of the actors in the
    films.

2   Tauber et al., "Kristen's Shocking Betrayal."

3   Caughey, "Gina," 126.

4   McClain, *Keeping Up*, 97.

5   Tauber, Lynch, and Strauss, "Brad and Angelina."

6   Beginning with this paragraph, some remaining sections of this chapter build on
    my earlier exploration of Brangelina: Díaz, "Brad and Angelina."

7   McCracken, *Culture*.

8   Denham and Lobeck, *Linguistics*.

9   Williams, "'Gilbo-Garbage.'"

10 Park, "Blame Bennifer."

11 "Separate Peace."

12 Zanessa: "Zanessa on the Red Carpet"; Robsten: Talarico, "Rob and Kristen";
    DiLively: "Scoop: Blake Lively"; Speidi: Silverman, "Speidi."

13 Garcia, "Inside."

14 Turner, *Understanding Celebrity*, 8.

15 Barbas, *The First Lady*; Hopper, *The Whole Truth*.

16 For more on taking sides in celebrity relationships, see Gamson, *Claims to Fame*.
    For more on "Team Aniston" and "Team Jolie," see Goldberg, "'Team Aniston.'"

17 Denham and Lobeck define blends ("also called portmanteaus") as words "made
    from putting parts of two words together" (*Linguistics*, 197).

18 "The Brangelina Fever."

19 Díaz, "Latinos."

20 Kuczynski, "Striking Back."

21 Alford, *Naming and Identity*.

22 Turner, "The Economy," 175.

23 Turner, Bonner, and Marshall, "The Meaning," 144.

24 Tauber, Lynch, and Strauss, "Brad and Angelina," 56.

25 Alford, *Naming and Identity*, 86, 18–19.

26 Coyle, "Jolie, Pitt."

27 Lai, "Glitter and Grain," 215.

28 "Production" of "authenticity" and "para-social interaction": Redmond, "Intimate Fame," 36; see also Ponce de Leon, *Self-Exposure*, and Barbas, *The First Lady*.

29 Turner, *Understanding Celebrity*, 8.

30 Cohabitating couples in the USA: 2010: 7,500,000; 2000: 5,500,000; 1990: 2,856,000; 1980: 1,589,000; 1970: 523,000; 1960: 439,000 (Kreider, "Housing").

31 DeBarros and Jayson, "Young Adults."

32 *People* 2019 Media Kit. From 2006 to 2010 women married for the first time at older ages than in previous years (see Copen et al., "First Marriages").

33 Shankar, "Reel to Real," 319.

34 Alford, *Naming and Identity*, 18.

35 For the use of a nickname demonstrating a close relationship, see Sapir, "Language," 15–16. For the use of celebrity nicknames by the media and public, see Caughey, "Gina."

36 Cave, "2005: In a Word."

37 Rein, Kotler, and Stoller, *High Visibility*, 15.

38 For more on the celebrity as a commodity, see Marshall, *Celebrity and Power*. For more on the celebrity's name as part of the commodity, see Turner, Bonner, and Marshall, "The Meaning and Significance."

39 For more on the celebrity's name as property, see Maurer, "Comment," 776–77. For more on the celebrity's name as capital, see Bourdieu, *Language*.

40 DeCordova, *Picture Personalities*, 9.

41 Dyer, *Heavenly Bodies*, 5.

42 Turner, "The Economy," 193.

43 "People Magazine Gets Pitt-Jolie Baby Pictures."

44 For more on linguistic and symbolic capital, see these works by Bourdieu: *Distinction*; *Language*, *Outline*; "The Political Field."

45 Smith, "Brad and Angelina's Twins."

46 Behind the September 11 issue (4.1 million single copies), the issue covering Princess Diana's death (3 million), and the issue covering the death of John F. Kennedy Jr. (2.8 million). Smith, "Brad and Angelia's Twins."

47 "First Photos"; "People Publishes First Photos of Brangelina Twins."

48 Unlike many of the celebrities that followed, Brangelina reportedly donated the money made from the sale of their children's photos to charity.

49 Izzo, "Forbes Just Announced"; Pomerantz, "Kristen Stewart."

50 Spitulnik, "The Social Circulation," 165.

51 McCracken, *Culture*.

52 Smith, "The New Brangelina."

53 Rizzo, "Jerry O'Connell."

54 See "Brangelina Take Berlin."

55 Turner, Bonner, and Marshall, "The Meaning and Significance," 144; Turner, "The Economy," 195.

56 Redmond, "Intimate Fame," 35.

57 *People* Staff, "Celebrity Name Game."

58 Coddington, Maxwell, and Palmer, "Celebrity Couple."

59 WikiHow, "Make Your Celebrity Couple Names."

60 Thomas, "Coined."

61 Murphy, "Cover Story."

62 Jordan, "Ellen and Portia's Wedding!"

63 Some much less-used names received an occasional mention in the magazines, such as Khlomar for Khloe Kardashian and Lamar Odom.

64 When the name Speidi was first used, media producers (including myself) suspected that reality television stars Heidi and Spencer Pratt coined the name themselves and suggested that friends who worked at the weekly magazines begin using it. It is possible that Kris Jenner ("momager" of the Kardashian sisters) did the same with the names Kimye and Khlomar. If this is the case, then reality television stars are taking back agency, as was the case with Desilu and Lenono.

65 Or interracial heteronormativity so long as one partner, preferably the male, is white—maintaining the acceptable trope of the available minority woman to the white man (see Beltrán and Fojas, *Mixed Race Hollywood*, and Marchetti, *Romance*).

66 Powdermaker, *Hollywood*, 23.

67 Redmond, "Intimate Fame," 31.

68 For example, McGahan, "How Did Beyoncé and Jay Z Meet?"

69 Willingham, "RIP Brangelina."

70 E.g., Aroesti, "The End of Brangelina"; Brody, "The End of Brangelina and the Rise of Acteurism."

Conclusion

1 Stelter, "Marriage May End."

2 Petersen, "The Gossip Industry," 205.

3   Dracklé, "Gossip and Resistance."

4   Bergmann, *Discreet Indiscretions*, 48.

5   Golshan, "President Trump's Cable News Obsession."

6   Trump and McIver, *How to Get Rich*, 179.

7   Wang, "Trump to Anchor Jorge Ramos."

8   Editorial, "Trump Can't Treat Press Like Paparazzi."

9   Cagle, "Women Speak Out"; Herbst, "7 Women Who Accused Trump."

BIBLIOGRAPHY

Adams, Char. "The Inside Story of Why PEOPLE Published Natasha Stoynoff's Account of Being Attacked by Trump." *People*, October 19, 2016. http://people .com/politics/the-inside-story-of-why-people-published-natasha-stoynoffs -account-of-being-attacked-by-trump/.

Adato, Allison. "Heidi's Secret: From the Maternity Ward to Lingerie Model in Two Months? Here's How Heidi Klum Did It." *People*, November 28, 2005.

Adato, Allison. "Slimmer and Wiser." *People*, September 26, 2005.

Adato, Allison, and Julie Jordan. "They're Breaking Speed Records, but Celeb Moms like Denise Richards Know That Getting Back in Shape after Baby—Whether It's the First or Fourth—Takes Sweat and Sacrifice." *People*, November 7, 2005.

Agee, James, and Walker Evans. *Let Us Now Praise Famous Men: Three Tenant Families*. 1939. Boston: Houghton Mifflin, 1960.

Ahmed, Sara. "Affective Economies." *Social Text 79* 22, no. 2 (Summer 2004): 118–39.

Ahmed, Sara. *The Cultural Politics of Emotion*. 2004. New York: Routledge, 2014.

Alcoff, Linda. "The Problem of Speaking for Others." *Cultural Critique*, no. 20 (Winter 1991–92): 5–32. http://www.jstor.org/stable/1354221.

Alford, Richard D. *Naming and Identity: A Cross-Cultural Study of Personal Naming Practices*. New Haven, CT: HRAF Press, 1988.

Alsultany, Evelyn. *Arabs and Muslims in the Media: Race and Representation after 9/11*. New York: New York University Press, 2012.

Andersen, Margaret L., and Howard Francis Taylor. *Sociology: The Essentials*. Belmont, CA: Thomson Higher Education, 2010.

Anderson, Benedict R. *Imagined Communities: Reflections on the Origin and Spread of Nationalism*. London: Verso, 1983.

Aparicio, Frances R. *Listening to Salsa: Gender, Latin Popular Music, and Puerto Rican Cultures*. Hanover, NH: University Press of New England, 1998.

Appadurai, Arjun. *Disjuncture and Difference in the Global Cultural Economy*. Middleborough, U.K.: Theory, Culture and Society, 1990.

Appadurai, Arjun. *Modernity at Large: Cultural Dimensions of Globalization*. Minneapolis: University of Minnesota Press, 1996.

Aroesti, Rachel. "The End of Brangelina: The Internet Reacts the Only Way It Knows How." *Guardian*, October 19, 2016. https://www.theguardian.com/culture/2016/oct/19/brangelina-trump-pepe-frog.

Askew, Kelly. Introduction to *The Anthropology of Media: A Reader*, edited by Richard R. Wilk and Kelly Askew, 1–14. Malden, MA: Blackwell, 2002.

Askew, Kelly. "Striking Samburu and a Mad Cow: Adventures in Anthropollywood." In *Off Stage/On Display: Intimacy and Ethnography in the Age of Public Culture*, edited by Andrew Shryock, 31–68. Stanford, CA: Stanford University Press, 2004.

Associated Press. "Brad Pitt Says He Hates Paparazzi." *Hollywood Reporter*, December 2, 2008. https://www.hollywoodreporter.com/news/brad-pitt-says-he-hates-123781.

Associated Press. "Justin Bieber Settles Lawsuit for Paparazzo Altercation." *Los Angeles Times*, March 16, 2016. https://www.latimes.com/entertainment/gossip/la-et-mg-justin-bieber-settles-paparazzo-suit-20160316-story.html.

Balassone, Merrill, and Gina Piccalo. "Lohan's Car Hit; Paparazzo Arrested." Home edition. *Los Angeles Times*, June 2, 2005.

Barbas, Samantha. *The First Lady of Hollywood: A Biography of Louella Parsons*. Berkeley: University of California Press, 2005.

Baron, Zach. "Stealing Fame." *New York Times*, June 5, 2013.

Bateson, Mary Catherine. *With a Daughter's Eye: A Memoir of Margaret Mead and Gregory Bateson*. New York: Morrow, 1984.

Baudrillard, Jean. "The Implosion of Meaning in the Media." In *Simulacra and Simulation*, 79–86. Ann Arbor: University of Michigan Press, 1994.

Baugh, John. "Linguistic Profiling." In *Black Linguistics: Language, Society, and Politics in Africa and the Americas*, edited by Sinfree Makoni, Geneva Smitherman, Arnetha Ball, and Arthur Spears, 155–68. London: Routledge, 2003.

Baugh, Scott. *Latino American Cinema: An Encyclopedia of Movies, Stars, Concepts, and Trends*. Santa Barbara, CA: Greenwood, 2012.

Behar, Ruth. "Believing in Anthropology as Literature." In *Anthropology Off the Shelf: Anthropologists on Writing*, edited by Alisse Waterston and Maria Vesperi, 106–16. Chichester, West Sussex, U.K.: Wiley-Blackwell, 2009.

Behar, Ruth. "Ethnography and the Book That Was Lost." *Ethnography* 4, no. 1 (2003): 15–39.

Behar, Ruth. "Ethnography: Cherishing Our Second-Fiddle Genre." *Journal of Contemporary Ethnography* 28, no. 5 (1999): 472–84.

Behar, Ruth. *An Island Called Home: Returning to Jewish Cuba*. New Brunswick, NJ: Rutgers University Press, 2007.

Behar, Ruth. "Searching for Home." *Aeon*, April 14, 2014. http://aeon.co/magazine/society/where-is-home-for-the-child-of-nomads/.

Behar, Ruth. *The Vulnerable Observer: Anthropology That Breaks Your Heart*. Boston: Beacon, 1996.

Beliso-De Jesús, Aisha. *Electric Santería: Racial and Sexual Assemblages of Transnational Religion*. New York: Columbia University Press, 2015.

Beliso-De Jesús, Aisha. "Santería Copresence and the Making of African Diaspora Bodies." *Cultural Anthropology* 29, no. 3 (2014): 503–26.

Belloni, Matthew. "Reese Witherspoon, Julianne Moore and Actress A-List on Nude Photo Hack, Renee Zellweger's 'Cruel' Treatment, Hollywood's Female Problem." *Hollywood Reporter*, November 28, 2014.

Beltrán, Mary, and Camilla Fojas. *Mixed Race Hollywood*. New York: New York University Press, 2008.

Benjamin, Walter. *The Work of Art in the Age of Mechanical Reproduction*. 1935. Translated by J. A. Underwood. London: Penguin, 2008.

Bergmann, Jörg R. *Discreet Indiscretions: The Social Organization of Gossip*. New York: Aldine de Gruyter, 1993.

Bernstein, Jacob. "The Baby Bump." *New York Times*, April 27, 2012. http://www.nytimes.com/2012/04/29/fashion/the-baby-bump.html?pagewanted=all.

Besnier, Niko. *Gossip and the Everyday Production of Politics*. Honolulu: University of Hawai'i Press, 2009.

Bird, S. Elizabeth. *For Enquiring Minds: A Cultural Study of Supermarket Tabloids*. Knoxville: University of Tennessee Press, 1992.

Bird, S. Elizabeth. "Introduction: The Anthropology of News and Journalism: Why Now?" In *The Anthropology of News and Journalism: Global Perspectives*, edited by S. Elizabeth Bird, 1–20. Bloomington: Indiana University Press, 2010.

Bird, S. Elizabeth. "Writing the Tabloid." In *The Tabloid Culture Reader*, edited by Anita Biressi and Heather Nunn, 246–58. Maidenhead, U.K.: McGraw-Hill/Open University Press, 2008.

Biressi, Anita, and Heather Nunn, eds. *The Tabloid Culture Reader*. Maidenhead, U.K.: McGraw-Hill/Open University Press, 2008.

Biskind, Peter. 1983. *Seeing Is Believing: How Hollywood Taught Us to Stop Worrying and Love the Fifties*. New York: Henry Holt, 2000.

Blankstein, Andrew. "Paparazzi Arrested while Taking Pictures during 'Bachelor' Taping." *Los Angeles Times*, March 1, 2010. https://latimesblogs.latimes.com/lanow/2010/03/paparrazi-arrested-while-taking-pictures-during-bachelor-wedding.html.

Blum, Virginia L. *Flesh Wounds: The Culture of Cosmetic Surgery*. Berkeley: University of California Press, 2003.

Boellstorff, Tom. *Coming of Age in Second Life: An Anthropologist Explores the Virtually Human*. Princeton, NJ: Princeton University Press, 2008.

Boggs, Carl, and Tom Pollard. *The Hollywood War Machine: U.S. Militarism and Popular Culture*. Boulder, CO: Paradigm, 2007.

Bok, Sissela. "Intrusive Social Science Research." In *Secrets: On the Ethics of Conceal-ment and Revelation*, 230–48. New York: Pantheon Books, 1982.

Bonilla, Yarimar. *Non-Sovereign Futures: French Caribbean Politics in the Wake of Dis-enchantment*. Chicago: University of Chicago Press, 2015.

Bonilla, Yarimar, and Jonathan Rosa. "#Ferguson: Digital Protest, Hashtag Ethnogra-phy, and the Racial Politics of Social Media in the United States." *American Eth-nologist* 42, no. 1 (2015): 4–17.

Boorstin, Daniel J. *The Image: A Guide to Pseudo-Events in America*. New York: Athe-neum, 1962.

Bourdieu, Pierre. *Distinction: A Social Critique of the Judgement of Taste*. Cambridge, MA: Harvard University Press, 1984.

Bourdieu, Pierre. *The Field of Cultural Production: Essays on Art and Literature*. Translated by Randal Johnson. New York: Columbia University Press, 1993.

Bourdieu, Pierre. *Language and Symbolic Power*. Translated by John B. Thompson. Cambridge, MA: Harvard University Press, 1991.

Bourdieu, Pierre. *On Television*. Cambridge, U.K.: Polity, 1998.

Bourdieu, Pierre. *Outline of a Theory of Practice*. Cambridge, U.K.: Cambridge Uni-versity Press, 1972.

Bourdieu, Pierre. "The Political Field, the Social Science Field, and the Journalistic Field." In *Bourdieu and the Journalistic Field*, edited by Rodney Dean Benson and Erik Neveu, 29–47. Cambridge, U.K.: Polity, 2005.

Boyd, Malcolm. *Christ and Celebrity Gods: The Church in Mass Culture*. Greenwich, CT: Seabury, 1958.

Boyer, Dominic, and Ulf Hannerz. 2006. "Introduction: Worlds of Journalism." *Ethnography* 7 (2006): 5–17.

"The Brangelina Fever." Reuters, February 6, 2006.

"Brangelina Take Berlin: The Globe-Trotting Couple Takes Their Family to Germany for Their Latest Adventure." *OK!*, October 13, 2008.

Braudy, Leo. *The Frenzy of Renown: Fame and Its History*. New York: Vintage Books, 1997.

Brettell, Caroline. *When They Read What We Write: The Politics of Ethnography*. West-port, CT: Bergin and Garvey, 1993.

Brody, Richard. "The End of Brangelina and the Rise of Acteurism." *New Yorker*, Sep-tember 20, 2016. https://www.newyorker.com/culture/cultural-comment/the-end-of-brangelina-and-the-rise-of-acteurism.

Brokaw, Francine. *Beyond the Red Carpet: The World of Entertainment Journalists*. San Clemente, CA: Sourced Media Books, 2013.

Brzeski, Patrick. "Oscars: Campaign Urges Nominees, Presenters to Wear Black Pin for 'Midnight Rider' Crewmember." *Hollywood Reporter*, February 28, 2014. https://www.hollywoodreporter.com/news/oscars-campaign-urges-nominees-presenters-684340.

Buch, Elana D. *Inequalities of Aging: Paradoxes of Independence in American Home Care*. New York: New York University Press, 2018.

Bucholtz, Mary. "Race and the Re-Embodied Voice in Hollywood Film." *Language and Communication* 31, no. 3 (2011): 255–65.

Bucholtz, Mary, and Qiuana Lopez. "Performing Blackness, Forming Whiteness: Linguistic Minstrelsy in Hollywood Film 1." *Journal of Sociolinguistics* 15, no. 5 (2011): 680–706.

Burns, Kelli S. *Celeb 2.0: How Social Media Foster Our Fascination with Popular Culture*. Santa Barbara, CA: Praeger/ABC-CLIO, 2009.

Byrne, Hugh. *El Salvador's Civil War: A Study of Revolution*. Boulder, CO: Lynne Rienner, 1996.

Cacho, Lisa Marie. *Social Death: Racialized Rightlessness and the Criminalization of the Unprotected*. New York: New York University Press, 2012.

Cagle, Jess. "Editor's Letter: Why PEOPLE Does Not Support Paparazzi Who Target Celebs' Kids." *People*, February 25, 2014. http://www.people.com/people/article/0,,20790683,00.html.

Cagle, Jess. "The Natasha Stoynoff Interview: Natasha Stoynoff Speaks to Jess Cagle in an Exclusive Video Interview on People/Entertainment Weekly Network." People TV, November 4, 2016. https://www.peopleewnetwork.com/video/people-features-the-natasha-stoynoff-interview-161104-people-peoplefeat-110.

Cagle, Jess. "PEOPLE Editor in Chief: Why We Printed Natasha Stoynoff's Story of Being Attacked by Donald Trump." *People*, October 13, 2016. http://people.com/politics/people-editor-in-chief-why-we-printed-natasha-stoynoffs-story-of-being-assaulted-by-donald-trump/.

Cagle, Jess. "'Women Speak Out': Powerful Stories from Survivors of Sexual Assault." *People*, May 24, 2017. https://people.com/human-interest/women-speak-out/.

Caldwell, John Thornton. "'Both Sides of the Fence': Blurred Distinction in Scholarship and Production (a Portfolio of Interviews)." In *Production Studies: Cultural Studies of Media Industries,* edited by Vicki Mayer, Miranda Banks, and John Caldwell, 214–30. New York: Routledge, 2009.

Caldwell, John Thornton. *Production Culture: Industrial Reflexivity and Critical Practice in Film and Television.* Durham, NC: Duke University Press, 2008.

Cameron, James, director. *Avatar.* DVD. Beverly Hills, CA: 20th Century Fox Home Entertainment, Lightstorm Entertainment, 2010.

Carr, David. "Paparazzi Cash In on a Magazine Dogfight." *New York Times*, November 4, 2002.

Carroll, Bret E. *American Masculinities: A Historical Encyclopedia*. Thousand Oaks, CA: Sage, 2003.

Caughey, John L. "Gina as Steven: The Social and Cultural Dimensions of a Media Relationship." *VAR: Visual Anthropology Review* 10, no. 1 (1994): 126–35.

Caughey, John L. *Imaginary Social Worlds: A Cultural Approach*. Lincoln: University of Nebraska Press, 1984.

Caughey, John, and LaRee Caughey. *Los Angeles: Biography of a City.* Berkeley: University of California Press, 1977.

Cave, Damien. "2005: In a Word. Scalito." *New York Times,* December 25, 2005. http://query.nytimes.com/gst/fullpage.html?res=9503E6D81530F936A15751C1A9639C8B63.

Chambers, Deborah, Linda Steiner, and Carole Fleming. *Women and Journalism.* London: Routledge, 2004.

"Charlie Sheen Cuts $12K Check for Paparazzo's Funeral." TMZ, January 10, 2013. http://www.tmz.com/2013/01/10/charlie-sheen-funeral-check-paparazzo-justin-bieber/.

Chavez, Leo R. *The Latino Threat: Constructing Immigrants, Citizens, and the Nation.* Stanford, CA: Stanford University Press, 2008.

Cherneff, Jill B. R. "The Legacy of Hortense Powdermaker." *Journal of Anthropological Research* 47 (1991): 373–478.

Childress, Erik. "CineVegas '05 Interview ('Standing Still' Director Matthew Cole Weiss)." EFilmCritic, May 27, 2005. http://www.efilmcritic.com/feature.php?feature=1488.

Cieply, Michael. "Death Raises Questions about On-Set Safety." *New York Times,* March 23, 2014. https://www.nytimes.com/2014/03/24/business/media/death-raises-on-set-safety-questions.html.

Clark, Judith. "Journalism: Theory, Practice, and Criticism." *Journalism* 4, no. 1 (2003): 50–75.

Claustro, Lisa. "E! Renews 'Keeping Up with the Kardashians.'" *Buddy TV,* November 13, 2007. https://web.archive.org/web/20071128144630/http://www.buddytv.com/articles/keeping-up-with-the-kardashians/e-renews-keeping-up-with-the-k-13667.aspx.

Clifford, James, and George E. Marcus, eds. *Writing Culture: The Poetics and Politics of Ethnography.* Berkeley: University of California Press, 1986.

Coddington, Rod, Allison Maxwell, and Chad Palmer. "Celebrity Couple Name Maker." *USA Today,* April 5, 2007. Accessed December 1, 2008. http://usatoday30.usatoday.com/life/people/2007-04-05-celeb-nicknames_N.htm.

"Complaint, Tatsha Robertson vs. People Magazine." 2014. Southern District of New York (14 CV 6759).

Constable, Nicole. *Romance on a Global Stage: Pen Pals, Virtual Ethnography, and "Mail-Order" Marriages.* Berkeley: University of California Press, 2003.

Cook, Deborah. *The Culture Industry Revisited: Theodor W. Adorno on Mass Culture.* Lanham, MD: Rowman and Littlefield, 1996.

Copen, Casey E., Kimberly Daniels, Jonathan Vespa, and William D. Mosher. "First Marriages in the United States: Data from the 2006–2010 National Survey of Family Growth." National Health Statistics Reports, Number 49, March 22, 2012, 1–22. https://files.eric.ed.gov/fulltext/ED575480.pdf.

Cottle, Simon. "Ethnography and News Production: New(s) Developments in the Field." *Sociology Compass* 1, no. 1 (2007): 1–16.

Cottle, Simon. "New(s) Times: Towards a Second Wave of News Ethnography." *Communications* 25 (2000): 19–42.

Couldry, Nick. *Media Rituals: A Critical Approach*. London: Routledge, 2003.

Couldry, Nick, and Anna McCarthy, eds. *MediaSpace: Place, Scale, and Culture in a Media Age*. London: Routledge, 2004.

Cowen, Tyler. *What Price Fame?* Cambridge, MA: Harvard University Press, 2000.

Cox, Aimee. "Afterword: Why Anthropology?" Hot Spots, Cultural Anthropology website, September 26, 2018. https://culanth.org/fieldsights/afterword-why -anthropology.

Cox, Aimee. *Shapeshifters: Black Girls and the Choreography of Citizenship*. Durham, NC: Duke University Press, 2015.

Coyle, Jake. "Jolie, Pitt Wed Privately at Chateau in France." Associated Press, August 28, 2014. https://apnews.com/52d1548e0df54e2a9889385c5f9b4cec.

"Crashes and Deception: Paparazzi on Getting Too Close." Associated Press, April 3, 2008.

Crenshaw, Kimberle. "Demarginalizing the Intersection of Race and Sex: A Black Feminist Critique of Antidiscrimination Doctrine, Feminist Theory and Anti-racist Politics." *University of Chicago Legal Forum*, no. 1 (1989): article 8.

Cryer, Max. *Curious English Words and Phrases: The Truth behind the Expressions We Use*. Wollombi, New South Wales: Exisle, 2012.

Curtin, Michael, and Kevin Sanson, eds. *Precarious Creativity: Global Media, Local Labor*. Oakland: University of California Press, 2016.

David, Sasha. "Self for Sale: Notes on the Work of Hollywood Talent Managers." *Anthropology of Work Review* 28, no. 3 (2007): 6–16.

Dávila, Arlene M. *Latinos, Inc.: The Marketing and Making of a People*. Berkeley: University of California Press, 2001.

Davis, Mike. 1990. *City of Quartz: Excavating the Future in Los Angeles*. London: Verso, 2006.

Davis, Ronald L. *The Glamour Factory: Inside Hollywood's Big Studio System*. Dallas, TX: Southern Methodist University Press, 1993.

DeBarros, Anthony, and Sharon Jayson. "Young Adults Delaying Marriage." *USA Today*, September 12, 2007. http://usatoday30.usatoday.com/news/nation/2007 -09-12-census-marriage_N.htm.

de Certeau, Michel. *The Practice of Everyday Life*. Translated by Steven Rendall. Berkeley: University of California Press, 1984.

DeCordova, Richard. *Picture Personalities: The Emergence of the Star System in America*. Urbana: University of Illinois Press, 1990.

Delgado, Richard, and Jean Stefancic. *Critical Race Theory: An Introduction*. New York: New York University Press, 2012.

Deloria, Vine. "Anthropologists and Other Friends." In *Custer Died for Your Sins: An Indian Manifesto*, 78–100. New York: Macmillan, 1969.

Denham, Kristin, and Anne Lobeck. *Linguistics for Everyone: An Introduction*. Boston: Wadsworth/Cengage Learning, 2010.

"Departures: Margaret Mead." *Us Magazine*, December 26, 1978.

Descartes, Lara, and Conrad Phillip Kottak. *Media and Middle Class Moms: Images and Realities of Work and Family*. New York: Routledge, 2009.

Díaz, Vanessa. "'Brad and Angelina: And Now . . . Brangelina!': A Sociocultural Analysis of Blended Celebrity Couple Names." In *First Comes Love: Power Couples, Celebrity Kinship and Cultural Politics*, edited by Shelley Cobb and Neil Ewen, 275–94. London: Bloomsbury Academic, 2015.

Díaz, Vanessa. "Donald Trump: People Magazine Reports Sexual Assault Accusation, Then Fawns over President Elect." *International Business Times*, November 28, 2016. https://chicano.ucla.edu/files/news/IBT_PeopleMagazine%E2%80%99s ShamelessPivot_112816.pdf.

Díaz, Vanessa. "Latinos at the Margins of Celebrity Culture: Image Sales and the Politics of Paparazzi." In *Contemporary Latina/o Media: Production, Circulation, Politics*, edited by Arlene Dávila and Yeidy Rivero, 125–48. New York: New York University Press, 2014.

Díaz, Vanessa. "Mary-Kate's Classroom Chitchat." *People*, November 18, 2004. http://www.people.com/people/article/0,,783509,00.html.

Díaz, Vanessa, and Anya Leon. "Selma Blair: Paparazzi Pics Provide a 'Scrapbook.'" *People*, November 1, 2011. http://people.com/parents/selma-blair-paparazzi -pics-provide-a-scrapbook/.

Discover Los Angeles. "The Guide to Spotting a Celebrity in LA." July 11, 2019. http://www.discoverlosangeles.com/blog/following-paparazzi-12-places-spot -celebrity-la.

Divito, Nick. "'Bachelor' Wedding Paparazzi Sue ABC." Courthouse News Service, March 9, 2010. https://www.courthousenews.com/bachelor-wedding-paparazzi -sue-abc/.

Douglas, Mary. *Purity and Danger*. London: Routledge, 1984.

Dracklé, Dorle. 2010. "Gossip and Resistance: Local News Media in Transition. A Case Study from the Alentejo, Portugal." In *The Anthropology of News and Journalism: Global Perspectives*, edited by S. Elizabeth Bird, 199–214. Bloomington: Indiana University Press, 2010.

Du Bois, W. E. B. *The Souls of Black Folk*. New York: Dover, 1903.

Dustmann, Christian, and Albrecht Christian Ekkehard Glitz. *Immigration, Jobs and Wages: Evidence and Opinion*. London: CEPR, CReAM, 2005.

Dyer, Richard. *Heavenly Bodies: Film Stars and Society*. New York: St. Martin's, 1986.

Dyer, Richard. *White: Essays on Race and Culture*. London: Routledge, 2017.

D'Zurilla, Christie. "Jesse James and a Paparazzo Tangle—And of Course There's Video." *Los Angeles Times*, April 1, 2010. https://latimesblogs.latimes.com

/gossip/2010/04/jesse-james-and-a-paparazzo-tangle-and-of-course-theres
-video.html.

D'Zurilla, Christie. "Kim Kardashian's $500,000 Vienna Ball Date Reportedly Goes
Awry." *Los Angeles Times*, February 27, 2014. http://articles.latimes.com/2014
/feb/27/entertainment/la-et-mg-kim-kardashian-vienna-opera-ball-richard
-lugner-date-20140227.

Editorial. "Trump Can't Treat Press Like Paparazzi." *Dallas Morning News*, November
18, 2016. https://www.dallasnews.com/opinion/editorials/2016/11/18/just-press
-issue-pool-reports-essential-government-transparency-informed-american
-electorate.

Eells, George. *Hedda and Louella*. New York: Putnam, 1972.

Espenshade, Thomas. "Immigrants, Puerto Ricans, and the Earnings of Native Black
Males." In *Immigration and Race: New Challenges for American Democracy*,
edited by Gerald D. Jaynes, 125–42. New Haven, CT: Yale University Press, 2000.

Espinoza, Galina, et al. "Mother Figures: How Do Hollywood's New Moms Bounce
Back into Shape? Sweat, Savvy Planning—And Lots of Expert Help." *People*,
February 10, 2003.

"EXCLUSIVE: Mel Gibson Busted for DUI." TMZ, July 28, 2006. http://www.tmz.com
/2006/07/28/exclusive-mel-gibson-busted-for-dui.

Fahrenthold, David. "Trump Recorded Having Extremely Lewd Conversation about
Women in 2005." *Washington Post*, October 8, 2016. https://www.washington
post.com/politics/trump-recorded-having-extremely-lewd-conversation-about
-women-in-2005/2016/10/07/3b9ce776-8cb4-11e6-bf8a-3d26847eeed4_story
.html.

Fellini, Federico, director. *La Dolce Vita*. DVD. Milan: Riama Film, Cinecittà, Pathé
Consortium Cinema, 1960.

Ferris, Kerry, and Scott R. Harris. *Stargazing: Celebrity, Fame, and Social Interaction*.
New York: Routledge, 2011.

Fincher, David, director. *Fight Club*. DVD. Beverly Hills, CA: Twentieth Century Fox
Home Entertainment, 1999.

Finn, Natalie. "Miley Cyrus: Justin Bieber Paparazzo Death Was 'Bound to Happen,'
Encourages the Biebs to 'Get Involved.'" *E! News*, January 2, 2013. http://www
.eonline.com/news/375318/miley-cyrus-justin-bieber-paparazzo-death-was
-bound-to-happen-encourages-the-biebs-to-get-involved.

"First Photos of Brangelina Twins Will Net Fortune." Associated Press, July 13, 2008.

Fox, Emily Jane. "Weight Watchers Pays Jessica Simpson to Diet." *CNN Money*, May
30, 2012. http://money.cnn.com/2012/05/30/news/companies/jessica-simpson
-weight-watchers/.

Fricke, Tom. 2006. "Imagining Vhebe: Of Friendship and the Field." *Michigan Quarterly Review* 45 (2006): 197–217.

Frost, Jennifer. *Hedda Hopper's Hollywood Celebrity Gossip and American Conservatism*. New York: New York University Press, 2011.

Fry, Hannah, and Laura Newberry. "'ᴇʀ' Actress Vanessa Marquez Shot and Killed by South Pasadena Police during Wellness Check at Home." *Los Angeles Times*, August 31, 2018. http://www.latimes.com/local/lanow/la-me-ln-marquez-20180831 -story.html.

Fuerbringer, Otto. "ᴘᴇᴏᴘʟᴇ: Second Prospectus." Unpublished document, 1973.

Galloway, Stephen. "Benedict Cumberbatch, Channing Tatum and Actor A-List on Hollywood Fame, Embarrassing Moments and Stage Poop." *Hollywood Reporter*, December 12, 2014.

Gamson, Joshua. *Claims to Fame: Celebrity in Contemporary America*. Berkeley: University of California Press, 1994.

Gans, Herbert J. *Deciding What's News: A Study of ᴄʙs Evening News, ɴʙᴄ Nightly News, Newsweek, and Time*. New York: Pantheon Books, 1979.

Ganti, Tejaswini. *Bollywood: A Guidebook to Popular Hindi Cinema*. New York: Routledge, 2004.

Ganti, Tejaswini. *Producing Bollywood: Inside the Contemporary Hindi Film Industry*. Durham, NC: Duke University Press, 2012.

Ganti, Tejaswini. "The Value of Ethnography." *Media Industries* 1, no. 1 (2014): 16–20.

Garcia, Jennifer. "Inside Kim Kardashian and Kanye West's Newlywed Life." *People*, July 30, 2014. http://www.people.com/article/kim-kardashian-kanye-west -married-life.

Garcia, John A. *Latino Politics in America: Community, Culture, and Interests*. Lanham, MD: Rowman and Littlefield, 2003.

Geertz, Clifford. "Deep Play: Notes on the Balinese Cockfight." In *The Interpretation of Cultures: Selected Essays*, 435–74. New York: Basic Books, 1973.

Gibson, Cristina. "Janet Jackson Flaunts Fabulous Figure at L.A. Concert: Find Out How She Did It!" *Us Weekly*, October 9, 2017. https://www.usmagazine.com /stylish/news/janet-jacksons-70-pound-weight-loss-details-w507846/.

Ginsburg, Faye. "Fieldwork at the Movies: Anthropology and Media." In *Exotic No More: Anthropology on the Front Lines*, edited by Jeremy MacClancy, 359–76. Chicago: University of Chicago Press, 2002.

Ginsburg, Faye. "Some Thoughts on Culture/Media." *ᴠᴀʀ: Visual Anthropology Review* 10, no. 1 (1994): 136–41.

Ginsburg, Faye D., Lila Abu-Lughod, and Brian Larkin, eds. *Media Worlds: Anthropology on New Terrain*. Berkeley: University of California Press, 2002.

Goldberg, Stephanie. "'Team Aniston,' 'Team Jolie' or 'Team Over It'?" ᴄɴɴ, August 14, 2012. http://www.cnn.com/2012/08/14/showbiz/celebrity-news-gossip /jennifer-aniston-angelina-jolie/.

Golshan, Tara. "President Trump's Cable News Obsession, Explained." *Vox*, February 8, 2017. https://www.vox.com/policy-and-politics/2017/2/8/14504150/trump -cable-news-obsession-explained.

Gornstein, Leslie. "Is Jennifer Aniston More of a Movie Star . . . or a Celebrity?"

ɛ! Online, August 16, 2012. http://www.eonline.com/news/338672/is-jennifer
-aniston-more-of-a-movie-star-or-a-celebrity.

Gregorian, Dareh. "Fired Black Editor of People Sues Magazine over Alleged Discrimination against African-Americans." *New York Daily News*, August 20,
2014. http://www.nydailynews.com/new-york/ex-black-editor-sues-people
-discrimination-claims-article-1.1911165.

Grene, David, and Richard Lattimore, eds. *Greek Tragedies*. Vol. 1. Chicago: University
of Chicago Press, 1960.

Grindstaff, Laura. "DI(t)Y, Reality-Style: The Cultural Work of Ordinary Celebrity."
In *A Companion to Reality Television*, edited by Laurie Ouelette, 324–44. Oxford:
Wiley Blackwell, 2013.

Grindstaff, Laura, and Susan Murray. "Reality Celebrity: Branded Affect and the
Emotion Economy." *Public Culture: Bulletin of the Project for Transnational Cultural Studies* 27 (2015): 109–36.

Guerra, Fernando J., Brianne Gilbert, and Mariya Vizireanu. "Paparazzi Data Brief:
2020 Los Angeles Public Opinion Survey Report." Los Angeles: Thomas and
Dorothy Leavey Center for the Study of Los Angeles, Loyola Marymount University, 2020. https://lmu.box.com/s/ikttvhzhbizhovjbt6dok6pxmp2eohdv.

Gupta, Akhil, and James Ferguson. "Culture, Power, Place: Ethnography at the End
of an Era." In *Culture, Power, Place: Explorations in Critical Anthropology*, edited
by Akhil Gupta and James Ferguson, 1–32. Durham, NC: Duke University Press,
1997.

Gürsel, Zeynep. "The Image Industry: The Work of International News Photographs
in the Age of Digital Reproduction." PhD diss., University of California, Berkeley, 2007.

Gürsel, Zeynep. "The Politics of Wire Service Photography: Infrastructures of Representation in a Digital Newsroom." *American Ethnologist* 39, no. 1 (2012): 71–89.

Gürsel, Zeynep. "U.S. Newsworld: The Rule of Text and Everyday Practices of Editing the World." In *The Anthropology of News and Journalism: Global Perspectives*,
edited by S. Elizabeth Bird, 35–53. Bloomington: Indiana University Press, 2010.

Gusterson, Hugh. *Nuclear Rites: A Weapons Laboratory at the End of the Cold War*.
Berkeley: University of California Press, 1996.

Gwaltney, John. "On Going Home Again—Some Reflections of a Native Anthropologist." *Phylon* 37, no. 3 (1976): 236–42.

Habermas, Jürgen. *The Structural Transformation of the Public Sphere: An Inquiry into
a Category of Bourgeois Society*. Cambridge, MA: MIT Press, 1972.

Hackett, Larry. "I Edited the People Writer Who Says Trump Groped Her. Here's
Why She Didn't Speak Out." *Washington Post*, October 14, 2016. https://www
.washingtonpost.com/posteverything/wp/2016/10/14/i-edited-the-people
-reporter-who-says-trump-groped-her-heres-why-she-never-came-forward
-before/.

Halbfinger, David M., and Allison H. Weiner. "As Paparazzi Push Harder, Stars Try to Push Back." *New York Times*, June 9, 2005.

Halbfinger, David M., and Allison H. Weiner. "Eye vs. Eye: Inside the Photo Wars." *New York Times*, July 17, 2005.

"Halle Berry Puts Paparazzi on Trial." TMZ, August 16, 2012. http://www.tmz.com /2012/08/16/halle-berry-paparazzi-on-trial-nahla-gabriel-aubry/.

Hamm, Liza. "Kirstie Alley Joins Jenny Craig—Again!" *People*, April 7, 2014. http:// www.people.com/people/article/0,,20803831,00.html.

Hankins, Joseph D. *Working Skin: Making Leather, Making a Multicultural Japan.* Oakland: University of California Press, 2014.

Hannerz, Ulf. *Foreign News: Exploring the World of Foreign Correspondents.* Chicago: University of Chicago Press, 2004.

Hannerz, Ulf. "Journalists, Anthropologists, and the Cosmopolitan Imagination." Paper presented at the American Anthropological Association annual meeting, Washington, DC, 2001.

Hannerz, Ulf. "Other Transnationals: Perspectives Gained from Studying Sideways." *Paideuma*, no. 44 (1998): 109–23.

Harrington, Maurine. "Confessions of Two ExFat Actresses." *People*, August 20, 2007.

Harrington, Walt. *Intimate Journalism: The Art and Craft of Reporting Everyday Life.* Thousand Oaks, CA: Sage, 1997.

Hart, Janet. "Prologue: Political Fables." In *New Voices in the Nation: Women and the Greek Resistance, 1941–1964,* 1–27. Ithaca, NY: Cornell University Press, 1996.

Harzig, Christiane, and Danielle Juteau Lee. *The Social Construction of Diversity: Recasting the Master Narrative of Industrial Nations.* New York: Berghahn Books, 2003.

Hasty, Jennifer. "Journalism as Fieldwork: Propaganda, Complicity, and the Ethics of Anthropology." In *The Anthropology of News and Journalism: Global Perspectives,* edited by S. Elizabeth Bird, 132–50. Bloomington: Indiana University Press, 2010.

Hasty, Jennifer. *The Press and Political Culture in Ghana.* Bloomington: Indiana University Press, 2005.

Hauser, Christine. "Writer for People Magazine Describes Forced Kiss by Trump." *New York Times*, October 13, 2016. https://www.nytimes.com/2016/10/14/us /politics/trump-people-natasha-stoynoff.html.

Henderson, Amy. "What Is the Origin of Hollywood's Red Carpet?" *Smithsonian,* October 25, 2013. https://www.smithsonianmag.com/smithsonian-institution /what-is-the-origin-of-hollywoods-red-carpet-180949038/.

Hennessy-Fiske, Molly. "UCLA to Pay $865,500 for Breaches of Celebrities' Medical Files; Settlement Also Calls for Staff Retraining and Measures to Prevent Future Privacy Abuses." *Los Angeles Times*, July 8, 2011.

Herbst, Diane. "7 Women Who Accused Trump, Including PEOPLE Writer, Tell Their Stories Onstage: 'I Feel Triumphant.'" *People*, January 11, 2019. https://

people.com/politics/people-writer-attacked-donald-trump-accuser-writes-play
-forcible-kiss/.

Herman, Edward S., and Noam Chomsky. *Manufacturing Consent: The Political Economy of the Mass Media*. New York: Pantheon Books, 1988.

Herwitz, Daniel Alan. *The Star as Icon: Celebrity in the Age of Mass Consumption*. New York: Columbia University Press, 2008.

Hesse, Barnor. "Counter-Racial Formation Theory." In *Conceptual Aphasia in Black: Displacing Racial Formation*, edited by P. Khalil Saucier and Tryon P. Woods, vii–x. Lanham, MD: Lexington Books, 2016.

Hill, Jane. "Language, Race, and White Public Space." *American Anthropologist* 100 (1998): 680 89.

Ho, Karen. *Liquidated: An Ethnography of Wall Street*. Durham, NC: Duke University Press, 2009.

Holbrook, Colin, Daniel M. T. Fessler, and Carlos David Navarrete. "Looming Large in Others' Eyes: Racial Stereotypes Illuminate Dual Adaptations for Representing Threat versus Prestige as Physical Size." *Evolution and Human Behavior* 37, no. 1 (2016): 67–78.

Holley, Val. *Mike Connolly and the Manly Art of Hollywood Gossip*. Jefferson, NC: McFarland, 2003.

Hopper, Hedda. *The Whole Truth and Nothing But*. Garden City, NY: Doubleday, 1963.

Horkheimer, Max, and Theodor W. Adorno. "The Culture Industry: Enlightenment as Mass Deception." 1947. In *Dialectic of Enlightenment*, 94–136. New York: Continuum, 1997.

Howe, Peter. *Paparazzi*. New York: Artisan, 2005.

Hughes, Sarah. "The Real Scandal: American Television's 38-Year Wait for a Black Female Lead Character." *Guardian*, October 22, 2012. https://www.theguardian .com/lifeandstyle/2012/oct/22/american-television-real-scandal.

Hunt, Darnell. "Race in the Writers' Room: How Hollywood Whitewashes the Stories That Shape America." Color of Change Hollywood, commissioned study, 2017. https://hollywood.colorofchange.org/wp-content/uploads/2019/03/COC _Hollywood_Race_Report.pdf.

Hunt, Darnell, and Ana-Christina Ramón. "Hollywood Diversity Report: Flipping the Script." Report. Los Angeles: Ralph J. Bunche Center for African American Studies at UCLA, 2015. https://irle.ucla.edu/wp-content/uploads/2017/11/2015 -Hollywood-Diversity-Report-2-25-15.pdf.

Hunt, Darnell M., Ana-Christina Ramón, and Zachary Price. "Hollywood Diversity Report: Making Sense of the Disconnect." Report. Los Angeles: Ralph J. Bunche Center for African American Studies at UCLA, 2014. https://socialsciences.ucla .edu/wp-content/uploads/2017/09/2014-Hollywood-Diversity-Report-2-12-14 .pdf.

Hunt, Darnell, Ana-Christina Ramón, and Michael Tran. "Hollywood Diversity Report: Busine$$ as Usual." Report. Los Angeles: Ralph J. Bunche Center for

African American Studies at UCLA, 2016. https://socialsciences.ucla.edu/wp
-content/uploads/2017/09/2016-Hollywood-Diversity-Report-2-25-16.pdf.

Hunt, Darnell, Ana-Christina Ramón, and Michael Tran. "Hollywood Diversity Report 2019: Old Story, New Beginning." Report. Los Angeles: UCLA College of Social Sciences, 2019. https://socialsciences.ucla.edu/wp-content/uploads/2019/02
/UCLA-Hollywood-Diversity-Report-2019-2-21-2019.pdf.

Hunt, Darnell, Ana-Christina Ramón, Michael Tran, Amberia Sargent, and Vanessa Díaz. "Hollywood Diversity Report: Setting the Record Straight." Report. Los Angeles: Ralph J. Bunche Center for African American Studies at UCLA, 2017. https://bunchecenterdev.pre.ss.ucla.edu/wp-content/uploads/sites/97/2017/04
/2017-Hollywood-Diversity-Report-2-21-17.pdf.

Hunt, Darnell, Ana-Christina Ramón, Michael Tran, Amberia Sargent, and Debanjan Roychoudhury. "Hollywood Diversity Report 2018: Five Years of Progress and Missed Opportunities." Report. Los Angeles: UCLA College of Social Sciences, 2018. https://socialsciences.ucla.edu/wp-content/uploads/2018/02/UCLA
-Hollywood-Diversity-Report-2018-2-27-18.pdf.

Huver, Scott. "R. J. Williams Revamps Young Hollywood." *Los Angeles Confidential*, November 2009.

In Touch, *Life and Style*, and *Closer* 2018 Media Kit. Accessed November 30, 2018. https://www.americanmediainc.com/sites/americanmediainc.com/files
/2018%20Media%20Kit%20-%20InTouch%2C%20L%26S%20and%20Closer
_0.pdf.

In Touch 2020 Media Kit. Accessed January 3, 2020. https://www.americanmediainc
.com/sites/americanmediainc.com/files/2020_iNTOUCH_MediaKit_1219.pdf.

Izzo, Michael. "Forbes Just Announced the Top 10 Highest-Paid Actresses in Hollywood." *Business Insider*, June 20, 2012. https://www.businessinsider.com/forbes
-names-kristen-stewart-highest-earning-actresssee-who-else-made-the-top-10
-2012-6.

Jackson, John L., Jr. "On Ethnographic Sincerity." *Current Anthropology* 51, no. s2 (2010): s279–87.

Janiewski, Dolores E., and Lois W. Banner. "Introduction: Being and Becoming Ruth Benedict and Margaret Mead." In *Reading Benedict/Reading Mead: Feminism, Race, and Imperial Visions*, edited by Dolores Janiewski and Lois Banner, vii–xv. Baltimore, MD: Johns Hopkins University Press, 2004.

Jares, Su Ellen. "Forget Academic Applause: Anthropologist Barbara Myerhoff's Research Won an Oscar." *People*, September 25, 1978.

Jermyn, Deborah. *Female Celebrity and Ageing: Back in the Spotlight*. New York: Routledge, 2014.

Johnson, Randall. "Editor's Introduction: Pierre Bourdieu on Art, Literature and Culture." In *The Field of Cultural Production: Essays on Art and Literature*, edited by Randall Johnson, 1–25. New York: Columbia University Press, 1993.

Johnson, Scott. "A Train, a Narrow Trestle and 60 Seconds to Escape: How 'Midnight

Rider' Victim Sarah Jones Lost Her Life." *Hollywood Reporter*, March 4, 2014. https://www.hollywoodreporter.com/news/midnight-rider-accident-sarah -jones-death-gregg-allman-685976.

Johnson, Zach. "Jessica Simpson: I'm 'So Excited' about $4 Million Weight Watchers Deal." *Us Weekly*, May 30, 2012.

Jones, Delmos. "Towards a Native Anthropology." *Human Organization* 29 (Winter 1970): 251–59.

Jordan, Julie. "Ellen and Portia's Wedding!" *People*, September 1, 2008.

Kaplan, H. Roy. *The Myth of Post-Racial America: Searching for Equality in the Age of Materialism*. Lanham, MD: Rowman and Littlefield Education, 2011.

Kast, Marlise Elizabeth. *Tabloid Prodigy*. Philadelphia: Running Press, 2007.

Keith, Amy. "Now She's Pregnant, Now She's Hot! Here's How the Famously Fit Actress Got Red Carpet Ready in Record Time." *People*, September 1, 2008.

Keith, Amy. "Tyra Banks Fights Back: You Call This Fat?" *People*, January 24, 2007.

Keith, Amy. "Why Tyra Lost 30 Lbs." *People*, September 21, 2009.

Kinon, Cristina. "E! Renews 'Keeping Up with the Kardashians.'" *New York Daily News*, November 13, 2007. http://www.nydailynews.com/entertainment/tv -movies/e-renews-keeping-kardashians-article-1.260586.

Kobal, John. *Gods and Goddesses of the Movies*. New York: Crescent Books, 1973.

Kottak, Conrad Phillip. *Prime-Time Society: An Anthropological Analysis of Television and Culture*. 1989. Walnut Creek, CA: Left Coast, 2009.

Kottak, Conrad Phillip. *Researching American Culture: A Guide for Student Anthropologists*. Ann Arbor: University of Michigan Press, 1982.

Kreider, Rose. "Housing and Household Economic Statistics." Division Working Paper. Washington, DC: U.S. Bureau of the Census, 2010.

"Kristen Bell Targets People Magazine on Twitter over 'Pedorazzi' Photos." *Huffington Post*, February 3, 2014. http://www.huffingtonpost.com/2014/02/03/kristen-bell -people-magazine-twitter_n_4717130.html.

Kuczynski, Alex. "Striking Back at the Empire: Wenner Media Takes On the Mighty Time Inc. in Transforming Us to a Monthly Magazine." *New York Times*, September 27, 1999. http://www.nytimes.com/1999/09/27/business/striking-back -empire-wenner-media-takes-mighty-time-transforming-us-monthly.html ?pagewanted=all&src=pm.

Laderman, Gary. *Sacred Matters: Celebrity Worship, Sexual Ecstasies, the Living Dead, and Other Signs of Religious Life in the United States*. New York: New Press, 2009.

Lai, Adrienne. "Glitter and Grain: Aura and Authenticity in the Celebrity Photographs of Juergen Teller." In *Framing Celebrity: New Directions in Celebrity Culture*, edited by Su Holmes and Sean Redmond, 215–30. London: Routledge, 2006.

Lambert, Molly. "The Kristen Stewart Mess: Forget It, Jake, It's Twilight Town." *Grantland*, August 6, 2012.

Lambert, Pam. "Hollywood Blackout: The Film Industry Says All the Right Things,

but Its Continued Exclusion of African-Americans Is a National Disgrace."
People, March 18, 1996.

Larson, Stephanie Greco. *Media and Minorities: The Politics of Race in News and Entertainment*. Lanham, MD: Rowman and Littlefield, 2006.

Lash, Scott, and Celia Lury. *Global Culture Industry: The Mediation of Things*. Cambridge, U.K.: Polity, 2007.

Lassiter, Luke Eric. "Authoritative Texts, Collaborative Ethnography, and Native American Studies." *American Indian Quarterly* 24, no. 4 (2000): 601–14.

Lawrence, Cooper. *The Cult of Celebrity: What Our Fascination with the Stars Reveals about Us*. Guilford, CT: skirt! Press, 2009.

Ledbetter, James. *Unwarranted Influence: Dwight D. Eisenhower and the Military Industrial Complex*. New Haven, CT: Yale University Press, 2011.

Leonard, Elizabeth. "'I Can't Believe I Did It!'" *People*, April 6, 2009.

Leonard, Elizabeth. "Kirstie Alley: 'I've Let Myself Go.'" *People*, March 18, 2009.

Leppert. Alice. "Momager of the Brides: Kris Jenner's Management of Kardashian Romance." In *First Comes Love: Power Couples, Celebrity Kinship, and Cultural Politics*, edited by Shelley Cobb and Neil Ewen, 133–50. New York: Bloomsbury USA Academic, 2015.

Lewis, Hillary. "'Midnight Rider': Sarah Jones Autopsy Reveals Details of Death." *Hollywood Reporter*, March 11, 2015. https://www.hollywoodreporter.com/news /midnight-rider-sarah-jones-autopsy-780791.

Linkof, Ryan. "The Public Eye: Celebrity and Photojournalism in the Making of the British Tabloids, 1904–1938." PhD diss., University of Southern California, 2011.

Lipsitz, George. *The Possessive Investment in Whiteness: How White People Profit from Identity Politics*. Philadelphia: Temple University Press, 1989.

Littlejohn, Georgina. "Why Wait for the Honeymoon! Kim Kardashian and Her Future Husband Kris Humphries Steal a Little Alone Time on Family Holiday in Tropical Paradise." *Daily Mail*, June 18, 2011. https://www.dailymail.co.uk /tvshowbiz/article-2004704/Meeting-Up-With-The-Kardashians-Kim -introduces-fianc-Kris-Humphries-family-clan-enjoy-luxurious-Pacific -getaway-island-Bora-Bora.html.

Loomis, Nicole Zsuzsanna. "Paparazzi." Master's thesis, University of Southern California, 2009.

Lull, James. "The Social Uses of Television." *Human Communication Research* 6 (1980): 197–209.

Lutkehaus, Nancy. Introduction to *Blackberry Winter: My Earlier Years*, by Margaret Mead, xi–xx. New York: Kodansha International, 1995.

Lutkehaus, Nancy. *Margaret Mead: The Making of An American Icon*. Princeton, NJ: Princeton University Press, 2008.

Lutz, Catherine A., and Jane L. Collins. *Reading National Geographic*. Chicago: University of Chicago Press, 1993.

MacKinnon, Catharine A. *Sexual Harassment of Working Women: A Case of Sex Discrimination*. New Haven, CT: Yale University Press, 1979.

"Mailbag: Body after Baby!" *People*, March 3, 2003.

Malkki, Liisa. "News and Culture: Transitory Phenomena and the Fieldwork Tradition." In *Anthropological Locations: Boundaries and Grounds of a Field Science*, edited by Akhil Gupta and James Ferguson, 86–101. Berkeley: University of California Press, 1997.

Mandel, Kwala. "Secrets from Red-Carpet Reporters." Yahoo!, February 22, 2012. https://www.yahoo.com/movies/bp/secrets-real-life-red-carpet-reporters -005534988.html.

Mankekar, Purnima. *Unsettling India: Affect, Temporality, Transnationality*. Durham, NC: Duke University Press, 2015.

Mansky, Jacqueline, and Michael Walker. "Oscars Red Carpet: A Brief History." *Hollywood Reporter*, March 7, 2014.

Marchetti, Gina. *Romance and the "Yellow Peril": Race, Sex, and Discursive Strategies in Hollywood Fiction*. Berkeley: University of California Press, 1993.

Marikar, Sheila. "Michael Lohan: Jon Gosselin's 'a Really Nice Guy.'" ABC News, July 23, 2009. http://abcnews.go.com/Entertainment/CelebrityCafe/story?id=8155155.

Márquez, John. "Latinos as the 'Living Dead': Raciality, Expendability, and Border Militarization." *Latino Studies* 10, no. 4 (2012): 473–98.

Marshall, P. David. *Celebrity and Power: Fame in Contemporary Culture*. Minneapolis: University of Minnesota Press, 1997.

Martin, Sylvia. *Haunted: An Ethnography of the Hollywood and Hong Kong Media Industries*. New York: Oxford University Press, 2017.

Maurer, Bill. "Comment: Got Language? Law, Property, and the Anthropological Imagination." *American Anthropologist* 105, no. 4 (2003): 775–81.

Mayer, Vicki. *Below the Line: Producers and Production Studies in the New Television Economy*. Durham, NC: Duke University Press, 2011.

Mayer, Vicki, Miranda J. Banks, and John Caldwell, eds. *Production Studies: Cultural Studies of Media Industries*. New York: Routledge, 2009.

Mazur, Allan. "U.S. Trends in Feminine Beauty and Overadaptation." *Journal of Sex Research* 22, no. 3 (August 1986): 281–303.

Mazur, Kevin, director. *$ellebrity*. Los Angeles: Run Rampant, 2012.

McAlister, Robert. *Wooden Ships on Winyah Bay*. Charleston, SC: History Press, 2011.

McCall, John C. 2004. "Nollywood Confidential: The Unlikely Rise of Nigerian Video Film." *Transition* 13, no. 95 (2004): 98–109.

McClain, Amanda Scheiner. *Keeping Up the Kardashian Brand: Celebrity, Materialism, and Sexuality*. Lanham, MD: Lexington Books, 2014.

McCracken, Grant David. *Culture and Consumption II: Markets, Meaning, and Brand Management*. Bloomington: Indiana University Press, 2005.

McDonald, John, and Robert J. Sampson, eds. *Immigration and the Changing Social Fabric of American Cities*. Thousand Oaks, CA: Sage, 2012.

McDonnell, Andrea M. "Just Like Us: Celebrity Gossip Magazines in American Popular Culture." PhD diss., University of Michigan, 2012.

McDonnell, Andrea M. *Reading Celebrity Gossip Magazines*. Malden, MA: Polity, 2014.

McG., director. *Charlie's Angels*. DVD. Culver City, CA: Columbia TriStar Home Entertainment, 2001.

McGahan, Michelle. "How Did Beyonce and Jay Z Meet? Jayonce Is a Little Hazy on the Details." *Bustle*, November 2, 2015. https://www.bustle.com/articles/120765 -how-did-beyonce-jay-z-meet-jayonce-is-a-little-hazy-on-the-details.

McNamara, Kim. *Paparazzi: Media Practices and Celebrity Culture*. Cambridge, U.K.: Polity, 2016.

Mead, Margaret. "'As Significant as the Invention of Drama or the Novel': A Famed Anthropologist Takes a Careful Look at 'An American Family.'" *TV Guide*, January 6, 1973.

Mead, Margaret. *Blackberry Winter: My Earlier Years*. 1972. New York: Kodansha International, 1995.

Mears, Ashley. *Pricing Beauty: The Making of a Fashion Model*. Oakland: University of California Press, 2011.

Meek, Barbra A. "'And the Injun Goes 'How!'': Representations of American Indian English in White Public Space." *Language in Society* 35, no. 1 (2006): 93–128. http://www.jstor.org/stable/4169479.

Meek, Barbra A. *We Are Our Language: An Ethnography of Language Revitalization in a Northern Athabaskan Community*. Tucson: University of Arizona Press, 2010.

Melas, Chloe. "People Magazine Faces Backlash after Publishing Donald Trump Cover." *CNN Money*, November 10, 2016. https://money.cnn.com/2016/11/10 /media/donald-trump-people-magazine-cover/index.html.

Mendoza-Denton, Norma. "Norteño and Sureño Gangs, Hip Hop, and Ethnicity on YouTube: Localism in California through Spanish Accent Variation." In *Raciolinguistics: How Language Shapes Our Ideas about Race*, edited by H. Samy Alim, John R. Rickford, and Arnetha F. Ball, 135–51. New York: Oxford University Press, 2016.

"Michael Lohan Marries Baby Mama—Lindsay Left in the Dark." *TMZ*, November 25, 2014. http://www.tmz.com/2014/11/25/michael-lohan-married-kate-major -lindsay-lohan-dad-wedding/.

"Mila Kunis Is on Top of the World." *Glamour*, August 2012.

Miller, Samantha. "Hollywood Blackout, the Sequel." *People*, April 2, 2001.

Mizejewski, Linda. *Pretty/Funny: Women Comedians and Body Politics*. Austin: University of Texas Press, 2014.

Mizoguchi, Karen. "Former PEOPLE Writer Natasha Stoynoff Speaks after Trump Controversy: 'We Cannot Be Silent Anymore.'" *People*, October 18, 2016. http:// people.com/politics/natasha-stoynoff-breaks-her-silence-since-donald-trump -controversy/.

Montag, Heidi, and Spencer Pratt. *How to Be Famous: Our Guide to Looking the Part, Playing the Press, and Becoming a Tabloid Fixture*. New York: Grand Central, 2009.

Morin, Monte. "Man Is Cited for Trespassing on Actor Brad Pitt's Property." *Los Angeles Times*, August 10, 2005. http://articles.latimes.com/2005/aug/10/local /me-pitt10.

Munn, Nancy D. *The Fame of Gawa: A Symbolic Study of Value Transformation in a Massim (Papua New Guinea) Society*. Cambridge, U.K.: Cambridge University Press, 1986.

Murphy, Meaghan. "Cover Story: Lindsay and Samantha: Inside Their Romance." *OK!*, October 13, 2008.

Nader, Laura. "Up the Anthropologist—Perspectives Gained from Studying Up." In *Reinventing Anthropology*, edited by Dell H. Hymes, 284–311. New York: Pantheon Books, 1972.

Nicolini, Jill. "Celebrity Photographer Killed While Following Justin Bieber's Car." Fox News, January 2, 2013. https://www.youtube.com/watch?v=yPNqmcyibU4.

O'Connor, Maureen. "Jennifer Garner's Harrowing Anti-Paparazzi Testimony." *The Cut*, August 14, 2013. https://www.thecut.com/2013/08/jen-garners-harrowing -anti-paparazzi-speech.html.

O'Donnell, Kevin, and Thailan Pham. "Lady Gaga: She Gained 25 Lbs . . . and Hid It 6 Ways!" *People*, October 8, 2012.

OK! 2019 Media Kit. USA edition. Accessed April 28, 2019. https://www.american mediainc.com/brands/ok.

Orth, Maureen. *The Importance of Being Famous: Behind the Scenes of the Celebrity- Industrial Complex*. New York: Henry Holt, 2004.

Ortner, Sherry B. "Access: Reflections on Studying Up in Hollywood." *Ethnography* 11, no. 2 (2010): 211–33.

Ortner, Sherry B. *Not Hollywood: Independent Film at the Twilight of the American Dream*. Durham, NC: Duke University Press, 2013.

Ortner, Sherry B. "Studying Sideways: Ethnographic Access in Hollywood." In *Pro- duction Studies: Cultural Studies of Media Industries*, edited by Vicki Mayer, Miranda J. Banks, and John Thornton Caldwell, 175–89. New York: Routledge, 2009.

Osborne, Robert. *80 Years of the Oscar: The Official History of the Academy Awards*. New York: Abbeville, 2008.

Page Six Staff. "Dating People Set Off a Buzz." *Page Six*, October 5, 2008. http:// pagesix.com/2008/10/05/dating-people-set-off-a-buzz/.

Palmer, Gareth. 2005. "The Undead: Life on the D-List." *Westminster Papers in Com- munication and Culture* 2, no. 2 (2005): 37–53.

Palriwala, Rajni. "Fieldwork in a Post-Colonial Anthropology: Experience and the Comparative." *Social Anthropology* 13, no. 2 (2005): 151–70.

"Paps Sue over 'Bachelor' Wedding Beat Down." TMZ, March 8, 2010. http://www

.tmz.com/2010/03/08/bachelor-jason-mesnick-wedding-abc-disney-lawsuit
-paparazzi-molly-malaney/.

Parada, Henry. "The Mestizo Refuses to Confess: Masculinity from the Standpoint
of a Latin American Man in Toronto." In *Troubled Masculinities: Reimagin-
ing Urban Men*, edited by Kenneth James Moffatt, 21–41. Toronto: University of
Toronto Press, 2012.

Park, Michael. "Blame Bennifer: Celeb Uni-Names Multiply." Fox News, June 13,
2005. Accessed December 1, 2008. http://www.foxnews.com/story/0,2933
,159302,00.html.

Pearl, Diana. "'Poor Donald!' Trump's Money Woes Detailed in 1990 PEOPLE Cover."
People, October 6, 2016. https://people.com/politics/poor-donald-trumps
-money-woes-detailed-in-1990-people-cover/.

Pearson, Ryan. "'Britney Beat': Paparazzi Are No Longer Faceless Pack Animals." Associated Press, April 3, 2008. Accessed September 20, 2012. http://www.foxnews
.com/story/0,2933,346212,00.html.

Pedelty, Mark. *War Stories: The Culture of Foreign Correspondents*. New York: Routledge, 1995.

"People Magazine Gets Pitt-Jolie Baby Pictures." Associated Press, August 1, 2008.

"People Published First Photos of Brangelina Twins." Associated Press, August 4, 2008.

People Staff. "Celebrity Name Game." *People*, November 23, 2005. http://www.people
.com/people/article/0,,1133516,00.html.

People Staff. "Diet Winners and Sinners of the Year: Here's the Skinny on Who Got
Fat, Who Got Fit, and How They Did It." *People*, January 10, 1994.

People Staff. "27 Photos of Ivanka Trump and Her Family That Are Way Too Cute."
People, November 9, 2016. Accessed November 1, 2018. https://people.com
/parents/ivanka-trump-and-jared-kushner-family-photos/.

People Staff. "Valerie Bertinelli on Gaining Weight: 'We Need to Take the Shame Out
of It.'" *People*, April 2, 2014. http://www.people.com/people/article/0,,20802656
,00.html.

PeopleStyle. "Melania Trump's First Lady Style: See Her Best Moments on the Campaign Trail." *People*, November 9, 2016. https://web.archive.org/web/2016
1129112547/https://people.com/style/melania-trumps-best-style-moments
-from-presidential-campaign/?xid=socialflow_twitter_peoplemag.

"People's West Coast Deputy in Trouble for Sleeping with Lady Staffer, but What
about His Men?" *Jossip*, October 6, 2008. Accessed December 19, 2014. http://
www.jossip.com/peoples-west-coast-deputy-in-trouble-for-sleeping-with-lady
-staffer-but-what-about-his-men-20081006/.

People 2019 Media Kit. Accessed April 28, 2019. https://static.people.com/media-kit
/assets/peop2019_ratecard.pdf.

Petersen, Anne Helen. "The Gossip Industry Producing and Distributing Star Images,
Celebrity Gossip and Entertainment News 1910–2010." PhD diss., University of
Texas, 2011.

Petersen, Anne Helen. *Scandals of Classic Hollywood: Sex, Deviance, and Drama from the Golden Age of American Cinema*. Kearny, NJ: Plume, 2014.

Peterson, Mark Allen. *Anthropology and Mass Communication: Media and Myth in the New Millennium*. New York: Berghahn Books, 2003.

Peterson, Mark Allen. "Getting to the Story: Unwriteable Discourse and Interpretive Practice in American Journalism." *Anthropological Quarterly* 74, no. 4 (2001): 201–11.

Petit, Stephanie. "Revealed: 6 People Who Corroborate Natasha Stoynoff's Story of Being Attacked by Donald Trump." *People*, October 19, 2016. http://people .com/politics/people-writer-attack-by-donald-trump-corroborated-six-named -sources/.

Petty, Richard, and Duane Wegener. "Attitude Change: Multiple Roles for Persuasion Variables." In *The Handbook of Social Psychology*, edited by Daniel T. Gilbert, Susan Fiske, and Gardner Lindzey, 323–90. Boston: McGraw-Hill, 1998.

Pham, Thailan. "Raven-Symoné Is Combatting Body Critics." *People*, January 15, 2009. http://www.people.com/people/article/0,,20252590,00.html.

"Photographers Sue! *Bachelor* Wedding Airs, abc Exploits Security's Attack on Photographers." x17 Online, March 8, 2010. https://www.x17online.com/2010/03 /photographers_sue_bachelor_wedding_airs_abc.

Pomerantz, Dorothy. "Kristen Stewart Tops Our List of the Highest-Paid Actresses." *Forbes,* June 19, 2012. https://www.forbes.com/sites/dorothypomerantz/2012 /06/19/kristen-stewart-tops-our-list-of-highest-paid-actresses/#38c2b24534ec.

Ponce de Leon, Charles. *Self-Exposure: Human-Interest Journalism and the Emergence of Celebrity in America, 1890–1940*. Chapel Hill: University of North Carolina Press, 2002.

Postman, Neil. *Amusing Ourselves to Death: Public Discourse in the Age of Show Business*. New York: Viking, 1985.

Powdermaker, Hortense. *After Freedom: A Cultural Study in the Deep South*. New York: Viking, 1939.

Powdermaker, Hortense. *Copper Town: Changing Africa. The Human Situation on the Rhodesian Copperbelt*. New York: Harper and Row, 1962.

Powdermaker, Hortense. *Hollywood: The Dream Factory. An Anthropologist Looks at the Movie-Makers*. Boston: Little, Brown, 1950.

Powdermaker, Hortense. *Stranger and Friend: The Way of an Anthropologist*. New York: Norton, 1966.

Puente, Maria. "Diana's Death: Did Tragedy Change Paparazzi Tactics?" *USA Today*, August 30, 2017. https://www.usatoday.com/story/life/2017/08/30/dianas-death -did-tragedy-change-paparazzi-tactics/533837001/.

Radcliffe-Brown, A. R. *The Social Anthropology of Radcliffe-Brown*. Edited by Adam Kuper. London: Routledge and Kegan Paul, 1977.

Randolph, Steven. "Pap Smear." *Vice*, April 30, 2012. https://www.vice.com/en_us /article/ex5bv4/pap-smear-0000179-v19n4.

Randolph, Steven. "Stalking the Paparazzi." *Vice*, May 4, 2012. https://www.vice.com /en_us/article/qbwj5v/stalking-the-paparazzi.

Rappaport, Joanne. "Anthropological Collaborations in Colombia." In *Anthropology Put to Work*, edited by Les Field and Richard G. Fox, 21–45. New York: Berg, 2007.

Real, Michael R. *Super Media: A Cultural Studies Approach*. Thousand Oaks, CA: Sage, 1989.

Redmond, Sean. "Intimate Fame Everywhere." In *Framing Celebrity: New Directions in Celebrity Culture*, edited by Su Holmes and Sean Redmond, 27–44. London: Routledge, 2006.

Rein, Irving J., Philip Kotler, and Martin R. Stoller. *High Visibility*. New York: Dodd, Mead, 1987.

Riding, Alan. "Public Likes Celebrity Photos but Hates the Photographers." *New York Times*, September 2, 1997. https://www.nytimes.com/1997/09/02/world/public -likes-celebrity-photos-but-hates-the-photographers.html.

Rizzo, Monica. "Jerry O'Connell: Anniversary to Be with In-Laws." *People*, July 15, 2008. https://people.com/celebrity/jerry-oconnell-anniversary-to-be-with-in -laws/.

Rock, Chris. "Chris Rock Pens Blistering Essay on Hollywood's Race Problem: 'It's a White Industry.'" *Hollywood Reporter*, December 12, 2014.

Rockwell, Donna, and David Giles. "Being a Celebrity: A Phenomenology of Fame." *Journal of Phenomenological Psychology* 40, no. 2 (2009): 178–210.

Roderick, Kevin. "People's Gold Problem." *L.A. Observed*, August 15, 2005. http:// www.laobserved.com/archive/2005/08/peoples_gold_pr.php.

Rodriguez, Phillip, director. *Los Angeles Now*. DVD. Alexandria, VA: PBS, 2004.

Rojek, Chris. *Celebrity*. London: Reaktion Books, 2001.

Rojek, Chris. *Fame Attack: The Inflation of Celebrity and Its Consequences*. London: Bloomsbury Academic, 2012.

Rosa, Jonathan. *Looking Like a Language, Sounding Like a Race: Raciolinguistic Ideologies and the Learning of Latinidad*. New York: Oxford University Press, 2019.

Rosa, Jonathan, and Vanessa Díaz. "Raciontologies: Rethinking Anthropological Accounts of Institutional Racism and Enactments of White Supremacy in the United States." *American Anthropologist* 122, no. 1 (2020): 120–32. doi:10.1111/ aman.13353.

Rosen, Marjorie, with Todd Cold, Lyndon Stambler, Sabrina Mcfarland, and Mary Huzinec. "Who's Winning, Who's Sinning: Diet Wars. You Think You've Got a Weight Battle? Celebs Like Oprah Winfrey, Dolly Parton and Jack Nicholson Have Problems That Are Off the Scale. Here's the Latest Skinny on Hollywood's Heavy Hitters." *People*, January 13, 1992. https://people.com/archive/cover-story -hollywood-takes-it-off-vol-37-no-1/.

Rothenbuhler, Eric W., and Mihai Coman. *Media Anthropology*. Thousand Oaks, CA: Sage, 2005.

Rudisill, Richard, Steven Joseph, and Peter E. Palmquist. *Photographers: A Sourcebook for Historical Research*. Nevada City, CA: Carl Mautz, 2000.

Rutenberg, Jim. "The Gossip Machine, Churning Out Cash." *New York Times*, May 21, 2011. https://www.nytimes.com/2011/05/22/us/22gossip.html.

Rutenberg, Jim. "WikiLeaks' Gift to American Democracy." *New York Times*, October 23, 2016. http://www.nytimes.com/2016/10/24/business/media/rutenberg -wikileaks-american-democracy.html.

Ruy, Frank, director. *Giving It Up*. DVD. New York: New Amsterdam Entertainment, 2008.

Samuels, David. "Shooting Britney." *Atlantic Monthly* 301, no. 3 (2008): 36–51.

Sanders, William B. *Gangbangs and Drive-Bys: Grounded Culture and Juvenile Gang Violence*. New York: Aldine de Gruyter, 1994.

Sanneh, Kelefa. "The Reality Principle: The Rise and Rise of a Television Genre." *New Yorker*, May 9, 2011.

Sanschagrin, Grover. "Paparazzi Success Secrets: Insider Tips, Patience, and Exclusivity." *Photoshelter* Blog, May 25, 2010. https://blog.photoshelter.com/2010/05 /paparazzi-success-secrets-insider-tips-patience-an/.

Sapir, Edward. "Language." In *Selected Writings in Language, Culture and Personality*, 7–32. Oakland: University of California Press, 1949.

Schneider, Karen, et al. "Too Fat? Too Thin? How Media Images of Celebrities Teach Kids to Hate Their Bodies." *People*, June 3, 1996.

Schutz, Alfred. *The Phenomenology of the Social World*. Evanston, IL: Northwestern University Press, 1967.

Schwartz, Margaret. "The Horror of Something to See: Celebrity 'Vaginas' as Prostheses." In *In the Limelight and under the Microscope*, edited by Su Holmes and Diane Negra, 224–41. New York: Continuum, 2011.

"Scoop: Blake Lively and Leo DiCaprio Heating Up in Europe." *People*, June 13, 2011.

"Scoop: Jessica Simpson's Slim-Down." *People*, July 30, 2012.

"Sean Burke: Renegade Master of the Paparazzi Reform Initiative." *Outlier TV*, September 22, 2015. https://podfanatic.com/podcast/the-people-series/episode /sean-burke-renegade-master-of-the-paparazzi-reform-initiative.

"Separate Peace: Bennifer One Year Later." *People*, January 17, 2005.

Serpe, Gina. "Gwyneth Paltrow, Chris Martin and Kids Out Together (Really) on Toy Run." E! Online, October 26, 2012. http://www.eonline.com/news/357591 /gwyneth-paltrow-chris-martin-and-kids-out-together-really-on-toy-run.

Serpe, Gina. "Honeymoon's Over? Busted *Bachelor* Paparazzi Prepare to Take on Jason and Molly." E! Online, March 1, 2010. https://www.eonline.com/uk/news /169433/honeymoon-s-over-busted-bachelor-paparazzi-prepare-to-take-on -jason-and-molly.

Serrin, Judith, and William Serrin. *Muckraking! The Journalism That Changed America*. New York: New Press, 2002.

Shankar, Shalina. "Reel to Real: Desi Teens' Linguistic Engagements with Bollywood."

Pragmatics: Quarterly Publication of the International Pragmatics Association 14, no. 2 (2004): 317–35.

Sheff-Cahan, Vicki, and Michelle Tauber. "'I Know What You're Thinking—I'm Fat!'" *People*, April 16, 2007.

Shira, Dahvi. "Raven Symoné: Only I Found Myself Attractive When I Was Heavy." *People*, January 6, 2011. https://people.com/bodies/raven-symone-weight-loss/.

Shohat, Ella, and Robert Stam. *Unthinking Eurocentrism: Multiculturalism and the Media*. London: Routledge, 1994.

Silverman, Stephen. "Speidi: The Next Tomkat and Brangelina?" *People*, May 9, 2008. Accessed December 1, 2008. http://tvwatch.people.com/2008/05/09/speidi-the -next-tomkat-branjelina/.

Silverman, Sydel. "American Anthropology in the Middle Decades: A View from Hollywood." *American Anthropologist* 109, no. 3 (2007): 519–28.

Slide, Anthony. *Inside the Hollywood Fan Magazine: A History of Star Makers, Fabricators, and Gossip Mongers*. Jackson: University Press of Mississippi, 2010.

Smith, Ben. "The New Brangelina." *Politico*, November 13, 2008. http://www.politico .com/blogs/bensmith/1108/The_new_Brangelina.html.

Smith, Stacy L., Marc Choueiti, and Katherine Pieper. "Inequality in 900 Popular Films: Examining Portrayals of Gender, Race/Ethnicity, LGBT, and Disability from 2007–2016." Los Angeles: Annenberg Foundation, 2017. https://annenberg .usc.edu/sites/default/files/Dr_Stacy_L_Smith-Inequality_in_900_Popular _Films.pdf.

Smith, Stacy L., Marc Choueiti, Katherine Pieper, Ariana Case, and Angel Choi. "Inequality in 1,100 Popular Films: Examining Portrayals of Gender, Race/ Ethnicity, LGBT and Disability from 2007 to 2017." Los Angeles: Annenberg Foundation, 2018. http://assets.uscannenberg.org/docs/inequality-in-1100 -popular-films.pdf.

Smith, Stephanie D. "Brad and Angelina's Twins Give People Its 4th Highest Selling Issue of All Time." *Huffington Post*, September 22, 2008. http://www.huffington post.com/2008/08/22/brad-and-angelinas-twins_n_120565.html.

Snyder, Robert W. "American Journalism and the Culture of Celebrity." *Reviews in American History* 31, no. 3 (2003): 440–48.

Sontag, Susan. *On Photography*. 1978. New York: Picador, 2010.

Soto Laveaga, Gabriela. *Jungle Laboratories: Mexican Peasants, National Projects, and the Making of the Pill*. Durham, NC: Duke University Press, 2009.

Sóuter, Ericka, and Marisa Wong. "Body after One Baby . . . or 2 or 3 or 4." *People*, November 7, 2005.

Spinney, Justin. "A Chance to Catch a Breath: Using Mobile Video Ethnography in Cycling Research." *Mobilities* 6, no. 2 (2011): 161–82.

Spitulnik, Debra. "Anthropology and Mass Media." *Annual Review of Anthropology* 22 (1993): 293–315.

Spitulnik, Debra. "The Social Circulation of Media Discourse and the Mediation of Communities." *Journal of Linguistic Anthropology* 6, no. 2 (1996): 161–87.

Squiers, Carol. "Class Struggle: The Invention of Paparazzi Photography and the Death of Diana, Princess of Wales." In *Over Exposed: Essays on Contemporary Photography*, edited by Carol Squiers, 269–304. New York: New Press, 1999.

Stallworth, Leo. "Justin Bieber Sued by Paparazzo for Alleged May 2012 Assault." KABC-7 News, June 26, 2013. https://abc7.com/archive/9153608/.

"Star Tracks: Curve Appeal." *People*, October 29, 2012.

"Star Tracks: Curves Ahead." *People*, November 7, 2012. http://www.people.com /people/gallery/0,,20645545_21238030,00.html.

"Star Tracks: Poolside Laugh." *People,* November 19, 2012.

Star 2019 Media Kit. Accessed April 28, 2019. https://www.americanmediainc.com /sites/americanmediainc.com/files/2019_Star_MediaKit_FINAL.pdf.

Stelter, Brian. "Marriage May End; Wedding Went On." *New York Times*, November 2, 2011.

Sternheimer, Karen. *Celebrity Culture and the American Dream: Stardom and Social Mobility*. New York: Routledge, 2011.

Stewart, Jon. "A Roc Nation in Crisis: Trouble in Beyadise." *The Daily Show*, Comedy Central, May 14, 2014. http://www.cc.com/video-clips/79e3zx/the-daily-show -with-jon-stewart-a-roc-nation-in-crisis—trouble-in-beyadise.

Stoynoff, Natasha. "Donald Trump Weds Melania Knauss." *People*, January 23, 2005. https://people.com/celebrity/donald-trump-weds-melania-knauss/.

Stoynoff, Natasha. "Physically Attacked by Donald Trump—A PEOPLE Writer's Own Harrowing Story." *People*, October 12, 2016. https://people.com/politics/donald -trump-attacked-people-writer/.

Stoynoff, Natasha, and Mike Lipton. "Happy Anniversary." *People*, January 16, 2016.

Strohm, Emily. "Valerie Bertinelli Wants to Get Back into That Tiny Green Bikini for Summer." *People*, June 1, 2012. https://people.com/bodies/valerie-bertinelli -weight-loss/.

Sturm, Circe. *Blood Politics: Race, Culture, and Identity in the Cherokee Nation of Oklahoma*. Berkeley: University of California Press, 2002.

Suchland, Jennifer. *Economies of Violence: Transnational Feminism, Postsocialism, and the Politics of Sex Trafficking*. Durham, NC: Duke University Press, 2015.

"Survey of Teens in the Greater Washington, D.C. Area." Report. Harvard University, *Washington Post*, Kaiser Family Foundation, October 1, 2005. http://www.kff .org/kaiserpolls/7406.cfm.

Sutherland, Jean-Anne, and Kathryn Feltey. *Cinematic Sociology: Social Life in Film*. Thousand Oaks, CA: Pine Forge, 2010.

Sutton, David E., and Peter Wogan. *Hollywood Blockbusters: The Anthropology of Popular Movies*. Oxford: Berg, 2009.

Swanbrow, Diane. "Presidential Campaigns Say as Much about U.S. Culture as Candi-

dates." University of Michigan News Service, October 15, 2012. http://www
.ns.umich.edu/new/releases/20880-presidential-campaigns-say-as-much-about
-u-s-culture-as-candidates.

Tabibian, Nikki. "On the Hollywood Industrial Complex." *Review and Debates at New York University*, May 13, 2017. http://reviewatnyu.squarespace.com/all/2017/5/12/on-the-hollywood-industrial-complex.

Talarico, Brittany. "Rob and Kristen Catch a Concert as a Couple." *OK!*, July 2010. https://okmagazine.com/news/rob-kristen-catch-concert-couple/.

Talmy, Steven. "Achieving Distinction through Mock ESL: A Critical Pragmatics Analysis of Classroom Talk in a High School." In *Pragmatics and Language Learning*, vol. 12, edited by Gabriele Kasper, Hanh thi Nguyen, Dina Rudolph Yoshimi, and Jim Yoshioka, 215–54. Honolulu: National Foreign Language Resource Center, University of Hawai'i at Mānoa, 2010.

Tauber, Michelle. "Raven Takes Flight." *People*, March 17, 2008. https://people.com/archive/raven-takes-flight-vol-69-no-10/.

Tauber, Michelle, and Jess Cagle. "Big Star." *People*, August 9, 2004.

Tauber, Michelle, Jason Lynch, and Chris Strauss. "Brad and Angelina: And Now . . . Brangelina!" *People*, May 9, 2005.

Tauber, Michelle, et al. "Kristen's Shocking Betrayal: Secrets and Lies." *People*, August 13, 2012.

Thomas, Karen. "Coined in the Realm of Celeb Couples." *USA Today*, April 5, 2007. http://usatoday30.usatoday.com/life/people/2007-04-05-celeb-nicknames_N.htm.

Topper, Martin D. "Anthropology and Mass Media: Or Why Is There a Margaret Mead, Daddy?" *Council on Anthropology and Education Quarterly* 7, no. 1 (1976): 25–29.

Traube, Elizabeth. "Secrets of Success in Postmodern Society." In *Culture/Power/History: A Reader in Contemporary Social Theory*, edited by Nichols Dirks, Geoff Eley, and Sherry Ortner, 557–84. Princeton, NJ: Princeton University Press, 1994.

Triggs, Charlotte. "He's Hired! Donald Trump Is Elected 45th President of the United States in Stunning Upset." *People*, November 9, 2016. https://web.archive.org/web/20190627022226/https://people.com/politics/2016-election-results-donald-trump-voted-president-of-the-united-states/.

Triggs, Charlotte. "My Front-Row Seat to History: PEOPLE Senior Editor Charlotte Triggs Watches Trump Win the Presidency." *People*, November 10, 2016. https://web.archive.org/web/20161110163846/https://people.com/politics/my-front-row-seat-to-history-people-senior-editor-charlotte-triggs-watches-trump-win-the-presidency/.

Trouillot, Michel-Rolph. *Global Transformations: Anthropology and the Modern World*. New York: Palgrave Macmillan, 2003.

Trump, Donald, with Meredith McIver. *How to Get Rich: Big Deals from the Star of the Apprentice*. New York: Random House, 2004.

Tuchman, Gaye. *Making News: A Study in the Construction of Reality*. New York: Free Press, 1978.

Turner, Graeme. "The Economy of Celebrity." In *Stardom and Celebrity: A Reader*, edited by Sean Redmond and Su Holmes, 193–205. London: Sage, 2007.

Turner, Graeme. *Ordinary People and the Media: The Demotic Turn*. Los Angeles: Sage, 2010.

Turner, Graeme. *Understanding Celebrity*. London: Sage, 2004.

Turner, Graeme, Frances Bonner, and P. D. Marshall. "The Meaning and Significance of Celebrity." In *The Tabloid Culture Reader*, edited by Anita Biressi and Heather Nunn, 141–48. Maidenhead, U.K.: McGraw-Hill/Open University Press, 2008.

Turner, Victor. "Ritual Symbolism, Morality, and Social Structure among the Ndembu." In *Ritual and Belief: Readings in the Anthropology of Religion*, edited by David Hicks, 94–103. Lanham, MD: AltaMira, 2010.

Ulhs, Yalda, and Patricia Greenfield. "The Value of Fame: Preadolescent Perceptions of Popular Media and Their Relationship to Future Aspirations." *Developmental Psychology* 48, no. 2 (March 2012): 315–26.

Ulmer, James. *James Ulmer's Hollywood Hot List: The Complete Guide to Star Ranking*. New York: St. Martin's Griffin, 2000.

Ulysse, Gina Athena. "Avatar, Voodoo and White Spiritual Redemption." *Huffington Post*, March 18, 2010. http://www.huffingtonpost.com/gina-athena-ulysse /emavatarem-voodoo-and-whi_b_418692.html.

Ulysse, Gina Athena. "Conquering Duppies in Kingston: Miss Tiny and Me, Field-work Conflicts, and Being Loved and Rescued." *Anthropology and Humanism* 27, no. 1 (2002): 10–26.

Ulysse, Gina Athena. *Downtown Ladies: Informal Commercial Importers, a Haitian Anthropologist, and Self-Making in Jamaica*. Chicago: University of Chicago Press, 2007.

Urciuoli, Bonnie. *Exposing Prejudice: Puerto Rican Experiences of Language, Race, and Class*. Boulder, CO: Westview, 1996.

U.S. Bureau of the Census. "Cohabiting Couples: Defined as Two Unmarried People of Opposite Sex Living Together, 1960–2010." Washington, DC. U.S. Bureau of the Census, 2010.

Us Weekly Staff. "Celebrity Body: Scary Skinny Bikini Bods." *Us Weekly*, January 22, 2010. https://www.usmagazine.com/celebrity-body/pictures/bony-bikini -bodies-2010211/6476/.

Us Weekly Staff. "Christina Aguilera's Body Evolution." *Us Weekly*, December 18, 2014. http://www.usmagazine.com/celebrity-body/pictures/christina-aguileras -body-evolution-2012104/34285.

Us Weekly Staff. "Khloe Kardashian's Body Evolution through Pregnancy, Weight Loss

and Relationship Drama." *Us Weekly*, February 21, 2019. https://www
.usmagazine.com/celebrity-body/pictures/khloe-kardashians-body-evolution/.

Us Weekly Staff. "Stars Who Love Their Bodies." *Us Weekly*, September 8, 2009. http://
www.usmagazine.com/celebrity-body/pictures/stars-who-love-their
-bodies-2009218/2032#ixzz1rx0GHYzQ.

Us Weekly Staff. "We're Tired of the Fat Jokes!" *Us Weekly*, October 16, 2009. http://
www.usmagazine.com/celebrity-body/pictures/were-tired-of-the-fat-jokes
-20091510/4629.

Us Weekly 2019 Media Kit. Accessed December 1, 2018. https://srds.com/mediakits
/UsWeekly-print/.

Valdivia, Angharad N. *Latina*. Illustrated edition. Cambridge, U.K.: Polity, 2010.

Valenzuela, Abel. *On the Corner: Day Labor in the United States*. Los Angeles: UCLA
Center for the Study of Urban Poverty, 2006.

Van Wolputte, Steven. "Hang On to Your Self: Of Bodies, Embodiment, and Selves."
Annual Review of Anthropology 33 (2004): 251–69.

Velasco, Juan. State of California, California Highway Patrol Traffic Collision Report
13-08-04052. Los Angeles. January 1, 2013.

Vigil, James Diego. *The Projects: Gang and Non-Gang Families in East Los Angeles*.
Austin: University of Texas Press, 2007.

Volkmer, Ingrid. *News in the Global Sphere: A Study of CNN and Its Impact on Global
Communication*. Luton, U.K.: University of Luton Press, 1999.

Wahl-Jorgensen, Karin. "News Production, Ethnography, and Power: On the Chal-
lenges of Newsroom-Centricity." In *The Anthropology of News and Journalism:
Global Perspectives*, edited by S. Elizabeth Bird, 21–34. Bloomington: Indiana
University Press, 2010.

Walton, Charles. State of California, California Highway Patrol Narrative/Supplemen-
tal Report 13-08-0452. Los Angeles. May 2, 2013.

Wang, Joy Y. "Trump to Anchor Jorge Ramos: 'Go Back to Univision.'" MSNBC, August 25, 2015. http://www.msnbc.com/msnbc/trump-anchor-jorge-ramos-go
-back-univision.

Ward, Pete. *Gods Behaving Badly: Media, Religion, and Celebrity Culture*. Waco, TX:
Baylor University Press, 2011.

Ware, Susan. *Letter to the World: Seven Women Who Shaped the American Century*.
New York: Norton, 1998.

Warner, Kristen. "Strategies for Success? Navigating Hollywood's 'Postracial' Labor
Practices." In *Precarious Creativity: Global Media, Local Labor*, edited by Michael
Curtin and Kevin Sanson, 172–85. Oakland: University of California Press, 2016.

Webb, Michael. *Happy Birthday, Hollywood! One Hundred Years of Magic: 1887–1987*.
Hollywood, CA: Motion Picture and Television Fund, 1987.

The Week Staff. "The $3 Billion Celebrity Gossip Industry: By the Numbers." *The
Week*, May 23, 2011. https://theweek.com/articles/484520/3-billion-celebrity
-gossip-industry-by-numbers.

Weir, Bill. "Paparazzi Wars: Jennifer Garner, Halle Berry Fight for Kids' Protection. Celebrity Mothers Testify in Favor of a Bill That Would Modify the Definition of Harassment." *Nightline*, ABC News, August 14, 2013. https://abcnews.go.com /Nightline/video/paparazzi-wars-jennifer-garner-halle-berry-fight-kids -19953087.

wikiHow. "Make Your Celebrity Couple Names." Accessed December 30, 2014. http:// www.wikihow.com/Make-Your-Celebrity-Couple-Names.

Williams, Linda Ruth. "Brangelina: Celebrity, Credibility and the Composite Uberstar." In *Shining in Shadows: Movie Stars of the 2000s*, edited by Murray Pomerance, 200–219. New Brunswick, NJ: Rutgers University Press, 2012.

Williams, Michael. "'Gilbo-Garbage' or 'The Champion Lovemakers of Two Nations': Uncoupling Greta Garbo and John Gilbert." In *First Comes Love: Power Couples, Celebrity Kinship, and Cultural Politics*, edited by Shelley Cobb and Neil Ewen, 13–28. New York: Bloomsbury USA Academic, 2015.

Willingham, A. J. "RIP Brangelina: 2006–2016." CNN, September 20, 2016. https:// www.cnn.com/2016/09/20/entertainment/brangelina-rip-timeline-trnd/index .html.

Wilson, Clint, Felix Gutierrez, and Lena Chao. *Racism, Sexism, and the Media: Multicultural Issues into the New Communications Age*. Thousand Oaks, CA: Sage, 2013.

Winerip, Michael. "People Magazine Still Has a Bikini Body." *New York Times*, May 24, 2009.

Winton, Richard. "Paparazzo Will Not Face Charges in Lohan Crash; Prosecutors Say There Is Not Enough Evidence That He Intentionally Hit the Actress' Car." Home edition. *Los Angeles Times*, December 29, 2005.

Winton, Richard, and Tonya Alanez. "Paparazzi Flash New Audacity: As Competition Grows, Photographers Trailing L.A.'s Celebrities Become More Aggressive." *Los Angeles Times*, October 16, 2005. http://articles.latimes.com/2005/oct/16/local /me-paparazzi16.

Wolmar, Christian. *Blood, Iron, and Gold: How the Railroads Transformed the World*. New York: Public Affairs, 2010.

Wood, Elisabeth Jean. *Insurgent Collective Action and Civil War in El Salvador*. New York: Cambridge University Press, 2003.

Yans, Virginia. "On the Political Anatomy of Mead-Bashing, or Re-Thinking Margaret Mead." In *Reading Benedict / Reading Mead: Feminism, Race, and Imperial Visions*, edited by Dolores E. Janiewski and Lois W. Banner, 229–48. Baltimore, MD: Johns Hopkins University Press, 2004.

Yee, Lawrence, and Jeremy Backlow. "People Editor-in-Chief Says Writer's Account of Trump Assault Is True, 'Good for the Public' to Read." *Variety*, October 22, 2016. https://variety.com/2016/biz/news/natasha-stoynoff-donald-trump-assault -people-magazine-jess-cagle-1201897872/.

Yoshida, Emily. "Sofia Coppola's Journey into the Heart of Low-Culture Darkness."

Grantland, June 24, 2013. http://grantland.com/hollywood-prospectus/sofia
-coppolas-journey-into-the-heart-of-low-culture-darkness/.

Yuen, Nancy Wang. *Reel Inequality: Hollywood Actors and Racism*. New Brunswick,
NJ: Rutgers University Press, 2017.

"Zanessa on the Red Carpet: Charlie St. Cloud Premiere Pics." *Hollywood Gossip*, July
21, 2010. http://www.thehollywoodgossip.com/2010/07/zanessa-on-the-red
-carpet-charlie-st-cloud-premiere-pics/.

Zelizer, Barbie. *Taking Journalism Seriously: News and the Academy*. Thousand Oaks,
CA: Sage, 2004.

INDEX

Note: Page numbers followed by *f* indicate a figure.

Obama, Barack, 46, 235, 238–39
Obama, Michelle, 235, 238–39
O'Connell, Jerry, 235
Odom, Lamar, 238, 269n63
O'Donnell, Rosie, 195
OK! magazine, 17, 24, 79, 199–200, 227, 237
Olsen, Ashley, 18, 21, 160, 164
Olsen, Mary-Kate, 18, 21, 160, 164, 178
One Direction, 237
Ono, Yoko, 225
ontologies, race and, 98–99, 112, 119–21, 262n10
Orth, Maureen, 14
Ortner, Sherry, 11
Oscars, 128, 245, 256n20
#OscarsSoWhite movement, 52
othering, 48, 60, 118, 175–76
Owen, Clive, 106

Paltrow, Gwyneth, 44, 60–61, 199–200
paparazzi: and beauty and appearance, 185–88, 199–200; boom, 47–48, 79–81; and celebrity couples, 221, 232; criminaliza-tion of, 36, 103, 115–18, 233–34; economics and ethics of, 76–94, 154–55, 216; institu-tional treatment of, 1–4, 7–10, 20, 95–121, 163–65, 178, 240, 246–50; lives and work of, 1–10, 33–75, 164, 246–50, 258n2, 258n9, 259n11, 259nn13–14; and red carpet space, 137–38, 147–49, 159–60; study of, 23–24. *See also* celebrity media
Paparazzi (Howe), 92
Paparazzi (McNamara), 46
Paparazzi Reform Initiative, 115–17
Papi (Lopez), 68
parasocial relationships, 219, 232. *See also* imaginary social relationships
Parker, Sarah Jessica, 203
Parson, Louella, 150–51, 176, 226
Parton, Dolly, 182
Pattinson, Robert, 60, 80, 218–19
Paves, Ken, 173
People en Español, 89, 132f

People magazine, 16–19, 79; author's work for, 11, 20–23, 26–28, 44–46, 129–32, 144, 160; beauty and appearance in, 181–200, 203–15, 266n7; and celebrity coupling, 219–40; and economics of celebrity media, 79–80, 265n12; gender and, 151–58; media production by, 4–6, 15–16, 70, 76–77, 163; paparazzi photos and, 116–17, 258n4; race in, 9, 90, 135, 169–72, 260n42; and red carpet space, 129–35, 139; study of celebrity and, 24–25; use of paparazzi photos in, 35, 48, 77
Perez Hilton, 24, 174
Petersen, Anne Helen, 248
Phillips, Wilson, 195
Piers Morgan, 245
Pimentel, Eduardo "Lalo," 62, 230f
Pimentel, Luiz, 185
Pink (singer), 77
Pinkett Smith, Jada, 105–7
Pink Is the New Blog, 24, 174
Pitt, Brad, 40–43, 76, 79–80, 90, 101, 135, 142, 163, 201, 221–23, 227–41, 245, 269n48
Players Club, The, 175
policing: of paparazzi, 1–3, 7, 57, 96–99, 116–17; of people of color, 97–100; of women's bodies, 9, 167–68. *See also* surveillance
Portman, Natalie, 137
Powdermaker, Hortense, 9, 13, 21, 229, 239
Pratt, Spencer, 225, 269n64
precarious labor, 4–12, 95–98, 119, 150–78, 249–50
pregnancy and media, 137, 142, 152, 161–64, 185, 188, 200–209
presidential election, 2016, 6
Production Culture (Caldwell), 10
"Pussy Grabber Plays, The," 249–50

queerness, 236–40, 259n30. *See also* sexuality
QuickTrim diet program, 214

race: and celebrity media, 4, 7–10, 151, 159, 164–76, 184, 250, 256n20, 260n42;

In **MANUFACTURING CELEBRITY** Vanessa Díaz traces the complex power dynamics of the reporting and paparazzi work that fuel contemporary Hollywood and American celebrity culture. Drawing on ethnographic fieldwork, her experience reporting for *People* magazine, and dozens of interviews with photographers, journalists, publicists, magazine editors, and celebrities, Díaz examines the racialized and gendered labor involved in manufacturing and selling relatable celebrity personas. Celebrity reporters, most of whom are white women, are expected to leverage their sexuality to generate coverage, which makes them vulnerable to sexual exploitation and assault. Meanwhile, the predominantly male Latino paparazzi can face life-threatening situations and endure vilification that echoes anti-immigrant rhetoric. In pointing out the precarity of those who hustle to make a living by generating the bulk of celebrity media, Díaz highlights the profound inequities of the systems that provide consumers with 24/7 coverage of their favorite stars.

"*Manufacturing Celebrity* presents fascinating ethnographic details and piercing social analysis on the production of 'celebrity' through sophisticated discussions of Latinx paparazzi, red carpet photographers, and women reporters exploited by the cultural dynamics of tabloid and mainstream news-making. This insightful book will be valuable to communication scholars, feminists, critical race scholars, media anthropologists, and general audiences interested in the representation and production of celebrity culture. Vanessa Díaz writes with a confident and distinctive scholarly voice."—**JOHN L. JACKSON JR.**, Walter H. Annenberg Dean of the Annenberg School for Communication and Richard Perry University Professor at the University of Pennsylvania

"Vanessa Díaz pulls back the curtain on Hollywood and the people who photograph and write about the movie stars of today and tomorrow. *Manufacturing Celebrity* is a must-read for anyone desiring keenly observed insights into the struggles of immigrants and women trying to catch some of the stardust in Hollywood's dream factory. Their stories reveal a Hollywood undergoing change that is often resisted as it grapples with the contemporary demographic reality of the United States."—**LEO R. CHAVEZ**, author of *The Latino Threat: Constructing Immigrants, Citizens, and the Nation*

VANESSA DÍAZ is Assistant Professor of Chicana/o and Latina/o Studies at Loyola Marymount University.

COVER ART: *Vengeance* premiere, Cannes Film Festival, 2009. Photo by Georges De Keerle / Getty.

DUKE UNIVERSITY PRESS
www.dukeupress.edu

ISBN: 978-1-4780-0943-6

SUPER-SOLDIER

THE

ANTIFA

COOKBOOK

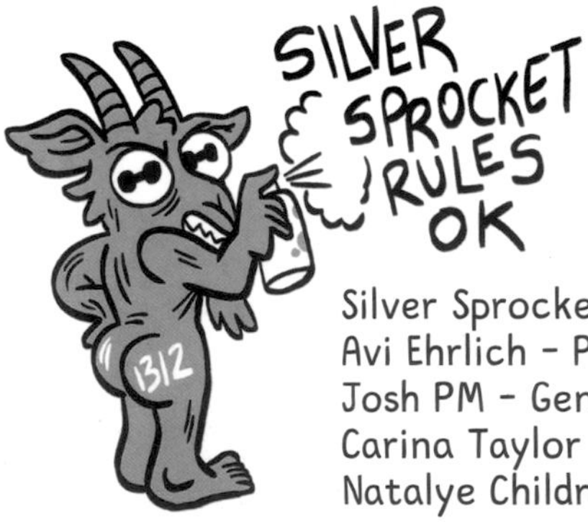

SILVER
SPROCKET
RULES
OK

Silver Sprocket
Avi Ehrlich – Publisher
Josh PM – General Manager
Carina Taylor – Production Designer
Natalye Childress – Copyeditor

PREPARING DISGUISE. GOING SILENT FOR NOW.

2

BUT WHEN YOU CENTER CAPITALISM IN OUR ACTIONS, YOU HYPERNORMALIZE THE LACK OF A DIALECTIC–

–I HEAR YOU, BUT OUR METHODS OF HARM REDUCTION HAVE TO BE BASED IN THE REAL WORLD–

...HI.

I'M HERE FOR THE MEETING?

SURE THING! WE'RE JUST GETTING STARTED– ALIX AND TEA WERE DEBATING OUR NON-BINDING RESOLUTION ON FORMING A SEARCH SUBCOMMITTEE TO DETERMINE POTENTIAL CANDIDATES FOR OUR EQUAL HOUSING ACTIONS WORKING GROUP. I'M MAX.

IT'S GETTING A *LITTLE* HEATED, AND AS FACILITATOR FOR TONIGHT WITH AN EYE FOR TIME, I'M GOING TO SAY WE TABLE THAT UNTIL WE BREAK OUT AFTER PIZZA. THANKS FOLX.

THAT'S IT FOR THE OLD BUSINESS.

ANY NEW BUSINESS?

3

LEVEL 00

WELCOME BACK, SECOND LIEUTENANT MARX.

WHOOOOOSH

AUTHO
PERSO
ONU

REPORTING FOR DUTY, GENERAL DISORDER, SIR!

9

CHIEF IS ALL OVER ME – *YOU COULDN'T INFILTRATE?*

CAP. "MOOSE"

NO SIR.

BC PD

NO PROBLEM.

THE GOOD NEWS IS: THE CITY GOVERNMENT HAS GRANTED US ACCESS TO A VAST SURVEILLANCE NETWORK!

OH! GREAT.

OH YEAH. CELL TRACKERS, FACIAL RECOGNITION, X-RAY TRUCKS, YOU NAME IT. AND NO OVERSIGHT!

MAKES SENSE! WE'RE THE GOOD GUYS.

BC PD

OUR INTEL SAYS ANTIFA IS GOING AFTER THE STATUE OF BARNABAS EARLE ON THE CAMPUS OF EARLE UNIVERSITY UPTOWN TODAY.

11

13

DISMISSED!

←EXIT←

HEY, MARX—

GENERAL DISARRAY! SIR!

NICE WORK OUT THERE LAST NIGHT, KID. I'M HERE TO TELL YOU—

YOU'RE GETTING THE CALL-UP.

THE SUPER-SOLDIER PROGRAM?

YOU'RE IN, MARX.

ARE YOU READY TO SEE WHAT WE *REALLY* DO HERE AT ANTIFA?

...AND HERE'S THE PSYCHOLOGICAL WARFARE DIVISION...

...WHERE MOST HOLLYWOOD MOVIES AND TELEVISION SHOWS ARE MADE.

GAY DOG 2

OUR CHEMICAL WEAPONS LAB...

...WHERE THE ADDITIVES TO VACCINES AND CHEMTRAILS THAT MAKE AMERICANS DOCILE AND SUSCEPTIBLE TO OUR PROPAGANDA ARE SYNTHESIZED.

WOWIE!

AND THE LAST STOP FOR YOU...

...THE SUPER-SOLDIER LAB.

LAB

WOOSH

Beep Beep

COME ON IN, MAX.

WE'VE BEEN EXPECTING YOU.

HEY, CAP.

MY BOY!

PRISONER HOLDING

GREAT HAUL ON CAMPUS THERE, DETECTIVE.

THANK YOU, SIR.

FUCK OFF, PIGS!

RUDE, AREN'T THEY?

I'D RECKON YOU COLLARED ABOUT 30 OF THEM, INCLUDING THE WORST OF THE WORST – *PRESS MEMBERS AND LEGAL OBSERVERS.*

THOSE RATS.

EXACTLY WHAT WE'D LIKE TO SEE. I FIGURE WE'LL HOLD THESE FOLKS AS LONG AS POSSIBLE.

PRESS

FOR *SOME REASON*, WE COULDN'T GET EVERYONE BOOKED UNTIL AFTER THE LAST ARRAIGNMENT OF THE DAY, SO THEY'RE GOING TO BE HELD ALL WEEKEND!

ANYHOW! I GOT SOME GREAT NEWS.

HAVE A SEAT.

THAT BIG PROMOTION YOU'VE BEEN GUNNING FOR?

CAPT. "MOOSE"

...IT'S YOURS.

...SERGEANT.

LEFT INDEX FINGER DISPENSES CONCRETE TO CLANDESTINELY CREATE DEADLY MILKSHAKE BRICKS

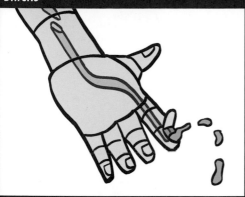

EYE CAMERA WITH ABILITY TO MALICIOUSLY EDIT AND POST VIDEO ON THE FLY WITH BRAIN SUPERCOMPUTER

LEFT THIGH CONTAINS FROZEN EGG COMPARTMENT FOR ANTI-POLICE PROJECTILES

RIGHT INDEX FINGER DISPENSES POISON WHEN SERVING COPS AT FAST CASUAL CHAINS

CONCEALED ROCKET BOOSTERS IN WRISTS TO HIT GROUND FASTER THAN NORMAL TO MAKE COPS LOOK BAD WHEN THEY DON'T EVEN TOUCH YOU

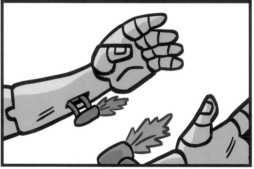

CHEST COMPARTMENT OF FALSE IDENTITY CARDS TO DISAVOW ANTIFA IF CAPTURED

UNION HALL #811
INT'L BROTHERHOOD OF PIPELAYERS,
STEAMFITTERS & STOOLMAKERS

ALRIGHT, FOLX!

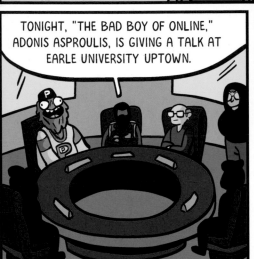

TONIGHT, "THE BAD BOY OF ONLINE," ADONIS ASPROULIS, IS GIVING A TALK AT EARLE UNIVERSITY UPTOWN.

THE SITE OF OUR RECENT TRIUMPH?!

WE CANNOT HAVE THAT.

IF HIS IDEAS WERE TO BREAK CONTAINMENT....

PEOPLE COULD START TO QUESTION OUR *COMMUNIST-MARXIST-SOCIALIST-MAOIST STALINIST-LENINIST-AUTHORITARIAN-RADICAL-ANARCHIST* IDEOLOGY.

PRES. OF ANTIFA

WE COULD LOSE OUR GRIP ON COLLEGE STUDENTS, THE *MOST RELIABLE TARGETS OF OUR ANTIFA MIND CONTROL!*

STOCK IMAGE

OUR MISSION TONIGHT:

DEPLATFORM ASPROULIS.

230TH STREET

EARLE UNIVE

FULL CANCELATION.

100% CENSORSHIP.

PRES. ANTIFA

SUPER-SOLDIER, WE'RE COUNTING ON YOU TO LEAD THE CHARGE.

DO YOU ACCEPT?

"PLUCKY"

YES, SIR!

ALRIGHT, PEOPLE!

COMMIS SIONER BO MAN

THERE'S SOME WRITER GIVING A TALK AT *EARLE U* TONIGHT.

DA COMMISH

YEAH, OKAY.

BC

...AND THOSE GODDAMN ANTIFAS ARE PLANNING ON SHOWING UP...SO WE GOTTA KICK THEIR ASSES.

OH! TOTALLY.

37

OH YEAH! NOW THAT YOU MENTION IT:

WE'RE THE, UH, DEFENDERS OF FREE SPEECH! AN IMPORTANT RIGHT, FOR AMERICANS.

WE *ARE* THE THIN BLUE LINE BETWEEN ORDER AND CHAOS.

A RESPONSIBILITY WE *ALL* TAKE SO, SO, SO SERIOUSLY.

THAT SAID, WHEN THEY'RE PROTESTING SOMEONE BESIDES THE COPS, WE CAN GO REALLY WILD AND NOBODY SEEMS TO CARE WHAT WE DO.

GREAT IDEA, MOOSE. GO NUTS!

WE'VE GOT ALL THAT COOL STUFF FROM *HOMELAND SECURITY.*

I'VE GOT OUR BIG LIST OF LAWS WE'VE GOTTEN AWAY WITH PRETENDING TO NOT KNOW IN PREVIOUS CASES, *THUS GRANTING US QUALIFIED IMMUNITY,* SO KEEP EVERYONE UP TO DATE.

DA COMMISH

YES, SIR!

BCPD

FROZEN EGG!

NOW!

BCPD BCPD

EARLE

BOX OFFICE

200 YEARS OF LEV STEIN HALL

ASPROULIS!

PREPARE TO BE...

...DEPLATFORMED.

PLEASE—!

45

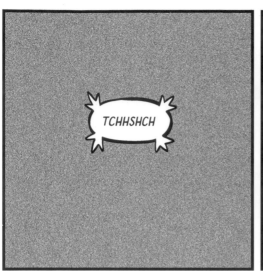

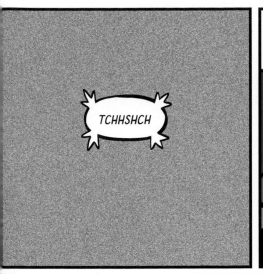

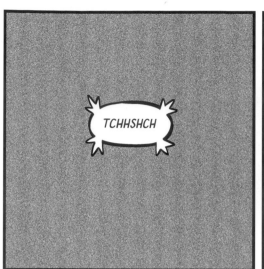

TCHHSHCH

OUR TOP STORY: AFTER A SUSTAINED EFFORT OF OVER SIX MONTHS OF DAILY PROTEST, THE MAYOR OF BIG CITY HAS MADE AN ANNOUNCEMENT.

BC1

THE POLICE HERE IN BIG CITY... ARE *NO MORE.*

AFTER 120 YEARS, THE BCPD IS TO BE DISBANDED, *EFFECTIVE IMMEDIATELY.*

RIP BCPD

SO I GUESS THAT'S THAT!

AFTER THE BREAK: *YOU WON'T BELIEVE WHAT THE PRESIDENT SAID THIS TIME!*

TCHHSHCH

53

PRETTY COOL, HUH?

YOU MIGHT HAVE HEARD OF BIG CITY'S NEW EXPERIMENT IN LAW ENFORCEMENT, POLICE 2. BUT WHAT ARE THEY?

I CAME TO THE BRAND-NEW BCPD2 HEADQUARTERS TO FIND OUT JUST THAT.

FWOOooo

IN GEOSYNCHRONOUS ORBIT ABOVE THE CITY, THE NEW SPACE STATION HEADQUARTERS PROMISES TO PUT A BRAND-NEW FACE ON LAW ENFORCEMENT.

I SPENT THE WEEK WITH POLICE 2 COMMISSIONER BOMAN, WHO SOME CITIZENS MAY REMEMBER FROM HIS TIME AS COMMISSIONER OF POLICE BEFORE THEY WERE DISBANDED.

SO. WHY SPACE?

WELL, OUR COMPSTAT TEAM SHOWED THAT OVER 100% OF NEGATIVE INTERACTIONS WITH POLICE WERE HAPPENING ON EARTH.

INTERESTING. SO THIS IS, WOULD YOU SAY, A NEW PAGE FOR LAW ENFORCEMENT?

THAT'S RIGHT.

ALSO, THIS HEIGHT IN ORBIT IS NECESSARY FOR SOME OF THE *NEW TECH* WE WERE ABLE TO OBTAIN WITH SOME *ANTI-TERRORISM GRANT MONEY.*

COMMISSIONER BOMAN EXPLAINED TO ME THAT THEY COULD TAP INTO ANY PHONE CONVERSATION ON EARTH – COURTESY OF EQUIPMENT PROVIDED BY TECH BILLIONAIRE MIKE LECKERSTEIN IN THEIR NEW SEMI-PRIVATE FUNDING ARRANGEMENT – KEEPING US SAFE WITH NONE OF THE BAGGAGE OF THE BCPD.

I DON'T HAVE ANYTHING ELSE!

THANKS SO MUCH.

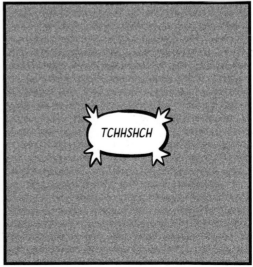

TCHHSHCH

55

THE FIGHT, ONCE AGAIN, HAS CHANGED.

RUNNING DIAGNOSTICS...

AND ONCE MORE, WE ARE OUTNUMBERED AND OUTGUNNED.

BUT IT'S NOT OVER. NOT BY A LONG SHOT.

THE FIGHT, ONCE AGAIN, HAS CHANGED.

DISRESPECTED ONCE MORE.

THE WHOLE DAMN WORLD HATES US AND WON'T GIVE US ANYTHING.

SO THE CYCLE STARTS ANEW.

THEY HIT US,

WE HIT THEM.

UNION HALL #811
INT'L BROTHERHOOD of PIPELAYERS, STEAMFITTERS & STOOLMAKERS

IT WAS FOOLISH TO THINK WE'D EVER WON.

YOU DIDN'T THINK WE HAD, DID YOU?

BECAUSE WE KNEW BETTER. WE KNEW...

...THE FIGHT IS NEVER OVER!

I'D LIKE TO SAY WE'RE READY FOR WHAT'S COMING.

BUT ALL I KNOW IS: I'LL MEET WHATEVER IT IS.

POLICE2: MURDER 1

ABOLISH BCPD 2

HEAD ON.

Matt Lubchansky is a queer nonbinary cartoonist and the Associate Editor of the Ignatz award-winning magazine and website *The Nib*. Their work has appeared in *The Nib*, *VICE*, *Eater*, *Mad Magazine*, *Gothamist*, *The Toast*, *The Hairpin*, *Brooklyn Magazine*, *New York Magazine*, *Food and Wine*, *Current Affairs*, and their long-running webcomic *Please Listen to Me*. They are the co-author of *Dad Magazine*, author of *Skeleton Party*, and co-editor of and contributor to *Flash Forward: An Illustrated Guide to Possible (and Not So Possible) Tomorrows*. Matt lives in Queens, NY, with their partner and one malignant police department. Matt is the 2020 Herblock Prize finalist.

The content of this book is obviously fiction. However, there are many things mentioned that are very, very real and within the power of your local police department. These are just a few that you may want to look up:

The 1997 National Defense Authorization Act's "1033 program" allows for the transfer of military equipment such as grenade launchers, Mine-Resistant Ambush Protected (MRAP) and Highly Mobile Multi-Wheeled (HMMWV) armored vehicles, and assault rifles. Since the program's inception, upwards of $5 billion of surplus military equipment has been transferred from the Department of Defense (DOD) to American law enforcement. While DOD oversight is a stipulation of the transfer, 1033 program information is not subject to any public review.

In fiscal year 2016, the Department of Homeland Security (DHS) awarded "Countering Violent Extremism" grants to 26 state and local government agencies as well as universities and nonprofits with little to no oversight. This program has continued in 2020 with another $10 million for "Terrorism and Targeted Violence Prevention." The NYPD's "intelligence and counterterrorism" budget is $189 million per year - this includes their unconstitutional surveillance of Muslims in the NYC metro area.

Since 1982's Supreme Court decision Harlow v. Fitzgerald, officers charged with constitutional violations have used the defense of "qualified immunity," which stipulates that by default, all government officials are immune from liability in civil suits if they violate your rights (unless the plaintiff can show hard proof of the violation - a difficult burden of proof). This includes if an officer violated the law intentionally.

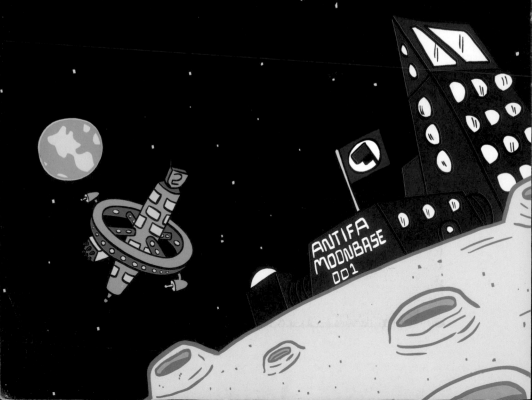

ANTIFA
MOONBASE
001